THE COVENANT OF GRACE

Matthew Henry

Matthew Henry's
Unpublished Sermons on

THE COVENANT OF GRACE

edited by
Allan Harman

CHRISTIAN HERITAGE

In memory of

J. A. Harman

A faithful minister of the gospel

Allan Harman is Research Professor at the Presbyterian Theological College, Melbourne. He is a well-known author in Australia and overseas. He has devoted his entire life to teaching the Old Testament and its languages to countless students in theological colleges across the world.

ISBN 1 85792 796 6

Published in 2002

by

Christian Focus Publications
Geanies House, Fearn, Tain, Ross-shire,
IV20 1TW, Great Britain
www.christianfocus.com

Cover Design by Alister MacInnes

Printed and bound by WS Bookwell, Finland

Contents

FOREWORD

Over forty years ago my father, the late Rev J. A. Harman, gave me a little book. It consisted of the manuscript of some of the sermons of Matthew Henry on the Covenant of Grace preached in Chester in 1691-92. He himself had been given it by the late Rev J. Campbell Robinson of St Kilda, Melbourne. Both men had served in the ministry of the Presbyterian Church of Eastern Australia for many years, and Mr Robinson, knowing my father's love of Matthew Henry's commentary, gave him this book prior to his death in 1952.

The book itself is small (the pages are only 8 cm by 14 cm) and the 174 leaves are written on both sides in Matthew Henry's neat handwriting. He nearly always used abbreviations, and included quotations in Greek, Latin and Hebrew. The first three sections (comprising 105 sermons) are missing, as the manuscript starts with *4. Pardon in the Covenant.*[1] The leaves have been bound together with a vellum cover.

On the front flyleaf there is a handwritten inscription:

These sermons of Mr Math. Henry,
on the Covenant of Grace,
were given to Henry James Stedman by
Mrs Brett of Westbrommich.
May 11th 1815.

The following is an extract from her letter to his father.

'Your account of your son Henry
pleases me. I wish his acceptance of that
volume of sermons on the Covenant, when
you have done with it; and present with it
my best respects and good wishes for his present and future happiness, and hope he will
maintain his steadfastness thro' all the

1. For the full list of the sermons see J. B. Williams, *Memoirs of the Life, Character and Writings of Rev. Matthew Henry* (Banner of Truth reprint, 1974), Note F, pp. 275-276.

temptations and trials of a changing world,
and inherit a kingdom that fadeth not.'
Amen.

Mrs Brett is a great-niece of Mr M. Henry.

Pasted inside the front of the book is a cutting from a bookseller's catalogue listing the volume for sale for £3 3s. My father understood that Mr Robinson bought it from this unnamed bookseller in 1929.

The series of sermons on the Covenant of Grace lasted from February 1691 to July 1692. He preached this series to provide comfort for God's people. Not only do we know the general outline of the missing sermons, but in this volume the final sermon is a summary of the whole.

In the 1950s when I was a student at Sydney University I started to transcribe the sermons, but I found it laborious work. Later I resumed it and managed to type up a few of the sermons. However, it was only when William and Carine McKenzie of Christian Focus Publications visited us in early 1998 that I received fresh stimulus to return to the task. I found that daily exposure to Matthew Henry's handwriting made it easier, and I have been able to complete the project

While Matthew Henry normally wrote in full sentences, at times he did not. I have occasionally inserted words (always in square brackets) to make it easier for the reader. Normally I have left the spelling without change, but in rare cases I felt it best to give the modern form. Throughout I have added footnotes, translating all the quotations in Greek, Latin and Hebrew. Some of these notes also relate to archaic English words, or references to people and events that would not be understood easily today.

Having read all these sermons several times I can testify to the blessing they have been to me. They are enfused with evangelical warmth, and we cannot read them without being challenged by them. I trust that they will be as great a blessing to others as they have been to myself.

Allan M. Harman
Presbyterian Theological College
Melbourne
September 2002

INTRODUCTION

There is hardly a better known name among biblical commentators than that of Matthew Henry. From the publication of its first volume (the Pentateuch) in 1706 to the present time, Henry's commentary has been repeatedly reprinted, translated into other languages, combined with the commentary by Thomas Scott to form Henry and Scott's commentary, or printed in an abridged form. It has been highly influential in under-girding the spirituality of a multitude of readers as they have used it for personal devotions or in preparation for teaching or preaching. Prominent Christian leaders such as George Whitefield and William Carey have testified to the influence it had upon them.

To take the case of Whitefield, shortly after his conversion he was in the practice of rising at five in the morning. On his knees he read from the English Bible, then his Greek New Testament, and finally he consulted Matthew Henry's commentary on the passage. Later his preaching was strongly influenced by Henry's exposition. Arnold Dallimore goes so far as to say that 'so fully had he drunk of the wells of Biblical exposition in Matthew Henry that much of his public utterance was little more than the thought of the great commentator – thought that had become assimilated in his own mind and soul, and poured forth spontaneously both as he prepared and as he preached his sermons'.[1] He could recall sayings of Henry,[2] and his list of rules for his College at Betheseda in Georgia included, among the books on divinity, the commentary of Matthew Henry.[3] When he penned his famous letter to John Wesley on the

---

1. Arnold Dallimore, *George Whitfield: The Life and Times of the Great Evangelist of the 18th Century Revival*, vol. 1 (Edinburgh: Banner of Truth Trust, 1970), p. 128.
2. Ibid., vol. 2, p. 168.
3. Ibid., p. 492.

subject of universal redemption, he did not give his own explanation of some biblical passages, but referred Wesley to commentators such as Ridgely, Edwards and Henry. His desire was that such treatises might show Wesley his error.[4]

But for the vast majority of readers Matthew Henry's life remains untold, and critical assessment of his work and ministry has been lacking. In presenting some of his hitherto unpublished sermons a brief account of his life and ministry should be given, along with an appreciation of him as a preacher as well as a commentator.

1. Matthew Henry's Life

The year in which Matthew Henry was born (1662) was a momentous one for the religious history of England. In that year over 2000 pastors were ejected from their livings in the Church of England because they refused to conform to the requirements laid upon them by the Act of Uniformity. This meant that these non-conformists who became Presbyterian or Congregationalist pastors were deprived of opportunities to minister publicly, and non-conformist students were excluded from Oxford and Cambridge Universities.

Matthew Henry's father, Philip Henry, had studied at Westminster School in London, and then proceeded for tertiary study to Christ's College, Oxford. This was the period in which the great Puritan leaders John Owen and Thomas Goodwin were exercising their most persuasive influence there. Philip Henry was settled as the Anglican pastor in the small village of Worthenbury in Flintshire near the Welsh border, and it was from that parish that he was ejected in 1662.

Being brought up in the home of such a godly father and pastor meant that Matthew Henry was from his earliest years exposed to deep religious commitment and training in the things of God. His father, with his own excellent educational background, was able to provide him with a broad general education, and specifically to ground him in the classical languages of Greek and Latin. Hebrew also featured on the agenda, and each day Matthew had to translate a passage from the Scriptures from the original language. Entry to

---

4. Ibid., pp. 567-568.

Oxford or Cambridge was closed to him, so his parents sent him to London when he was twenty-three years of age to study law at Gray's Inn. It was not that his parents or he himself considered that he would ever pursue a legal career, but this was an opportunity to continue his education. He also was able to listen to some of the best conformist preachers such as Tillotson and Stillingfleet. It is not known which non-conformist preachers he heard in the London area, but he certainly identified with the non-conformist cause, as he showed by visiting Richard Baxter in prison. His sense of call to the Christian ministry gradually deepened and though he seems to have considered entering into the ministry of the Church of England, by 1687 he had decided to accept a call to a non-conformist congregation.

Henry chose to go to Chester in the west of England, entering into the pastorate of a congregation that did not have its own building. This lack was rectified by the opening in 1690 of its own chapel. His ministry was not confined to Chester, but he moved widely around the local area preaching in many localities. Various attempts were made to induce him to leave Chester, but it was not until 1712 that he accepted a call to the congregation in Hackney, London. His growing literary work was a factor in this move, as he was producing many other works quite apart from his commentary.[5] He was not spared to exercise a long-term ministry there, for he died in 1714 at the age of fifty-two.

2. Matthew Henry the Commentator

The Reformation brought a tremendous change in regard to biblical exposition. The medieval practice of allegorising the text was set aside in favour of grammatico-historical exegesis. This meant that an expositor approached a biblical passage and worked through it in the original language. Questions of grammar and philology were discussed and the passage was placed in its historical context. Only then was the teaching of the passage set out and also utilised in later

---

5. He set out in writing his eleven reasons for accepting the call to Hackney. See J. B. Williams, *The Lives of Philip and Matthew Henry* (Edinburgh: Banner of Truth Trust, 1974), pp. 104-108.

theological formulations. John Calvin brought to the task his skills as a renaissance scholar and his commentaries on the biblical text became the model for later commentaries. By Matthew Henry's time there were not only the Reformation commentaries to be exemplars, but those from the post-Reformation and Puritan periods.

The commentary of Matthew Henry fits easily into the category of Puritan exposition of Scripture. Many of the great Puritans had already died before he was born, but through his father he had contact with their ideas and works. His commentary is thus representative of what was at the essence of Puritan biblical study and exposition. Underlying all the Puritan efforts were the basic presuppositions of the divine nature of the Bible and the fact that biblical doctrine was the teaching regarding God and what duty he required of man. The Puritans clearly taught that man unaided by the Holy Spirit could not understand biblical teaching, for it was spiritually discerned.[6]

In commencing his great task Matthew Henry thought it necessary to spell out the six great principles that were his presuppositions. They were:

1. That religion is the one thing needful.
2. That divine revelation is necessary to true religion.
3. That divine revelation is not now to be found nor expected anywhere but in the Scriptures of the Old and New Testament.
4. That the Scriptures of the Old and New Testaments were purposely designed for our learning.
5. That the Holy Scriptures were not only designed for our learning, but are the settled standing rule for our faith and practice.
6. That therefore it is the duty of all Christians diligently to search

---

6. For an excellent discussion of the Puritan exposition of Scripture see J. I. Packer, 'The Puritans as Interpreters of Scripture', in *A Quest for Godliness: The Puritan Vision of the Christian Life* (Wheaton: Crossway Books, 1990), pp. 97-105. It is also available in a slightly different form in Puritan Papers vol. 1 1956–1959, ed. D. Martyn Lloyd-Jones (Phillipsburg: P & R Publishing, 2000), pp. 191-201.

> the Scriptures, and it is the office of ministers to guide and assist them therein.[7]

Even before he started on his *Exposition*, Matthew Henry was in the habit of writing on Scripture. He also drew attention to this fact in his preface:

> It has long been my practice, what little time I had to spare in my study, from my constant preparations for the pulpit, to spend it drawing up expositions upon some parts of the New Testament, not so much for my own use, as purely for my own entertainment, because I knew not how to employ my thoughts, and time more to my satisfaction.[8]

In December 1700 he sent some of these expositions to his friend, Rev. Samuel Clark, with the following sentences regarding it:

> I leave it [the publishing] to you, and resolve to follow Providence, having often reflected with most comfort upon that which has been least my own doings. The work has been, and still is, to me its own wages, and the pleasure recompense enough for all the pains. You will please let me know, as there is occasion, what is done concerning them; if they return to the place from whence they came, they shall be heartily welcome. I shall not repent my writing of them, and I hope you will not repent the reading of them though they go no further.[9]

It is not clear why there was no progress on publication of it for another four years. On 12 November 1704 he began to write his notes on the Old Testament, which he completed on 18 July 1712. Then he worked on the New Testament, reaching the end of Acts on 17 April 1714. He was not spared to write any further, and

---

7. Matthew Henry, *Exposition of the Old and New Testament* (London: James Nisbet, 1880), vol. 1, pp. iii-v.
8. Ibid., vol. 1, pp. v-vi.
9. J. B. Williams, op. cit., p. 302.

others took over the task. They based their work on notes he had made, including almost complete ones on the Epistle to the Romans. He left some brief jottings on other epistles and there were also some shorthand notes of public and private expositions.[10] In all, four volumes appeared during his lifetime, starting with the Pentateuch in 1706, while he had just completed volume 5 before his death on 22 June 1714.

There is a clear connection between Matthew Henry's commentary and his pastoral ministry. From the outset he lectured twice every Sunday to his congregation, and the content of many passages covered in his exposition was the basis of sermons. If comparison is made between his sermons and his exposition of a particular text, the relationship can be seen very quickly. Here is one example only, taken from his commentary on John 14:27:

> When Christ was about to leave the world he *made his will*. His soul he committed to his Father; his body he bequeathed to Joseph, to be decently interred; his clothes fell to the soldiers; his mother he left to the care of John; but what should he leave to his poor disciples, that had left all for him? Silver and gold he had none; but he left them that which was infinitely better, his peace. *'I leave you*, but I leave *my peace* with you. I not only give you a title to it, but put you in possession of it'.

This is how he had dealt with the same verse in his first sermon on 'Peace', preached on 24 January 1692 (see p.77 in this volume):

> When our Lord Jesus was about to leave the world he made his will. His soul he committed to the hands of his Father (Luke 23:46). His body he bequeathed to Joseph of Arimathea to be decently interred, yet not so as to see corruption. His clothes fell to the soldiers that crucified him (Luke 23:34). His mother he left to the care of the beloved disciple (John 19:26). But what should he bequeathe to his poor disciples, who had forsaken all to follow him? Silver and gold he had none to leave them, but he left them that which was infinitely better than thousands of gold and silver.

---

10. For a list of those who completed the exposition of the New Testament, see J. B. Williams, op. cit., p. 308.

The influence of Matthew Henry's commentary is not hard to find, but there is no detailed analysis available of the impact it had on other preachers and writers. Dr Leslie Church, who abridged the commentary so that it could be published in a single volume,[11] suggests that the hymns of William Cowper 'were undoubtedly inspired by the spirit and even the phrasing of Matthew Henry'.[12] Certainly many of Charles Wesley's words in his hymn 'A charge to keep I have' seem to be borrowed from Matthew Henry's commentary on Leviticus 8:35, on which text he says:

> We have every one of us a charge to keep, an eternal God to glorify, an immortal soul to provide for, needful duty to be done, our generation to serve; and it must be our daily care to keep this charge, for it is the charge of the Lord our Master, who will shortly call us to an account about it, and it is at our utmost peril if we neglect it.

Another testimony to Matthew Henry's worth as a commentator comes from William Jay. In his autobiography when he is speaking about commentators he says this:

> But for private and pious use I never found anything comparable to Henry, which, as old John Ryland said, 'a person cannot begin to read without wishing he was shut out from all the world, and able to read it through, without stopping'.[13]

In writing to Miss Harman, one of his correspondents who had sent him a copy of Richard Baxter's life, he thanks her for the gift and then says: 'Henry says – it is impossible to read the book of Psalms and not be inflamed or ashamed by the perusal. I say the same about this work'.[14]

---

11. *Matthew Henry's Commentary in One Volume*, ed. Leslie F. Church (Grand Rapids: Zondervan, 1961).
12. Ibid., p. vii.
13. *The Autobiography of William Jay* (Edinburgh: Banner of Truth Trust, n.d.), pp. 124-125. The quotation from John Ryland comes from the 3rd edition of his *Contemplations* published in 1777, p. 371.
14. Ibid., p. 235-37. For other testimonies to the influence of Henry's *Exposition*, see J. B. Williams, op. cit., pp. 235-37.

3. Matthew Henry the Preacher

From an early age Matthew Henry's heart was turned towards the work of the ministry. He was touched spiritually at a very young age by his father's preaching. Philip Henry encouraged his children to prepare for the Lord's Day by spending an hour together every Saturday afternoon. At these times Matthew Henry presided, and if he thought his sisters had cut short their prayers he would gently reprove them!

After his period of study in London he returned to his parents' home at Broad Oak (a farm near where his father had ministered before his ejection) in June 1686 and immediately preached on several occasions. The way his preaching was received, and the effect it had on a notoriously godless couple, seem to have confirmed his sense of calling to the ministry. On a visit to Chester he was invited to preach and did so on several consecutive evenings. The dissenters who heard him issued an invitation to him to become their pastor. After consulting his father he accepted the invitation, but sought a little time as he wished to return to London for some months. It was there that he was ordained privately by a gathering of Presbyterian ministers on 9 May 1687. He commenced his ministry at Chester on Thursday 2 June 1687 by giving the normal Thursday lecture.

From that time onwards Henry was busy with preaching and lecturing in his own congregation and at many other places near Chester. Within his own congregation at nine o'clock on Sunday morning in addition to psalm singing and prayer, he both lectured on a portion of the Old Testament (that is, gave an exposition) and also preached a sermon. The same sort of pattern was followed in the afternoon, though he lectured on the New Testament at this service. During the course of his ministry at Chester he went through the whole of the Bible with his congregation more than twice. On Thursday evening he also lectured, and his expositions on Scripture questions took twenty years. While the actual attendances at these various services is unknown, yet the fact that his congregation grew until it had over 350 communicants testifies to the appreciation of his ministry.

His diary reveals that he was also extremely active in preaching in villages around Chester. In Moldsworth, Grange, Bromborough, Elton and Saighton he preached every month, but even more frequently in Beeston, Wrexham, Stockbridge and Darnal. Each year he paid a visit to Nantwich, Newcastle and Stone, and towards the end of his ministry in Chester he went every year on a preaching tour in Lancashire. Shrewsbury, Market Drayton and Stafford were also on his list of preaching appointments. On several occasions he went to London, preaching at various places on the way, and in the metropolis he preached practically every day of his visit.

In planning his preaching at Chester Matthew Henry was very systematic.[15] His first series of sermons was on the misery of being in a sinful state. He followed on with sermons dealing with conversion, and this took him two years. Then came a series of sermons in which he laid down the biblical pattern of Christian conduct, expressed in twenty statements that he expounded with an appropriate text for each head. After that he wanted to bring comfort to God's people and therefore entered on his long series on the covenant of grace, in which he dealt in order, with God in the covenant, Christ in the covenant and the Holy Spirit in the covenant. At the end of this series, as with all his other ones, he preached a sermon or two summarising the content of the preceding sermons and recapitulating the main points.

In many respects Matthew Henry's sermons were typical of the Puritan period.[16] The Puritans believed that preaching is vital in that it is the unfolding of God's Word so that its teaching is plain to the minds of hearers. It is the principal way God has ordained of bringing his life-giving Word home to humans. Zwingli began the practice of regular and consecutive exposition of Scripture, but it was the Cambridge Puritans who developed it most fully. Matthew Henry

---

15. For a list of his sermons, see J. B. Williams, op. cit., note F, pp. 273-293.
16. For discussion of Puritan preaching see Peter Lewis, 'The Puritan in the Pulpit' in his book *The Genius of Puritanism* (Haywards Heath: Carey Publications, 1975), pp. 19-52; J. I. Packer, 'Puritan Preaching' in *A Quest for Godliness*, op. cit., pp. 277-289.

followed in their shoes as he opened up the Scriptures to his hearers. Like the other Puritans he was not averse at all to doctrinal preaching, for he held to the evangelical and reformed position of the Protestant Reformation and believed wholeheartedly that the theology of the Scriptures is to be preached to sinners and saints.

Three further points should be made about his sermons. First, he was methodical, not only in planning and preparing his sermons, but also in his presentation of the biblical content. Peter Ramus, a Huguenot academic, had taught that analysis is the key to understanding, and the Puritans took this point up and utilised it with their orderly presentation of material. This was intended to make the matter plain to hearers and to help them to remember it better. Secondly, Matthew Henry followed the other Puritans in always seeking to press home the teaching of Scripture to his hearers. His sermons never ended without some practical application. The teaching of Holy Scripture was not just of theoretical concern but something that should move hearers to action. Thirdly, there is one respect in which Matthew Henry differs from his Puritan predecessors. Whereas they often chose to deal with a particular topic and preached week after week from the same text, he chose to preach from different texts even if he was dealing with the same subject. This gave greater variation to his preaching, and brought out even more broadly the biblical teaching on the matter at hand. It is not surprising that his preaching appealed to so many in his day, and delivered with simplicity and wonderful turns of phrase, they struck home to the consciences of hearers.

4. Matthew Henry's Sermons on the Covenant of Grace

Anyone already familiar with Matthew Henry's commentary or his other works will find here the same delightful style. He knew his Bible exceptionally well, referring in these sermons to all the biblical books with the exception of 1 Chronicles, Obadiah, Haggai and Philemon. He studied the Scriptures intently, and organised his material methodically. Constantly he illustrated, not by lengthy stories, but by phrases and references that crystallised his points. Above all, he presses home the truth to his listeners (and readers). He also knew and utilised the great Christian writings from the early church down to his day.

There are remarks on biblical passages that many readers will recognise from his commentary, for, as already pointed out, clearly his sermon preparation lay behind much of his other writing. Many notable expressions like these occur:

> God's beloved ones are the world's hated ones and we are not to marvel at it.

> When we come for the pardon of our sins we must come with a Christ in the arms of our faith and love.

> In the want of the faith of assurance live by the faith of adherence. Are you in doubt about your spiritual state? Put the matter out of doubt by a present consent – if I never did, I do it now.[17]

> Every transgression in the covenant doth not put us out of covenant. Especially understand that our salvation is not in our own keeping but in the hands of the mediator.

> We have *all* received the gospel. Salvation is a *common* salvation (Jude 3). All have need to receive, even the most worthy. All are welcome to receive, even the most unworthy, if they come and seek it in the right way.

> Assure yourselves none shall come to heaven hereafter but those that are fitted for it by grace here. 'Tis only the pure in heart that shall see God (Matt. 5:8; Heb. 12:14).

> Believe that you have a holy God above you, a precious soul within you, and an awful eternity before you, either of weal or woe.

> Grow upwards in heavenly mindedness, downward in humility. Be pressing forward. The way to grow in grace is to use what we have. The Word is the means of our growth. Make daily use of it (2 Tim. 3:17).

---

17. This seems to have been a favourite saying of his, as he used it when he was describing his own spiritual situation when he was only ten years old. See J. B. Williams, *op. cit.*, p. 5.

Some of Matthew Henry's sermons have been previously available, as they are printed in his *Complete Works*.[18] Most of those sermons are ones preached on special occasions such as funerals or ordinations of ministers. However, in this book we have a consecutive series of sermons on a particular theme, accompanied by a closing sermon that summarises the content of the whole series. They are testimony to a faithful gospel preacher, who, with a mind and heart set on the things of God, sought to unfold the riches of Scripture. They are not just relics of the past, but will speak God's Word to the present-day reader just as Matthew Henry's *Exposition* continues to do.

Allan M. Harman
Presbyterian Theological College
Melbourne
July 2002

---

18. *The Complete Works of Matthew Henry: Treatises, Sermons, and Tracts* (Grand Rapids: Baker Book House, 1997).

4

Pardon in the Covenant

20 Dec. 1691

4. PARDON IN THE COVENANT

For I will be merciful to their unrighteousness and their sins and iniquities will I remember no more (Heb. 8:12).

These words conclude that summary of the New Covenant, which the Apostle here sets down from Jeremiah 31:31, etc. Though all covenant privileges be eminently included in that of God's being to us a God, and we need desire no more to make us happy, yet that we might have strong consolation, and might more distinctly view our comforts and take comfort from them, the particulars included in that general are severally set before us. Sin having multiplied our wants and sorrows, free grace hath in the New Covenant provided a salve for every sore, a remedy for every malady. As in the prescriptions of duty, though their two great commandments of love to God and love to our neighbour include all God requires of us (Matt. 22:37-40) in one word (Gal. 5:14), yet these generals are branched out into many particulars, in compassion to our infirmities, which being often mistaken in our practical inferences.

This in the text though put last, is not the least considerable. 'Tis mentioned as the foundation of all the rest, *for* I will be merciful. Other benefits and privileges flow from this. See Romans 11:27; Ezekiel 36:33. 'Tis sin that keeps God and man at a distance, hinders good things from us (Isa. 29:1, 2). 'Tis a partition wall, and therefore no good [is] to be expected till this partition wall be taken out of the way. Observe the method (Hos. 14:2), *Take away all iniquity*, and then give good. We must date our ruin from our sin, and then date our rise from our pardon – they shall all know me – *for I will be merciful*. Sin disfits us for the knowledge of God. We cannot know him with comfort till sin be pardoned (Luke 1:77).

Observe in the text:

1. The wound opened. *Unrighteousness, sins, iniquities*, three words noting the same thing, all plural,

   a. to set forth the unsearchable fulness and riches of pardoning mercy. Thus in the proclamation of God's name (Exod. 34:5-7) no room [is] left for doubting. [We are] forgiven *all* trespasses (Col. 2:13) be they never so many, never so great.
   b. to set forth the unsearchable wickedness of our hearts and lives. What abundance of guilt have we contracted, how many ways, in how *many things* have we offended (Jas. 3:2)? We owe ten thousand talents.
      i. *Unrighteousnesses*. All sin is unrighteousness, ἀδικία,[1] 'tis injustice, omissions, commissions. 'Tis the perverting of that which is right (Job 33:27). 'Tis a wrong to God, 'tis the withholding of our dues, 'tis contrary to that rectitude and uprightness in which God at first made man. It may be meant only of sins against our neighbour, transgressing the law of justice and honesty, which God is concerned in though the wrong be done immediately to our neighbour, because the law we break is his, and so he is reflected upon.
      ii. *Sins*, ἁμαρτιῶν,[2] errors, missings of the mark, shooting short, or over, or wide to the right hand, [or] to the left. The glory of God is the mark we should aim at. By sin we miss that mark (Rom. 3:23).
      iii. *Iniquities*, ἀνομιῶν,[3] transgressions of the law (1 John 3:4), illegalities, irregularities, want of conformity to the law. It includes both original and actual sin, the non-conformity of our natures, the non-conformity of our actions to the law of God, swerving from the rule. The Word of God is the rule. As far as we turn aside from that we sin. 'Tis good looking upon sin under that notion, and

---

1. Greek, 'injustice, unrighteousness'.
2. Greek, 'sins'.
3. Greek, 'lawless deeds'.

'twill help both to discover sin to us, and to break our hearts kindly for it. If this be our case, have not we need of pardon, transgressing in our sins (Lev. 16:21)?

2. The remedy applied, and that's a pardon.
[In] two ways [it is] expressed.

a. *I will be merciful*, which speaks the freeness of the pardon. It comes from mercy, mere mercy (ἵλεως ἔσομαι,[4] I will be propitious; the ἱλαστήριον,[5] the mercy seat). Misery is the proper object of mercy. Sin implies misery as the certain consequent of it.

The opposite to mercy is *wrath*. I will be merciful, i.e. I will not be angry (Luke 18:13), but in Christ propitious and will graciously receive. And this mercy is dispensed in a way of sovereignty – mercy to whom I will (Rom. 9:18).

b. I *will remember them no more,* i.e. not remember it against them (Ps. 79:8), to charge them with it, to condemn them for it, an act of oblivion, [they] shall be past, all cleared. 'Tis a high expression of the fulness of pardoning mercy, and this [is] conveyed by the covenant, verse 10. It implies sanctification. *Nihil est novi quod vet. rem in memoriam reducat* (Grot[ius]).[6]

Doct[rine] That pardon of sin is one of the most precious privileges of the covenant of grace. One great benefit of the New Covenant is forgiveness of sin.

Here I shall endeavour (by the divine assistance) to show:

---

4. Greek, future tense of the verb 'to be', 1st person singular, together with the adjective 'propitious', 'forgiving'.
5. Greek, 'the covering of the ark of the covenant' which was sprinkled with atoning blood on the Day of Atonement (Heb. 9:5).
6. The Latin quotation comes from Hugo Grotius (1583–1645), a Dutch literary figure and scholar. The translation is: 'There is nothing new which can bring the old things back to mind'.

1. What pardon of sin is.
2. How 'tis a privilege of the covenant of grace.
3. That it is a most precious, an *unspeakable* privilege.
4. The application of the doctrine.

For the first, what pardon of sin is. 'Tis requisite rightly to understand the nature of it.

1. It is not any real change in the sin. Sin is the transgression of the law. Now:

   a. Pardon doth not make the sin not to have been – for that's a contradiction. Pardon doth not make a man absolutely innocent. Though Peter was pardoned it cannot be said but that he did deny his Master. This is a thing that doth remain. That which is done cannot be absolutely undone again. Indeed there are some expressions in Scripture which come something near to this (Jer. 50:20) but that must be understood in respect of the consequence of sin. Christ did not die to verify contradiction.

   b. It doth not make it not to have been sin, an irregularity offensive to God and deserving wrath. Sin appears *sin* even after it is pardoned. It would be a reflection upon God and altogether inconsistent with the holiness of his nature not to hate sin, or at any time to be reconciled to sin. As the action so the obliquity[7] of the action doth remain. He *cannot behold iniquity* (Hab. 1:13).

2. But it is a relative change in the sinner. Pardon has relation to guilt. Now guilt is an obligation to punishment resulting from the obliquity and irregularity of an action. Pardon doth not take away the desert of sin but only the actual ordination of it to condemnation.

---

7. *Obliquity*, an archaic English word meaning 'turning aside from moral character'.

Def[inition] Pardon of sin is an act of God's free grace whereby to a repenting, believing sinner for the sake of Christ and his righteousness that obligation to punishment which ariseth from the sinfulness of his heart and life is dissolved and ceaseth; or this: 'tis a gracious act of God discharging the sinner by the gospel promise or grant from the obligation to punishment upon consideration of the satisfaction made by Christ accepted by the sinner and pleaded with God.[8]

'Tis a judicial act – [it] supposeth a law broken. If no sin, [there is] no need of pardon. Now:

1. It is an act of God as the supreme rector and governor of the world, who is offended, and whose law is broken by sin, he's the party wronged (Rom. 8:33). None can forgive sins but he (Mark 2:7). Many can forgive themselves easily enough. Their quarrel with themselves is soon over, but that's no forgiveness. Others may forgive us the wrong done them by our sins, and yet God [may] not forgive us. 'Tis a flower in his crown to forgive sin. See how he glories in it (Isa. 43:25), *I even I*. 'Tis not a pardon but a cheat which doth not come under the broad seal. 'Tis an act of power, great power (Num. 14:17), an act of prorogation.[9] Therefore we are taught to go to him for it as a Father. *Our Father, forgive us*. Christ is said to forgive sin (Luke 5:24) for he is God, and to him all judgment is committed. But the act of pardoning is usually and fitly ascribed to the Father, for Christ's sake (Eph. 4:32).

   See what evil there is in sin which none but God himself can remove, and in this he is God and not man (Hos. 11:9), a none-such[10] God (Mic. 7:18). As he gives so he forgives like himself and it is his glory (Prov. 25:2). When he would proclaim his name he makes himself known as a God of pardons (Exod.

8. In a marginal note Matthew Henry refers at this point to Richard Baxter's *Aphorisms*, p. 166 as the source of the definition.
9. *Prorogation*, 'the act of a sovereign discontinuing a legislative assembly without dissolving it'.
10. i.e. a God unlike any other.

34:6, 7). These words, *and will by no means clear the guilty*, some read as an expression of mercy, *evacuando non evacuabit visitans iniquitatem*,[11] emptying, he will not empty when he visits, not stir up all his wrath (Jer. 30:11). The Pope cannot forgive sin. 'Tis a delusion.

2. It is an act of his free grace. Therefore he saith, *I will be merciful*, *freely by his grace* (Rom 3:24), δωρεὰν τῇ αὐτοῦ χάριτι,[12] two expressions of the same thing. He adds *freely*, the more to magnify grace. [There is] nothing in us to move him to it, but a great deal on the contrary. Joseph found grace in the eyes of his master (Gen. 39:4) but there was a reason for it, verse 3. Lest any should think that so we find grace in God's eyes he prefixeth *freely*. Without any motive in us, he thus loved us, *ex mero motu*,[13] *because* he loved us (Deut. 7:7, 8). His free love eternally determining was the cause of his free love actually conferring these distinguishing mercies. He doth it not for your sakes (Ezek. 36:32) because he promised himself any advantage by it, as princes pardon criminals to transport them, not for their importunity sake but his own sake (Isa. 43:23). Though faith and repentance are required as conditions, yet 'tis free. The pardon of a malefactor [is] nevertheless free for his being required to plead it upon his knees at the bar, and say, God bless the king. Χηαρίζομαι[14] is a word used for the forgiveness of sin (Col. 2:13; 3:13).

3. It is for the sake of Christ and his righteousness in consideration of the satisfaction made by him, and yet an act of *grace*, *free grace*, free as to us though purchased by Christ. 'Twas free grace that accepted the satisfaction for us, vicarious, Christ paid the *tantundem*,[15] not the *idem*,[16] the value not the strict debt.

11. Latin, 'emptying, he will not empty when he visits iniquity'.
12. Greek, 'as a free gift by his grace'.
13. Latin, 'out of pure feeling'.
14. Greek, 'I show grace to, I forgive'.
15. Latin, 'just that amount'.
16. Latin, 'the same'.

We are justified freely and yet it is διὰ τῆς ἀπολυτρώσεως[17] (Rom. 3:24), for the sake of the redemption that is in Jesus through his blood (Eph. 1:7), and yet according to *grace*, the riches of grace. He was made sin for us, i.e. a sacrifice for sin (2 Cor. 5:21). All our pardons come streaming to us in his blood. 'Tis he that is the propitiation (1 John 2:2) – died for the redemption of the transgressors under the first testament (Heb. 9:15).

4. It is by the promise or grant of the gospel. That's the charter of our pardons. There God has declared his mind and will. That's the act of indemnity. 'Tis by virtue of that that we are pardoned. That's the New Covenant. 'Tis in that that Christ is set forth to be a propitiation (Rom. 3:25). In the pardon of sin there is no change in God; the change is in us. If a malefactor, that has long stood out, at length come in and claim the benefit of the indemnity there is no change in the king. The king pardoned him conditionally when he passed the act, his coming in interested him in that.

5. It is to a repenting believing sinner. Faith and repentance are the conditions. There is a possibility of pardon before, but no actual pardon, no immediate interest till the conditions be fulfilled. But it is God by his Spirit that works these conditions wherever they are that the purpose of God according to election may stand which is secret to us. His revealed will is that we repent and believe or else no pardon [is] to be had (Mark 1:15).

6. It is the *dissolving* of an *obligation* to punishment – or a discharge from it. By the law we are charged, by our pardon we are discharged.

   a. There is an obligation to punishment resulting from the sinfulness of our hearts and lives. The sin that *dwells* in us, the sin that is *committed* by us, is worthy of death. Sin is the work, death

17. Greek, 'through the redemption'.

the wages (Rom. 6:23) – death temporal, spiritual, eternal. Sin [is] the conception, death the birth (Jas. 1:15). Sin [is] the seed sown, death the harvest (Gal. 6:8). Sin lies at the door (Gen. 4:7). The law hath tied a knot between sin and death, sin and the curse (Gal 3:10). Sin is a bond (Acts 8:23). We are by the righteous sentence of the law bound to answer it – as a malefactor bound over to the assize. Upon the breach of the law we become obnoxious to the penalty. Believe this with application to yourself and your own sin, original, actual, drunkenness, lying, yea and vain thoughts. Wrath comes upon the children of disobedience (Col. 3:6), ὑπόδικος τῷ θεῷ[18] (Rom. 3:19), liable to a process.

b. When sin is pardoned the obligation is dissolved and becomes void and of none effect. Upon the commission of the sin by the sentence of the law we are bound over to punishment. Upon our sincere repentance and faith by the grant of the gospel we are freed from that bond.

[In] several ways this is expressed in Scripture.

i. Sin is not imputed (Ps. 32:2; 2 Cor. 5:19). It is not laid to the charge of the sinner. Though all good be justly forfeited, the forfeiture is not taken. All evil [is] deserved, but the evil [is] not inflicted. The expression is used in Shimei's petition for pardon (2 Sam. 19:19), *impute not iniquity*, i.e. do not deal with me as a criminal. He confessed his fault but deprecated the punishment. Iniquity is imputed when the sinner is called to an account for it, judgment laid to the line (Isa. 28:17).

ii. God doth not *enter into judgment* with the sinner. So the expression is (Ps. 143:2), i.e. doth not deal with the sinner according to his desert, doth *not mark iniquity* (Ps. 130:3), doth not arraign him as a criminal at the bar, doth not prefer

18. Greek, 'answerable to God'.

an indictment against him. There's a *nolle prosequi*[19] entered.

iii. The sinner *shall not die* (2 Sam. 12:13), i.e. not die eternally, not be separated from God and from his love and favour and blessing as thou hast deserved. The sentence of the law is gone forth against thee but it shall not be executed. The law entails death upon sin, but the gospel cuts off the entail. 'Tis true the disease is mortal of itself, but pardoning mercy hath taken off the malignity of it.

iv. God's anger is *turned away* (Isa. 12:2). Sin provokes the holy and righteous God to anger (Isa. 1:4). He is angry with the wicked every day (Ps. 7:11). When sin is pardoned the anger ceaseth (Ps. 85:3; Hos. 14:4), the enmity [is] slain (Eph. 2). The soul becomes the object of his love – no more frowns in his face but smiles. The curse [is] reversed and a blessing [is put] in the stead of it. The sinner [is] received graciously – kissed as the returning prodigal. Thus pardon is often expressed.

v. Iniquity *shall not be the ruin* (Ezek. 18:30). Iniquity hath a direct tendency to ruin. It's the high road to it. Now pardon interposeth [and] prevents that ruin. Though [we are] corrected yet not ruined. [There is] help even for self-destruction (Hos. 13:9). Means [are] devised that the banished, though wilfully banished by themselves, should not be for ever expelled (2 Sam. 14:14), not punished with everlasting destruction, the due desert of sin.

vi. There is *no condemnation* (Rom. 8:1). Their being in Christ Jesus secures them from condemnation. He doth not say, there is no accusation against them nor nothing in them that deserves condemnation, for there's a great deal. He doth not say there's no self-condemnation, for they are taught to judge themselves. He doth not say there's no affliction to them, no, nor that there's no displeasure with

---

19. Latin, 'to be unwilling to prosecute'.

that affliction – but, no *condemnation* – i.e. no ordination or obligation to the wrath and curse due for sin – *rectus in curia.*[20]

I shall further open the nature of pardon of sin from several Scripture similitudes which do illustrate it. When sin is pardoned

1. we are acquitted from it as it is a doctrine thus in the Lord's Prayer, *forgive us our debts*. Sin is a debt. Pardon of sin is the remitting of a debt. Rent is withheld. Duty to God, to our neighbour, to ourselves, is rent. Where this is withheld there's debt contracted, a trust committed to us and not performed, mercies received and no returns. Our first father ran us in debt, and like sorry debtors we are apt to run further and further into debt. This debt is upon record (Job 14:17). Now when sin is pardoned this debt is remitted, [and] we receive an acquittance so as no more to stand charged with the debt. And the acquittance is grounded upon the satisfaction, which Christ our surety has made by dying for us. Thus sin is said to be blotted out (Isa. 43:25), as a debt is blotted out when it is either paid or pardoned. To some more is forgiven, to others less (Luke 7:47, 48, 50). David prayed, *blot out [all mine iniquities]* (Ps. 51:1). Thus acquittance saves us from prison, 'tis our plea to the arrests of the law and our own consciences. Though the debt be great to ten thousand talents, yet it's all remitted to the utmost farthing! The handwriting [is] cancelled (Col. 2:14).

2. we are eased of it as it is a burden. Sin is a burden, which will if not removed in time sink us in hell. If we be not sensible of this burden 'tis a sign we are *in sin*, as in our element, [as] a man in the air and water feels not the pressure of it, a sign we are spiritually dead. A dead man feels no weight, but if alive 'tis heavy. See how David complains (Ps. 38:4; 40:12). Those that are convinced of sin are weary and heavy-laden under it (Matt.

20. Latin, 'made right in the court'.

11:28). Now pardon easeth us (Hos. 14:2, *take away [all iniquity]* – or lift off as a burden). Sin is said to be laid *upon Christ* (Isa. 53:6), and so taken off from us. By faith we cast this burden upon the Lord Jesus, and so find rest to our souls. When iniquity is taken away the soul is quiet (Zech. 3:9).

3. we are cleansed from it as a blot. Sin leaves a spot and stain upon the soul, which renders it loathsome to the pure and holy God. The enlightened soul is sensible of it. 'Tis a deep stain. Now pardon washeth it off, removes the filth. David prays for washing (Ps. 51:3, 7). God promiseth washing (Ezek. 36:25) though as *scarlet and crimson* (Isa. 1:18), a deep dye, a double dye, dyed in the wool of original corruption, the many threads of actual transgression, yet [it becomes] *as wool and snow*. The blood of Christ is the fountain opened (Zech. 13:1). 'Tis he that purgeth away our sins (Heb. 9:14). [He] washed us from them in his own blood (Rev. 1:5; compare chap. 7:13, 14). And the consequent of this is, thou art *all fair* (Cant. 4:7), all the spots being taken away in justification. There seems to be an allusion to the ceremonial washings. Ceremonial defilements [are] typical of moral [defilements] (Heb. 9, 13, 14).

4. we are cured of it as a wound. Our sins are wounds (Ps. 38:5), painful, weakening, mortal. These wounds often stink and are corrupt through our foolishness. When the sin is pardoned the wound is cured. See it in David's prayer (Ps. 41:4), in his praise (Ps. 103:3), in God's promise (Hos. 14:4). The healing virtue is in the blood of Christ under the wings of the Son of Righteousness (Mal. 4:2). The wounds of sin are like the bitings of a fiery serpent. We are cured as the stung Israelites by looking upon the brazen serpent (John 3:13, 14; see Isa. 33:24). Blessed be God there is balm in Gilead, [there is] a physician there (Jer. 8:22). When the wound is cured, the pain, the peril ceaseth.

5. 'tis *covered* as a thing forgotten (Ps. 32:1). God is said *to hide his face* from it (Ps. 51:9). David, in a sense of the filth and stain

that he had contracted, desires that God would turn his eyes *from* that sin, lest that should turn his heart against the soul. He deprecates the displeasure which God has at sin and sinners. He is said to cast it behind his back (Isa. 38:17). In the language of the text he *remembers it no more,* i.e. to judge, and condemn for it. Men forgive but cannot forget. When God forgives, he forgets. 'Tis covered as nakedness is covered that the shame of it may not appear (Rev. 3:18). Many cover their sins themselves and cannot prosper (Prov. 28:13). [They] cover them with fig-leaves, excuses, pretences, [they] hide it as Adam. God covers it when he pardons it as with *the coats of skin*, the robe of Christ's righteousness which hides all our deformities.

6. 'tis blotted out as a cloud, as a thick cloud (Isa. 44:22). Sin is as a cloud [which] intercepts the beams of the sun, [and] comes between us and its light and influence. It's a partition wall. 'Tis a black cloud, [that] threatens a storm, a deluge. When 'tis pardoned this cloud is *blotted out*, as a thick cloud soon dispoiled by the sunbeams and no sign of it remains (Job 7:9). Thus God takes away all iniquity (Hos. 14:2), casts it into the depths of the sea (Mic. 7:19), not near the shoreside where 'twill appear again at low-water, but *into the depths of the sea* – past recall – alluding to the Egyptians drowned in the Red Sea. Thus God is said to remove our sins from us as far as east is from the west (Ps. 103:12), i.e. as far as it can be.

7. the quarrel that it raised between us and God is taken up. Pardon of sin is called reconciliation (2 Cor. 5:19). It is the ending of a controversy. Sin begets a controversy (Hos. 4:1). When the sin is pardoned the quarrel is over, atonement is made, there's peace with God (Rom. 5:1). God lets fall his action as it were. He shall make peace (Isa. 27:5). He calls to us to reason with him (Isa. 1:18), to plead with him (Isa. 43:26), which speaks his willingness to be reconciled. When we consent to the terms, he *is* reconciled. The enmity is slain. When God pardons sin he is said to be pacified (Ezek. 16:63).

To conclude. If this be pardon of sin,

1. Admire it. Well may we say, Who is a God like unto you (Mic. 7:18)? Let this goodness of God pass before you this day.
2. Make sure an interest in it. See that your sins be pardoned. Do not rest in an unpardoned state.

27 Dec. 1691

FOR I WILL BE MERCIFUL TO THEIR UNRIGHTEOUSNESS

D[octrine] That pardon of sin is one of the most precious privileges of the covenant of grace.

For the second. That pardon of sin is a privilege of the covenant of grace.

The forgiveness of sins is

1. an article of our creed, *I believe the forgiveness of sins*, that there is such a privilege purchased by the blood of Christ, promised in the everlasting gospel. It comes in among the privileges that pertain to the Catholic Church, which is by the blood of Christ sanctified and cleansed (Eph. 5:26, 27).
2. an article of our covenant. So it comes in here and when we say, 'I believe the forgiveness of sins' we mean more than a barren assent to the truth. It includes a consent to the tender.[1]

For the understanding we must distinguish

1. of two covenants that God hath made with man.

   a. A covenant of works – made with our first parents in innocency wherein *life* was promised upon condition of *perfect, personal and perpetual* obedience. Do this and live, i.e. continue happy. Now

      i. when Adam was taken into this covenant he needed no pardon – *for God made man upright* (Eccles. 7:29). There was a perfect purity and rectitude in his nature, his

1. i.e. acceptance of the gospel offer.

understanding clear, his will complying, his affections regular, all in frame. He was created in God's image. That in us which needs pardon is the devil's image. He that is innocent needs not to be justified. That was a covenant of friendship, not a covenant of reconciliation which supposeth a quarrel. Therefore there needed no mediator. Adam in his innocent estate dealt with God immediately. There was no cloud to interpose or interrupt his communion – no fracas, no wrath, but all clear.

ii. in case of failure the covenant promised no pardon. That covenant left no room for repentance (Gen. 2:17, *thou shalt surely die*), and therefore when Adam had eaten forbidden fruit he fled from God, and hid himself (Gen. 3:8), in a sense of his guilt, having no encouragement to hope for pardon, like the malefactor while the hue and cry is in pursuit of him. And if God had not presently revealed a Saviour, the seed of the woman that should break the serpent's head, Adam had sunk in despair. The law could not do it (Rom. 8:3).

b. A covenant of grace, and it is in and by this covenant that pardon and forgiveness is to be had, a better covenant established upon better promises, for the redemption of the transgressions that were under the first testament (Heb. 9:15). This is a plank thrown out after shipwreck, as the valley of Achor for a door of hope (Hos. 2:15). This is a covenant of reconciliation, supposeth man fallen, and so guilty and obnoxious, and needing pardon. 'Tis a remedial law.

2. between the Old Testament and the New Testament dispensation of the covenant of grace. The covenant of grace was for substance the same under both, but differing in the manner of dispensation.

a. The Old Testament saints received remission of sins – we find it often prayed for by the saints, often promised by God. 'Twere endless to instance particular places, especially in the prophets. The ceremonial law was founded upon and did suppose a possibility of reconciliation. Though the remission of the external punishment did then appear most obvious, yet the removal of God's wrath and the more spiritual consequents of that wrath were doubtless eyed by the true penitents, who looked through the ceremonial purifications by the washings and the ceremonial atonements by the sacrifices to spiritual cleansing and reconciliation.

b. The way and method of this remission was very darkly revealed to them in and by the sacrifices which could not possibly take away sin (Heb. 10:4). The malignity of sin is spiritual, and not removable by *carnal ordinances* and therefore those that did the service were not perfected by it as pertaining to the conscience (Heb. 9:9; 10:1). They could not receive the atonement with any assurance further than they looked at Christ through those sacrifices. The clearest revelation of remission of sins that we have in the ceremonial law was the Day of Atonement (Lev. 16:21), but in that there was a remembrance of sins every year (Heb. 10:3) and the repetition argued imperfection. All that were forgiven were forgiven for Christ's sake, though he were not then exhibited, and the faith the saints lived by was acted upon the revelation they had, and the faith working in obedience to the institutions they were under.

c. The nearer gospel times drew on, the more light they had concerning the terms of forgiveness (as Isa. 1:10-18; 55:7, 8) and the satisfaction of Christ as the ground of remission more fully revealed (Isa. 53; Dan. 9:24). Thus was the church led on by degrees to the knowledge of this mystery.

d. [This mystery] which now under the gospel is brought to light, and yet which is most clearly made known in the gospel is the ground of our pardon, namely, the death of Christ, remission *through his blood*. The law discovered the wound, but the gospel opens the remedy, the substance figured and typified by all the legal shadows, a dispensation of more light and liberty, yet yields us firmer footing for our faith to rest upon.

And blessed be God that this is the dispensation that we are under. The approach of this dispensation was the great argument to persuade to repentance (Matt. 3:2; 4:17).

3. between the external and the internal administration of the covenant of grace.

   a. Pardon of sin is freely offered to all upon their faith and repentance. This is the external administration, the tender and offer of the covenant proposals. Thus the covenant is administered in the visible church. As far as the sound of the gospel goes, so far goes the offer of pardon upon repentance – not forgiveness to all absolutely, whether they repent or no. 'Twould not consist with the holiness of God to make so unlimited a distribution of his favours.

But [there is] forgiveness to all that repent and believe.

   i. Forgiveness to all sinners. Repentance and remission must be preached among all nations (Luke 24:47). The sacrifices of atonement were instituted only for Israel, but Christ being come he is the propitiation for the sins of the whole world (1 John 2:2). The gospel excludes none that do not by their own unbelief and impenitency exclude themselves. Pardon [is] proclaimed even to the sinners of the Gentiles, that had been afar off. The first offer made to the Gentiles was by Peter (Acts 10:43). The chief of sinners was not excepted (1 Tim. 1:15, 16). Pardon upon repentance was offered even to those that had embrued[2] their hands in the blood of Christ (Acts 2:38) and Christ's dying prayer for them (Luke 23:34) warranted the offer. If any man sin, [we have an advocate with the Father, Jesus Christ the righteous] (1 John 2:1).

   ii. Forgiveness of all sins, unrighteousness, sins, iniquities, though for number many, for nature heinous, yet all forgiven. Upon repentance the blood of Christ cleanseth from all sin

2. *Embrued* or *imbrued*, 'to soak or drench (especially in blood)'.

> (1 John 1:7), and if we confess, God is faithful to cleanse us from *all* (v. 9). Paul had his blasphemy and persecution pardoned (1 Tim. 1:13), all trespasses (Col. 2:13). We have the rule and the only exception (which strengthens the rule) is Matthew 12:31, 32. The exception is the *blasphemy against the Holy Ghost*, therefore unpardonable because it is a sin against the highest and most convincing evidence that is appointed for the cure of unbelief. When a man is convinced that the miracles of Christ and his resurrection are true in fact, and yet shall be so far from taking them for a divine attestation as deliberately to determine in his heart that it was by the power of and by collusion with the devil that these works were done, and so make that the refuge of an obstinate unbelief, this is blasphemy against the Holy Ghost. Which means can possibly be used to convince such a man? What greater evidence can be expected? The Spirit works on men as intellectual agents – and as those that reject Christ's satisfaction will find no other sacrifice (Heb. 10:26), so that those who reject this evidence will find no other. 'Tis such a foundation of infidelity as a man cannot be beaten out of, as a man may from the disbelief of matter of fact. Certainly those have not committed this sin that believe Christ is the Son of God, and would fain have an interest in him, nor those that are afraid they have committed it. For 'tis a sin that hardens the heart with a resolute resistance of Christ. See Baxter of this sin, p. 35, etc. that Hebrews 6:6 speaks of the impossibility of the sinner's repenting, implying if he could repent they were pardoned.[3]

This excepted, the offer is free and general.

1. 'Tis written in the Scriptures as with a sunbeam in the Old

---

3. The reference can be located in *The Practical Works of Richard Baxter* (London: George Virtue, 1838), vol. 2, p. 331.

Testament (Isa. 1:16-18; 55:7, 8; Ezek. 18:30; 33:15, 16), [and] in the New Testament (Acts 2:38; 3:19; 13:38, 39; Matt. 6:14). The Scripture tells us how this privilege was procured for us (Eph. 1:7), on what we are to build our hopes of it, viz. the blood of Christ. [It] tells us on what terms 'tis proposed to us – repent, believe in Christ, go and sin no more, forgive others. We are not left to grope our way to peace and pardon, in the dark as the poor heathen, who laboured under invincible uncertainties about the way of reconcilement to the offended deity (Acts 17:23). But the way is plain, the work cut short in righteousness, the directions clear, the assurances firm. What would we more? The act of indemnity [is] signed, published, ratified.

2. Ministers [are] sent with authority to preach this (Luke 24:17). See their commission (John 20:23), *whosoever sins ye remit*. 'Tis not an authoritative but a declarative power, the act of indemnity being now past by the resurrection of Christ (Rom. 4:25; cf. Dan. 9:24). The apostles are sent and in them all succeeding ministers [are] to proclaim the jubilee, *to remit sin*, i.e. to assure the penitent of the remission of their sins according to the gospel and *to retain sin,* i.e. to cut off the impenitent from pardon. This is called binding and loosing (Matt. 16:19; 18:18), binding the guilt upon the unbelievers, as Peter did upon Simon Magnus, loosing it from them that believe. This extends to church censures.

3. The sacraments are seals of this offer, to assure us that God is in earnest in the proposal. Baptism is *for the remission of sins* (Acts 2:38; 22:16), i.e. it seals the proposals. Do not children need the forgiveness of sins? Are not they capable of it? Cannot God convey the privilege absolutely to them and the church can convey it but conditionally to any, and so it may to children upon their parents believing? Sacraments [are] apportioned to the external, not to the internal administration of the covenant of grace. They were instituted that we might have strong consolation (Heb. 6:17, 18). The Lord's Supper is a seal of our pardon, if we

repent and believe (Matt. 26:28). If not, we do but bind on former guilt.

Thus pardon of sin is a covenant privilege, as it is offered to all in the covenant.

a. Bless God for this offer. If yet in doubt about the forgiveness of thy sins, yet be thankful that there is forgiveness with God (Ps. 130:4), that pardon of sin is to be had.

b. Be encouraged to accept of it. The command is to you all to repent (Acts 17:30) and the promise as large upon repentance. Sense of this should melt us into a return.

c. Pardon of sin is effectually assured to all true believers. Others may be pardoned but they are pardoned – those that are not only in profession but in power in covenant with God. Though in strength of grace but little children, yet if truly born again their sins *are* forgiven (1 John 2:12). All that believe are justified (Acts 13:39), if their faith be true and sincere, a heart-purifying, a working faith. 'Tis one of the links in the golden chain (Rom. 8:30, if called, *then justified*). That is the order – not justified from eternity, but *elected* to be justified. Their justification was not actually but causally in the death and resurrection of Christ, as the effect in a meritorious cause not yet legally applied till you believe. You heard before what's the meaning of pardon of sin, the obligation to punishment ceaseth and becomes void.

Three questions I would answer concerning it:

Question 1. If believers have all their sins pardoned why then are they taught to pray every day for the pardon of their sins in the Lord's Prayer?

What do we mean when we pray for pardon?

A[nswer] Though believers are in a justified state yet they must pray for the pardon of their sins.

1. We must pray for the pardon even of the sins which we have some good hopes through grace are pardoned. David after he

was told that his sin [was] taken away (2 Sam. 12:13) yet prayed earnestly for pardon (Ps. 51:1, 2, 7, 9; Ps. 85:7). He prayed for the pardon of the sins of his youth (Ps. 79:8, *former iniquities*). The prodigal after he had received the kiss which sealed his pardon yet went on with his confession.

We must pray:

a. For the continuance of our pardon. As in daily bread, though we have it by us, we pray to God to give it to us, i.e. to continue it, so for daily pardon. We must pray for that which we are sure of, pray that God would not reverse that pardon, nor withdraw his loving kindness – that God would remember them no more – that the obligation to punishment once cancelled may never be again revived – that mercy vouchsafed may be more than a reprieve, that sin may never be imputed – forgive, forget.

b. For the consequents of our pardon viz. freedom from the penal evils which are the fruits of sin, that favour of God, the good things which our sins have kept back from us, the joy of God's salvation and his free spirit (Ps. 51:12). Those do not always come presently though the sin be taken away.

c. For the comfort of our pardon – that God would make us to hear joy and gladness (Ps. 51:8), not only pardon our sins but tell us that they are pardoned – sprinkled from an evil conscience (Heb. 10:22). This comfort may be clouded, and even pardoned sins may set themselves in array, and we may be made to possess them (Job 13:26) and then it's time to pray, 'Lord pardon them'. The pardon may pass in the court of heaven and not yet in the court of conscience.

d. For the completing of our pardon. Justification is not complete till the day of judgment and when we shall be openly acknowledged and acquitted,[4] when the times of refreshing shall come (Acts 3:19). Probably this explains that Matthew

4. 'Openly acknowledged and acquitted'. This is a quotation from the Westminster Shorter Catechism, Ques. 38.

12:32 of forgiveness in the world to come, and this is to be prayed for.

2. We must pray for the promised pardon of our renewed sins. Even justified persons have need to be daily praying for forgiveness. He that is washed hath need to wash his feet (John 13:10). There is a fountain opened that's always running (Zech. 13:1) and we have need of it.

   a. Those that are in a justified state yet are daily sinning *in many things* (Jas. 3:2; Eccles. 7:20; 1 John 1:5). Even God's children have their spots (Deut. 32:5), mixtures in the best duties – wine with water – sins of infirmity – nay, such fall sometimes into gross sins, as David, [or] Peter. We are not yet perfect – corrupt nature remains and will be working.
   b. Those sins are displeasing to God. Though they do not, they shall not, prevail to dissolve the state of justification, yet they are offensive to God. Though a true believer shall never again be a child of wrath, yet he may be a child under wrath (see 2 Sam. 11:27). Though God be reconciled to the sinner, he is not, he cannot be reconciled to the sin. His spirit is grieved (Eph. 4:30).

3. We are therefore to pray for the pardon of them – eminently and virtually all the sins of believers are pardoned in the imputation of Christ's righteousness which is the foundation of remission, but not formally and explicitly. They cannot be remitted before they are committed, no nor before they are expressly or implicitly repented of, since that would be a license to sin – *sins are passed [over]* (Rom. 3:25). There's a pardon ready but it must be sussed out, a righteousness ready but it must be pleaded (1 John 2:1). We are sinning daily and therefore must be repenting daily. God will be sought unto even for promised mercies (Ezek. 36.37). We turn the grace of God into wantonness and abuse his mercy if we become unconcerned about our sins because there's pardon ready. There is forgiveness that thou may be feared (Ps. 130:3,

4). You that through grace have your sins pardoned yet must live a life of repentance and watchfulness. After every fall be doing your first works (Rev. 2:5). Bless God there is a fountain opened, a pardon office erected, and be daily using it. Have recourse to the fountain. The covenant of grace is herein well-ordered yet there's provision made in case of failure. Every transgression in the covenant doth not put us out of the covenant.

Question 2. If all the sins of believers be forgiven them, what's the meaning of their afflictions? Is not the obligation to punishment dissolved?

A[nswer] 'Tis plain that even pardoned persons are afflicted. Man is born and born again to troubles, and it is a ruled case that even where the eternal demerit of the sin is remitted yet the temporal punishment may be inflicted (as 2 Sam. 12:13, 14) which derogates nothing from the honour of pardoning mercy (see Ps. 99:8). God sometimes may and doth afflict, not in reference to sin (as John 9:3) but he afflicts none but where there is sin. Christ had sin imputed. If there had been no sin there would have been no trouble. Pardoned persons die, and that's part of the wages of sin – and often suffer other outward trouble. Though pardoned [they are] yet afflicted. The body [is] dead because of sin (Rom. 8:10).

1. These afflictions are not the challenges of vindictive justice, to satisfy that. No, Christ has made full satisfaction for all that believe. There needs no additional satisfaction. They are not the effects of the rigorous justice of the law of works, as unremedied. They do not come from God's hatred against their sins – not from the covenant.

2. But they are the chastisement of a fatherly displeasure. Some dispute whether they should be called *punishments*. All chastisements are punishments; they are called punishment (Ezra 9:13), judgments (1 Cor. 11:31; 1 Pet. 4:17). There's a place

reserved in the covenant for these chastisements (Ps. 89:31), the rod of men (2 Sam. 7:14). There are rebukes which implies a fault (Rev. 3:20), fatherly corrections which are not but for some fault (Heb. 12:6, 7).

But what doth God intend in them.

a. He designs to assert the honour of his own covenant as in the case of David – to discover to all the world that he hates sin wherever he finds it. [He] will not, cannot, allow of it, no not in his own people (Amos 3:2). Therefore begin at the sanctuary (Ezek. 9:6). Those that shall not burn in hell for sin for ever yet are burnt in the hand for sin now (see Num. 14:20, 21). God is jealous of his own honour.

b. He designs to bring sin to remembrance and to embitter it to us (Job 13:26). Afflictions revive the remembrance of forgotten sins. 'Tis like the crowing of the cock to Peter. It helps to soften the heart and make it tender. It had this effect upon Ephraim (Jer. 31:18). This is the voice of the rod and of him that has appointed it. Afflictions are calls to repentance. We are chastened that we may not be condemned (1 Cor. 11:32).

c. He designs to reform and amend our hearts and lives, to reduce us from our strayings, to purge out corruption (Isa. 27:9). 'Tis not a destroying fire but a refining fire (Isa. 48:11) to purify the graces, that being provided they may be improved (Job 23:10). When God chasteneth he teacheth (Ps. 94:12), teacheth with briar and thorns. The same afflictions [are] designed for hurt to the wicked, for good to the godly (Gen. 24:5, 9).

Ques[tion] 3. If all the sins of believers be pardoned, whence is it that many true believers want the sense of that pardon and walk uncomfortably?

1. 'Tis God's pleasure it should be so. His favours are his own and he may dispense them as he pleaseth. [He] often speaks peace when he doth not make us to hear joy and gladness. [He] seems

to hide his face and withdraw the tokens of his love – to keep the soul humble and watchful, and to sweeten the comfort when it doth come – to prevent returns to folly, that the broken bones may never be forgotten, but better care taken for their future.

2. 'Tis generally through their own defaults – their ears are deaf to the peace that is spoken.

    a. 'Tis owing to their mistakes in the nature of pardon and repentance – they fear they are not pardoned because they do not sorrow for sin so much as they should, and who doth? Is it sincere? Understand that there may be a heart of flesh when yet there is much remaining hardness. Sin may be pardoned and yet there may be outward trouble and inward bitterness.
    b. Means of obtaining it are neglected, meditation and self examination, ordinances. There's need of diligence to get assurance (2 Pet. 1:10). We lose it by our slothfulness. The ordinance of the Lord's Supper is appointed for this end that we might get the comfort of our pardons. It is a sealing, assuring ordinance.
    c. The evil heart of unbelief hath a great stroke, distrust of God and hard thoughts of him, living off from a dependence upon Christ and looking for that in ourselves which is to be had in him only. We miss of comfort because we seek it in ourselves and lean too much to our own performances.
    d. Careless walking clouds that sense of pardon, gives just occasion to question our sincerity and provokes God to hide his face. When God's children grow heedless, rest in duty done and not minding how [they] misspend time, trifle with unsuitable company, no wonder if they lose the sense of pardon and put out the light of their comforts. These joys are reserved for those that keep close to God.

Watch against these things that hinder the sense of your pardons. Next to the happiness of a pardon is the comfort of knowing it.

[undated]

FOR I WILL BE MERCIFUL(i)

Doctrine That pardon of sin is one of the most precious privileges of the covenant of grace.

Application 'Tis a doctrine we are all of us interested in – for we have all sinned. Whether we are willing to own it or not we are all *guilty before God* (Rom. 3:19), all *concluded* under sin (Gal. 3:22). When a disease is epidemical every one is concerned to enquire into the methods of cure and therefore let us seriously endeavour to bring what hath been said home to ourselves.

Use 1. Give God the glory of his pardoning mercy and be often mentioning it to his praise. His goodness is his *glory* (Exod. 33:18, 19; 34:6, 7). He doth himself glory in it (Isa. 43:25; Prov. 25:2), and we should ascribe glory to him accordingly. Be affected with it, adore, admire pardoning mercy. What hath been said should raise our wonder. In the day of complete pardon the Lord will be *admired* (2 Thess. 1:10). If the sins of pardoned saints be (as some think they will) mentioned in that day, it will be only to increase the wonder. When such sins appear pardoned we should begin our heaven now in wonder.

To raise your admiration consider:

a. Who it is that *pardons* sin – 'tis God himself. The party wronged against when the injury is committed, it is he whose law is broken, his authority violated, his goodness slighted, his bowels spurned at by the sin which he pardons. 'Tis the law maker, the sovereign prince, none but he can pardon. 'Tis he that is the God of pardons (Neh. 9:17).

To afford you with wonder consider:

i. He is an omniscient God, and yet a pardoning God. Many times princes are content to pardon offences, because they cannot come to the knowledge of them, but God knows all the wickedness of our hearts and lives and yet pardons. [He] knows more than our own hearts know (1 John 3:20; Ps. 90:8). He *sees our ways* and yet is *ready to heal* us. It increaseth the wonder (Isa. 57:18). Princes pardon a crime sometimes, when if they knew all they would not. But God knows all the sins and all the transgressions in all the sins, and knows how prone we are to return to folly again, and yet he pardons.

ii. He's a holy and righteous God, and yet a pardoning God. He doth not only see all our sins, but he hates them all. They are contrary to his nature. He cannot endure to look upon iniquity and yet he has found out a way to pardon sin without impeachment of his justice. Though he is not, he cannot be reconciled to the sin, yet he is, he will be reconciled to the sinner. When he proclaimeth himself a God pardoning sin he subjoins a declaration of his justice (Exod. 34:6, 7). *[He] will by no means clear, visiting the iniquity [of the fathers upon the children]*.[1] [There is] no respect of persons with God, yet – not as David pardoned Absalom.

iii. He's a powerful, mighty God – and yet a pardoning God. Princes sometimes pardon because they cannot punish. David pardoned the sons of Zeruiah but because they were too hard for him (2 Sam. 3:39). But there's no weakness in God's arm. He can reach the stoutest, the biggest sinner with the messengers of his wrath. Oppositions made to him are but like briars and thorns before a consuming fire and yet he offers peace (Isa. 27:4, 5). He can frown a sinner into hell, punish with a word – and yet he pardons.

---

1. This sentence is a literal translation of part of the Hebrew text of Exodus 34:7. The AV and other translations insert in italics the word 'guilty' as the object of the verb 'by no means clear'.

b. How and after what manner he pardons. He is *God and not man* in his pardons, as in many other things (see Hos. 11:9). If all the patience and compassion in the world were crowded into the bowels of one man, yet that would be too weak to pardon you. Thou hast outsinned the compass and extent of all created patience and mercy, but I am God and not man.

'Tis in this especially that God will have us to know that his thoughts are not as our thoughts, nor his ways as our ways (Isa. 55:7, 8, 9). If we had been wronged and abused and had power to avenge ourselves, our thoughts and ways would be of nothing but that revenge, but it is not so with God.

'Tis in pardoning sin that God shows himself a none-such God[2] (Mic. 7:8). *Who is a God like into thee?* Thence the Maccabees had their name.[3] Com[pare] Exod. 15:11. We should thus adore God as a pardoning God, and we shall see cause enough for it if we consider:

i. How *free* his pardons are. We are justified *freely* (Rom. 3:24). He pardons *ex mero motu*.[4] [There is] nothing in us to move him to it, unless it be the misery we are in, which is the object of mercy. He forgives *for his own sake* (Isa. 43:25), not for our sakes be it known to us. He forgives because he will forgive, because he delighteth in tender mercy. That's the reason rendered (Mic. 7:18). When he afflicts he doth it not from the heart (Lam. 3:33). We force him by our provocations to take his rod in hand, but when he pardons he doth it for reasons fetched from within himself. His goodness doth but take occasion from our badness to be so much the more glorious. Where sin abounds grace doth much more abound in pardoning (see

---

2. i.e. 'a god unlike any other'.
3. The Maccabees were the leaders of Judah in the last two centuries BC. Here one of the possible derivations is given of the name 'Maccabee'. It could be a word made up from the initial letters of four Hebrew words in Exodus 15:11, 'Who is like you, O LORD, among the mighty?'
4. Latin, 'out of pure feeling'.

Isa. 43:24, 25; 57:17, 18). She went after her lovers and forgat me [said the Lord], therefore I will allure her (Hos. 2:13, 14). When God forgives 'tis that he may make his mighty power known (Ps. 106:8).

ii. How *full* his pardons are. Princes' pardons are often times for special reasons of state clogged with a multitude of provisory exceptions and limitations. Many offenders, [and] many offences particularly [are] excepted, but God's pardons are full.

(1) He pardons great sins. Man forgives *pence* but God forgives *talents*, ten thousand talents. Though iniquities reach up to the heavens the mercy of God reacheth beyond the heavens. His goodness overflows our crimes. There's pardon with God, even for *the rebellious also* (Ps. 68:18). Though sins have been as scarlet and crimson (Isa. 1:18), no stain [is] too deep for pardoning mercy to fetch out, no wound so desperate but the grace of God can cure it. Mountains [are] swallowed up as well as molehills in the depth of the sea.

(2) He pardons *all* sins, forgives *all* trespasses (Col. 2:13), *iniquity, transgression and sin* (Exod. 34:7), leaves not a drop in the cup of wrath and cancels all your obligations and dischargeth *all the debt* (Matt. 18:32). This is admirable indeed, considering how many, how mighty our transgressions are. [He is] *plenteous* in mercy, *abundant* in goodness – [O the] *riches* of his grace.

iii. How *frequent* his pardons are. Man pardons some few offences, now and then one, but he's apt to be weary, witness Peter's question (Matt. 18:21), but God *multiplies* to pardon (Isa. 55:7). *Many a time turned he his anger away*. 'Tis spoken of Israel (Ps. 78:38). He hath granted renewed pardons for renewed provocations. There's healing mercy with God even for backsliding sinners, that have returned to folly even after God hath spoken peace.

Former pardons are with men an argument against further pardons. Our law allows not the benefit of clergy more than once, but God's thoughts are not as ours. With him former pardons are a good plea for further mercy. Moses urged it and it prevailed, *as thou hast forgiven this people from Egypt* (Num. 14:19; Ps. 85:2, 4). Besides the first pardons there are after-pardons, and 'tis very admirable that there should be daily pardons for daily offences. [We are] encouraged to pray every day, 'forgive us our debts'. A pardon office [is] erected, a fountain opened.

iv. How *firm* his pardons are. [They are] pardons that are not, that cannot be recalled. The scope of the parable (Matt. 18) is not to show the possibility of the revocations of a pardon, but the necessity of our forgiving our brother to that pardon. When God pardons sin he casts it into the depth[s] of the sea (Mic. 7:19). Man forgives but he does not forget. When God forgives sin *he remembers it no more*. 'Tis blotted out as a cloud and of which no footstep remains. His gifts and pardons are without repentance (Rom. 11:29). 'Tis not in the power of any creature to reverse that pardon which the Creator has granted.

These pardons will be a plea that will certainly stand good at the great day. We may venture our soul upon them. Sin is *separated* as far as from east to west (Ps. 103:11, 12).

v. How *forward* he is to pardon. He is ready to forgive (Ps. 86:5), swift to show mercy. Man pardons but he must be importuned, and pressed for it, is generally very backward to it. But God is easy to be entreated. He's loath to punish. 'Tis his strange act (Isa. 28:21). He comes out of his place to punish (Isa. 26:21), for the place where he sits is the mercy seat. He has his eye upon us, to observe whether we are looking towards him, and if there be any penitent motions he is aware of them and is ready to meet us with a pardon. He looketh upon men (Job 33:27), [he] hearkens and heareth (Jer. 8:6), like the father of the prodigal, a lively representation of God's readiness to forgive (Luke 15:20). David did but sincerely purpose to confess and God forgave (2 Sam. 12:13; Ps. 32:5). He offers his pardons, beseecheth us to be reconciled, proposeth terms very easy and reasonable (Jer. 3:12, 13). Even an outside repentance hath prevailed for a reprieve, a remission of the temporal punishment as in the case of Ahab (1 Kings 21:29) and Nineveh (Jonah 3:10), a sign he is forward to forgive.

vi. How *faithful* and just he is in pardoning. This is admirable indeed, that infinite wisdom hath so ordered matters that it's become an act of righteousness in God to pardon sin (Rom. 3:25, 26). [He is] faithful and just to forgive (1 John 1:9). He doth not only pardon sin but he has been graciously pleased to oblige himself by promises to pardon our sins, so to make himself though not a debtor to us yet a debtor to his own truth. His justice is wonderful in that he pardons our sins for the sake of Christ's satisfaction, his righteousness imputed to us, made ours.

Promises of pardon [are] written, sealed, abundantly ratified and confirmed that we might have strong consolation. Provision [is] made to reconcile pardoning mercy with rectorial justice. The ends of government and the honour of God's dominion [are] preserved – mercy and truth are met together (Ps. 85:10).

Well, may we not say now, *Who is a God like unto thee pardoning iniquity?* 'Tis a sign we never experienced the riches of pardoning mercy if we do not admire it and be affected with it. Behold what manner of love (1 John 3:1). Wonder at the dimensions of it (Eph. 3:18), and let this:

1. Encourage our prayers. Is there all this riches of grace in pardoning mercy? Act faith upon this in your petitions for pardon. [There is] no room left for doubting.

2. Engage our praises. Speak of it to the glory of God. Render the calves of your lips.[5] The abundant riches of pardoning mercy call for abundant returns of praise and thankfulness.

Use 2. Make it sure to yourselves that your sins are pardoned. While I speak to men I speak to sinners, that are concerned in this doctrine. You have all sinned. The question is whether your sins be pardoned or no – as rightly a question as you can put to your own consciences. And yet how many are there that did never seriously propose it to themselves, yet have lived many years in this world, filling their measure of guilt by repeated transgressions and never yet considered of a way to empty that measure. The Lord touch the consciences of such.

I believe you would, all of you, desire to know whether your sins be pardoned or no.

1. You cannot search the records of heaven, nor look into the secret of the divine decrees. Say not, *Who shall ascend into heaven?* (Rom. 10:6, 7, 8). That needs not, we have the rules of trial in the Word, which is as a touchstone, a lamp and a light, not only to direct but to discover.

2. You must therefore search the register of your own hearts. Examine the state of your souls. Pardon is in itself only a relative change, but 'tis always accompanied with a real change by which 'tis known. In general, the character of one that's pardoned we have (Ps. 32:2), *in whose spirit there is no guile,* i.e. none reigning and predominant. David himself had some remainders of it, but the power of it was broken. For the main he was upright. 'Tis this sincerity that is our gospel perfection.

[There is] no guile, viz. in the work of repentance, which is the condition of our pardon, no allowed, approved guile.

Those have their sins pardoned who have done that which the

5. This is a quotation from Hosea 14:2.

Word requires as the condition of pardon. I shall therefore tell you what that is. Are you asking the question [in] Acts 2:37, or that [of] Micah 6:6, 7? I shall endeavour to answer it from the Word – and you must not expect any new directions, but the old plain truths (allu [de to] 2 Kings 5:11, 12; Gal. 1:9). And when I have told you what is required you'll see what you have to do that you may have your sins pardoned and whether you have done it or no.

Three things are required of all those that would have their sins pardoned, and are wrought in them. You shall see what they are from the Word of God, and that will be the major proposition. Your own conscience must make the minor, and then the conclusion will follow of itself, either one way or other.[6]

In order to [gain] that forgiveness of sin:

1. There must be a *sincere repentance* for all our past sins. [There is] no remission without repentance. They go together in the offer (Luke 24:47), [and] in the application (Acts 5:31). We are commissioned to offer pardon upon no other terms, and we cannot, we dare not make the terms easier (Acts 3:19). 'Tis the constant tenor both of the Old Testament and the New (Ezek. 18:30). Many [passages] serve to the same purpose. You'll easily acknowledge that it will by no means stand with the honour of God and of his government to pardon sin to those who do not repent of it. Pardon cannot be welcome to those who do not repent. Till we feel the weight of a burden we cannot reckon it a kindness to be eased of it. We reckon it but reasonable among men (Luke 17:3, 4, *if he repent forgive him*).

   You must repent, that is,

   a. You must be sensible of your sins. Know your abominations, and know them with a concernedness. See sin, so as you never yet saw it. Sin must appear sin (Rom. 7:13). Taste bitterness in sin, know and see that as an evil thing and a bitter

6. Matthew Henry is using the language of logic, in which there is a major premise, a minor premise and then a conclusion.

thing to depart from God (Jer. 2:19; 4:18). Sin becomes as the waters of Marah[7] to your repenting soul, or as the waters of jealousy,[8] that bitter water which causeth the curse. You must feel weight in sin, weary and heavy-laden (Matt. 11:28), pricked to the heart for it (Acts 2:37), as a man sensible of his sins. To repent is to be *convinced* of sin, original sin, actual sin,

- to be convinced of the fact of sin, that we have done so and so, without denying or dissembling.
- of the fault of sin, that we have done ill in doing so, without excusing or extenuating.
- of the folly of sin, that we have done foolishly in doing so, made a foolish bargain (Ps. 73:22).
- of the filth of sin, that we have been defiled in our own ways, have brought a stain upon our souls.
- of the fountain of sin, that all this comes from the corrupt nature, shapen in iniquity (Ps. 51:5; Job 14:4).
- of the fruit of sin, that the wages of every sin is death (Rom. 6:23), of our sin in particular.

This must be else [there is] no pardon. A tribunal must be erected in our own souls, process entered, the evidence examined, the matter brought to an issue.

b. You must be sorry for your sins (Ps. 38:18), godly sorrow (2 Cor. 7:9, 10, 11), the heart must be rent (Joel 2:13), broken (Ps. 51:17), the soul afflicted (Lev. 16:29) and it must be a kindly sorrow. Look upon a pierced Jesus and mourn and be in bitterness (Zech. 12:10). Peter wept bitterly. I lay not stress upon the outward expressions but upon the inward impressions. Deep waters do not make the greatest noise. Be sorry for your sins as when you have lost your labour, made a

7. Cf. Exod. 15:23.
8. Cf. Num. 5:21-31.

bad bargain – as Micah when he left his gods (Jude 18:24). Sorrow for all, though pleasant, gainful, fashionable, seemingly little.

c. You must loathe your sins and yourselves because of them. There must be a hatred and detestation of sin as that which is contrary to you. To repent is to fall out with sin, to be put out of conceit with it. Repentance is a change of your mind. Sin that was among your delectable things is now ranked with your detestable things. Job upon this score quarrelled with himself (Job 42:6; so Ezek. 6:9). To repent is to begin a quarrel with our own souls. What a wretch was I to sin against such a God, against so much light and love? 'Tis hard to persuade people to fall out with themselves but it must be, a quarrel with corrupt self, or else no pardon.

d. You must lay them open before God in a free and full confession. Declare your iniquity (Ps. 38:18). 'Tis the only way to pardon (1 John 1:9; Prov. 28:13). This David did and sped well (Ps. 32:3, 4, 5). Be particular in your confession – *this evil* (Ps. 51:4), thus and thus have I done (Josh. 7:19), and it must be with a suitable feeling – not as a tale that is told – but with holy shame and blushing (Ezra 9:6). In case of wrong done [there must be] confession to man and restitution.

This is the repentance required. 'Tis not saying, 'God forgive me', or 'Lord have mercy upon me', that will qualify us for the forgiveness of sins. 'Tis not hanging down your head like a bulrush, but there must be the contrition of soul.

2. There must be a *sincere repentance* upon the merit of Christ as our righteousness wherein to appear before God. [There is] no peace in any other way (Rom. 5:1). Those that are weary and heavy-laden must come to Christ (Matt. 11:28). Come to the Father by him (Heb. 7:25). There must be

a. a conviction of the insufficiency of our own and the all-sufficiency of Christ's righteousness. We must see ourselves not only in a miserable condition but in a hopeless condition, unable of ourselves to get out of that condition. Acknowledge that we owe more than ever we are able to pay. See the ability and willingness of Christ to save the believer. Believe the report of the gospel concerning him, that faithful saying (1 Tim. 1:15), and believe it with the application that he both can and will make you clean.

b. a consent to the terms on which he is offered to us in the gospel. Accept the proposal, touch of the top of the golden sceptre, *kiss the Son* (Ps. 2:12) in token of the resignation of yourselves to him. Come under the healing wings of the Son of Righteousness. Fly to Christ for refuge as the poor guilty malefactor (Heb. 6:18). Be found in Christ (Phil. 3:9). Lord, I am willing to be ruled and saved by thee.

c. a confidence in him and in his righteousness, trusting in him, as having enough in his satisfaction and the atonement made by him to answer the demands of God's justice and the desires of our souls. When we come for the pardon of our sins we must come with a Christ in the arms of our faith and love. Make him our friend. [There is] no seeing the face of God with comfort out of Christ. The Jews came short of justification by going about to establish their own righteousness (Rom. 10:3). 'Tis a rock that multitudes split upon. If any man sin we have an advocate, a propitiation (1 John 2:1, 2). Away to that fountain. Take hold of the horns of the altar (Ps. 71:16).

3. There must be a *sincere resolution* by the grace of God to go and sin no more. This is another thing required, else no pardon – not only repent but *turn* (Ezek. 18:30), else we do but mock God (see John 8:11). Cease to do evil and learn to do well (Isa. 1:16, 18; Isa. 55:7; Prov. 28:13). What can be more reasonable than this? Contrition for sin is a mere mockery if it be not accompanied with a conversion from sin. There's no pardon but a curse to those that say, I shall have peace though I go on (Deut. 29:19). In vain do we pretend to be sorry of what we have done if we be not firmly resolved to do so no more (Job 34:32).

This resolution against sin implies

a. a strong engagement against remaining corruptions. The axe of justification must be laid to the root of them. If they be harboured and festered and allowed of, if we approve of that inclination which is in us to evil, and are willing to have it gratified, there's no peace. If all goes one way in the soul it's a bad sign, for all will not go the right way. Whenever the guilt of sin is pardoned though the doing of it remains, the power of it is broken. Where the iniquities are forgiven the diseases are healed (Ps. 103:3). When God pardons sin he *subdues the iniquities* (Micah 7:19).

b. a full purpose against actual transgressions, binding the soul with a bond against every evil work and way – from a conviction of the great evil of sin – casting it away with detestation and abhorrence (Hos. 14:8). This must be deliberate, not a flash but a settled resolve. Such a resolution will ordinarily blunt the edge of a temptation, a resolve against sin as sin, which will be a universal resolve and a well-principled resolve.

You too know what we must do that we may have our sins pardoned, and now brethren,

1. Have you done this? Conscience, speak the truth in the presence of God. Can you witness to such affections as these about your sins? What faith? What repentance? What fruit of them? One evidence of the sincerity of this is our readiness to forgive others that trespass against us. See Matthew 6:14, 15. Wrath and malice and rancour and bitterness evidence great hypocrisy. In other things we can tell whether we repent – why not in this?
2. Will you do this? You see the way chalked out to you plainly. Will you walk in it? The promise of pardon upon repentance should be a prevailing inducement with us to repent (Matt. 4:17). Delays are dangerous. Today if you will hear his voice harden not your heart (Heb. 3:7). Make it sure to yourselves that you truly repent. Believe the gospel and then the Scripture. Make it sure to yourselves that your sins are all pardoned.

24 Jan. 1692

FOR I WILL BE MERCIFUL(ii)

D[octrine] That pardon of sin is one of the most precious privileges of the covenant of grace.

Use 3. Accept the gospel offer of pardon. The offer is general, let the application be particular. Do not give sleep to your eyes nor slumber to your eyelids till you have some comfortable evidence of your interest in this unspeakable privilege. Press after a share in this blessedness. Most people are enquiring for *any good.* Do not content yourselves with any good (Ps. 4:6) but reach after *all good*, all the good which is included in pardon of sin.

You have been told what you must do that you may have your sins pardoned. Take it in two words.

1. Accept the pardon in a covenant way; submit to the grace of the Lord Jesus. Take it and thank Christ for it, not any merit or righteousness of your own. Even the faith by which it is received is the gift of God (Eph. 2:8). How it stuck with the Pharisaical generation (Rom. 10:3). Receive the remission of sins in a dependence upon Christ, his merit for your purchase of it, his Spirit for the application of it. 'Tis he that gives repentance and remission (Acts 5:31).
2. Accept the pardon upon covenant terms, with the removal of the guilt of sin by pardoning mercy. Be willing to have the power of it broken by renewing grace. Will you submit to the grace of Christ, submit to his government – a Prince and a Saviour? And this is the law of his kingdom, *let the wicked forsake his way* (Isa. 55:7). There must be an abhorrence of every sin, and a stedfast reflection to walk closely with God.

But I see, in this case 'tis much more easy to direct than to persuade, to tell people what they shall do than to prevail with them to do it. Pardon of sin is richly offered. Now there are two sets of people to be dealt with:

1. Presuming sinners, that slight the offer, that are unconcerned about their sins, careless of pardon, indifferent whether they have their sins pardoned or no, put off seeking after it, ready to say as Laodicea (Rev. 3:17), as Ephraim (Hos. 12:8), so pleased with a self-acquittment that you are not concerned whether God acquit them or no (Prov. 30:20).
2. Despairing sinners, that put away the offer because they think it doth not belong to them. They say, there is no hope; no! (Jer. 2:25) and so *pine away* in their iniquities (Ezek. 33:10). [They] think their iniquities [are] too great to be pardoned (Gen. 4:13 margin).[1] These are like the two rocks (1 Sam. 14:4), on one or the other multitudes split and perish.

Let me therefore speak a few words to each, to persuade them to accept the offer of pardon. Let us reason together (Isa. 1:18). The objections of both are very unreasonable. Let us *plead* together (Isa. 43:26). What words shall I choose out?

1. To startle and awaken the careless. I speak to those that are under the guilt of sin and take no care to get it removed, [who] never yet seriously asked, 'What shall I do?'

Fools make a light matter of sin (Prov. 14:9). 'Tis the general distemper of the careless world, as persons in debt many times [are] unconcerned about their debts. Augustus Caesar sent for the pillow of one that died deep in debt, concluding there must need be some strange narcotic virtue in that pillow or else a man so much in debt could never sleep upon it. I wonder what pillows people sleep upon

---

1. The margin of the AV gives the following translation of this verse: 'Mine iniquity is greater than that it may be forgiven.'

that are so much in debt to God's justice by sin and take no care about it, as if the debt would pay itself, or time would pay it. Let's inquire into the cause and cure of this carelessness.

That which makes the generality so careless is

a. their ignorance. They do not know *what is sin*, so think themselves not guilty. They do not know *what sin is* and so think there is no danger. [They] know not that they are wretched (Rev. 3:17), know not what a precious privilege pardon is, *if thou knewest* (John 4:10). They know not neither *will* they understand (Ps. 82:5), and that's the reason *they walk on in darkness*.

b. their infidelity. 'Tis a practical atheism that is at the bottom of it. When they are told that if their sins be not pardoned they are undone, would they neglect so great a concern if they did really believe it? It doth not profit them for want of faith like Lot's sons in law (Gen. 19:14).

c. their inconsideration. They know and say they believe but they do not lay it to heart, and the reason of this inconsideration is [that] they are too full of other things, carnal mirth and jollity, the care and cumbrances of the world fills them. Bad company draws away their hearts, or they think it's time enough yet. [They] put off the concern to a more convenient season, as Felix (Acts 24:25). People think they shall fare as well as their neighbours.

Now to awaken you out of this carelessness I must entreat you to consider. You can be considerate enough in other things that are but trifles to this. For the Lord's sake consider a little:

i. What need you have of pardon, you are guilty, filthy, wounded, obnoxious. [You have] no righteousness of your own (Ps. 50:21; 1 John 1:5, 9). Whether you believe it or no, so it is. You have sinned and you cannot disown it.

ii. Think what your condition is while your sins remain unpardoned. God is your enemy. He is angry with you every day (Ps. 7:11) and his wrath is increasing, while you go on in your impenitency (see v. 12), *if he turn not*, which implies mercy in case he do turn, but if not, he will *whet his sword.* While you abide under the guilt of sin you abide under the wrath of God (John 3:36), treasuring up wrath (Rom. 2:5). Every sin thou committest adds to the account, and will inflame the reckoning. The whole creation is at war with thee. All the curses of the law stand in full force against thee. An unpardoned sinner is a matter for a curse to operate on.

All thy enjoyments are cursed to thee. Guilt stains all the beauty, and embitters all the greatness of the creature. Every affliction has a sting in it. 'Tis guilt that is *the wormwood and gall* in the affliction and the misery. 'Tis that that makes the cross so heavy. There is *no peace* (Isa. 57:21) except it be that rotten peace which is worse than trouble. Sacrifice [is] an abomination (Prov. 15:8; Isa. 1:11). The roaring lion has full power over you. The sin thou liest under is his image and he will own it. The smell of the everlasting fire is already upon you.

Sirs, do you believe this? That till your sins are pardoned God is against you, *I even* I (Ezek. 5:8). Assume that time will not better your condition. It's but going worse while you continue in your neglect. You are sleeping on the top of a mast.

iii. Consider upon what reasonable terms pardon is offered to you. You are not required to bring thousands of rams, no, only acknowledge thine iniquity (Jer. 3:12, 13). *Repent and turn* (Ezek. 18:30). The sacrifice of God is a broken spirit (Ps. 51:17). Could you with confidence ask an offer of pardon upon easier terms? Nay, tis not only offered you but you are counselled to accept of it (2 Cor. 5:20) and have all possible assurances given you of the sincerity of the offer.

This will aggravate the condemnation of sinners and render it the more intolerable, that pardon was offered them upon such easy terms and they would not accept it. How will this exasperate the never-dying worm and pour oil into the inextinguishable flame (Prov. 1:24, 25)? 'Twill for ever justify God and every mouth will hereby be stopped. If you had been required to do some great thing (allu[de to] 2 Kings 5:13).

iv. Consider what a great deal of work you have to do to get your sins pardoned, what a deceitful heart is to be examined, crooked ways to be considered, nests of wickedness to be searched into and discovered, a tedious web to be unravelled. That which makes many so careless is [that] they presume upon the grace of God, turn it into wantonness, as if a pardon were soon obtained, as if a cold, 'God forgive me', or, 'Lord have mercy upon me', would expiate for the sins of their whole lives, or the reading of the absolution over them would send them to heaven without control.

Believe it, pardon is not so easily had. There's many a high thought to be humbled, a hard heart to be softened, a heart of stone melted, a long account to be cast up. The gate of repentance is a strait gate, the way to pardon is a narrow way (Matt. 7:13). Therefore, *strive to enter* (Luke 13:24). Lazy seeking will not do. The longer 'tis put off the harder it grows (Heb. 3:13).

v. Consider what a little time you have to be doing it in. People are tempted to put off the great work, thinking it's time enough yet, but the judge standeth before the door. You know not how few sands may yet be in the glass. You see others as likely to live as you gone into eternity. They have no lease of their lives, not the youngest, not the strongest. Death may surprise you before you are aware in an unpardonable state. Persons in debt sometimes comfort themselves with this that the creditor cannot take out execution perhaps till next term, or next court-day, and so long they are safe, but we are no day secure from the arrests of death. Now is the accepted time (2 Cor. 6:2), no time your own but the present time. You have lost a deal of time already, and have spent that time in filling the measure of guilt which you should have spent in emptying of it.

vi. Consider how happy you will be if your sins be pardoned. You are made for ever. Let this work be upon your hope. Do not neglect so *great a salvation* (Heb. 2:3). When pardon is offered you all blessedness is offered you, pardon and peace, joy, comfort, the favour of God – [they are] all your own if sin be pardoned. 'Tis the foundation of all the privileges of the New Covenant. Believe the favour of God to be better than life, and you will labour after that favour.

vii. Consider what will come of it if you live and die in an unpardoned state. You are certainly undone for ever. Salvation itself cannot save the finally impenitent. *You shall die in your sins* (Joh. 8:24), a terrible word. Better die in a dungeon than die in our sins, to have the sins of youth lie down with us in the dust (Job 20:11), iniquities upon the bones (Ezek. 32:27).

How dreadful will unpardoned sins look in the judgment of the great day, when we must give account to everything done in the body (2 Cor. 5:10), all appearing against us and no plea, no advocate, nothing to bring us off? If no pardon in this world 'tis certain [there is] none in the world to come, and then there remains nothing but a certain fearful looking for of judgment and fiery indignation (2 Cor. 5:11).

And now what say you to it, you careless ones? What thoughts have you of sin and the pardon of it? I can but lay these thoughts before you. 'Tis your concern to lay them to heart. You cannot but say that you have a fair offer. Do not put it away from you. Say not, it's time enough yet. Choose the good and refuse the evil. If you stood condemned at man's bar how welcome would the news be. Think of these things as you will think of them shortly.

2. To comfort and encourage the despairing. It may be I speak to some that are truly sensible of their sins, and concerned about them and desire nothing more than to have them pardoned but distrust pardoning mercy, think their iniquities [are] too great to be pardoned. *Come now* and let us *reason together* (Isa. 1:18).

'Tis against the will of God that you should pine away in your iniquities (Ezek. 33:10, 11). He has made sufficient provision for your encouragement. There's enough in the Word for faith to fasten upon – firm footing. Therefore be not faithless but believing. Judas repented but he despaired, and it was his ruin. In true repentance there must be an eye to the mercy of God in Christ. Think as bad as you will of sin, provided you do not think it unpardonable. Though your sins have been many, mighty, repeated, deeply aggravated, yet return and repent and they shall all be pardoned.

This is good news, like rain to the new mown grass, but what assurance of it? Assurance enough.

a. The mercy of God is infinite mercy. We dare not set bounds to this mercy. 'Tis almighty mercy, his *power* is great in pardoning sin (Num. 14:17) and is any thing too hard for him? Our sins are but finite, being the sins but of finite creatures, but his mercy is infinite, being the mercy of an infinite God. You have heard the proclamation of his name, and it is encouraging enough (Exod. 34:6, 7). Mercy and forgiveness belong to him (Dan. 9:9). Mercy is his delight. He is swift to show mercy. He hath said it, he hath sworn it, he has *no pleasure in the death of sinners* (Ezek. 33:11). He had rather they would turn and live than go on and die. He meets returning penitents (Jer. 31:18, 19, 20). The Ninevites took encouragement purely from this (Jon. 3:9) and it sped well.

We are *men* in sinning (Hos. 6:7) but he is God and not man in pardoning (Hos. 11:9). You cannot deny the goodness of God if you consider your own experience of it. Mercy hath reprieved you this long and done you good. The methods of providence towards you have been such as abundantly evidence his goodness. Argue from thence, if the Lord had been pleased to kill me he would not have done so much for me (Judg. 13:23).

b. The merits of Christ's death are of inestimable value. Did we expect pardon for sake of anything in ourselves? Our expectations must need rise or fall according to the value thereof, but the merits of Christ being of infinite worth no room is left for doubting. His blood is *the blood of God* (Acts 20:28). The price paid down received its value from the dignity of him that paid it. If an estate be claimed we reckon the payment and acceptance of a valuable consideration is a good plea. When we plead the merit of Christ we plead a valuable consideration. And there is an infinite sufficiency (1 John 1:7, *from all sin*). He is able to save to the uttermost (Heb. 7:28), to the uttermost of sins, of sinners, especially because of his *intercession*. There's much in that (1 John 2:1, 2).

c. The invitations of the gospel are free and gracious. All that are weary and heavy-laden are called to come to Christ (Matt. 11:28). He is our David ready to entertain all that are in *distress* or in *debt* or *discontented* with themselves and their sins (1 Sam 22:2). The golden sceptre is yet held out, and whosoever will may come. The proclamation of pardon is published. It excludes none that do not by their unbelief and impenitency exclude themselves. Gospel offers are serious. God is in earnest.

d. The promises of the New Covenant are sure and precious. There's footing firm enough for faith in the promises. This is in the text if there were no more, word upon word for our encouragment. The promises [are] large and unlimited (Isa. 1:18), *as scarlet and crimson* – a deep dye, a double dye, in the wool of original corruption, in the many threads of actual transgressions. Yet there is mercy. He will abundantly pardon (Isa. 55:8). And these [are] the Word of God or are they not? If they are, are they not true, eternally true and dare you question them? 'Tis unbelief that staggers at the promises. We have line upon line to this purpose. The promises [are] sealed in the sacrament of baptism (Acts 2:38), in the Lord's Supper (Matt. 26:28), that we might have strong consolation (Heb. 6:18), too strong to be borne down by unbelief.

e. The experience of all ages confirms this. Great sinners have found mercy and why may not we? Never any true penitent from the beginning of the world to this day missed of pardon – Manasseh (2 Chron. 33:12, 13), though as to the temporal punishment the Lord would not pardon (2 Kin. 24:4), yet the eternal demerit was remitted; Mary Magdalene out of whom was cast seven devils yet much was forgiven (Luke 7:39, 48), the Corinthians (1 Cor. 6:11, 12), Paul (1 Tim. 1:13-16); even those that had a hand in crucifying Christ (Acts 2:23, 38). One would not be afraid to venture after so many instances, especially when none can be produced to the contrary.

Hearken to this poor desponding soul. There is balm in Gilead, the wound is not incurable. Thy case is sad but not desperate, there is *hope in Israel*.

1. Chide yourselves for your disquietments. It is your infirmity (Ps. 77:10). Do not allow yourselves in it. Be not proud of your doubts.
2. Charge yourselves to believe (Ps. 42:5). Venture upon Christ and the covenant of grace and be positive in it.

Use 4. By way of exhortation to those who through grace have their sins pardoned. I hope I speak to many such who being justified by faith have peace with God. The Apostle grounds an exhortation upon this privilege (1 John 2:12). Take heed of abusing this privilege. Do not make ill use of it (see Rom. 6:12). Your pardon is but pretended if from thence you take encouragement to sin.

Are your sins pardoned?

1. Be very thankful. Look upon it as an unspeakable privilege and value it accordingly. Put it in the imprimis[2] of the receivings. See Psalm 103:1, 2, 3. When you are mentioning your mercies mention this as the spring of all. Think how much was forgiven and how freely. This use we should make of the remembrance of

---

2. Latin, 'first', 'chief'.

past sins to have our hearts thereby enlarged in thankfulness. Read the book and see it crossed. Paul would not hold in the midst of his discourse (1 Tim. 1:16, 17). See every pardon flowing to you in the blood of Christ and let that enlarge your heart in thankfulness (see Rev. 1:5).

2. Love much. If you be truly thankful you will be studying what you shall render (Ps. 116:12), and the thing that you are to render is *love*. Those to whom much is forgiven should love much (Luke 7:42, 43). Sense of the riches of that privilege cannot but enlarge your heart in love. The love of Christ must needs constrain us to love him again.

   And this love should engage us to and encourage us in all manner of gospel obedience. It should be oil to the wheels, our bonds loosed (Ps. 116:16). He loved us and washed us. Those who have their sins pardoned should think nothing too much to do, too hard to suffer, too dear to part with for God. If we are at any time called out to hard service, sense of pardon should carry us through it.

3. Be very careful to preserve the sense of your pardon. Be chary of your comforts, do nothing to disturb them. Unbelief and careless walking oftentimes cloud our evidences. We lose the comfort of pardon when we return to those sins that were pardoned. Be not on every occasion calling the evidences in question. Take heed lest the noise of this world's hurry drown the voice of joy and gladness. Keep up a relish of the sweetness of pardoning mercy.

4. Be oft remembering with regret even pardoned sins. Let sin be ever before you, even pardoned sins. So David's was and yet [see] Psalm 51:3. Never think a kind thought of sin, though pardoned. The prodigal after he had received the kiss which sealed the pardon yet went on with his confession (Luke 15:20, 21). Sorrow for pardoned sins is kindly, and flows from love to

God. There is a holy shame and blushing which follows upon God's being pacified (Ezek. 16:8; Ps. 38 title[3]).

5. Bear afflictions cheerfully. Sense of *sin* should make us *patient* under afflictions (Lam. 3:39; Mic. 7:9), but sense of *pardon* should make us *cheerful,* not so much as say, 'I am sick' (Isa. 33:24). Be of good cheer (Matt. 9:2). If sin be pardoned the sting of the affliction is taken out, there's no harm in it, no wrath in the cup, no curse with the cross, sick but not in sin.

6. Go and sin no more. If your sins be indeed pardoned, you have repented of them, and then you have tasted bitterness in them. Have you done so? If you have indeed you'll have little mind to it another time. Gratitude obligeth us not to return to sin again (John 8:11; Ps. 85:8). For peace and pardon's sake have no more to do with sin. When your wounds have been healed, will you run another venture? God is not mocked. Do not think that a pardon is a licence to sin. Think what was the price that purchased your pardon and then take heed of dallying with it. Do not trample under foot the blood of the covenant (Heb. 10:29).

7. Be ready to forgive others. Sense of pardon of sin should help to weaken our spirits, and to make us gentle and easy to be entreated. Them that have found mercy should show mercy. 'Tis the Apostle's argument (Col. 3:12, 13; Eph. 4:32). Think what a great debt was forgiven you (Mat. 18:32). Be not of a revengeful implacable spirit. Do not lie at watch to take advantage against a brother. Be not extreme to mark what is done amiss.

8. Rejoice in hope of the glory of God (Rom. 5:1, 2). Justification is an earnest of glory (Rom. 8:3). Go thy way and eat thy bread with joy (Eccles. 9:7). Hath God pardoned thee? He has not done with thee. Long for the day when you shall be openly acknowledged and acquitted, your pardon proclaimed before all the world and the comfort of it completed, when the times of

---

3. The title of Psalm 38 is: *A Psalm of David, to bring to remembrance.*

refreshing shall come (Acts 3:19). If sin be pardoned every bar in the way of thy happiness is removed. See an account of the future happiness of those that are justified, that are washed in the blood of Christ (Rev. 7:14, 15, 16, 17).

5

Peace in the Covenant

24 Jan. 1692

PEACE IN THE COVENANT

Peace I leave with you. My peace I give unto you, not as the world giveth, give I unto you (John 14:27).

Our Lord Jesus is here in this chapter as the long expected *consolation of Israel* speaking good words and *comfortable* words to his poor disciples whom he was now leaving overwhelmed with a multitude of sorrows and exposed to a multitude of dangers in an evil, malignant world. Among many other refreshing words this in the text is not the least considerable. *Peace I leave with you.* Com[pare] chapter 16:33. When our Lord Jesus was about to leave the world he made his will. His soul he committed to the hands of his Father (Luke 23:46). His body he bequeathed to Joseph of Arimathea to be decently interred, yet not so as to see corruption. His clothes fell to the soldiers that crucified him (Luke. 23:34). His mother he left to the care of the beloved disciple (John 19:26). But what should he bequeathe to his poor disciples, who had forsaken all to follow him? Silver and gold he had none to leave them, but he left them that which was infinitely better than thousands of gold and silver. Two things:

1. His pattern (1 Pet. 2:21) particularly of humility (John 13:1, 15) when he was ready to depart and it is a pattern without a blot.

2. His peace in the text – the former to make us holy, this to make us happy. Those and those only may expect an interest in his peace that conform to his pattern. Thus careful was our dear Master of his poor disciples in a world of doubts and sorrows. The pattern resolves doubts and the peace ends the sorrows. After his resurrection he pronounced peace *to them* (John 20:21) but that they might have strong consolation it is here made a legacy and consigned to us by will.

The covenant of grace is called διαθήκη[1] which properly signifies a *testament*. Christ is the Testator. The text is a comfortable item in the testament. *Peace I leave with you*, which is full to show that *peace* is conveyed to us in the New Covenant or testament.

Observe:

1. What the legacy is. 'Tis *peace, my peace*. 'Tis called Christ's peace, the peace that he enjoyed, spiritual peace, that he purchased by the merit of his death – the peace that he preached (Eph. 2:17) – that peace that by the promises and prophecies of the Old Testament was annexed to his kingdom and government. 'Tis his therefore, he has power to bequeath it. He is the appointed trustee of peace. He is the Prince of Peace (Isa. 9:6). He is the peace (Mic. 5:5).
2. To whom it is bequeathed – to *you* – you that believe in me. You, my disciples and followers, them that are likely to be most exposed to trouble, *you* in distinction from the unbelieving world that has no part nor lot in this matter, *you* that are the sons of peace and so are capable subjects disposed for reception of such a blessing. See Luke 10:5, 6. When ministers preach peace none but the sons of peace that are qualified can claim the benefit. To *you*, viz. not only in their personal capacity but as they were the representatives of the whole church. As in precept, so in promise. What was said to them was said to all (Matt. 13:6). *You* – and all that are like you in all generations, not for you only (John 17:20).

   The repetition is very emphatical. I leave it with you. I give it to you a present grant, which doth actually confer an interest that we might have abundant encouragement. I *give* it, and what's freer than a gift? When Christ ascended on high he *gave* gifts (Eph. 4:11) and this was one of his gifts. Ministers may preach peace and pray for peace but it's Christ's prerogative to give peace. He's the Lord of peace himself (2 Thess. 3:16).

---

1. Greek, 'covenant', and only rarely 'testament' (see Heb. 9:16-17).

Question What is that *peace* which our Lord Jesus here bequeathes?

Answer Peace is taken generally for *all good.* 'Twere endless to mention particular instances. *Peace be to you* was the usual Hebrew salutation. When Christ leaves his peace with his disciples he leaves them all good. 'Tis hard to know what is good for a man in this life (Eccles. 6:12), but he that doth know hath assured all good to those that are his. He to whom God has given Christ, how shall he not with him give every thing else (Rom. 8:32)?

All good, i.e. all needful good, all that which our poor souls stand in need of, all the purchased good, all the promised good, all that which is truly and really good, that which is good for your better part, for the eternal state. The fountain of all good, viz. the favour of God. No *good* thing shall he withhold (Ps. 84:11). Whatever we want we may be sure it is not good for us, or else we shall have it. Whatever good we have 'tis Christ's – my peace – see all flowing from his fulness!

2. Peace is taken especially for love and reconciliation. Now what is that peace which Christ has left to his people:

a. Negatively – not peace with the world, neither the god of this world, nor the men of the world. [There is] no peace for the seed of the woman either with the serpent or with the serpent's seed since the old enmity was put (Gen. 3:15). We must not expect it. God's beloved ones are the world's hated ones and we are not to marvel at it (1 John 3:13), the hatred, cruel, restless. So that is not *the peace* here meant. This is not Christ's peace. He had it not, he was despised and rejected of men, persecuted to the death, and those that bear his image must not expect better usage in the world than he had (Matt. 10:24, 25; John 13:16).

Nay, our master has expressly forewarned us of the contrary

(John 16:33). Our way to heaven lies through many tribulations (Acts 14:22). We must suffer persecution (2 Tim. 3:12). You may sooner reconcile fire and water, light and darkness, than the seed of the woman and the seed of the serpent. The experience of all ages seals to it. Christ came to send a sword, the sword of persecution (Matt. 10:34, 35, 36).

We are called out of the world, [we] are not of it. God can make even enemies to be at peace (Prov. 16:7). The gospel sets us at a distance from the world, crucifies us to the world and the world to us, and therefore we must look for the world's hatred (John 15:18, 19). But blessed be God there's no real evil in it – better an enemy than a friend to the world. Even this [is] for good and we shall get *through* it.

b. Positively, what is the peace that Christ here leaves to those that are his? It had need be something very good that must countervail all this trouble that he hath left them and so it doth abundantly.

i. Peace with God. That's Christ's peace, the peace that he came to make. When the first begotten was brought into the world 'twas with an olive-branch of peace (Luke 2:14), *on earth peace*. The counsels of the covenant are *counsels of peace* (Zech. 6:13). This peace is left with and given to all the saints. It notes not only the making of the peace, at our first reconciliation, but the maintaining and keeping up of the peace ever after. Being justified by faith we *have peace* with God (Rom. 5:1). God is said to be *reconciling* the world (2 Cor. 5:19), which notes a continued act, carrying on the work of reconciliation from one degree to another. q.d.[2] Whoever are your enemies I bequeath God to them for a friend. That peace I leave with you.

Our Lord Jesus has bequeathed to all his people:

(1) An interest in the love and favour of God. Jesus Christ

2. Latin abbreviation, *quasi dicas*, 'as if, as it were'.

was the beloved Son of his Father, God was well-pleased in him, and he has bequeathed to us an interest in the same love, and acceptance (Matt. 17:5, *in whom),* so that we become joint heirs with Christ (Rom. 8:17, *heirs of God*). [He] empowers us to make use of his name and interest at the throne of grace. The Father loveth the Son (John 3:35) and the Son has made over that interest in his Father's love to all his friends (John 14:21; 16:27), owns them for his brethren (John 20:17*), My Father and your Father, my God and your God.* Therefore [it is] ours because [it is] his. He hath undertaken for the Father, and hath commission so to do (John 16:15). My father *will* love him (John 14:23), will honour him (John 12:26), *my peace I give unto you*, q.d., you that believe, take this upon the word of the faithful witness, whoever hates you my Father will love you. He undertakes for it, and this is a precious legacy.

(2) An access to the throne of grace (Eph. 2:18). He has left with all the saints a door open, *a new and a living way* to the Father (Heb. 10:20). He has settled an intercourse between us and God, and left that to us as a precious privilege. He founded it in the merit of his death, that rent the veil. He keeps it up in the prevalency of his intercession as our advocate with the Father. He has assured us of an answer of peace to all our prayers (Ps. 85:8).

(3) A ready way to take up a quarrel in case any happen. He's left us a plea to urge, a promise to fasten upon. He's bequeathed to us a fountain open, in which to wash our feet daily (John 13:10). He having delivered us from condemnation undertakes that we shall not come into condemnation (John 5:24). There is inexhaustible treasure of merit in the Lord Jesus, and 'tis given us to make use of it as there is occasion.

Thus he has given us peace with God.

ii. Peace with our brethren. He has left this peace to his church, and it is a precious legacy. He died not only to bring God and man together, but to bring the saints nearer together (Eph. 2:14, 15), to gather them all together in one (Eph. 1:10; John 11:52). The reign of Christ [is as] peaceable as Solomon's (Isa. 11:6, 7; Ps. 72:7). Jerusalem [became] a vision of peace. This was Christ's legacy and it had a strange effect. Before the death of Christ how often do we find the disciples quarrelling about trifling things, but afterwards how frequently is it repeated, they were all with one accord.

This peace Christ has left to his church, i.e.

(1) He hath prescribed it. He has made it the law of his kingdom, the livery of his family (John 13:34, 35), enforced the prescriptions with the most endearing motives, set before us his own example. He's called us to peace (1 Cor. 7:15). We have line upon line to this purpose. [There is] no one duty more pressed in the New Testament than this.

(2) He hath prayed for it, that they all may be one (John 17:21, etc). He has left us that prayer for our encouragement to believe that peace shall be upon Israel, for it is a granted prayer, he was always heard, so that it amounts to a promise and is a specimen of the intercession he ever lives to make in heaven for us.

(3) He hath poured out his Spirit to work all his people into a peaceable frame. Observe how the text comes in, verse 26. There's a promise of the *comforter* and then follows, *peace I leave with you*. Where the Spirit is peace is, for wrath and malice grieves him. The Spirit slays the enmities, subdues and conquers all those corruptions which break the peace.

How comfortable is this to those who mourn for the divisions of Reuben. Our Master has bequeathed peace to his church, and he will see to the executing of his own will.

But observe 'tis *my peace*, that's peace with truth. There is the devil's peace (Luke 11:21). The Christian religion is first pure, then peaceable (Jas. 3:17).

3. Peace in our own bosoms – peace within, and that's the *peace* I take to be here meant, because of what follows in the close of the verse, *let not your heart be troubled.* 'Tis such a peace as is opposite to fear and trouble of heart, which was the distemper they were now under, such a peace as keeps the heart and mind from trouble and discomposure.

And this is that which I shall speak more largely to.

Doct[rine] That peace of conscience is a previous privilege of the New Covenant which belongs to true believers. Inward peace is a legacy that Jesus Christ has left disciples. If a friend make his will we are ready to ask, pray what has he left me? If you be indeed the friends of Christ he has left you his peace.

Show 1. What this inward peace, this peace of conscience is. I shall endeavour to open it you a little, though despairing full to explicate it, for it passeth all understanding (Phil. 4:7, πάντα τὸν νοῦν[3]). Plato talked much of his νοῦς[4] but here it's over-matched. 'Tis the white stone and the new name which none knows but they that receive it (Rev. 2:17). 'Tis joy that a stranger doth not intermeddle with.

> 'Peace of conscience is a just and rational quietness and tranquility of soul arising from a believing sense of our justification before God.'[5]

3. Greek, [surpasses] the mind.
4. Greek, 'mind'.
5. No indication is given of the source of the quotation.

1. It is seated in the soul. 'Tis an inward thing, 'tis a peace that doth not terminate in the sensitive faculties, but affects the heart and more refined powers. [It] reacheth the innermost recesses (Ps. 94:19). 'Tis gladness in the heart (Ps. 4:7) and therefore:

a. It is sound and solid. 'Tis a substantial peace, peace that hath reality in it, not like the laughter of the fool while the heart is sorrowful (Prov. 14:13). 'Tis such a peace as is joined with truth in the inward parts. The peace of the hypocrite is *a lie in his right hand,* a rotten peace and so it will appear at last.

b. It is secret and unseen. 'Tis meat that the world knows not of (allu[de to] John 4:32). The richest mines lie most out of sight, and the deepest waters make the least noise. The laughter of the fool is like the crackling of thorns, [it] makes a great noise (Eccles. 7:6). The life of comfort which the saints have is a hidden life (Col. 3:3). There may be a cloud upon the countenance through outward trouble when there's sunshine in the heart.

c. It is safe and secure. Being lodged in the soul 'tis not exposed, as that is which we carry in our hands. This peace being spiritual, will last (see John 16:22, *Your heart shall rejoice*, and then follows, your joy *no man taketh from you)*. The upper region is not hurried with the storms and tempests of this lower region.

2. It is a quietness and tranquillity of soul. 'Tis the satisfaction of the spirit concerning itself and its own state. 'Tis the evenness of the soul (see Isa. 32:17, *quietness and assurance forever*). Quietness comes short of *assurance.* There may be *good hope through grace* (2 Thess. 2:16) where there is not full assurance. The day may be calm and the air serene though the sun do not shine out.

The opposite to it is disquietment and uneasiness, when a man vexeth himself with the reflection upon something past, the view of something present, or the fear of something future. Now the soul is then at peace

a. when we can look back with quietness and see all our past sins pardoned, no cloud of guilt to come between us and God, the books crossed so that through grace nothing we have done amiss can come against us. While sin is set in order before us it fills us with terror and confusion. When it is cast in the depth[s] of the sea, there is peace.

b. when we can look inwards with quietness and see our present state good, the spirit witnessing with our spirits that we are the children of God (Rom. 8:16). While a man sees himself under wrath and the curse his mind cannot but be uneasy, but when he sees that wrath and curse removed he is quiet then. That's taken away which raised the storm, and then there's a calm presently.

c. when we can look forward with quietness and see our future happiness safe. 'Tis hoping and quiet waiting for the salvation of the Lord (Lam. 3:26). This peace enters into that within the veil and casts anchor there, and so is quiet. It is a freedom from that spirit of bondage which works to fear (Rom. 8:15).

3. It is a just and rational quietness. A wicked man may have some kind of quietness, but it is a stupidity and senselessness. 'Tis unjust and irrational, like the quietness of a stick or stone. That's not peace of conscience but searedness of conscience (1 Tim. 4:2). This peace of conscience is the result of a self-debate, and deliberation with ourselves not prejudging the cause as bribed and biassed by self-love, or carelessly taking the matter for granted, but examining ourselves, trying our case, and the pronouncing a judgment accordingly. There's as much difference between these two as between skinning a wound over whilst it festers within, and searching it to the bottom and then healing it, the one a palliative, the other a perfect cure. We therefore call it *peace of conscience*. Conscience is that faculty of the soul by which we make a judgment of ourselves and our own state and actions. He is not acquitted, that for the present absconds and evades his trial, but he that takes his trial and so comes off well. Conscience is a court in our own souls.

4. It supposes our justification before God. That which breaks the peace is *sin*. Till sin is removed in justification there can be no true peace. If [there is] no peace with God, [there's] no true peace with ourselves (see Rom. 5:12). We must stand or fall by God's judgment. That is indeed our case which it is in his judgment. His knowledge is the rule of truth, his will the rule of good acts. Those are acquitted indeed whom he acquits. That's a rotten peace of the devil's speaking which is not founded in justification. Therefore *mercy* and peace are put together (Jude 2). Till we have found mercy with God we cannot find peace in ourselves. And *grace and peace* often.

5. It ariseth from the sense of that justification. A man cannot have the comfort of his justification till he has in some measure the knowledge of it. Hagar had a well of water by her and knew it not (Gen. 21:16, 19). So many that are justified before God upon their faith and repentance yet are not clear in the evidences of it. God sometimes speaks peace, and we do not perceive it (Job 33:14; Acts 3:19, *that your sins may be blotted out* ὅπως ἄν[6] *that the times of refreshing may come* viz. into your souls – so Lightfoot[7]).

Further to show then what peace of conscience is,

a. It is the counterpart or copy of our pardon. It supposeth the original and is our assurance of it, attested a true copy by the blessed spirit. 'Tis our receiving *the atonement* (Rom. 5:11, i.e. the comfort of the atonement). 'Tis the reflex act of faith. Having repented of my sins and believed in Christ, I then believe that, according to the promise of the covenant, my sins are pardoned and all's well, and hence must needs result

---

6. Greek, 'in order that'.

7. John Lightfoot (1601–1675), Anglican rector and Master of Catherine Hall, Cambridge, was a member of the Westminster Assembly (1643–1647). He was a noted biblical scholar especially in the area of Hebrew studies. His greatest work was *Horae Hebraicae et Talmudicae* (six volumes, 1658–1678).

abundant satisfaction and quiet especially following upon that uneasy sense of sin and sorrow for that weariness which evermore goes before the pardon. Peace of conscience is that cheerfulness which follows upon pardon (Matt. 9:2).

b. It is the composure of our spirits. Peace is the fixation of the soul, the gathering in of the thoughts and affections and the establishing of them upon God. Sense of guilt and wrath puts the soul into a hurry, peace composeth it. It is the staying of the mind. That's peace, peace (Isa. 26:3), fixed (Ps. 112:7).

Now I have what I would have, that which fills and satisfies me. God is mine and Christ mine and I have enough. Those powers and faculties which were suffered to run roving in pursuit of lying vanities are now all summoned in to be bestowed upon God the only adequate object of the soul's desires.

c. It is the calm of our fears. Fear hath torment (1 John 4:18). Peace of conscience easeth that torment. Where true peace is there's that which will answer all the formidable suggestions of fear – *though the earth be removed* (Ps. 46:2). *All earthly success* and supports withdrawn, though Satan accuse, the law condemn, the roaring lion seek to devour, yet where this peace is the soul is armed against them. *If God be for us [who can be against us?]* (Rom. 8:31). This peace is armour of proof against those fiery darts which enflame the soul (Ps. 3, 5, 6; 27:1, 3; Heb. 13:6).

d. It is the rest of our souls, like the rest of the labourer after his day's toil, like the rest of the needle and the pole star[8] after a tremulous and fluctuating motion. This is the rest promised (Matt. 11:28, 29; Jer. 6:16). The love, desire, delight have found an adequate object, and are satisfied in it. This is my rest for ever, here I will dwell with a complacency. This is part of the Sabbath which remains for the people of God (Heb. 4:9),

8. The *needle*, the magnetised end of the pointer on a compass; the pole star is the north star.

an acquiescence in Christ and his righteousness. Here I cast anchor. The more the soul has been hurried with conviction, the sweeter is this rest. Return unto thy rest, thy Noah[9] (Ps. 116:7). When the body can find no rest in the world, but tossed with tempests, the soul finds rest in God, and in the promises.

e. It is a reconciliation with ourselves. Where sin is and the man is sensible of it, it cannot but produce a quarrel, a self-loathing and abhorrence. The man's uneasy to himself. Now this peace takes up that quarrel. When the filth we have contracted is washed off, the bad bargain we have made recalled, the danger we have incurred prevented, the curse we lay under removed, now that man begins to be easy to himself. Though there always remains a humility and a jealousy ariseth, yet that self-indignation ceaseth. When Mary Magdalene had been quarrelling with her hair, the instrument of her sin, Christ sends her away in peace (Luke 7:48, 50).

f. It is the rejoining of broken bones. Conviction breaks the bones. This peace sets them in joint again (Ps. 51:8), not only cured but rejoicing, stronger and easier than ever. This peace is a man's rejoicing in himself alone (Gal. 6:4). 'Tis joy and peace in believing (Rom. 15:3). This joy [is] terminating in God as the head of it, the gladness of our joy, and prevailing to sweeten the bitter cup, and to counter-balance all the sorrow and afflictions of this world (Hab. 3:17, 18). And is not this a very precious legacy, which Christ has left his people? If this be that peace, happy is the people that is in such a case.

9. The Hebrew word Noah means 'rest'.

31 Jan. 1692

PEACE I LEAVE WITH YOU

Doctrine That peace of conscience is a previous privilege of the New Covenant belonging to true believers.

Show 2. That this is a privilege of the New Covenant belonging to true believers.

1. 'Tis not the privilege of vain philosophy (Col. 2:8). The Stoics[1] boasted of it as the privilege of their sect, to be free from the hurries and discomposures of passion, priding themselves in a pretended apathy, and an obstinate refusal to lay anything to heart, as if either the integrity or felicity of man consisted in a conformity to stocks and stones in senselessness. 'Tis a brutish way of curing the gout by cutting off the leg. That ease, that self-enjoyment which they fancied to result from this abdicating of human affections the pious soul is blessed with by the regulating and sanctifying of them and that which they in vain sought in the dictates of a blind philosophy, the true believer hath happily found and securely enjoys in the covenant of grace.
2. 'Tis not the privilege of worldly prosperity. Peace is that which the busy world pretends to seek though very preposterously in their self-disquieting pursuits. They are very solicitously casting anchor in the loose sand but upon the first blast the anchor slips and comes home, and the safety of the ship is hazarded. But the covenant of grace is the Rock in which the true believer casts anchor and so enters into that within the veil (Heb. 6:19; see Matt. 7:24-27). He was a fool that expected peace in full barns (Luke 12:19, 20). If inward peace were the privilege of worldly

1. The Stoics were a philosophical school founded in Athens by Zeno (335–263 BC), and in the first and second centuries AD Stoicism became the dominant philosophy of the Romans.

prosperity then those that have most of the world would have most of this peace. But we see the contrary (Ps. 127:2; Eccles. 4:6, 8). Witness the disquiet of Haman in the court, Ahab in the throne. Peace is not a flower that grows in the mind.

But we have found the way of peace.

1. It is a privilege of the New Covenant. Since Adam ruined and fell there could be no peace in the covenant of works, because [there is] no pardon. If some further provision had not been made by free grace man must have been when he was turned out of paradise, a fugitive and a vagabond. But the covenant of grace is the ark in which the wandering dove may find rest for the sole of her foot. The law shows the wound but what peace in that unless we could see the remedy? See Heb. 10:2, 3. The gospel brings in the better hope.

Let's see how inward peace, or peace of conscience, is a privilege of the New Covenant.

a. It is bought with the blood of the covenant. Peace of conscience is part of Christ's purchase. Nothing but that which reconciled us to God could truly and safely reconcile us to ourselves. 'Tis by the blood of the covenant that the poor sinking perishing prisoners are brought out of the pit wherein is no water and become prisoners of hope (Zech. 9:11, 12). We had by sin forfeited our title to peace. Christ by dying took off the forfeiture and restored our title.

Christ was troubled in spirit that we might have peace of spirit. His soul was exceeding[ly] sorrowful even unto death that our souls might be exceeding[ly] joyful even unto life, eternal life. He bore the load of our sins (1 Pet. 2:24) to ease us of the burden which we must otherwise have sank under to eternity.

Christ by dying removed that guilt which breaks the peace, unstung afflictions and death and disabled them to break the peace of his people. How should we value this peace which was purchased at so dear a rate! Nothing less than the merit of Christ can satisfy a convinced conscience, and still the storms which guilt has raised.

b. It is built upon the foundation of the covenant. That's a lethargy, not peace, which is not grounded and bottomed upon the covenant of grace.

i. Upon the truths of the covenant. In those the *understanding* finds peace. Abstracted from the revelations of the Gospel how unsatisfying are the results of the most rational enquiries, and how much at a loss doth the soul remain after all. 'Tis the New Covenant that furnisheth out truths satisfying to the understanding, objects agreeable to the faculty, which contributes much to the peace of the soul. Gospel-truths are *worthy of all acceptation* (1 Tim 1:15). That truth which will satisfy the understanding must be clear and certain, great and concerning, truth which we are interested in. Mr. Selden[2] on his death-bed professed in all his reading he never found that which he would rest his soul upon but in the Scripture, particularly Titus 2:11, 12.

ii. Upon the tenders of the covenant so rich, so real, so sure, so suitable. That there is a Saviour is a truth satisfying to the understanding, but unless this Saviour may be mine the peace is but imperfect. *I will give you rest*. There's an offer on which the peace is bottomed. Not only Christ given for us, but Christ given to us. The covenant of grace being all our salvation is *all our desire* (2 Sam. 23:5) which notes the soul's complacency in it, *loving* this salvation (Ps. 40:16), not only approving of the covenant but acquiescing in the covenant. If God be to me a God, I have enough. Here is inward peace founded upon the covenant. This was the meaning of Abraham's laughter

2. John Selden (1584–1654) trained in law and practised in London. However, he had wide interests including history, oriental studies and Judaism. He was a member of parliament for Oxford University and also participated in the Westminster Assembly.

when God took him into the covenant (Gen. 17:17). This is *embracing* the promises (Heb. 11:13) with joy and satisfaction, glorying in the proposals of the New Covenant (Isa. 45:25). The lines are fallen in a pleasant place if God be my portion (Ps. 16:5, 6).

c. It is bequeathed in the promises of the covenant, how in the text 'tis left as a legacy. Peace I *leave with you*. The leaving of it as a legacy bespeaks:

i. The friendliness of the giver. Legacies are tokens of love and kindness, not as other contracts upon a valuable consideration. This peace comes freely to us though it was dearly purchased by the Lord Jesus. Christ is a friend to believers (Cant. 5:16), and he showed himself so when he left them this legacy. 'Tis to convince us that he loves us and is concerned for our ease and quiet, our happiness, not only in the other world but in this. This peace is of his creating (Isa. 57:19), creation is out of nothing. There's nothing in us to merit or challenge such a gift, but it is of his own good will. There's none of the seeds of peace in our hearts by nature till he sows them there, plants the flourishing cedar in the wilderness (Isa. 41:18, 19, 20). This should very much sweeten and endear this gift to us. 'Twas a love-token left us by a dear friend.

ii. The firmness of the gift. His leaving of it to us makes it sure, for it is not in the power of all the men on earth or all the devils in hell to overthrow and invalidate the will and testament of the Lord Jesus. The promise is *sure to all the seed* (Rom. 4:16).

(1) The will is written. There are nuncupative wills[3] which are more liable to dispute, but the New Testament of our Lord and Saviour Jesus Christ is written. We have it in black and white. Not only the great things of the

---

3. *Nuncupative*, an older English word used mainly to describe wills that were not written.

law but the great things of the gospel [are] written to us. That which is written remains, that the saints might in all ages be ascertained of the truth of it, and that no room might be left for the doubting.

(2) The will is published. Ministers are sent to proclaim peace, peace to him that is afar off and to them that are nigh (Isa. 57:19), to tell all the sons of peace what their Master has left them that they may put in their claims. Ministers are messengers of glad tidings. Their errand is to comfort the Lord's people (Isa. 40:1, 2).

(3) The will is sealed. The sacraments are seals of the New Testament in the blood of Christ (Matt. 26:28). Wine makes glad the heart. That's the intent of the ordinances, instituted to assure true believers of this peace.

(4) There is an executor named, one to administer to true believers those comforts which their Master bequeathed to them, and that is the Holy Ghost (see the verse before the text). His office is to comfort, to speak peace to the saints and to make them hear it, to create this peace. *He shall take of mine* (John 16:15) as executor, and he is faithful to his trust.

(5) The Testator is dead. That's necessary to the validity of the will (Heb. 9:16, 17). He died to give life to the testament. 'Twas but a little after he made this will that he died to empower us to claim our legacy. He had a great estate to dispose of, and many poor relations to dispose of it to, and he did it and died to confirm it. The sacrament which is the confirmation of the will is the commemoration of the death.

(6) The will is proved. The broad-seal of heaven is annexed to it, by his ascension and reception into glory. He had power given him over all flesh (Matt. 28:18; John 17:2). When the apostles were sent to preach peace they had a power given them to work miracles for the confirmation of their preaching, which was the probate of the will. The Testator himself rose from the dead and

went to heaven to prove his own will, and this that we might have strong consolation (Heb. 6:17-20).

2. It belongs to true believers. 'Tis not a privilege that lies in common to all but is inclosed for the benefit of believers, those that by a lively faith are not only in profession but in truth in covenant with God, such as truly consent to the gospel offer, such as are sanctified. The name will not serve turn,[4] if that be all.

a. It belongs to all true believers not that they have all the present possession of it. Many a child of light walks in darkness (Isa. 50:10). The sons of peace may be long under trouble and yet I say it belongs to them for

i. they have all a title to it. Wherever there is grace there is a title to peace. They are all interested in the promise of it, and 'tis certain that in this case a promise without possession is better than possession without a promise. Light is sown for the righteous. 'Tis sown in the promise, and it will come up again in due time (Ps. 97:11). A legacy left to a child is for him till he come to age.

ii. they have all a foundation laid for it. Where the image of God is stamped upon the soul in grace and holiness there is that wrought which has a direct tendency to this peace. All true believers have their sins pardoned, their peace made with God, and he that has laid such a foundation will certainly build upon that foundation and will not neglect the work of his own hands. Where the soul is brought into a conformity to the will of God there is a disposition to peace. Those principles are imbibed and rooted which necessarily conduce to the silencing of fears and the preserving of the peace. All that have received the Spirit as sanctifier have received the beginning of that good work which will be performed, sealed with the Spirit of promise (Eph. 1:13).

---

4. *Serve turn*, 'to be sufficient for the purpose'.

iii. There are very few believers but they have some degrees of it. There may be light, day-light, growing light where there is not yet the clear sunshine. Where there are not sensible comforts and strong consolations yet there may be a silent satisfaction in the covenant of grace, spiritual supports where there are not spiritual suavities, some glimmerings of peace though scarce discernible through the cloud of troubles and temptations, *perplexed but not in despair* (2 Cor. 4:8, 9). What is it that keeps them from despair but some degree of this peace? Though there be thorns in the flesh there is grace sufficient (2 Cor. 12:9).

iv. If they want[5] it, 'tis their own fault. The legacy is left them but they do not sue it out by prayer. Peace is the fruit of the lips, praying lips (Isa. 57:19). God will be sought unto, for promised mercies. They put a bar in the way of their peace by their careless walking, and then they may thank themselves if they want peace. The condition of this peace is that they return not to folly (Ps. 85:8). If they do, they forfeit their peace.

v. They shall all be sure of it at last. Their trouble and disquietment will certainly end well at last. The dark and cloudy morning may prove a fair sunshine day. Though for a small moment God may forsake yet he will gather with everlasting loving kindness (Isa. 54:7, 8). Though the Israelites indeed may be left to wander a great while in a vast howling wilderness yet they shall get through it at last to Canaan. Clouds will be scattered and comforts will return, for the promise is very sure, though the performance seem slow (Ps. 37:37, *the end is peace*).

b. It belongs to true believers only. As far as those who reject the gospel offer and persist in unbelief they have no part or lot in the matter (Isa. 48:22; 57:21). We have no warrant to speak a word of peace to any that are going on still in their trespasses

5. *Want*, here in the sense of 'lack'.

(Jer. 6:14). Those who are at enmity with God can never have any true peace in their own bosoms. The building can never be reared without a foundation.

i. Wicked people may have peace but they have no cause for it. They may be free from inward disturbances and disquiet, and fancy their condition to be good but 'tis because of their ignorance (Rev. 3:17). Have they any cause for peace that are lying under the wrath of God, the curse of the law, held in the devil's snares and led captive by him at his will? [They have] little reason to rejoice. Their peace is like the sleep of a man in a lethargy. 'Tis not peace but senselessness and stupidity. They think their condition [is] good because they do not know how bad it is. [They are] dead in sin (Eph. 2:1) and so feel nothing. Their laughter [is] like the laughter of some in some kind of convulsion. 'Tis their disease. What hast thou to do with peace (allu[de to] 2 Kings 9:18, 22)? They go like an ox to the slaughter (Prov. 7:22, 27). A wound in the vitals though most perilous is not always most painful. 'Tis like him that sleeps on the top of a mast (Prov. 23:34).

ii. They may have the devil's peace but they have none of Christ's peace. While the strong man armed keeps the palace his goods are in peace (Luke 11:21). All goes one way in the soul. No opposition [is] given to the destroying rule of Satan, and he is careful that they have no disturbance while they are in his drudgery. They lay themselves to sleep, and 'tis his interest to rock the cradle. Freedom from the trouble of sin without the freedom from the guilt and power of sin is the devil's peace and confirms the sinner's slavery and strengthens the chain.

iii. They may have peace of their own speaking, but they have no peace of God's speaking. There are many that say, I shall have peace though I go on (Deut. 29:19), but is there ever a word in all the Bible to encourage such a surmise? Babylon had peace of her own speaking (Rev. 18:7), and it did but aggravate her ruin. Self-created peace will in the end prove a self-deceiving, self-destroying peace. He that said, *'Soul, take thine ease'* was soon pronounced a fool for saying so (Luke 12:19, 20).

iv. They may seem to have peace but they have no real peace. The heart may be sorrowful in the midst of their laughter (Prov. 14.13). 'Tis but from the teeth outward. You know not what secret twitches and reproaches those feel that seem to lead the merriest lives. There's many a one whose heart condemns him yet doth not proclaim the sentence upon the house top, doth not feel quietness in his belly (Job 20:20, 22).

v. They may have some kind of peace for the present but it will certainly end in trouble, either in trouble that will mend them or in trouble that will end them, either convictions in this world or confusion in the other will put a dismal period to this rotten peace. The iniquity will be hateful at last (Ps. 36:2). He shall *lie down in sorrow* (Isa. 50:11). What will his hope, his peace, be when God shall make the soul to wander (Job 28:8).

By all this it appears that true peace belongs only to true believers.

Show 3. That this is a precious privilege, a privilege of inestimable value. Take heed of thinking meanly of the legacy that Christ has left us. Prize it highly, not to mention the precious blood that purchased it, the precious benefits it is founded upon. Let us only consider the precious fruits and effects of it. This peace is a precious privilege for,

1. It is satisfying to all our desires. He that has this peace may truly say that he has enough. His condition [is] good and he knows it. What would he more? 'Tis all our desire (2 Sam. 23:5). 'Tis thus that a good man is satisfied from himself (Prov. 14:14). The soul dwells at ease (Ps. 25:13) where it would be. Here will I dwell for I have desired it. See Psalm 37:4, *he shall give you*. Those that by faith suck from the breasts of consolation are satisfied

(Isa. 66:12). The soul that has this peace is in its centre, returns to its rest (Ps. 116:7). This [is] the contentment of the soul in God and he is insatiable indeed whom an all-sufficient God cannot content.

2. It is silencing to all our fears, and our fears many times are more tormenting to us than present griefs. This peace sets us above all the fear of evil tidings (Ps. 112:7). Our groundless apprehensions of trouble to come many times ruffle and unhinge us more than anything else. This peace is the fixation of one foot of the compass in the centre of the promise, and then the motion of the other to the several points of the compass is even and regular and undisturbed. Where this peace rules in the heart events are quickly expected, nothing can come much amiss. 'Tis not the wind in the air, but the wind in the earth that makes the earthquake.

3. It is securing in all our dangers. We live in a perilous world in which we are continually exposed. Now this peace of God keeps the heart (Phil. 4:7, φρουρήσει,[6] keep as in a garrison or stronghold). Perhaps it doth not keep the body or the estate, but it keeps *the heart*, the main fort, keeps it from anxious, perplexing care. Com[pare] verse 6. This peace keeps trouble from *the heart*. This peace is the soul's quiet committing of itself to the protection of God, and acquiesing in his care. 'Tis dwelling in the secret place of the Most High (Ps. 91:1).

4. It is solacing in all our sorrows. There's not only safety but joy in this peace. When clouds and darkness are round about us the soul that enjoys this peace has a Goshen.[7] Be the times never so black, the Israelites indeed have light in their dwellings. This bears up the spirit under the heaviest pressures, keeps the head above water in a storm. When pressed above measure the testimony of conscience is not only a support but a rejoicing (2 Cor. 1:12).

---

6. Greek, 'it shall guard, hold in custody'.

7. *Goshen*, the area of Egypt in which the Israelites lived. See Gen. 46:28-9.

This comforted Paul at the bar (Acts 23:1; 24:16). How pleasant is it to have the bird in the bosom sing sweet.

5. It is sweetening to all our comforts. As trouble of conscience and disquiet of soul embitters the sweetest comforts, and puts wormwood and gall upon them, so peace of conscience sweetens the most common. 'Tis this peace of conscience that is a continual feast (Prov. 15:15). We read of a long feast that Ahasuerus made (Esther 1) but what was that to the feast of a good conscience. Those feasting days were mixed with trouble, but this continual faring sumptuously every day.

6. It is emboldening in our approaches to God (1 John 3:21). If we have peace in our bosoms, with what holy courage may we draw near to God. 'Tis a sense of guilt and wrath that damps and discourageth us, a sense of pardon and reconciliation brings us into the presence of God with a humble confidence (Rom. 5:16). This opens the lips, gives us παρρησία.[8]

7. It is encouraging under the censures of men. When men condemn us, if our own hearts acquit us, how easy is it? And how little do we need to matter [with] man's day (1 Cor. 4:3, 4)?[9] This was it that encouraged Job when his friends condemned him (Job 27:5, 6). He that is at peace with himself may the better bear the quarrels of other people.

8. It is enlarging to the heart in all manner of obedience. 'Twill oil the wheels and make them go on smoothly. This will make us run the ways of God's commandments (Ps. 119:32). The temple was built in a time of peace. As with the church in general so with particular believers. Times of rest should be edifying times.

9. It is an ease to the soul in a dying hour. This peace unstings death and takes off the terror of it. Those that can depart in peace may

---

8. Greek, 'boldness' (especially in speech). Acts 4:29.
9. Cf. AV margin at 1 Corinthians 4:3, 'man's day'.

sing old Simeon's song (Luke 2:29). What can be dreadful in death to one that knows how to look beyond it with comfort? This eased Hezekiah (2 Kings 20:3).

10. It is an earnest to the soul of the glory that shall be revealed. 'Tis the foretaste of heaven, a glimpse of that light, a foretaste of those rivers of pleasure. Peace of conscience is attained upon earth. 'Tis glory begun. What's heaven but this peace perfect and uninterrupted? 'Tis full of glory (1 Pet. 1:8), like the cluster of grapes which the Israelites had in the wilderness.

7 Feb. 1692

PEACE I LEAVE WITH YOU(ii)

Doct[rine] 1. That inward peace is a precious privilege of the covenant of grace belonging to true believers.

Applic[ation] We are ministers of *the New Testament*. Our work is to direct poor souls in claiming the legacies which the Lord Jesus Christ has left them, and from this text I must address myself by way of exhortation to those sorts of people. Suffer these words of exhortation.

Exh[ortation] 1. To those that want this peace though they have a title to it – to troubled saints – whose souls are cast down and disquieted, to whom the legacy doth belong, but they have it not, and who pine in the want of it.

Q[uestion] Who have a title to this peace?

A[nswer] 1. Those that are of broken and contrite heart have a title to this peace – that are weary and heavy-laden – to such belongs the promise of reviving (Isa. 57:15), of rest (Matt. 11:28). These have a title to this peace that have been and are truly disquieted for their sins – comforts belong to the mourners (Matt. 5:4; Isa. 57:18). God's method is first to wound and then to heal (Hos. 6:1), first to break the bones by conviction, then to make them rejoice (Ps. 51:8). Poor soul, has not sin been thy grief and burden? Hath it not lain heavier than anything also? If so peace belongs to you.

2. Those that are at war with sin have a title to this peace, that have broken their league with it, and renounced their allegiance to it, and though it remain yet which do not allow its reign have a right

to peace (Rom. 8:13 ye *shall live,* i.e. be comforted). If the force of the soul be raised and kept up in opposition to the usurped power of sin, though the Canaanites do remain in the land as thorns in the eyes, we may take the comfort of the victory begun.

3. Those that are the willing disciples of Jesus Christ have a title to this peace. The legacy is left to them, that submit to Christ's teachings, deny themselves, and follow him, trust him with their dearest interests, love him, serve him, sit at his feet, desire his favour, endeavour to please him, are ready to leave all for him, would not quit their relation to him for thousands of gold and silver. Those are Christ's disciples indeed, and though labouring under much weakness and darkness, yet to them pertains this peace.

Now there are many who thus have a title to peace, yet have not possession of it, have not that quietness and tranquillity of mind which belongs to Christ's disciples. Their spirits are overwhelmed (Ps. 77:2, 3), sorrow fills their heart (John 16:6), their spirit wounded (Prov. 18:14), troubled and afraid (John 14:27), their flesh and their heart failing (Ps. 73:26).

These troubles and disquietments which break the peace are reducible to two heads which require a distinct consideration. This trouble arises either from the outward condition, or from the spiritual state.

1. This peace is often broken by outward troubles, this quietness of soul often disquieted by crosses in the secular concerns. This is sometimes the real ground which 'tis pretended to be upon spiritual accounts. At least it begins here. Some have their peace broken by pain and sickness of body, their bone and their flesh is touched, and they let it reach the soul and spirit, and disquiet and disease that it makes them fretful and disconsolate, that they cannot enjoy God or themselves, especially if it be tedious. Others by losses and crosses in their estates. They do not thrive in the world. They go behind hand in their trade, and see others

enriched, themselves impoverished, and this is a constant disturbance to them. Others by afflictions in their relations. Comfort they should have in them is embittered, like gall and wormwood. Unequally yoked, it may be, the relation that should be a meet help is a cross. No children, or sickly children, or (which is worst of all) wicked children, on these accounts, many of God's people walk heavily and in bitterness. Near and dear relations [are] taken away, who were the desire of their eyes, the circumstances aggravating, for this they sorrow as if there were no hope. The best saints have their share of these and the like troubles (Eccles. 2:1, 2) and when they put on the Christian [they] did not put off the man, therefore cannot but be sensible of them. [There is] no arguing against sense (as Mr Baxter[1] said), but that which I am pressing upon you is that you let none of these troubles break your peace. Hold fast your tranquillity, and let not that go, however it goes without. Keep your peace within (John 14:1). Let it not be within the reach of any outward affliction to rob you of your inward peace, or interrupt that quietness which arises from a sense of pardon. Soon said (you'll say) but not so soon done. Will you take some directions, in the observance of which by the grace of God you may keep the peace notwithstanding all the occasions of sorrow or fear? Apply them to your particular grievance. I now speak not to sinners (Isa. 33:14) but to those come out of their sins.

a. Weigh the causes of your troubles in the balances of right reason. Show yourselves men. Do not lie poring upon the trouble but search into the cause. *Why art thou cast down* (Ps. 42:11)? Many of our fears and sorrows would vanish before such a test. Think, is it worthwhile to break my peace for such a thing as this? *Dost thou well to be angry for a gourd* (Jonah 4:8, 9)? Sense represents our troubles black and heavy and so we are borne down upon that supposition. Reason will discover them not to be as bad as was

1. Richard Baxter (1615–1691), Puritan pastor and author.

apprehended. The work of reason is to correct the errors of fancy. How often is our peace broken by the creatures of our own fancy, and fear then plays the tyrant. [There are] many instances of it – ceaseless jealousies create [for] us more disturbances than real evils. Arraign them, examine them, try them (Isa. 51:12, 13).

b. Turn your troubles into the right channel. Fire is good in its place but hurtful out of it. Are you in sorrow, turn it into sorrow for sin, your fear into the fear of God. This would be so far from breaking the peace that it would strengthen it. 'Tis not the sorrow in itself that works death, but *the sorrow of the world* (2 Cor. 7:10). The breaking of a vein stops excessive bleeding by revulsion, so godly sorrow cures the sorrow of the world. If you have your eye upon your sins you'll see more occasion for sorrow than in any affliction. 'Tis better thus to divert than to dam up the stream. David doth so often. This would drown the sense of the trouble, as the report of a cannon drowns the whisper.

c. Eye the providence of God in all events. An acquiescence in the regular and steady measures of God's counsel would keep the heart calm and even under all the seemingly irregular and unsteady motions of events. That which keeps your peace is the staying of the mind upon God (Isa. 26:3). This kept Eli's (1 Sam. 3:18), and Job's (Job 1:21; 23:4), and David's [minds] (Ps. 39:9; see 2 Sam. 15:25, 26). The wisdom of providence should make us submit in reason, the sovereignty of providence should make us submit in duty, the irresistibleness of providence should make us submit in point of interest.

d. Limit the expectations from and affections to the creature. Take heed of overloving and overvaluing anything in this world. Inordinate affection in the enjoyment lays a foundation for inordinate affection in parting – as David to Absalom – like the sway of a pendulum as far as you draw it aside one way, when you quit your hold so far will it force itself t'other way. When we make an idol of any creature, no wonder if we part with it as Micah did with his gods (Jude 18:24). Do not promise yourselves that in this world which is not in it. The disciples promised themselves worldly pomp and grandeur with their Master, and that made them grieve so to hear of his cross. Do not lay too much weight upon a bruised reed.

e. Live by faith upon the covenant of grace. Faith is the great conservator of the peace. 'Tis promised (John 14:1), [and] approved (Ps. 27:13). Dwell much upon the promises. Apply them to your particular case. When creature confidences fail and comforts are drawn dry, act faith upon them. Covet that rock of ages, that well of living water (thus David, 2 Sam. 23:5). You have heard of some that have made many a meal's meat upon the promises when they have wanted[2] bread. Act faith upon the great article of the covenant that God is to us a God. When all's gone, God is not gone. Mother, 'Is God dead?' said the little child to the disconsolate mother. See Isaiah 41:10; 43:2, 3. Do not perish for thirst when there's a well of salvation so near. Live by faith (Hab. 2:4; Ps. 73:26).

f. Look unto Jesus (Heb. 12:1, 2, 3). Look to Christ dying, rising again, interceding. See him unstinging every affliction, bearing the heavy end of the cross. Look to his patience (John 18:11, *not as I will but as thou wilt*). Derive strength from Christ to bear you up under every burden. He can still the storm, and quiet the tempest, be it never so turbulent. Behold the exaltation of Christ as his advancement, as your concernment. 'Tis in Christ that we have peace (John 16:33), he is our peace (Eph. 2:14) when the Assyrian comes (Micah 5:5).

g. Think much of your mercies. While we observe only what makes against us, we sink under the thought but if we would withal observe what makes for us we should find strength to silence all disquieting thoughts. This kept Job's peace (Job 2:10). Look over your experiences. Remember your song in the night (Ps. 77:5, 6). Let not the sense of one's afflictions drown the sense of a thousand mercies. You cannot say but that God has been good to you, your mercies undeserved,

---

2. *Wanted*, here 'lacked'.

your afflictions deserved. Especially think of soul mercies. Has God not pardoned thy sin, healed thy soul, and is that not enough to quiet thee (Isa. 33:6; Matt. 9:2)?

h. Cast your burden upon the Lord by faithful and fervent prayer. Prayer is a salve for every sore. Unbosom yourselves to him. 'Twill be an ease to your spirits. 'Tis your prescribed, approved means of relief (Phil. 4:6, 7). The way to rejoice evermore is to pray without ceasing (1 Thess. 5:16, 17). Hannah found prayer to be [her] heart's ease (1 Sam. 1:18). This throws the cares upon God, who cares for us (Ps. 55:22). This is the appointed way of rolling our way upon the Lord (Ps. 37:5). 'Tis good in prayer to be particular in spreading your case to God. He knows it before, but he would know it from us. Eye him as a Father in prayer.

i. See all your troubles working together for your good (Rom. 8:28). God will give the expected end and it will be good. The potion is bitter, the operation severe but it is in order to a cure (*afterwards it yields [the peaceable fruit of righteousness]* Heb. 12:11). It is not intended for a consuming but a refining fire. You know not perhaps the particular intendment but you'll know (John 13:7), and when you come to heaven you will see that you could not have been without it. In other things the well-grounded expectation of a good issue much easeth the fatigue of a hazardous adventure.

j. Keep your eye fixed upon the joy that is set before you. Think of the many mansions (John 14:1, 2), the land of the living (Ps. 27:13). This is an excellent preservative of the peace to converse within the veil. If the anchor be cast there we are kept steady. See 2 Corinthians 4:17, 18. That weather [may be] foul and ways dirty, but home is not far off, and all's quiet and well there. [There are] no storms in the upper region. That's a happiness suited to all our burdens. Relief [is] there for every distemper. It's all thy own, regard not thy stuff then (all[ude to] Gen. 45:20). Our happiness is lodged in a safe and quiet place. Live upon that happiness.

2. This peace is often broken and disturbed by our doubts and fears about our spiritual state and condition. There is a fear concerning our spiritual state which is our duty, a quickening fear, a fear of diligence, a fear of coming short (Heb. 4:1; Phil. 2:12). Happy is the man that thus feareth always (Prov. 28:14). But there is a fear that is our burden, and our enemy, a disquieting fear, a fear of amazement, such a fear as breaks our peace. 'Tis culpable in you that have the root of the matter and have a title to peace. Such are many times *cast down and disquieted*, walk in darkness and have no light (Isa. 50:10), [who] never had any settled peace or have left it.

Let us endeavour to open:

The Case. 1. The disciples of Christ that are at peace with God many times want peace of conscience, that is:

a. Convictions of guilt are strongly set home. The wound is opened, and bleeds afresh. David, a man after God's own heart, yet complains of broken bones (Ps. 51:8) upon this account. Sin is set in order and appears exceeding[ly] sinful. Job when he was old was made to possess his iniquities (Job 13:26). Self-accusations appear very legible, the remembrance of the sin and of all the aggravating circumstances revived. The more saving knowledge, the worse sin appears and the more horrid if it do not appear pardoned.

b. Doubts concerning our spiritual state prevailing – is the Lord among us or not? – knows not whither he goes (John 12:35), giving up all for gone, *free among the dead* (Ps. 88:5), of that society, number and company; questioning that testimony of the Spirit which we have sometimes had the experience of – was it not a delusion, a mere cheat? This must needs be uneasy to those who know the mercy of a sinful state, to be ready to conclude themselves among that number.

c. The favour of God suspended. Though God love his people with an everlasting love yet the sense of that love may be withdrawn for a time. And a believer at such a time may be ready to conclude that God has departed from him, as David (Ps. 13:1), Job (ch 13:24), Heman (Ps. 88:14), Jonah (ch. 2:4), [or] Christ himself upon the cross (Matt. 27:46). [They] cannot get a good look from God, though even then his right hand sustains them. The earth has the sun's influence when the light of it is wanting. 'Tis but for a small moment [that the favour of God is suspended] (Isa. 54:7, 8).

d. The joy of the Lord interrupted – not those sweets as formerly in communion with God, not that sensible intercourse, not that comfort which used to arise from it. The beloved has withdrawn himself – was gone, was gone (Cant. 5:6; 3:2, deserted). The bridegroom gone, and can the children of the bride chamber rejoice? Nay, comforts embittered, the soul refusing comfort, remembering God and troubled (Ps. 77:3). His remembering of God was not the cause of his trouble, but the ineffectual means of his relief.

e. Evidences for heaven eclipst – no comfortable look within the veil – the title to glory on all occasions questioned (Ps. 77:3), the Spirit not witnessing with our spirit, the light of grace not appearing, grace exercised and yet not discovered, seed sown yet it lies hid under the clods. The heart seems to be hardened (Isa. 63:17).

f. The very terrors of the Almighty may set themselves in array. God may perhaps appear as an enemy (Job 6:4; Ps. 88:15, 16, 17; Lam. 3:3), [as] a horror of darkness upon Abraham (Gen. 15:12). Such may sometimes be the condition of God's dear saints and servants, and it is a sad condition. Ask those that know what it is, and they will tell you so. This want of peace 'tis not to the same degree in all, but more or less of disquiet and dejection of spirit is to be found one time or other in good people. God permitting it for trial, to keep us humble, to teach us the fellowship of Christ's suffering, to sweeten his returns.

The Cure. 2. Is it thus with any of you? You want this peace and you would fain have it, would you? Why, 'tis God only who can cure the wounded spirit. If he speak trouble, who can command peace (Job 34:29)? If ever thou hast any true peace it must be the work of creating power (Isa. 57:14).

But ordinarily God works by means, and uses not to be wanting to us if we do our endeavour. You would fain have peace of conscience. Will you be at the cost of it? Are you willing to take pains for it? There is an excellent direction given (Isa. 50:10), *trust in the name of the Lord*, that name (Gen. 17:1; especially Jer. 23:6). *Stay upon his God.* In the want of the faith of assurance live by the faith of adherence. We suppose you do desire this peace of conscience, this quietness and tranquillity of soul.

a. Search for secret guilt and repent of it before the Lord. It must be a diligent search (Ps. 77:6). Beg of God to discover it to you (Job 34:31, 32), to show you what crooked path you turned aside to when you went out of the way of peace. Inquire for the Achan, the Jonah, and deal with it as an anathema. Search and try (Lam. 3:40). Be strict and impartial in this search. Give conscience leave to speak faithfully – perhaps some duty omitted, some sin committed, and that provoked God to withdraw. If you do find any such wonder not at your want of peace, but immediately break off from it. Maintain no secret haunts of sin. Perhaps you returned to folly after peace [was] spoken formerly, and that has broke the peace again. Consider if your affections be not carried out too much towards the world. If conscience reproach you not, conclude it a trial and proceed accordingly.
b. Be peremptory in the closing act. Are you in doubt about your spiritual state? Put the matter out of doubt by a present consent – if I never did, I do it now. Keep hold of God whatever comes of it. If there may be hope (Lam. 3:29), resolve to trust God though he slay you (Job 13:15). Venture upon that in the way of obedient believing, and if I perish *I perish* (Esther 4:16). I'll not quit my hold of Christ let what will come of it. If I give off from him, I shall certainly perish, I can but perish if I throw myself upon him (allu[de to] 2 Kings 7:3, 4). Thou

mayest take great comfort in such a resolution, for never was any one sent to hell with a resolution to venture all in the hand of Christ.

c. Dwell much in your thoughts on the goodness of God's nature. Even at Mount Sinai he proclaimed his goodness (Exod. 34:6, 7). Hard thoughts of God ruin our peace. Believe that God is love (1 John 4:16), inclined to help his creatures. He has said it, he has sworn it, that he has no delight in sinners' death (Ezek. 33:11). He is not extreme to mark iniquities. Let God be amiable in your eyes. That would answer many of Satan's suggestions who plays the old game (Gen. 3) to beget in us hard thoughts of God. Even in our repentance we must have an eye to God's goodness (Joel 2:13).

d. Observe what makes for you as well as what makes against you. Do not put comfort away from you, nor make that to be against you which is for you. Do not deny the grace of God in you. Though you labour under much weakness yet take the comfort of sincerity. *This I will call to mind* (Lam. 3:21) that it is of the Lord's mercies that we are not consumed, etc. (vv. 23, 24). You cannot say but that you desire the favour of God more than anything else – that Christ is the fairest of ten thousand in your eyes. You dishonour God when you disown that which is the work of his own hands. Though you want peace you would not change conditions with prospering sinners.

e. Do not look for that in yourselves which is to be had in Christ only. We seek our peace in our own performances, and bottom it there, and because we find them weak and imperfect our peace fails us. Depend only on the merit of Christ [and] cast anchor there. The hypocrite weaves his hope out of his own bowels and they prove like the spider's web (Job 8:14). The true Christian builds all upon Christ. God leaves you in the want of this peace to make you glad to be beholden to Christ for it. 'Tis not in us to answer the demands of the broken covenant of works. 'Tis not in us to deal with God immediately, to do anything of ourselves that is good. It must be all had in and from Christ.

f. Understand aright the tenor of the New Covenant. Much of our troubles and fear and doubt is owing to our ignorance and mistake about the covenant of grace that we are under. Understand how *well-ordered* it is (2 Sam. 23:5). We are under grace and not under the law (Rom. 6:14), grace that accepts the willing mind. Sincerity is our gospel profession. What is required of us shall be wrought in us. Every transgression in the covenant doth not put us out of covenant. Especially understand that our salvation is not in our own keeping but in the hands of the mediator. Study the Scripture [on] the extent of the covenant.

g. Transfer all your cares and burdens to the Lord Jesus, by an obedient faith. Dwell much in your meditations upon the death and resurrection and undertaking of Christ (Rom. 8:34). Trust him with the management of all your pleas and all your conflicts. *But thou shalt answer, Lord, for me* (Herbert).[3] Never expect peace but when you are found most near to Jesus Christ. He has *borne our griefs and carried our sorrows* (Isa. 53:4). What need we load and entangle ourselves with them? Let your care be to please Christ in holy, humble walking, and then cast all your other cares upon him.

h. Abound more in the duty of praise. We are very much enemies to ourselves by the neglect of it. When you are doubting the certainty of your covenant interest turn those doubts into praise for the possibility of an interest. Thankfulness for what we have would help us to the comfort of it. Paul took this course (Rom. 7:24, 25). Whatever your troubles be you cannot deny but that you have matter for praise, if you had but a heart.

i. Be diligent and constant in the use of the means. The Word was written that our joy might be full (1 John 1:4). Read it, hear it, study it . Wait at wisdom's gates, a daily duty. Do not let slip any opportunity. Lie at the poolside. Be much in prayer.

---

3. The quotation is from the English poet George Herbert (1593–1633). It comes from his poem 'The Quip', which can be found in *The Temple and the Priest to the Temple* (London: J. M. Dent, n.d.), pp. 110-111.

God will be sought unto for this as other promised mercies. Plead with God. Though the answer[s] do not come presently, abide by it. Peace is the fruit of your lips (Isa. 57:19). The sacraments are means of peace. Keep close to the Lord's Supper. It is a sealing ordinance. To say I am under doubts, therefore I will not come, is to say, I am sick, therefore I will not take physic.[4] Keep in good company. Open your case to a faithful Master that you may be free with a word spoken to your particular case, [that you] may be blessed for good. Remember the days of old (Ps. 77:5), former evidences, experiences. Only take heed to trusting to means.

j. Be willing to wait God's time. He is wise and knows how to dispense his gifts. Let patience have its perfect work unto long suffering. Wait upon the Lord though he hide his face (Isa. 8:17). Comfort is not your Christ. Your case is not singular. 'Tis but for a small moment (Isa. 54:7, 8). The vision is yet for an appropriate time (Hab. 2:3, 4). Be not short-spirited. Light is sown and it will come up again, though it seem long. The joy of harvest will abundantly recompense the cares and pains and tears of the sadness.

4. *Physic* 'medicine'.

14 Feb. 1692

PEACE I LEAVE WITH YOU(iii)

D[octrine] 2. That inward peace is a precious privilege of the covenant of grace belonging to true believers.

Exh[ortation] 2. To those that pretend to this peace but have no title to it. There are many that lay claim to this peace to whom it doth not belong. This as other desirable and excellent things hath its counterfeits. Something like it that is not it. With such multitudes are deceived, and the more precious a jewel is the worse it is to be deceived with its counterfeit.

There are three kinds of false peace.

1. The security of the hardened sinner who takes searedness of conscience for peace of conscience (1 Tim. 4:2) and senselessness for quietness. Conscience strove long, but the sinner stifled it, and now it's silent, and this he takes for peace. I shall have peace though I go on (Deut. 29:19). A resolute banishing [of] all thoughts of God and the soul and eternity are the ground of this peace. See a description of this peace [in] Job 15:25, 26, 27. 'Tis a peace that consists with, nay, is grounded upon war with God, and that's a dismal peace. The calls of the Word, the terrors of the law make no impression. His heart is as hard as stone (allu[ude to] Job 41:24), (he) strengthened himself in his wickedness (Ps. 52:7). Thus they do that go on in a way of open profaneness, drinking in iniquity like water (Job 15:16), bidding defiances to God himself. Do I speak to any such? Believe it sinner.

   a. Thy case is very sad. 'Tis the devil's peace while he as an armed man keeps the palace (Luke 11:21). Thou art sleeping at the pit's brink. Hell will be hell indeed to those that go sleeping thither. While thou art sleeping thy damnation slumbereth not (2 Pet. 2:3). Thy courage is but fool-hardiness, and so it will appear at the last, when the fire of hell will soften those that would not be softened by the fire of the Word. Thou wilt then be undeceived when it is too late, and feel that which thou wouldest not believe. 'Twill then appear in vain to fight it out with God (Isa. 27:4, 5). See thy case described (Prov. 7:22, 23) and tremble at the consequents.

b. Yet blessed be God, thy case is not desperate, yet there is hope. The Almighty can make a hard heart soft, send his Word and melt thee though frozen never so hard. He can fetch water out of the rocks, and speak life to the dead. Only be persuaded to quit thyself like a man, and allow thyself the liberty of consideration. *Awake thou that sleepest* (Eph. 5:14). Be persuaded to look before thee. Dost thou know that thou hast a soul, that thou must be somewhere forever, that thou must die, and after death the judgment? Consider those then that forget God. Say not a little sleep (Prov. 6:9, 10).

2. The sensuality of the voluptuous worldling that builds his peace upon his outward prosperity as that fool (Luke 12:19). Because their houses are safe, from fear their hearts are so, and they feel no bands, no not in their death (Ps. 73:4). As in the days of Noah (Luke 17:26). They eat the fat and the sweet (Amos 6:3-6). They put away sorrow from their hearts, and roll themselves in pleasures, and this they call peace. This is the peace that *the world gives* (Eccles. 11:9). 'Tis to the body, the sensitive appetite, the belly filled (Ps. 17:14). It never affects the soul, therefore [it is] not true peace. Be persuaded not to rest in this peace. See Psalm 119:70.
Consider but these two things:

a. what a little thing will disturb it. When affliction comes that will ruin this peace, it will fall in a storm. See how soon Belshazzar's mirth was marred (Dan. 5:6). Sinners in Zion are afraid (Isa. 33:14; comp. vv. 15, 16). A small matter will awake a sleeping lion. If conscience come to be startled, guilt stare thee in the face, the world will give thee small relief. [You will be] consumed with terrors (Ps. 73:19; comp. v. 5). In straits even in the fulness of his sufficiency (Job 20:22).

b. what a little time will put a period to it – this night (Luke 12:20), sudden destruction (1 Thess. 5:3). What will become of the world's peace when death strips thee of all, and thou shalt carry nothing away with thee? – *but know thou* (Eccles. 11:9). 'Tis but for a moment (Job 20:5). All that will remain on the other side [of] death will be the tormenting remembrance that thou in thy lifetime receivedst thy good things (Luke 16:25; see Isa. 50:1).

3. The self-flattery of the formal hypocrite that lays his claims higher and pretends to peace of conscience arising from pardon, thinks his spiritual state and condition to be good – makes him rich (Prov. 13:7; Rev. 3:17), flatters himself in his own eyes (Ps. 36:2) as if all were well with him. This is a common mistake and fatal to thousands, yet [they] please themselves with a fool's paradise. They say they have peace, they do not doubt of their happiness, perhaps none more confident than they. The hypocrite has his hope (Job 27:8) and it bears his charges to the very gate of heaven, but there fails him (Luke 13:25, 26).
I would endeavour two things.

1. To discover the hypocrite's peace, to distinguish it from this peace that Christ gives, that they may not take that which counters for gold.

a. The hypocrite's peace comes cheap and easy, but saints' peace is laboured for. 'Tis easy building upon the sand, but building upon the rock requires pains (Luke 6:48, *digged deep*) by an impartial and strict examination. You have peace. How did you come by it? What did it cost you? What did [you] not part with for it? What search, what godly sorrow? What pains did you take for it? Perhaps you easily took the thing for granted and called that *peace*, and so light come, light go. There can be no true peace without great diligence in examination, and great humiliation for sin.

b. The hypocrite's peace is built upon the sand (woven out of his bowels). The saint's peace is built upon Christ the Rock. Everything but Christ is sand – general mercy, common privileges, external performances, a righteousness of his own (Matt. 7:22). That's true peace which is derived from the Prince of Peace. Many derive it from their profession, their name to live (Matt. 3:9), their place among God's people as if that would secure them partial reformation, as Judges 17:13.

c. The hypocrite's peace will consist with a beloved sin. The saint's peace works in a real hatred to every sin. It never breaks the rotten peace to maintain a correspondence with sin, for when the peace was made there was a reserve for that (2 Kings 5:18), a proviso that there should be no squares,[1] the beloved sin must be harboured. If secret haunts of sin are kept up under the cloak of a visible profession, the peace is none of Christ's peace. If the heart goes after the covetousness, or the pride or the uncleanness, and these be allowed of, though you sit before God as his people sit, you have no true peace. See Isaiah 33:15, 16. Till you have sincerely quitted the love of every sin there is no peace (Isa. 57:21).

d. The hypocrite's peace makes him proud and self-conceited. The saint's peace makes him humble and denying. See the language of the hypocrite (Isa. 65:5, *I am holier than thou*). The language of the true Christian is 1 Timothy 1:15. I have *need of nothing*, saith Laodicea (Rev. 3:17). *I am poor and needy*, saith David (Ps. 40:17). The hypocrite takes the glory of his peace to himself. The true Christian gives it all to Christ, sees Christ making their difference, and does not boast. [There is] nothing to boast of, said Mr Cook,[2] not a word of works. The veriest dunghill worm that ever went to heaven, said Mr Baxter.[3]

1. *Square* is probably used here as in Shakespeare in the sense of a 'rule'.
2. The person referred to is probably the Puritan John Cook, the Solicitor General under the Commonwealth period.
3. Richard Baxter (1615–1691), the Puritan pastor and author.

e. The hypocrite's peace makes him slothful and careless. The saint's peace makes him watchful and diligent. The hypocrite rests in his attainments, sits down contented, neglects his guard, is off his watch, lies open like the field of the slothful. The true Christian is pressing forward (Phil 3:12, 13), uses his peace as an argument against sin and to duty. He that thinks he has grace enough 'tis a bad sign he has none at all in truth.

Well, try by these things and be faithful in the search. What will it avail you to have a peace that will stand you in no stead when you have most need of it?

2. To direct your feet into the paths of true peace (Luke 1:79). I would not beat you off from your false peace and then leave you without peace. No, blessed be God there is a path of peace opened. Will you walk in it? Know the things of peace (Luke 19:42).

a. The path of deep humiliation and sorrow for sin. The way to rear the building high is to lay the foundation low. The more particular we are in our repentance for sin the more likely to have the sense of a pardon and the more sensible[4] the contrition is the more sensible the consolations are likely to be (Ps. 126:5, 6; Matt. 5:4).

b. The path of dependence on Jesus Christ. There's no true joy and peace but in believing (Rom. 15:13). Receive Christ Jesus the Lord and walk in him. [There's] no rest for the soul but in the beloved Lord Jesus. Disclaim all reliance upon your own righteousness, and say, none but Christ (Phil. 3:3) as this is the meaning of that Scripture. The doctrine of justification by faith is the best friend to true peace. Justification expected by works must needs leave the soul at great uncertainties.

c. The path of delight in God (Ps. 37:4). The more the soul is brought into an acquaintance with God, and an acquiescence in him and his goodness the surer, the sweeter, the safer the

4. *Sensible* here means 'touching the senses or feelings'.

peace is. Return to him as your rest (Ps. 116:7). Let your souls be satisfied in him and take not up with anything short of him.

d. The path of diligence and sincerity in all manner of gospel obediences. Give diligence to make your election sure (2 Pet. 1:10). 'Twill not got without diligence, diligence in prayer, meditation, reading the Scripture, self-examination, attendance upon ordinances, watchfulness against sin, and strictness in your thoughts, words and actions (Ps. 119:165).

Exh[ortation] 3. To those that have this peace and have cause for it, whose sins are pardoned and they know it, whose peace is made and they have the comfort of it. Their evidences clear and unclouded, who though perhaps they have not full assurance yet have good hope through grace, enough to quiet their spirits, and to maintain a humble expectation of the glory that is to be revealed, and to keep them from fainting under outward troubles.

Do I speak to such? Suffer a word of exhortation.

1. Be very thankful to God for it. You have great reason to be so. Speak of it to his praise (Col. 3:15). Has he given thee grace? Thou hast great reason to be thankful, but especially if he has withal given thee peace. See it to be his gift, the gift of his love (2 Thess. 2:16, *loved us and given us*). Outward peace is a great mercy, and calls for our thankfulness (Ps. 147:14), much more inward peace. See it coming from God, 'tis of his creating (Isa. 57:19), of his ordaining (Isa. 26:12), of his speaking (Ps. 85:8). Admire his love herein.

Consider it

a. as a rich mercy, a precious privilege. Think how sad this is to want his peace, how sweet it is to have it. Think of the value of the blood that purchased it (Isa. 53:5, *the chastisement of our peace*), the virtue of the spirit that wrought it. 'Tis a heaven upon earth. In giving you this peace he has given you a cordial for the relief in all your straits, a foretaste of the rivers of pleasure.

b. as a distinguishing mercy. God has herein dealt better with you than with many of his own dear people, who walk in darkness and whose evidences are clouded. Distinguishing mercies are hugely obliging (John 14:22).

'Twas not because you were better than they, but because your Heavenly Father saw you weaker than they and less able to bear it. Think when and how the peace was spoken – perhaps or ever you were aware. Tell others what God has done for your souls (Ps. 66:16).

2. Walk humbly with God. Thou standest by faith, i.e. by a dependence on Christ not in any strength of thine own, therefore *be not high-minded* (Rom. 11:20). Do not bear too high a sail while the gale is so strong, for you are yet at sea, and there's great danger in being puffed up (2 Cor. 12:7). Ezekiel and Daniel that had most intimate converse with heaven are most frequently called *Son of Man* to keep them humble. What hast thou that thou hast *not received* (1 Cor. 4:7)? Let boasting be for ever excluded. 'Tis an excellent thing to have a low spirit in the midst of high attainments. Spiritual pride is apt to steal upon us and like a dead fly to spoil the most precious pot of ointment. Therefore watch against it. When you are pleasing yourself with your peace, let your delight terminate in God and make him the *gladness of your joy*. Take heed of forgetting the Lord thy God. When your face shines put on the veil of humility.

3. Abound in fruit bearing. 'Tis summer time with you and therefore should be a time of fruitfulness. When the church had rest 'twas edified (Acts 9:31). Times of peace should be growing times, and being thus planted by the rivers of water bring forth their fruit in its season (Ps. 1:3). Hath God delivered your eyes from tears? – walk before the Lord (Ps. 116:7, 8, 9). Study why you shall render. Let peace be oil to the wheels of your obedience (Ps.

119:32). The temple was built at a time of peace. You have now an opportunity, a price put into your hands. This joy of the Lord will be your strength (Neh. 8:10). [Be] up and be doing then. Be daily getting ground of your corruptions, getting nearer to God. Be busily working out your own salvation.

4. Be very careful to preserve this peace. 'Tis a precious jewel; take hold of losing it. Let this peace *rule in your hearts* (Col. 3:15). All other interests [must] be made to truckle[5] to this. Keep this peace and this peace will keep thee (Phil. 4:7).

   a. Be not apt to arraign your evidences. 'Tis the unbelief of God's Israel that upon every difficulty suggests, *Is the Lord among us or is he not* (Exod. 17:7)? *You have not received the spirit of bondage again* (Rom. 9:16). Be daily suspecting your strength, and suspecting your steps but be not upon every slight occasion suspecting your states when once the point is settled. Remember the days of old.
   b. Abstain from all appearance of evil (1 Thess. 5:22). Take heed of sin and every thing that looks like it. Do not return to folly after God hath spoken peace (Ps. 85:8). All sin is folly but especially sin after peace spoken. Keep at a due distance from it. 'Tis folly to sport at the pit's brink. The fly that plays with the flame hazards her wings. It's good keeping out of harm's way. In a doubtful case keep the safer side, and take heed of doing any thing to offend conscience (Acts 24:16). Have your conversation in simplicity and godly sincerity (2 Cor. 1:12).

5. Evidence this peace in your carriage and behaviour. Make it to appear that you have this quietness and tranquillity:

   a. by a sober cheeerfulness in all your converse. It becomes those that are at peace with their own consciences to show it.

5. *Truckle*, 'submit', 'accept an inferior position'.

A merry heart makes a cheerful countenance (Prov. 15:13). None have such reason to live cheerful lives as true believers. You contradict your peace by your prevailing melancholy. Make it to appear that you have found wisdom's ways of pleasantness. *Eat thy bread with joy* (Eccles. 9:7). *Serve the Lord with joyfulness* (Deut. 28:47). *Tristis es & felix.*[6]

b. by a holy contempt of the pleasure of sin, looking upon them with a holy scorn. The pleasure of this peace should put our mouths out of taste to all other pleasures, as looking at the sun dazzles the eyes to other objects. Offer these things to those that know no better. This foretaste of the milk and honey of Canaan should spoil our relish of the garlic and onions of Egypt (Heb. 11:25). No man having drunk old wine desires new (Luke 5:39). Shall I leave my sweetness (allu[ude to] Jude 9:11)?

c. by a joyful bearing of afflicting providences. Let the pleasure of this peace prevail to sweeten every bitter cup. Let it silence your complaints (Isa. 33:24), keep you from fainting and preserve your spirits in an even frame under all the unevenness of providence. It ill becomes you to fret at every little cross, as if your peace were bound up in the creature. Sustained by this peace rejoice in the Lord when the fig tree doth not blossom (Hab. 3:17, 18).

d. by a gracious readiness to suffer for righteousness sake if God call you to it. Venture to a prison in banishment for the testimony of Jesus armed with this peace. This will make sufferings easy, to have the bird in the bosom sing sweet. When men reproach us while we have this peace what need we matter it? Sometimes God gives special comforts to prepare us for trials. Those that were to be the witnesses of Christ's agony to prepare them for that must be the witnesses of his transfiguration.

e. by a believing triumph over death and the grave. Have you this peace? Be not afraid to die. So *death where is thy sting* (1

6. Latin, 'you are sad and happy'.

Cor. 15:55)? Even in the darksome valley fear no evil (Ps. 23:4). This was Paul's rejoicing when he had received the sentence of death (2 Cor. 1:12). Christ died to deliver us from the fear of death (Heb. 2:14). Be not then again entangled in it. Either the fear of death will conquer our peace or our peace will conquer our fear of death.

6. Be very tender to those that want this peace. Pity them, pray for them, do not confuse them, take heed of condemning *the generation of the righteous* (Ps. 73:13, 14) as Job's friends condemned Job. Those that have less peace than you may perhaps have more grace. *Look not upon me because I am black* (Cant. 1:6). We must take heed with what eye we look upon the people of God when they are in their blackness, for though black yet comely, verse 5, black in themselves but comely in Christ, black in their own apprehension but comely in God's acceptance. Take heed of quenching the smoking flax. God is very angry with the prophets that make those sad whom God would have to be comforted (Ezek. 13:22; 34:4; a brand is set upon the watchmen, Cant. 5:7).

7. Prepare for trouble. The calm is an opportunity to get ready for a storm. You have peace, 'tis well. Be not too confident that it will be always. So Psalm 30:6, 7. Let not him that putteth on the harness boast as he that puts it off. You are yet in the wilderness, yet at sea. What cloud you may yet come under you cannot tell, but it's good to provide for the worst. Lay up a stock of comforts, evidences, experiences against such a day. God may see cause to withdraw. Think it not strange if he should, but arm yourselves for a state of desertion. Get the faith of adherence strengthened that you may have that to live by when the faith of assurance fails.

8. Let present peace quicken your longings after the eternal peace. Here the peace enters into peace, then we shall enter into peace (Isa. 57:2). We are here tasting the sweetness of the cisterns but there we shall be satisfied from the fountain (Ps. 37:37). Our

peace here is liable to interruption and disturbance, but that's a quiet region. Love and long for the approaching of our Lord. Think, if the foretaste be so sweet what will the feast be? If the bunch of grapes that meets us in the wilderness be so grateful,[7] what then will the full vintage be in the heavenly Canaan. Do long for *that* peace of God which passeth all understanding. Who would be fond of a world of trouble that is upon the borders of such a world of peace?

7. *Grateful*, here in the sense of 'pleasing'.

6

Grace in the Covenant

21 Feb. 1692
σύν θεῷ[1]

6. GRACE IN THE COVENANT

And of his fulness have all we received
and grace for grace (John 1:16).

These are supposed to be the words not of John the Baptist, whose testimony concerning Christ is recorded (v. 15), but of John the Evangelist, and their coherence is plain with the close of the 14th verse. He was *full of grace and truth*, which he proves (v. 15) by the witness of John, and here in the text applies, for the comfort of true believers, of that fulness have we all received – the fulness of grace and truth, i.e. true grace which came by Jesus Christ (v. 17).

The knowledge of God is incomparably the best and most desirable knowledge, which we should every one of us with a holy contempt of everything else labour after (Phil. 3:8). To know what he is in himself and what he is to his people – and the best knowledge of this is that which is gotten by experience. He is full of grace and truth, for we have received of his fulness, *all we*, i.e. all we that have believed in him.

Doct[rine] 1. That there is a fulness in the Lord Jesus Christ.

1. As God. He is a perfect being – El Shaddai,[2] a God all-sufficient – *in him dwelleth all the fulness of the godhead bodily* (Col. 2:9; 1 John 16:15). This proves that he is truly God, for he had *the fulness, all the fulness* of the godhead – not some portion of the divinity, such as the deluded Gentiles falsely attributed to their idols, but all the fulness – God equal with the Father (Phil. 2:6, 7). Therefore [he is] said to be the Son of God – the

1. Greek, 'with God'.
2. Hebrew, 'God all-sufficient', or 'God all-powerful'. From the Latin translation *omnipotent* is derived the English 'almighty'.

first-begotten of the Father. As in ordinary generation the fulness of the human nature is communicated, so of the divine nature in the eternal ineffable generation. Hence he is said to *be Light of Light, very God of very God* – one with the Father.

Now,

a. This fulness *dwelleth* in him – not sojourneth in him – but dwelleth, as at home – alluding to God's dwelling between the cherubims in the tabernacle of the testimony (Ps. 80:1). It dwells as in its proper seat, not for a time but for ever. The body of Christ is therefore called the temple (John 2:21), *the image of God* (Col. 1:15; Heb. 1:3).
b. It dwells in him *bodily* – σωματικώς.[3] God has many ways of being present with his creatures, but 'twas in a peculiar manner that he dwelt in the human nature of Christ. *Bodily*, i.e. even in the body of Christ the word was made flesh and so dwelt (John 1:14). Bodily, i.e. substantially and essentially, not in clouds and ceremonies, as the Shekinah between the cherubim (see Col. 2:17). *The body is Christ* is opposition to the shadows. Under the O[ld] T[estament] God dwelt in the temple typically, but he dwells in Christ bodily – personally, and we receive of the fulness (2 Pet. 1:4).

2. As mediator, and so it's here spoken of. He hath a fulness, i.e. a sufficiency – according to the good pleasure of the Father (Col. 1:19), *all fulness*, i.e. all sufficiency.

a. For himself – to qualify him for the undertaking. The Spirit was poured upon him *without measure* (John 3:34) – not as upon the prophets of old, *some of* the Spirit (Num. 11:17). No, he was anointed above his fellows (Ps. 45:7). He hath the seven spirits (Rev. 3:4), i.e. a fulness of the Spirit.

---

3. Greek, 'bodily'.

He hath a fulness:

i. For his prophetical office – a fulness of knowledge and truth. He has lain in the bosom of the Father from eternity (John 1:18). He knew all things, knew the will of the Father perfectly. God gave him the Urim and the Thummim[4] – anointed him to preach the gospel (Isa. 61:1). [He has] a fulness of compassion on the ignorant and on them that out of the way (Heb. 5:2; Mat. 11:29), a full commission, he teacheth as one having authority. [His] credentials [are] under the broad seal of heaven. None teacheth like him. He's of quick understanding (Isa. 11:3).

ii. For his priestly office. He is ordained (Heb. 5:1). He hath somewhat to offer, and he has offered it. He is a merciful and faithful High Priest (Heb. 2:17), able to save to the uttermost (Heb. 7:25). The anointing of Aaron with plenty of ointment signified the abundant graces that Christ was qualified with for the execution of his priestly office. There was a sufficiency in that sacrifice which he offered to make atonement for sin. The mercy seat was as long and as broad as the ark, signifying the full answer given to the demands of the law by the merit of Christ's death.

iii. For his kingly office. He hath a fulness of wisdom, righteousness and strength (Micah 5:4). Christ is called David (Hos. 3:5). David was anointed with a horn of oil, not a vial, as Saul, noting the fulness of gifts and graces that Christ should be adorned with (Ps. 72:1, 2, etc.). He had a fulness of power to subdue his chosen people to himself and to rule them with his golden sceptre, a fulness of power to restrain and conquer his implacable enemies,

---

4. The Urim and Thummim were stored in the high priest's breastplate. They were probably precious gems, but the manner in which they communicated the mind of God is not made clear in the text of the Old Testament. The words themselves most probably mean 'light' and 'perfection', and the divine revelation may have involved some visible authenticating sign or special miraculous light.

a crown is given to him (Rev. 6:2), all judgments [are] committed to the Son (John 5:22), not only authority to judge but ability.

Thus had Christ an ability for the discharge of his work. Those that are called of God to any work shall be qualified for it. Hence it was that the good pleasure of the Lord prospered in his hand (Isa. 53:10). None other but he was fit. No shoulders but his could bear the government.

3. For us. He received that he might give. Compare Psalm 68:18 with Ephesians 4:8. The anointing runs down from the head to the skirts of the garments (Ps. 133:2). He received as our trustee, and he hath a *fulness* for us, as Joseph the great treasurer of corn not for himself but for the people, so Christ. He is *a horn of salvation* (Luke 1:69). A horn [de]notes plenty – all that which Christ received as mediator was for the good of the church, to which he is the head of vital influence. See John 17:2, 8, 19.

   a. He hath a fulness of wisdom for us. Treasures of *wisdom and knowledge* [are] hid in him (Col. 2:3) – not hid from us but hid for us, for he is made of God unto us wisdom (1 Cor. 1:30). In this respect [he is] greater than Solomon. All true wisdom is conversant about him, communicated by him. The doctrines he teaches make us wise to salvation (2 Tim. 3:15). See wisdom's preparations (Prov. 9:1, 2, 3). He hath provided for us a spirit of wisdom and revelation (Eph. 1:17). He can give an understanding, [he can] open the blind eyes.
   b. He hath a fulness of righteousness for us, wrought out by the merit of his death. He is *Jehovah our righteousness* (Jer. 23:6). He hath brought in an *everlasting righteousness* (Dan. 9:24), a fountain (Zech. 13:1). [He] hath wherewithal to discharge us from the great debt, like the coats of skin large enough to cover us, he is made of God unto us righteousness. *By one offering he has perfected* (Heb. 10:10). There's no defect in Christ's satisfaction. Being made by an infinite person

it is of infinite value. He has rest for all that are weary.

c. He hath a fulness of strength for us – strength that is made perfect in weakness (2 Cor. 12:9), *strengthened with all might, according to his glorious power* (Col. 1:11). [There's] strength for our spiritual work, our spiritual warfare. He is our strength – [he] gives strength and power unto his people. Hence we read *of the power of his might* (Eph. 6:10).

d. He hath a fulness of comfort for us. He is not only our strength but our song. He is the consolation of Israel. There is enough in Christ to furnish all his people with strong consolation and to crown them with everlasting joys. He hath a treasury of cordials, suited to all the necessities and exigencies of his people. He hath healing under his wings (Mal. 4:2).

This fulness that is in Christ as mediator is:

i. A complete fulness. 'Tis *all* fulness. We read of the *fulness* of the world (Ps. 24:1) but that is not *all* fulness. 'Tis not satisfying to the soul. 'Tis but like the fulness of a blown bladder, 'tis full of wind, full of vanity and vexation of spirit – but – *ye are complete in him* (Col. 2:10, compare v. 9). 'Tis a fulness that answers all the needs and desires of the soul – supply *all* your wants (Phil. 4:19). 'Tis substance (Prov. 8:21).

ii. A continuing fulness, a fulness that can never be exhausted, can never be drawn dry. 'Tis not the fulness of a cistern but the fulness of a fountain – able to the uttermost, to the uttermost of times (Heb. 7:25) – always flowing and yet ever full – *the same yesterday* (Heb. 13:8). He *ever* lives to make intercession. The water of purification was to be *running water* (Num. 19:17, Heb. living waters) – like the sun's fulness of light, as full now as it ever was (Ps. 19:5, 6).

iii. It is a communicative fulness. Christ has not only a sufficiency wherewithal to supply us but a readiness to supply us. He was born in an inn which receives all passengers. He is a fountain opened (Zech. 13:1), not a spring shut up. 'Tis offered to us (Isa. 55:1), nay we are invited to accept of it (Prov. 9:4, 5). 'Tis said to *dwell* in him (Col. 1:14). A man's dwelling place is not only his safe place, but the place where he may be found. In Christ we may find what we want. You'll be sure to find him at home.

Use 1. Give Christ the glory of his fulness. Speak of it to his honour. Admire the wisdom of the Father in treasuring up all the fulness of his hand, his kindness to us in it, for he is bone of our bone. 'Twas a mercy to Jacob's family that the store-keeper was one of themselves. Wonder at the inexhaustibleness of Christ's fulness. O the depth (Rom. 11:33)!

2. Apply yourselves to him accordingly. See the emptiness of the creature, it's insufficiency to help and supply you. 'Tis not in it. Come off from your dependence on it, lower your expectations from it, do not spend your money for that which is not bread (Isa. 55:2). It pleased the Father that in him should all fulness dwell. Let it please you. Have recourse to him. Count all but loss that you may win Christ (Phil. 3:8). Marry him and it's all your own.

3. Live upon Christ's fulness. Having found the fulness make daily use of it. Do all in the hand of Christ (Col. 3:17). To you to live must be Christ (Phil. 2:21). Spend upon this stock. Fetch in strength from heaven to enable you to do what you have to do in religion. Be every day drawing water out of this fountain. Why are you so empty while Christ is so full? So poor while he is so rich? Take his counsel (Rev. 3:20).

Doct[rine] 2. That all true believers receive grace for grace from the fulness that is in Jesus Christ. The covenant which is the channel or conduit pipe by which this fulness that is in Christ communicates itself to believers among other things conveys grace to them. The usual salutation in the Old Testament was *Peace be unto you,* but when the mystery of our redemption was more clearly manifested the apostles in their benedictions prefixed grace as the only foundation of peace (Rom. 1:7). Grace then is in the covenant, which is therefore called a covenant of grace – grace and truth (John 1:17).

Show 1. What that *grace* is which is received.

a. Grace is *the good will* of God manifested towards us, the root and foundation of all good – *good will towards men* (Luke 2:14), unworthy, undeserving men. 'Tis the favour of God, the light of his countenance (Ps. 4:6), *that loving kindness* which is better than life, the good will of him that dwelt in the bush (Deut. 33:16). This true believers receive. All that good you have or hope for flows from this grace. And it is from Christ's fulness. What interest we have in the favour of God 'tis at second hand by virtue of our union with Christ, God's beloved Son (Matt. 3:17; 17:5). Are we accepted, it is in the beloved (Eph. 1:6, ἐχαρίτωσεν ἡμᾶς,[5] *made us favourites*). He had a fulness of the divine favour, and from him we receive it, not only reconciliation but loving kindness.

'Tis from Christ's fulness that we receive:

i. Gracious visits. [There's] no communion between God and man but in Christ. When God manifests himself to the soul 'tis through Christ (John 14:23). You have sometimes experienced those visits. What favour there was in them! You owe it to Christ – *that they may be one in us* (John 17:21). [There's] no fellowship with the Father but in the Son (1 John 1:3). It amazeth and astonisheth us to think of God out of Christ but God in our nature is Emmanuel, God with us. This is promised in the covenant (Rev. 3:20; Ps. 36:7, 8).

ii. Gracious answers. The returns of prayers are owing to the fulness of Christ's intercession. 'Tis from his fulness that we have the comfort of *a throne of grace* (Heb. 4:16). The fulness of that which his blood speaks on our behalf,

5. Greek, 'he has freely given us'.

the fulness of that smoke of the incense with which the prayers of the saints are perfumed. The return is given for the name's sake in which we come (John 16:13).

iii. Gracious comforts. Our good hope is *through grace* (2 Thess. 2:16), and that we receive from Christ's fulness, for he is the consolation of Israel. God is to us *the God of comfort*, as he is the *Father of our Lord Jesus Christ* (2 Cor. 1:3), all the consolation that is *in Christ* (Phil. 2:1). Our consolations are then strong when they are grounded upon the merit of Christ's death.

iv. Gracious supplies. Help in time of need comes from grace (Heb. 4:16), and its all from Christ's fulness (Phil. 4:19, *by Christ Jesus*). For soul, for body, what there is of the grace and favour of God in these is owing to Christ's fulness – supplies of strength (Phil. 4:13, *through Christ strengthening me*). 'Tis the supply of the spirit of grace (Phil. 1:19).

v. Gracious deliverances, begun, completed. There is grace that is to be brought us shortly and that must come from Christ's fulness (1 Pet. 1:13). Eternal life is the gift of grace through Jesus Christ our Lord (Rom. 6:23). He is made of God unto us redemption. Our glorification is owing to the fulness of Christ's mediation, his loving to the end.

This grace believers receive. 'Tis called grace because it is free (Rom. 11:6, *not of works*). Our whole salvation from first to last is carried on in a way of grace (Eph. 2:5, 8). Cry, 'Grace, Grace' (Zech. 4:7), and it all comes from Christ's fulness. He consigns over to us an interest in his Father's love and favour.

b. Grace is the *good work* of God wrought in us, the saving change which is necessary to salvation. 'Tis sanctification (1 Cor. 6.11), the new creature (2 Cor. 5:17), the new man (Eph. 4:24), the new heart (Ezek. 18:31). Grace is the regular motion of the soul and all its powers and faculties towards God. This [is] the good work (Phil. 1:6), the conformity of the soul to the will of God. 'Tis called grace because it comes to us from the favour of God, and recommends us to the favour of God. 'Tis the hidden man of the heart which is in the sight of God of great price (1 Pet. 3:4).

Now believers *receive* this grace. 'Tis given to them. What have we that we have not received (1 Cor. 4:7)? *By the grace of God* (1 Cor. 15:10). Whatever we have had or hope to have of this grace we have received it, and must expect to receive it from Christ.

In the external administration of the covenant, grace is offered to all (Prov. 1:23). In the internal administration 'tis effectually applied to all true believers.

See what it is that is granted.

i. The planting of grace. 'Tis God that begins the good work, lays the foundation. Wheresovever there is a change wrought 'tis of his working, the Lord's planting (Isa. 61:3). Hence 'tis called a new creation (Col. 3:10; Eph. 2:10). Creating work is God's work (Isa. 41:19, 20). 'Tis he that opens the blind eyes, softens the hard heart, changeth the bent of the will and affections. 'Tis owing to this power that the sea flies, that Jordan is driven back.

'Tis promised in the covenant to all that seek it. Nay, *how oft is he found of those that sought him not.* See Deuteronomy 30:6, [*the* LORD *thy God*] *will circumcise the heart*, take off that which hinders, the superfluity of naughtiness. The great command is, thou shalt love the Lord thy God. The great promise is, I will circumcise thy heart to love me. See Ezekiel 11:19, *I will put a new spirit*. The great duty is to make us a new heart (Ezek. 18:31). The great promise is he'll make it for you and the great heart maker is the only heart mender. O but there's a great deal of opposition, why, *he'll take away the stony heart*. The opposition shall be conquered, the enmity slain (Ezek. 36:26). See Ezekiel 36:27, *I will – and you shall*. There's the sovereignty of grace dealing with men as men, working a change upon the will (Ps. 110:3). See Hosea

2:14, *Therefore I will allure her*.

'Tis the great article of the New Covenant (Heb. 8:10), *I will put my laws in their minds*. That's grace, when a counterpart of the law is written in the heart. God can write the law upon stone. 'Tis a disposition of the Spirit to obey the will of God, so that the soul becomes the epistle of Christ (2 Cor. 2:2, 3). Duty becomes natural to the new nature. Faith is the gift of God (Phil. 1:29), the work of God, of his glorious power (Eph. 1:19, 20; 2:8).

The particular performance of the promises of first grace is determined by the election of grace (Eph. 1:4; see John 6:37), but so that they never failed any poor soul that pleaded them and trusted to them.

ii. The preferring of grace. Grace is a plant that will wither if it be not kept alive by constant care. God has promised not only to plant grace but to water it. He has provided in the covenant of grace for the keeping of the heart and mind (Phil. 4:7). 'Tis the power of God in the promise of the covenant that keeps a spark of grace alive in the sea of corruption, in the midst of so many temptations. *Kept by the power of God* (1 Pet. 1:5). We are kept in the hands of the Father (John 10:28, 29). That good part shall never be taken away (Luke 10:42). As 'tis with natural, so with spiritual life. 'Tis God that holdeth our souls in life. There's a promise of the covenant to this purpose (Jer. 32:40*, they shall not depart*). God will not forsake the work of his own hands, will keep them *from falling* (Jude 24), uphold them with his right hand in their combats, under their burdens.

iii. The exercise of grace. Where the habits of grace are planted, yet without renewed quickening influences from on high for the drawing out of these graces into action nothing will be done. We act but as we are acted. Grace acts in as close a dependence upon God as a God of grace as nature doth upon him as a God of nature (allu[de to] Acts 17:28). This is granted by the covenant. The Spirit helpeth our infirmities (Rom. 8:26). He wakeneth morning by morning (Isa. 50:4), [he is] their arm every morning (Isa. 33:2). The best man is no more than what the grace of the covenant makes him every day. He works all our works in us (Isa. 26:12), both to will and to do (Phil. 2:13). All our sufficiency is in him (2 Cor. 3:5). The exercise of grace in resisting temptation is his gift (Eph. 6:10, 11) in the performance of duty. From me not only the root but *the fruit* (Hos. 14:8; Cant. 4:16).

iv. The increase of grace. Growth in grace is a great duty (2 Pet. 3:18), and it is also a promised mercy. There's that in the covenant. *He that hath clean hands shall be stronger and stronger* (Job 17:9; Prov. 4:18). Grace doth then increase when the habits of it are more confirmed and strengthened, the actings of it quickened and invigorated. Gracious aversions, dislikes and oppositions more fixed and resolute. Less apt to be shaken. Gracious inclinations, dispositions and affections more lively, frequent and fervent. Here's grace growing, and this is had from the covenant. 'Tis God that is the dew (Hos. 14:5). 'Tis not our industry but his pound that gains ten pounds. All our growth in grace is received from promise of the covenant (Matt. 25:29*, to him that hath shall be given*). This is very comfortable to the bruised reed and smoking flax that the day of small thing shall not be despised, but he will give more grace (Jas. 4:6).

v. The comfort of grace. Grace has that in it which being agreeable to the divine nature and will cannot but bring abundant satisfaction to the soul, and a complacency in its conformity (in some measure) to the eternal mind, and its hope of glory that shall be revealed. Now all this we receive. Grace, and peace the fruit of it, is from God the Father and from our Lord Jesus Christ. This is one of the grants of the covenant that we shall be satisfied with God's likeness. *The work of the righteous shall be peace* (Isa. 32:17).

vi. The consummation of grace. The covenant of grace assures us of the completing of the growing light in the perfect day (Prov. 4:18), the performance of the good work unto the day of Christ (Phil. 1:6), till we all come to the perfect man (Eph. 4:13). That which is perfect shall come (1 Cor. 13:10), and this will be the gift of God. We must cry, Grace, Grace to the top-stone (Zech. 4:7). Should God leave us at last we should certainly come short, but faithful is he that has called us, true to his word who will also do it (1 Thess. 5:24). He will give grace and glory.

And this is that grace which is granted to believers in and by the New Covenant.

28 Feb. 1692

FROM HIS FULNESS HAVE ALL WE RECEIVED AND GRACE FOR GRACE ...

D[octrine] That all true believers receive grace for grace from Christ's fulness.

Show 2. How is *grace* received *from Christ's fulness*.

1. It is *received*. What have we that *we have not received* (1 Cor. 4:7). 'Tis a gift, a free gift. The philosophers called their good qualities and dispositions πράξεις, *habitus*.[1] 'Twas enough to them that they had them. Christianity teacheth us to call them δώσεις, *gifts* (Jas. 1:17). They called them *virtues*, as if they were the products of our natural *powers* but we must call them *graces* wrought in us by the gift of God.

   a. Grace is not born in us. No, we were *shapen in iniquity* (Ps. 51:5). We brought into the world with us corrupt depraved degenerate natures. We were called transgressors from the womb (Isa. 48:8). We brought into the world with us a carnal mind (Rom. 8:7). [We] derive corrupt natures from the loins of our first parents. Faith and love and other graces are flowers that do not grow in nature's garden. Jews and Gentiles [are] all born under sin (Rom. 3:9-19). That which is *born of the flesh is flesh* (John 3:6; Job 14:4; 1 Cor. 15:49). We all by nature bear the image of the earthy. Adam lost the image of God's holiness for himself and all his posterity and then begat a son in his own likeness (Gen. 5:3). Even the children of saints are born in sin. Grace doth not run in the blood. Inherent holiness is not propagated, which yet doth not impede the

---

1. The Greek word πράξεις means 'actions, business', and the Latin *habitus* means 'habits', 'dispositions'.

propagation of federal[2] holiness. Though the seed of believers are born polluted it doth not therefore follow that they are not born privileged. David who acknowledgeth the corruption his mother bore him in (Ps. 51:5) yet pleads the privilege his mother bore him to (Ps. 116:16, the son of thy handmaiden; so Ps. 86:16). Though a wise man do not beget a wise man, yet a freeman begets a freeman. I was born free, saith Paul. We are all born diseased and impotent, but being born of believers we are born by the pool-side, not always under the internal but always under the external administration of the covenant. Israel as the seed of Abraham were transgressors from the womb, but as the seed of Abraham, to them pertained the adoption (Rom. 9:4). Those who will not admit this blessing of Abraham to come upon the Gentiles must expunge it out of their Bibles (Gal. 3:7, 14; Acts 2:39).

b. Grace is not acquired by us. Means indeed are to be used, ordinances attended on, but if not in temporals much less in spirituals can we say, 'my might and the power of my hand hath gotten it' (Deut. 8:17). 'Tis our duty to work out our own salvation, but still it is God that works in us (Phil. 2:12, 13). Where there is true grace 'tis not owing to the *improvement* of natural powers or any preparation of our own to dispose us *for* the reception of grace. No, the preparation as well as the performance is from God. (Prov. 16:1; Ps. 10:17). That, whatever it is which distinguisheth us from others is owing not to our free will but to God's free grace, yet so that the ruin of those that perish in a graceless state lies at their own door. All that we have is received – *omnia desuper*[3] – all things come of thee (1 Chron. 29:14), all our sufficiency (2 Cor. 3:5). The saints have been ready to acknowledge it (1 Cor. 15:10, *by the grace of God*). Though Paul [was] a great scholar, a man of great natural parts, yet [he] lives upon alms. This is a good text to try doctrines by.

2. *Federal* comes from the Latin *foedus*, 'bond', 'covenant'.
3. Latin, 'all things come from above'.

Arminianism makes grace a servant of man's goodness. Antinomianism makes it a servant to man's badness.[4]

2. We have *all* received it – ἡμεῖς πάντες[5] (John 1:16).Not only all we apostles as some understand it (see Lightfoot[6]). John the Baptist bore witness of him (v. 15), and we, we disciples, were next appointed to preach and proclaim him. See Ephesians 3:8; 1 Corinthians 3:10. But all we believers – all that see his glory (v. 14) – see it by faith. All that have grace have it from him. We have *all* received. The gospel salvation is a *common* salvation (Jude 3). All have need to receive, even the most worthy. All are welcome to receive, even the most unworthy, if they come and seek it in the right way.

a. This is abasing to the proud. The greatest saints have *received.* Those that have never so much are beholden to Christ for it all. The apostles themselves were receivers (*freely you have received*, Matt. 10:8). All stand upon the same level (Col. 3:11). Jews, scholars, rich, honorable must be beholden to Christ for all they have. We can none of us say we have no need of these supplies, as Laodicea (Rev. 3:17). There's no getting to heaven for the wisest, [for] the greatest man in the world, without grace received from Jesus Christ. Though we have Abraham to our father, have external privileges and performances, yet all that will not bring us to heaven without grace.

b. This is encouraging to the humble. We have all received grace – not all the children of men. Many are yet in a graceless

---

4. Arminianism gets its name from Jacobus Arminius (1560–1609), who deviated from orthodox reformed teaching by asserting (among other things) that Christ died for all men, God's saving grace is not irresistable, and that it is possible for true Christians to fall from grace. Antinomianism (Greek, 'against the law') teaches that the law has no place in the life of the believer.

5. Greek, 'we all'.

6. John Lightfoot (1601–1675), Anglican rector and Master of Catherine Hall, Cambridge, was a member of the Westminster Assembly (1643–1647). He was a noted biblical scholar especially in the area of Hebrew studies. His greatest work was *Horae Hebraicae et Talmudicae* (six volumes, 1658–1678).

state, but all believers – all, i.e. all that have seriously sought it, all that desired it, all that came thirsting to the waters for it (Isa. 55:1), all that were willing to submit themselves to the sanctifying workings of the blessed Spirit, all that sincerely consented to the covenant of grace. We have *all* received. The offer is general. Whoever will, let him come (Rev. 22:17).

i. Though we be never so many and numerous. There's grace enough to be had for us all from the Lord Jesus. 'Twas foretold that the number of believers should be great (Isa. 60:4, 5, 8), and 'twill appear so when they come all together (Rev. 7:9). Now Christ has enough for all, *every* sorrowful soul (Jer. 31:25). There's more oil than vessels, though the vessels [are] not a few (2 Kings 4:3, 6). The water out of the rock supplied all the thousands of Israel. He gives to *all* (Jas. 1:5), not as charity is directed to seven and to eight (Eccles. 11:2). There's enough in the covenant for all that believe – a feast to all nations (Isa. 25:6), [he's] rich to all (Rom. 10:12). Christ's feeding multitudes with the blessed bread signifies the multitudes that are supplied with grace. We may be ready to object, Whence shall we have bread for so great a multitude (Matt. 15:33)?

ii. Though we be never so mean and unworthy. Though low and despised in the world yet the covenant of grace hath provisions for us. Though mean in parts and gifts and other endowments, yet meanness is no bar. This is one thing in which rich and poor meet together – every valley filled (Luke 3:5) – partakers of the same benefit (1 Tim. 6:2). Women and children were fed by Christ among the 5000. The King will see his guests and will let none go unprovided for.

iii. Though we be never so miserable and empty – empty of knowledge, empty of grace (tohu and wohu,[7] Gen. 1:2), yet we have received from Christ, without money and

7. *Tohu* and *wohu* are transliterations of two Hebrew words that occur in Gen. 1:2: 'without form and void'.

without price (Isa. 55:1). The poor and the maimed are fetched in to the feast. Former barrenness and badness is no bar to this grace if we be truly penitent and come for grace. Poor and blind and naked are invited to Christ (Rev. 3:17, 18). Paul that had been a blasphemer yet received this grace. There's gifts received even for the rebellious (Ps. 68:18).

c. We have all received it *from Christ's fulness*. All God's good will towards us, his good work in us is owing to Christ and his fulness. The fulness that he has he has for us. If the clouds be full of rain they empty themselves (Eccles. 11:3; Rev. 8:3, ἐδόθη αὐτῷ ἵνα δώσῃ[8] he received that he might give, was filled that he might fill). 'Tis he that *filleth all in all* (Eph. 1:23), is made of God unto us sanctification (1 Cor. 1:30; see Col. 2:19). He *fills the treasures* (Prov. 8:21). All the good that is in us we have from Christ, who has not only a fulness of abundance, the fulness of a cistern, as Stephen is said to be full of the Holy Ghost, but a fulness of redundance, the fulness of a fountain, overflowing for us. He is a great trustee that all men may honour the Son.

i. Grace is purchased by the fulness of Christ's merit. Though to us it comes freely yet Christ paid for it. We had forfeited grace by our first father's abuse of the stock, quit under his hand. [There's] no way of taking off the forfeiture but by the satisfaction of Christ's blood. He *gave himself for us* that he might purify us (Titus 2:14). See Romans 5:6, 8. Christ died *for the ungodly* to make atonement for their ungodliness, and observe the fruit of that atonement, verse 15 *the grace of God*, i.e. the favour of God towards us and *the gift by grace*, the work of God in us, *hath abounded.* Therefore the more plentiful pouring out of the spirit of grace was deferred till after the ascension of Christ that it might appear to God the fruit of the purchase made

8. Greek, 'it was given to him that he might give'.

by his death, and the pleading of that purchase by his intercession. Hence we are said to be sanctified as well as justified by the blood of the covenant (Heb. 10:29; so Heb. 13:20, 21, through the blood of the everlasting covenant makes you perfect).

ii. Grace is proffered in the fulness of Christ's promises. The fruits of Christ's purchase are laid up for us in the promises, whence we are to draw as we have occasion. By this we partake of a divine nature (2 Pet. 1:4), open thy mouth wide (Ps. 81:10). 'Tis from these promises that an active faith fetcheth in supplies of grace. These promises are free and full, and they are all Yea and Amen in Christ. The promises to all are a gracious proclamation, tendering grace, to all believers. They are a gracious charter conveying and assuring grace – breasts of consolation.

iii. Grace is wrought by the fulness of Christ's Spirit. 'Tis the blessed Spirit that effectively changeth the nature, plants good dispositions and affections, through sanctification of the Spirit and sprinkling of the blood of Christ (1 Pet. 1:2). He abides in us by the Spirit (1 John 3:24; 4:13). Hence we are said to have the Spirit of Christ (Rom. 8:9) and that Spirit [is] poured out (Prov. 1:23; Isa. 44:3), noting the fulness of the Spirit, so that we are said to be one spirit with him (1 Cor. 6:17).

iv. Grace is communicated by the fulness of Christ's ordinances, which we therefore call the means of grace – outward and ordinary means. These in themselves are empty things but they have a fulness in them to true believers. They are wells of salvation (Isa. 12:3; Ps. 87:7). The Word sacraments, and prayer, these are the golden pipes by which the oil is conveyed to the lamps from the olive trees (Zech. 4:12). Thus ministers are said to come in the fulness of the blessing (Rom. 15:29; 2 Cor. 6:11, 12, *not straitened in us*). What fulness there is in ordinances. 'Tis Christ that puts it into them and he must be owned in all that we receive by them.

Show 3. What's meant by the expression here used, *grace for grace*, χάριν ἀντὶ χάριτος? The phrase [is] somewhat singular, and creates some puzzles to interpreters, but all agree it [is] very significant to set forth the riches of believers' receivings. Several ways it is understood. I love to give Scripture its full latitude and therefore shall take in all the probable senses, and you'll find each of them illustrating the doctrine.

1. It notes the *freeness* of this grace – *grace for grace*, i.e. grace for grace's sake (Grot[ius]).[9] 'Tis *gratia gratis data*,[10] as Romans 12:6, χαρίσματα κατὰ τὴν χάριν.[11] So Ephesians 3:7, δωρεὰν τῆς χάριτος.[12] [See also] Romans 3:24.

   a. It is a gift. Whatever grace, whatever measure of grace we have, 'tis given to us. 'Tis given to us to believe (Phil. 1:29). Christ himself, the spring and fountain of all grace, is the gift of God (2 Cor. 9:15; John 4:10), and whatever we have that's good 'twas given to us in and with the Lord Jesus. Grace to us for the sake of grace to Jesus Christ. So Cameron.[13]
   b. It is a free gift. 'Tis for the sake of grace, not for the sake of merit. We deserve nothing but wrath, but for the sake of grace that Christ may be glorified. 'Tis of his own good pleasure (Phil. 2:13), not of the will of the flesh or the will of man (John 1:13), but of his own will (Jas. 1:18). To glorify the Spirit as a free agent, blowing where and when he listeth (John 3:8). If it were of works 'twould not be grace (Rom. 11:6). Thus is the doctrine of free grace insisted on. The good work is grace, but lest there should be any suspicion of previous deserts in

---

9. Hugo Grotius (1583–1645) was a Dutch jurist and statesman who also wrote on biblical and theological subjects.
10. Latin, 'grace freely given'.
11. Greek, 'gifts according to grace'.
12. Greek, 'the gift of grace'.
13. John Cameron (1579–1625), though born and educated in Glasgow, spent most of his life in France, though he was for one year (1622) Principal of Glasgow University.

us, he adds, for grace's sake, not for your sakes be it known to you (Ezek. 36:32).

He loves because he will love. 'Tis for his own sake. He works for his own name. It becomes a God to act by sovereignty for he is his own end. What he doth for his people 'tis *ex mero motu.*[14] He has made us accepted, ἐχαρίζωσε,[15] he hath graced us, for what end, why to the praise of the glory of his grace (Eph. 1:6), that every crown may be thrown at the feet of free grace. Comp. Eph. 2:6, 7, and every song [shall] be sung to that humble tune (Ps. 115:1).

2. It notes the *fulness* of this grace. Grace for grace, i.e. abundance of grace, as skin for skin (Job 2:4), i.e. all that a man had. We receive from Christ abundance of grace, plenteous redemption (Ps. 130:7, 8). He rains righteousness (Hos. 10:12). He that is the desire of all nations fills the house with glory (Hag. 2:7).

a. There's enough for all. He fills all things (Eph. 4:10) and yet is not himself emptied. Like the light of the sun, one has never the less for another's partaking of it. Ask the saints that have received from Christ whether they have not found him a full fountain. There's no danger of loss by inviting others, as Philip (John 1:45), [there's] bread enough (Luke 15:17).

b. There's enough for each. True believers have a sufficiency of grace (2 Cor. 12:9), a God of grace that is to them a God all-sufficient (Gen. 17:1).[16] Drink you, drink abundantly (Cant. 5:1). Be earnest after more and more grace. There's enough, [for] we are not straitened in him. 'Tis a cup that runs over (Ps. 23:5), above what we are able to ask or think (Eph. 3:20). Those that drink of this water shall never thirst. 'Tis

---

14. Latin, 'out of pure feeling'.

15. Greek, 'he has freely given'.

16. The reference to Gen. 17:1 concerns the use of the name El Shaddai, one of whose suggested derivations gives the meaning 'the God who is all-sufficient'.

satisfying to the soul (John 4:14; comp[are] John 6:35). He gives to all liberally. The streams of grace run not only wide but deep. As when the 5000 were fed, 'twas not every one a little, which was the most that Philip counted on, but they did all eat and were *filled*. Every one has as much as he would (John 6:7, 11, 12). Grace is rained down like the manna. He that gathered little had no lack (2 Cor. 8:15). If we have but a little 'tis because we are straitened in ourselves. 'Tis the will of our Master that every weary soul should be satiated (Jer. 31:25), the hungry filled with good things (Luke 1:53).

c. It notes the serviceableness of this grace – *grace* for the promoting of grace, grace to be used and exercised.
   i. For ourselves – grace for grace, i.e. gracious vouchsafements from Christ for gracious actings by us – grace to be employed in gracious exercises. We have received a talent, not to bury it but to trade with it, to lay it out for our Master's honour and our own comfort, and the charge is, Occupy till I come (Luke 19:13). We have gracious works to do, and we have received grace to do them with. We receive knowledge to teach ourselves.
   ii. For others. Lightf[oot][17] understood it of the apostles who received grace, i.e. the office of the apostleship, and gifts qualifying them for that office and wherefore had they these betrustments but that they might propagate grace to others and bring them to the knowledge and obedience of grace, to advance grace in the thoughts and affections of others. Ministers are concerned to receive grace. 'Tis applicable to each of us. We have received grace for the benefit of others, to do good with it, to minister grace (Eph. 4:19). See Romans 12:6, etc. There is a manifold grace, but we are only stewards of it (1 Pet. 4:10, 11). As in the first so in the second creation we are created to work. The sun hath his light but not for himself, but to enlighten the world, and we are bid to *shine as lights* (Phil. 2:15, comp[are]

17. See footnote 6.

Matt. 5:16). We received grace that our speech and our whole conversation might be with grace, that free grace may be glorified. Christ himself received that he might give (Eph. 4:8; Ps. 68:18).

d. It notes the substitution of NT grace in the room of OT grace, grace for grace, Beza,[18] i.e. grace instead of grace (Chrysostom, Homilies[19]). As there is a righteousness and a righteousness, a faith and a faith, temple and temple, sacrifices and sacrifices, circumcision and circumcision, etc. so there is grace and grace. There was *grace* under the OT. The gospel was preached then (Gal. 3:8), but the dispensation is now improved and perfected, and we have a NT grace, instead of that a glory which excelleth (2 Cor. 3:10).
   i. Discoveries of grace are now more clear. Gospel grace was then made known by dark types and prophecies. Christ did then as it were stand behind the wall, look forth at the windows, show himself through the lattice, as some understand Cant. 2:9, but now the substance is come, and the clear light shineth (2 Cor. 3:13, 18). The morning clouds are dispelled. So dark were the discoveries of grace then that multitudes sought justification by the works of the law (Rom. 10:3). But now grace and truth are come (John 1:17). Truth stands here opposed not to the falsehood but the shadows. So that without the NT substance the OT shadows could not be perfect (Heb. 11:40).
   ii. Distributions of grace are now more plentiful. The Spirit is now more fully poured out, both in regard of extent and in regard of energy. Then the house was filled with glory, but now the earth is filled with glory. The partition wall is broken down. We live in a time of improvement and reformation

18. Theodore Beza (1519–1605) was Calvin's successor in Geneva as the leader of Reformed Protestantism. Matthew Henry is most probably referring to Beza's Latin notes on the Greek New Testament published in 1556.
19. The reference is to the Homilies of John Chrysotom of Antioch (c. 347–407). Chrysostom's discussion can be found in Homily 14 on Jn. 1:16.

(Heb. 9:10), promises [are] more spiritual, life and immortality [are] brought to light. We are under the dispensation of the Spirit.

e. It notes the augmentation and continuance of grace – *grace for grace*, i.e. one grace after another, one grace because of another, that later because of the former. We receive grace for grace, one grace a pledge of more, foundation grace for edifying grace. *He that has begun the good work will perform it* (Phil. 1:6; 2 Cor. 3:18, *from glory to glory*). We may be sure he will. Those that have true grace have that *for more* grace.

i. 'Tis the beginning of more. 'Tis in order to more, as the setting of the root is in order to the fruit, the planting of us in the house of the Lord in order to our flourishing (Ps. 92:13). The morning light is in order to the perfect day. Though there be great remaining darkness, yet the light is growing (Prov. 4:18). The laying of the foundation is in order to the building and far be it from our thoughts, the infinite wisdom should come under the imputation of the foolish builder that began to build and was not able to finish. The forming of the embryo is in order to the perfect man. When God gives a principle of true grace to any soul 'tis in token of what he intends further for the soul. He has not done with it.

ii. 'Tis an assurance of more, not only as it has a tendency to more, for grace wherever it is growing, but as it qualifies us for more, and evidenceth our special interest in the promise of more, for as for God his way is perfect. To him that has more shall be given (Matt. 25:29). Take this in part.

f. It notes the agreeableness and conformity of grace in the saints to the grace that is in Jesus Christ – χάρις ἀντὶ χάριτος[20] – grace in us answering to grace in the Lord Jesus Christ, as in

20. Greek, 'grace instead of grace'.

the impression upon the wax answers the seal line for line, figure for figure, as the child answers the Father limb for limb. The grace and holiness of Christ is the exemplary cause of the grace and holiness of the saints. Some think this is the meaning of ὑστερήματα[21] (Col. 1:24), the empty space of the seal filled up the wax. We are predestinate to be conformed *to the image of his Son* (Rom. 8:29; [see also 1 John 2:6; 4:17]). That Spirit that the saints are acted by is the Spirit of the Son (Gal. 4:6). Believers are in this measure spirited as Christ was spirited (Rom. 8:9).

i. This speaks of the duty of the saints which is to labour to be like Christ. Press after conformity to him. Be pure as he is pure (1 John 3:3). Labour to exemplify the holiness of the Lord Jesus in a holy conversation (1 Pet. 1:15). Show forth his virtues (1 Pet. 2:9). Tread in the steps of the Lord Jesus, the steps of his humility, weakness, love, self-denial, contempt of the world. Grow more and more like Christ.

ii. This speaks the privilege and honour of the saints that beholding by faith the glory of Christ they are changed into the same image. A Christian indeed is a living picture of Christ. The progress of grace is an approach towards Christ's image, and the perfection of grace in glory is the completing of that image (1 Cor. 15:49). 'Tis called the measure of the stature of the fulness of Christ (Eph. 4:13), not Christ personal but Christ mystical. The perfection of the church is the fulness of Christ (Eph. 1:23). Allus[ion] to the growth of Christ's natural body (Luke 2:52). When he shall appear we shall be perfectly like him (1 John 3:2).

21. Greek, 'the things lacking'.

6 Mar. 1692

OF HIS FULNESS HAVE ALL WE [RECEIVED]

Doct[rine] That all true believers receive grace for grace from Christ's fulness.

Use 1. By way of trial and examination. It concerns us all to enquire whether we have received grace from Jesus Christ or no, and to be strait in the enquiry. For,

a. It is a thing of very great consequence. 'Tis the concernment of our souls, our everlasting concernment. 'Tis the one thing needful, the good part (Luke 10:42). 'Tis not needful we should be rich in the world, but it is needful we should have grace else we are undone for ever. 'Tis the root of the matter (Job 19:28). God gives glory to none but those to whom he giveth grace (Ps. 84:11).

b. It is a thing in which it is an easy matter to be mistaken, and therefore you had need be jealous over yourselves. The heart is deceitful in nothing more than in its opinion of itself. Men are easily persuaded to have a good opinion of themselves and their judgments are commonly biased in their our favours. Many think they have received grace for grace from Jesus Christ when really they have not (Prov. 13:7; 30:12; Rev. 3:17). [This is] a common mistake.

i. We are apt to mistake common grace for saving grace. There are portions given to the sons of the concubines who are sent away, and have no part nor lot in the inheritance of the children of promise. Common gifts of knowledge and utterance are received from Christ and many take these for grace – common illuminations (Heb. 6:4), prophesying in Christ's name (Matt. 7:22). These common graces are given for the edification of others and of themselves so as to leave them inexcusable. But grace is beyond gifts (1 Cor. 12:31).

ii. We are apt to mistake counterfeit grace for true grace, pretence for realities, shows for substance, *the form of godliness for the power of it* (2 Tim. 3:5; Heb. 3:1), *the name to live* for the life indeed. Many an hypocrite hath personated the true Christian so long to deceive others that at length (like Perkin Warbeck in another case[1]) he comes to believe it himself. Many a foolish unthinking soul takes counters for gold, and so deceives itself to its own ruin. A plausible profession of faith not contradicted by any thing appearing serves to give a right to the sacraments and church privileges, for the stewards of the mysteries cannot search the heart, and multitudes take up with this as entitling them to heaven and happiness.

Believe it (sirs), all is not gold that glistens, all is not grace that pretends to be so. We are therefore concerned to look within – and search. The qu[estion] is whether we have *grace* or no. Did you ever upon serious consideration and due trial settle the point in your souls? The Word of God is the touchstone. Try by that.

Two ways *grace* may be considered.

1. As a privilege, and it is a great privilege, given in a distinguishing way to some and not to others. Now have you received this privilege? Justification is to be tried by sanctification, being evermore concomitants.

Our receiving of this privilege may be tried by these four evidences.

a. Our seeking of it. Wherever God hath given true grace he hath given truly to desire it. Were you ever yet so fully convinced

---

1. Perkin Warbeck (c. 1474–99) was a pretender to the English throne. He claimed to be Richard, Duke of York, and landing in Cornwall from Ireland in 1497 he raised an army but fled when confronted with the forces of Henry VII. Upon his capture he confessed to being an imposter and identified himself as being a native of Tournai in present-day Belgium.

of the excellency of grace as to *thirst* after it (Isa. 55:1), nay, to *hunger and thirst* (Matt. 5:6)? The strongest natural desires [are] satisfied with nothing less than meat and milk. Grace is the favour of God. Did you ever desire that more than anything else (Ps. 4:6)? 'Tis the image of God. Did you ever desire the saving knowledge of God's ways? Did you ever ask for grace? But how? Was it not coldly and indifferently? Have you sought diligently (Heb. 11:6), knocked for it (Matt. 7:7), cried after it, searched for it (Prov. 2:3, 4), sought it more than the things of this world, as Solomon (2 Chron. 1:10)? If you were put to the choice either to have riches without grace, or grace without riches, which would you choose? Grace is too precious a privilege to be thrapped[2] upon those that slight it and have no desire of it. What value have you for grace?

b. Our submission to it. The privilege of grace is like the privilege of government which carries with it a restraint to exorbitant motions. You are pleased it may be, with the light of grace, and are *willing for a season to rejoice in that light*, but are you pleased with the law of grace? What work is wrought upon the will? Are you willing *in the day of power* (Ps. 110:3) as well as in the day of privilege? [God] delivers into it (Rom. 6:17). Are your souls laid under the command of grace? Were the everlasting doors ever yet thrown open to receive the King of glory? Have you cordially submitted to the discovery of grace, the dictates of grace? This was the first breathing of grace in Paul (Acts 9:6; *the obedience of faith*, Rom. 1:5; Acts 6:7).

c. Our satisfaction in it, in the good will of God towards us (Ps. 4:7, 8), his good work in us, satisfied with present likeness (Ps. 17:15), though still desiring more of grace, yet never desiring more than grace. Let me have grace and I have enough, though I had nothing else. True grace evermore allays the thirst after earthly things. Silver and gold has little in it truly

2. *Thrapped*, 'to bind on'.

desirable to one that has received grace for grace. Those that have the privilege take a humble complacency in it.

d. Our sorrow for that corruption which is opposite to it. This gracious mourning for sin is very consistent with that holy rejoicing in God. Where the *spirit of grace* is poured out it immediately follows they shall look unto him whom they have pierced and *mourn* (Zech. 12:10). Where grace is, sin is embittered, and sorrowed for with an eye to Christ pierced. God gives *grace to the humble* (1 Pet. 3:5), to those who lie low before him in a sense of their corruptions. 'Twas an evidence that Paul with his mind served the law of God when the body of death was such a burden to him (Rom. 7:24).

2. As a principle. Grace in the heart is a root (Matt. 13:21). 'Tis the spring (John 4:14) out of which are the issues of life (Prov. 4:23), an active principle – as the seed – and principles are known by their operations, the tree by its fruits (Matt. 7:20). Grace is life, and where there's life there is a principle of motion and action.

Grace where it is in truth is

a. an enlightening principle. Wherever there is true grace there is something of knowledge. Many deceive themselves with their good meanings, though they be blind meanings. An ignorant soul can never be a good soul (Prov. 14:2). What light can you witness to? The question is whether you see ought? What do you know of God and Christ and your souls and another world? As in the creation of the world so in the new creation the first thing is *light* (2 Cor. 4:6). Are you *light in the Lord* (Eph. 5:8)? Do you desire knowledge and labour for it? Are the scales fallen from your eyes? This cuts off many ignorant people that know nothing of the things of God, are dark even in the land of light.

b. a transforming principle. Grace is a change (2 Cor. 3:18). It follows up that light. Those that have grace are not what they have been. They are transformed (Rom. 12:2). 'Tis an inward change. Grace changeth the thoughts, affections, desires, designs. 'Tis a universal change. The whole man is changed. Words, actions, employment, company [are] all new (2 Cor. 5:17). That man is not the same he was. The stream is turned against the natural bent.

c. a resisting principle, active in its opposition to temptation, corruption and everything that is contrary to it. Grace is armour (Eph. 6:11, etc). It maintains a conflict, the spirit lusteth against the flesh (Gal. 5:17). Even then when 'tis brought into captivity yet it struggles. Where grace is all [it] doth not go one way in the soul. The devil will be alluring, and a deceitful heart will be starting aside, but grace will enter its protest and give its strongest opposition to all sinful revolts and rebellions.

d. a working principle. Where there is grace 'twill be putting on a man to good duties. 'Twill work in prayer, meditation, charity, etc. We are created unto *good works* (Eph. 2:10). 'Tis a root which will bring forth fruit. The same duties which were done before by grace are done after another manner. Grace is the *fervency of the Spirit* in every duty – the life and vigour of it. Where there is that true grace the inside of religious performances is minded more than the outside. Grace overcomes oppositions and discouragements. 'Tis oil (Ps. 45:7), the anointing (1 John 2:27), [that] supples the members, makes us lively and agile in that which is good. 'Tis oil to the lamps to keep them burning, 'tis oil to the wheels to keep them moving. You that say that you have grace, what do you do with it? What fruit doth it bring forth? Where grace is, duty becomes easy.

e. a depending principle. Wherever grace is it is received not only in its rise but in its growth and action. All that have received grace from Christ live upon him daily. To me to live is Christ (Phil. 1:21). Grace lives and acts in a dependence upon Christ. I live *yet not I* (Gal. 2:20). I laboured *yet not I* (1 Cor. 15:10). Wherever true grace is the soul is brought to go out of itself and to live upon Christ, to stand in the strength of the Lord, that strength of his grace (2 Tim. 2:3). Go forth not in any strength of our own (Ps. 71:16).

f. a fixing principle. Wherever grace is it is to the soul as the ballast of the soul. The heart is established with grace (Heb. 13:9). Thoughts and affections, desires and designs [are] fixed – fixed to religion, fixed in it. Those that are giddy and wavering, off and on, like the morning cloud, it's a sign they have not this grace. Where God has given grace he hath given *a nail* in his holy place (Ezra 9:8), [and] gathered in the wandering soul.

g. a growing principle. Like the shining light (Prov. 4:18), [it is] more and more strong. 'Tis a seed of immortality. Grace where 'tis true is growing. The growth [is] not always alike, sensible, but those who think they have grace enough and need no more 'tis to be feared have none at all in truth. Paul pressed forward (Phil. 3:13, 14). If the house of David be established it will grow stronger and stronger, like a grain of mustard seed.

h. an aspiring principle, not after great things in this world but great things in t'other world. Those that have true grace aim at no less than glory. Grace makes unseen things its scope (2 Cor. 4:18; Phil. 3:14). [It] intends to make heaven, without loss, nothing more than heaven out of religion. Grace sets the affections on the things above (Col. 3:1).

Use 2. By way of exhortation and counsel.

1. To those that want grace. I fear I speak to many such who have been long under the offers of grace, enjoying the means of grace, and yet are void of a true principle of grace. [They] are acted by other principles. [They] live by sense, walk after the flesh, fleshly wisdom, which stands opposed to the grace of God (2 Cor. 1:12). Those that want grace have reason. Will you use it? In order to your being saints, be men.

a. Be sensible of your want of grace. Acknowledge your own emptiness. Observe how it is with you when a temptation is to be resisted, a duty performed, an affliction born, and you'll see what want there is of grace, how unready to every good work, how weak is thy heart. The light and power of nature will not go through with that which must be done if ever we mean to get to heaven. How soon will the water be spent in that bottle! See your wound incurable by any physic[3] that nature can administer, the disease inveterate, obstinate to nature's methods. Moral philosophy cannot cure you.

b. See the excellency and desirableness of grace. 'Tis compared to gold and silver and rubies (Prov. 3:14; 8:19). 'Tis an ornament (Isa. 52:1), a diadem of beauty to the soul. Grace is the glory of the soul (Ps. 45:13, 14). Grace is that which renders us (1) amiable in the eyes of God, of great price (1 Pet. 3:4). God is pleased with his own image upon the soul. 'Tis compared to pleasant spices (Cant. 1:12; 4:13, 14, 16). 'Tis this that makes the soul precious in God's sight (Isa. 43:9). (2) fit for every ordinance and every providence. 'Tis grace that prepares us for every good work, doing work, suffering work. When the Spirit is poured out upon us then and not till then we shall walk in God's statutes (Ezek. 36:27). Grace is therefore called the anointing because by it we are set apart to every thing that's good. As kings, priests, prophets were anointed, grace qualifies a man for every employment or condition. (3) meet to partake of the inheritance of the saints in light. Grace is that which qualifies us for glory. 'Tis the first resurrection. 'Tis the wedding garment. Assure yourselves none shall come to heaven hereafter but those that are fitted for it by grace here. 'Tis only the pure in heart that shall see God (Matt. 5:8; Heb. 12:14). Heaven would not be heaven to a graceless unsanctified soul. To see and enjoy God, to be for ever free from sin, and to be engaged in holy work and holy company, would this be heaven to a graceless soul? How weary are such of perfect Sabbaths, much more of the long Sabbaths? [There is] no getting to heaven without being born again (John 3:3).

And is not grace desirable then? Believe that you have a holy God above you, a precious soul within you, and an awful eternity before you, either of weal or woe. You'll say, Blessed

---

3. *Physic*, 'medicine'.

and holy is he that has part in the first resurrection (Rev. 20:6; Ps. 119:1).

c. Be earnest with God in prayer for grace. If you be convinced of the desirableness of it you cannot but desire it (John 4:10). Offer up those desires to God in prayer, for God will be sought unto even for promised mercies (Ezek. 36:37). Be importunate in this request, as one that will have no say. *I will not let you go* (Gen. 32:26). Plead your own indigence,[4] not to affect God but to affect yourselves. In your impotency beg for grace as a hungry man for bread, Say, 'Lord I am undone without it'. Those desires that used to be carried out toward other lying vanities must all be summoned into that laid out here. Give the gold to whom you wilt. Plead the promises. Lay hold on it by faith (Ezek. 36:25, 26). If there be anything within you that will not say 'Amen' to this prayer, check and crucify it. God never yet said 'Seek in vain'. Especially when we pray for spiritual blessings, plead the errand of Christ into the world (Titus 2:14), [and] the work of the Spirit which is to sanctify.

d. Apply yourselves by faith to Christ's fulness as it is exhibited to us in the New Covenant. Take Christ's counsel (Rev. 3.18; Isa. 55:1). Believe the revelation of the Word concerning the riches of Christ and his readiness to give out to us. Say not, 'How shall I go to Christ into heaven?' No, the Word is nigh you (Rom. 10:8). 'Tis Christ in the promise that you are to close with. Come to him as Joseph's brethren, to him for corn, humbled, submissive. Receive Christ and his fulness, give up yourselves to him. You must be beholden to him for all the grace you can expect from God. See this fountain ready to you, a fountain opened. Draw water out of it. Christ has substance for those that come to him (Prov. 5:21).

e. Be diligent in attending upon the means of grace. Grace is the gift of God, but ordinarily he works by means. Read the Scriptures and good books, and pray over and think over

4. *Indigence*, 'poverty'.

what you read. Be constant to public means. Wait at wisdom's gates (Prov. 8:34). Lie at the pool-side, waiting for the stirring of the waters. The Word is called the word of grace. 'Tis the seed of the new birth (1 Pet. 1:23). Ordinances are the golden pipes by which the oil of grace is conveyed. Lay hold on every opportunity [and] make the best you can of every sermon, and every Sabbath. Lay your souls under the power of every word. Let the word of the Lord come, the searching word, the commanding word.

2. To those who have received grace from Christ's fulness. I hope I speak to some such who though labouring under much folly, and weakness and corruption, yet can witness in some measure to a change, who though oft stumbling yet are in the way, that have a law in the mind warring against the law in the members (Rom. 7:22).

a. Let God have all the glory. Own all to come from Christ's fulness, and speak of it to his praise. Do not take the glory to yourselves, or your own improvement of natural powers. 'Twas not you that made yourselves to differ. Do not give the glory to the means. 'Tis not in the minister. He's but an earthen vessel. *Why look ye to us* (allu[ude to] Acts 3:12)? Run up all the streams to the fountain (1 Cor. 15:10), not unto us [O Lord, not unto us, but unto thy name give glory] (Ps. 115:1). Every crown must be cast down before the throne (Rev. 4:10). 'Tis for this end that God plants the trees of righteousness (Ps. 92:14, 15) that he may be glorified (Isa. 60:21; 43:21). Show forth the praises of him that called you (1 Pet. 2:9). Think of the distinguishingness of the gift – to us and not to others (John 14:22). [Think of] the design of it – that you might glorify him. Think what your condition was when God gave you grace – how helpless, how deplorable, cast out in the open field. What comeliness you have, it is of God's putting upon you (Ezek.16:14). Admire his love, preventing[5] love.

5. *Preventing*, older English from the Latin, *prevenio*, 'I go before'.

Who am I, O Lord God [2 Sam. 7:19]? So many [are] passed by. Let Christ be magnified. 'Tis for grace's sake.

b. Do you take the comfort? Have you grace, [then] let *peace* accompany it. If God hath given you grace he hath done more for you than if he had given you a world to possess and enjoy and do what you would with. The Spirit that is your sanctifier is the comforter. Is it not a special token for good, a mark of the divine favour? If God have given you grace he will preserve it and carry it on (Phil. 1:6). [He] will not neglect the work of his own hands. This is [a] matter of comfort in reference to outward wants and burdens. Grace is clothing for the soul when it may be the poor body wants clothing, poor in the world but rich in faith (Jas. 2:5), and that's *true riches* which will make you rich towards God.

c. There's duty required from you. The new creature was created for work. If God has given you grace he has qualified you for his service, and he did not give you such qualifications for nothing.

   i. Preserve grace. Have you grace, take heed of losing it. God has promised to preserve it, but we must not therefore be secure but fear. Grace is a jewel which we are in danger of being robbed of, and therefore should stand upon your guard. Lay hold on wisdom and retain it (Prov. 3:18). Resolve by the grace of God still to hold fast your integrity (Job 2:3) and never let go (Job 27:5). The design of Satan is to rob us of our grace.

   ii. Use grace. Be daily drawing *it out* into exercise. Have your conversation in the world by the grace of God (2 Cor. 1:12). Do everything with your grace – your religious duties, pray and sing psalms with grace (Col. 3:16). Let your ordinary converse be *with grace* (Col. 4:6). Review all your mercies, bear all your crosses with your grace. Do even common actions after a godly sort (3 John 6). Draw out into exercise the suitable graces. The talents were given you not to be buried but to be traded with. More shall be given to him that hath and useth what he hath, else you receive *the grace of God in vain* (2 Cor. 6:1). Let grace direct and rule you in everything.

iii. Grow in grace. Press after more degrees of grace (2 Pet. 3:18). Be still adding, with a holy covetousness (2 Pet. 1:5, etc). Let the habits of grace be more strengthened, the actings of it more quick and lively. Pray to God to increase your faith (Luke 17:5). Let your growth be uniform. Grow in every grace. See 2 Corinthians 8:7. Grow upwards in heavenly mindedness, downward in humility. Be pressing forward. The way to grow in grace is to use what we have. The Word is the means of our growth. Make daily use of it (2 Tim. 3:17). *Build up yourselves – praying [in the Holy Ghost]* (Jude 20). Abide under the influences of the Son of Righteousness (Mal. 4:2). Get something by every sermon. Aim at getting, as those thriving tradesmen by every market.

iv. Do what you can to promote and propagate grace in others. Let your candle light others, and your zeal provoke them to love and to good works. Take special care of those that are under your charge. Instil good principles into them betimes. You cannot give them grace but you may bring them to the means. How busy are sinners to propagate their corruption (Prov. 1:11), and shall we do nothing to propagate grace? Let your light shine. Be exemplary.

v. Long for the perfection of grace in glory. Grace is here but weak and imperfect struggling with corruption, but there the work shall be completed, corruption conquered. Let the perfect weakness of grace which you are sometimes mourning over, the perfect comforts of grace which you are sometimes reposing in make you thirst after the completeness of grace, there where the weakness shall be no more, and the comforts perfected and uninterrupted.

13 Mar. 1692

GRACE

For this is the covenant that I will make with the house of Israel after those days saith the Lord, I will put my laws into their minds and write them in their hearts (Heb. 8:10).

That which is here mentioned as the first and great article of the New Covenant is that which implies *grace* in the covenant, a good work wrought in us by the power of the divine grace. The law [is] written in the heart. Observe:

1. Who makes this covenant. 'Tis *I, the Lord*, who acts herein by sovereign power, acts as the Father of spirits.

2. With whom it is made – *with the house of Israel.* Not Israel according to the flesh but Israel according to the Spirit. True believers are the Israel of God, set apart for God (Ps. 4:3). As Israel [they] have God's special presence with them as Israel had. The adoption and the glory pertains to them.

3. When it's made – *after those days*, in gospel times when life and immortality are brought to light, after the expiration of the OT dispensation.

4. The promise itself – *I will put my laws*. Christ came to abolish the moral law as a covenant of works, but not to cancel or repeal it as a rule of duty (Matt. 5:17). There is a law of faith (Rom. 3:27). But 'tis here promised that this law shall be written in the heart.

Doct[rine] That it is a precious privilege of the New Covenant belonging to true believers that God will put his laws into their minds and write them in their hearts.

Show 1. What is the meaning of this promise.

Some understand it of the bringing of the law to the mind of man, Ham[mond].[1] Whereas the OT duties were therefore good because they were commanded, the NT duties are therefore commanded because [they are] good, rational, thus the Word is *nigh thee* (Rom. 10:8).

But it is rather to be understood of the bringing of the mind of man to the law.

Two things are here promised in general.

a. The opening of the understanding to know the will of God. This is the meaning of putting the laws into their minds – εἰς τήν διάνοιαν αὐτῶν[2] – into their *understandings* – for God deals with men as men, as rational creatures (Hos. 11:4). [He] doth not lead people blind-fold to heaven. He puts the law into their understanding.

i. We are by nature ignorant of our duty and apt to mistake about it, the natural man, ψυχικὸς δὲ ἄνθρωπος[3] (1 Cor. 2:14), *the man with a soul*, all the powers and faculties of a soul yet if they be not renewed with grace he *receiveth* not the things of the Spirit of God. We are blind (Rev. 3:17), and in nothing more blind than about our duty because there the understanding is most apt to be bribed and biased by corrupt affections. Hence it is that we put *darkness for light* (Isa. 5:20), choose the evil and refuse the good.

The unsanctified understanding puts wrong constructions upon the law in favour of a beloved lust. To this is owing the

---

1. The reference is almost certainly to the Anglican divine Henry Hammond (1605–1660). He was nominated to the Westminster Assembly but did not take his seat. In 1653 he published *A Paraphrase and Annotations upon all the Books of the New Testament*.

2. Greek, 'into their mind'.

3. Greek, 'the unspiritual man', in contrast with 'the spiritual man'.

good conceit that multitudes have of themselves and their spiritual state, *alive without the law* (Rom. 7:9). See the case of the heathen, though many of them were great scholars (Rom. 1:21), and it is a common case (Eph. 4:18).

ii. The great work of the Spirit in conversion is to open the understanding (Acts 26:18), to make known God's words (Prov. 1:23), not only concerning truth, but concerning duty, not only what is to be believed but what is to be done. All true believers have the law in some measure put into their minds. Though ignorant and foolish enough in other things yet they have the necessary knowledge of good and evil, are brought to know that which they did not know, or did not acknowledge before. The imaginations are captivated (2 Cor. 10:5).

God gives to believers to understand the law.

1. The spirituality of the law. This he puts into their minds, that the law is *spiritual* (Rom. 7:14), that it reaches the heart and lays a restraint upon the inward man, forbids spiritual wickedness, requires spiritual worship and spiritual obedience (John 4:24), spiritual washing (Jer. 4:14). The Pharisees, though they were doctors of the law, did not understand this (Matt. 25:23). The putting the law *into the mind* rectifies this mistake, discovers heart sins to be avoided, heart duties to be done. These are the wonders of the law (Ps. 119:18).
2. The sanctity of the law. The enlightened understanding discovers the law to be holy, and the commandment *holy* (Rom. 7:12). How can it be otherwise when it is the law of a holy God, the declaration of his holy will? Where the law is *put into the mind* that holiness is discovered to be in it which was not seen before, that it is consonant to the eternal law of good and evil. Before, the understanding was ready secretly to cavil of the equity of it, but now 'tis subscribed to. Thy Word is very pure (Ps. 119:140).

3. The breadth of the law. When God puts the law into the mind the understanding is opened to discern the extent of it, that the commandment is exceeding[ly] *broad* (Ps. 119:96). [It] obliges the whole man, all that we are, and all that we have, and all that we do. Natural, civil, religious actions come under the rule of this law. Till the law is put into the mind we are apt to construe it with limitations, exemptions and provisos, and to say we have done no wickedness (Prov. 30:20). What harm is there in such or such a thing, but when God gives us to understand the extent of the law then we see there is harm in it. Till the law is put into the mind, we are apt to justify ourselves in a partial obedience, but the renewed understanding takes in every iota (Luke 16:17).
4. The bindingness of the law. When the law is put into the mind the understanding discovers the authority of the law-maker, the strictness of the commands and the severity of the penalty. When the law is put into the mind 'tis put there as in the hand of the Lord Jesus (1 Cor. 9:21), enjoined by his authority, to whom all authority is committed, enforced by his arguments taken from his love which strengthens the obligation. 'Til the law is put into the mind there appears not that *cogency* in it. 'Tis looked on as a thing indifferent (yea, has God said, Gen. 3:1), whether it be obeyed or no. But when this *understanding* is given the law is observed with the *whole heart* (Ps. 119:34 and v. 4).

b. The bowing of the will to comply with the will of God, and this is the meaning of the later phrase, *I will write them in*, or, *upon their hearts*. The understanding and the will are as the two tablets of the soul in which the law is written. 'Tis to have a gracious frame and disposition of spirit inclining us to obey the will of God. 'Tis to be reconciled to our duty, the will melted into the will of God.

i. We are by nature *unwilling* to that which is good. The carnal mind is enmity against God (Rom. 8:7). There is a contrariety in our corrupt wills to the will of God. The heart [is] stubborn and perverse, starting aside like a broken bow. As he called them, so they went from him (Hos. 11:2). [They] will not hearken (Ps. 81:11), [and] *give a withdrawing shoulder* (Neh. 9:29 [AV] marg.). They seem to *give* the shoulder in profession, but really it is a withdrawing of the shoulder. Children of Belial, that will not endure the yoke, break the bonds in sunder, like the *deaf adder* (Ps. 58:4, 5). The authority of the command though great and sacred makes no impression, our tongues are our own, who is Lord over us? This is the law in the members, the law of sin. It's written in the heart, and all lies in subjection to that. Bewail the corruption of the will, that's the main fort.

ii. The work of the Spirit in conversion is to make us willing. That's *writing the law in the heart*. This is the new nature which hath new inclinations and aversions. Thy people shall be willing (Ps. 110:3). This is the taking away of the heart of stone, and giving a heart of flesh. See Ezek. 11:19, 20; 36:26, 27. The enmity is slain, the opposition in some measure checked, and the will becomes complying. *Lord, what will thou have me to do* (Acts 9:6)? There is an affection to that which is good. The man loves that which before he was loath to. See Romans 8:2. Adam in innocency had the law written in his heart, but his fall broke the tables, and defaced the writing. Some characters nevertheless then are remaining in the heart of man by nature, which appear in natural conscience (Rom. 2:14, 15), *the work of the law*, i.e. natural conscience that doth that to them which the law doth to those that have it, enjoining good, and forbidding evil. *The work of the law* is not the work that the law commands, but the work that the law doth. Now the blessed spirit in believers writes the law the second time (allu[ude to] Deut. 10:1, 4). (Some think that the writing of that here was the first writing that ever was.) While we remain in a natural condition sin is written *in the tables of the heart* (Jer. 17:1), but now old things are past away (2 Cor. 5:17). This is a considerable part of the divine nature (2 Pet. 1:4).

The law written in the heart is:

1. Ready to us. That which is in the heart is near and at hand. The rule is not far to seek, when we have occasion for it (see Ps. 27:8), ready for us as a guide when we know not what to do. 'Tis a word behind us, whispered in our ear (Isa. 30:21), ready to us as a monitor when we are about to do amiss, stepping in with water to quench the fire of Satan's darts [and] kindles, O *do not this abominable thing* (Jer. 44:4). When the law is written in the heart God's judgments are laid before us (Ps. 119:30), always in our view, as the copy in the view of the learner.

   The law written in the heart is our companion to talk with, to advise with. See Proverbs 6:21, 22; Psalm 119:98. Perhaps it alludes to the phylacteries that were appointed by the law (Deut. 6:8, 9), that they might have the law continually in their view. The hearts of the saints are the phylacteries in which the law is written (comp[are] Prov. 3:3; 4:20, 21). That which is there enjoined as a duty is here promised as a privilege.
2. Dear to us. That which is written in our hearts is of precious encouragement to us. When the law is written in the heart 'tis prized and loved. When God promises to write the law in our hearts the meaning is that he will bring us *to love* our duty, to love the command. *O how love I thy law* (Ps. 119:97), sweeter than honey and the honeycomb (Ps. 19:10). The law is obeyed of choice, not constraint. *This* I do because I love to do it. 'Tis the inclination of the heart to God's testimonies (Ps. 119:36), so that obedience becomes in a manner *natural* to the new nature (Phil. 2:20, *naturally care*). The Word is said to *dwell in us* richly (Col. 3:16) as a man at home where he's welcome. Let the Word of the Lord come.
3. Ruling in us. The heart is the commanding part of the man. Out of it are the issues of life (Prov. 4:23). Now to have the law written in the heart is to have all the motions both

of the inward and outward man commanded by it. The heart is the root, the fountain. Writing the law there casts salt into the spring, makes the root sweet. The heart is the throne. The writing of the law in the heart is the setting up of the will of God in the throne in our souls, his interests the commanding interests. The law may be in the mouth, and make no change in the life (Ps. 50:16, 17), but if the law be in the heart that will change the whole man. 'Tis written there not only as an epistle to inform us, but as an edict to command us.

Show 2. That this is a precious privilege of the New Covenant belonging to true believers.

a. It is promised in the New Covenant – in the OT administration of it (Deut. 30:6), in the NT administration here in the text. 'Tis herein *well-ordered* that what is required in the covenant is promised in the covenant. 'Tis well for us it is so. We are so weak and impotent, our faculties so sadly depraved, that we cannot do the things that we would. Why, do as well as you can and you shall have strength (Phil 2:12, 13; Prov. 1:23, *I will* and *you shall*). There shall be a counterpart of the law written in the heart. You shall have not only the light given you but the eye to see it, not only the law, but the will to comply with it. There are promises to grace and promises of grace. God works faith by the promises.

b. It belongs to true believers. Indeed, it is given to believe. The law of faith is written in the heart, and with that other laws. See how this grace is given out (John 6:37; comp[are] v. 44). All true believers have the law written in their hearts. 'Tis their undoubted character. See 2 Corinthians 3:2, 3. We have there the description of a true Christian. He is *the epistle of Christ* as a man's mind is seen in his epistles. Believers are Christ's image – and *our epistle*. The ministry of the Word is the ordinary means by which this privilege is conveyed – *ministered by us*. And the epistles of Christ are *manifestly declared, known and read.* Where there is the law in the heart, 'twill appear in the life (Ps. 116:10, *written with the Spirit*). The word of itself is but the pen, 'tis the Spirit that guides the hand, written with the finger of God, not in stone as the moral law (Exod. 34:1) but in the heart which is made a heart of flesh, tender, easily receiving impressions. Salt put under a stone gives it no relish, as it doth to flesh. This work is not perfected at first but by degrees.

c. It is a precious privilege to those that have it. Happy they that have the law in their books and in their ears (Ps. 89:15), but thrice happy they that have it in their hearts. The law is an inheritance (Deut. 33:4). The nearer, the surer this inheritance is, the better it is. Bibles may be taken out of our hands. It's good having the Word in our hearts.

i. It is good evidence. It's good to have the law written in the heart for its evidence

1. of our new birth. We are born with no other law in our hearts but the law of sin and death. That which is born of the flesh is flesh, and will be so (John 3:6). The writing of the law in the heart is that which is born of the Spirit and that is Spirit, [it] makes us spiritual. This is walking after the Spirit (Rom. 8:1), serving the law of God with the mind (Rom. 7:25). Which way doth the stream go? Wherever there's grace there's a principle ready to close with the will of God – an evidence of our sonship.
2. of our conformity to the Lord Jesus. He had the law in his heart (Ps. 40:8), the law of the mediatorship. The work was hot and hard, but the law in his heart carried him through it. If the law be written in the heart God is to us a God. So it follows. 'Tis this that makes us the epistle of Christ. 'Tis this that is grace *for* grace, answering to grace in Jesus Christ, spirited as Christ was spirited.
3. of our title to glory. Preparedness for heaven is the best evidence of our title to it. The writing of the law in the heart is that which

makes us meet for glory. 'Tis by this that we are *wrought* to the self same thing (2 Cor. 5:5). What's heaven but everlasting holiness, of which present sanctification is an earnest? There they rest not day nor night. Heaven would not be heaven to one that has not the law of love and praise written in his heart.

ii. It hath a good influence.

1. Upon the easiness of our religion. 'Tis this that makes the yoke of Christ an easy yoke, that the neck is fitted to it (Matt. 11:30). Duty is done with pleasure and delight when the law is written in the heart (Ps. 40:8). Where the love of God is shed abroad in the heart there it is that the commandments are not grievous (1 John 5:3). 'Tis like Moses's mother nursing her own child. Till the law is written in the heart every religious duty goes against the grain. 'Tis perfect drudgery, but when once the man is brought to love his duty the hardest pieces of it seem nothing, like Jacob's service for Rachel. Study is a pleasure to one that has a disposition to learning, but it's a punishment to one that has not. Prayer is a delight to one that has the law of prayer written in his heart, otherwise it's a task. It becomes in a manner natural.
2. Upon the evenness of our religion. There are many whose goodness is as the morning cloud. They are off and on in duties, an aguish[4] religion, hot and cold, and the reason is they have not the law in their hearts. They do not act from a principle for that would settle them. An hypocrite doth his duty from some external motions, and therefore moves no longer than those last, as the clock only while the weights are at it. A true Christian has τι ἔνδον.[5] Where the law is written in the heart, the obedience will be universal, for the same principle which will carry a man to one duty will carry him to another. And it will be uniform, not for a start. See what God said of a people in a good mind (Deut. 5:29, *such an heart*).

4. *Aguish*, 'shivering' 'malarial'.
5. Greek, 'something inside' (Luke 17:21).

3. Upon the purity of our religion. The law written in the heart will be our preservation from the defilement of Satan's temptations. This will be armour of proof in the day of battle (Ps. 119:11, *that I may not sin*). 'Tis this that will invigorate our resistance and make us more than conquerors. The law of his God is in his heart and thence it is that none of his *steps shall slide* (Ps. 37: 31) – *none*, i.e. very few, or, he shall never so slide as not to recover his feet and get up again. The law in our books will not keep us from sin if we have not the law in our hearts.
4. Upon the perseverance of our religion. What's the reason of the apostasy of so many who begun well but this, they never had the law in their hearts. They never acted from a principle. When the fear of God is in the heart that will be a preservative from apostasy (Jer. 32:40). That which is written remains, especially that which is written in the tables of the heart. If apostatising times should come nothing but a principle would bear us out. See Ps. 119:30, 31. 'Tis this that is the root; for want of this many wither (Matt. 13:21).

Use 1. Enquire whether you have the law written in the heart. It concerns us all to enquire, for our holiness and happiness depends upon it.

Shall I ask you,

a. What is sin to you? Where the law is written in the heart nothing is more bewailed than past guilt, nothing more dreaded than returns to folly. The law discovers sin. Those that make a light matter of sin have none of the law in their hearts. Have you tasted bitterness in sin? What care do you take to avoid it? The reigning love of the world cannot consist with the law of God there. Is sin mortified, crucified, kept under? When a temptation comes, to go into wicked company, to lie, or take God's name in vain, or cheat, what kind of resistance do you make? From what principles do you refrain [from] sin? Is it as Joseph (Gen. 39:9)?

b. What is Christ to you? Where the law is in the heart Christ is precious, and very dear. Do you see the need of Christ? Do you live upon him? The more we have of the law in our hearts the more we see the insufficiency of it to make a righteousness for us, and therefore go out of ourselves. Blessed be God for Christ (Rom. 7:25). Where the law is in the heart Christ is submitted to as Prophet, Priest and King with cheerfulness.

c. What are religious duties to you? What inclination have you to them? Are you indifferent to them or desirous of them? What is the ordinary frame and temper of your souls in praying, hearing? Do you say, What a weariness is it (Mal. 1:13), like Doeg (1 Sam. 21:7) when will the Sabbath be gone (Amos 8:5)? Listless to them, lifeless in them. What pleasures do you take in ordinances? Are they not dry, tasteless things to you or can you witness to some pleasures and delight in them? What's a day in God's courts to you? Is it what it was to David (Ps. 84:10)? Are Sabbaths your burdens or your blessings? Where the law of prayer is written in your heart prayer is a delight. The heart is ready to close with calls to it. Is it so with you?

2. Endeavour to get the law written in your heart. 'Tis the work of the Spirit and his sovereign agency, and we can do nothing to merit it. 'Tis God that works in us to will and to do, but it must be done in God's way.

a. Prize this privilege. Prefer it before anything else. The law of God, especially the law in our hearts, should be better to us than thousands of gold and silver (Ps. 119:72). Put a value upon it. Desire such a change of your nature. The first thing towards grace is desire of grace. See your want and thirst after supply. 'Tis a privilege to have the Word written in our hearts, written to us (Prov. 22:20), much more written in us.

b. Put this promise in suit by faithful and fervent prayer. Promises were given to be pleaded and so was this. Lay your souls by faith and prayer under the work of the Spirit. This covenant is a testament, sue out your legacy. Though your hearts be hard, 'tis not the first time that God has written upon stone. Instance in particular graces according as your corruptions and temptations are, I am passionate, Lord. Write the law of meekness upon my heart. Pray David's prayer (Ps. 119:34, 35, 36) and often el jireh.[6] The God of holiness will be ready to answer those prayers. Plead his honour.

c. Meditate much on the written Word. God works by means (Ps. 1:3). Let not the great things of the law be as strange things to you (Hos. 8:12). The law written in the heart doth not supersede the law in the book but is consonant to it. Improve all helps for understanding the Scriptures and searching into them. Love your Bibles. Converse much with them. Turn what you read and hear into blood and spirits. Lay up what you hear in your hearts, as leaven (Matt. 13:33).

d. Make daily use of the law written in your hearts. That's the way to have more written and more legibly, hearken to the dictates of the law in your hearts. Do not dare to offend an enlightened conscience (Acts 24:16). Listen to the voice behind you. Be ready to discourse of it, and let discourse of that kind be pleasant and natural. When the Word is put into the heart it is put into the mouth (Isa. 59:21). Walk according to this rule. In everything you do in religion make it appear that you act from a principle.

---

6. *el jireh*, Heb. 'God will see [to it]', cf. Gen. 22:14.

7

Access in the Covenant

20 Mar. 1692

7. ACCESS IN THE COVENANT

For through him we both have an access by one Spirit unto the Father (Eph. 2:18).

This access is mentioned as a special privilege of the New Covenant belonging to true believers not here only but [in] Romans 5:2 and Ephesians 3:12, and challengeth a distinct consideration.

The Apostle is here opening that great mystery of the calling in of the Gentiles, and incorporating them with the Jews in the mystical body of Christ. Thus the two sticks became one in the hand of the Lord.[1] Having instanced in several privileges they were joint partakers of, both [are] made one new man, verse 15, both reconciled unto God, verse 16, both had peace preached to them, verse 17, he mentions this among the rest, [that] both have an *access* to God, and thence infers, verse 19, *you are no more strangers*. Thus was the middle wall of partition broken down, a mystery hid from ages and generations.

In the text observe:

1. The privilege itself enjoyed – an access unto the Father – προσαγωγήν[2] – not only an entrance but an introduction, a leading by the hand as it were, as in princes' courts. Those that are to have an audience with the king are to be conducted and introduced by some courtier. We have a manuduction.[3]

   – *to the Father*, to God as Father. We are all near to God as Creator (Acts 17:27), but this is an access to him as a Father, an admission into the relation and to the privileges of sons.

---

1. The allusion is to what Ezekiel was told to do with two sticks and the interpretation that follows (Ezek. 37:18-28).
2. Greek, 'access' (Rom. 5:2).
3. *manuduction*, 'guidance by the hand'.

2. The persons partaking of this privilege – *we both* – both Jews and Gentiles that believe. 'Tis not an engrossed privilege appropriated to some exclusive of others, but common to all believers. Hitherto the visible way of access was open to the Jews only (Ps. 76:1). 'Twas among them that God recorded his name. The children of Israel were a people near unto him (Ps. 148:14), and he to them. No nation [was] like them (Deut. 4:7). The Gentiles were afar off (Eph. 2:17). Those that were uncircumcised were not admitted to partake of temple privileges. They must keep their distance.

But now that hedge is taken down, and in point of access to God there is neither circumcision nor uncircumcision (Col. 3:11; Gal. 5:6). All true believers have access, all that are *reconciled unto* God, verse 16, all the spiritual Israel, the *spiritual* seed of Abraham.

3. The way and method of our partaking of it:

a. *Through him*, δί αὐτοῦ,[4] i.e. Christ, verse 13, through him as the door (John 10:9), through him as the way (John 14:6). The deluded Gentiles had their *dei minores*,[5] their inferior deities by whom they had access to the supreme numen,[6] as the Papists have their saints and angels, but we have our access through Christ, the alone mediator (1 Tim. 2:5), the middle person.

b. *By one spirit* – ἐν ἑνὶ πνεύματι.[7] 'Tis a spiritual access, and not to be understood after a corporal and carnal manner. 'Tis by the Spirit. Christ having opened a way for us, the Spirit brings us into the way and leads us in it. [He] makes intercession for the saints (Rom. 8:27) and it is one and the same Spirit that leads all the saints, as all the members of the body are acted and animated by the same soul. There is not

---

4. Greek, 'through him'.
5. Latin, 'lesser gods'.
6. Latin, 'a divine being'.
7. Greek, 'by one spirit' (1 Cor. 12:13).

one spirit for the Jews and another for the Gentiles. 'Tis one and the same Spirit of adoption that rules in all the saints.

Doct[rine] That it is the unspeakable privilege of all true believers that they have through Christ access to the Father by one Spirit.

This is a privilege of the New Covenant. 'Tis in that covenant that we come near to God. 'Tis a privilege offered to all in that covenant (2 Cor. 6:17). 'Tis conveyed and granted to all true believers. Others may have [other things, but] they have not access.

Show 1. What this access to the Father is, and what is implied in it. 'Tis προσαγωγή.[8] The verb is used [in] 1 Peter 3:18, *that he might bring us to God* – that he might *lead*, or *introduce* us to God. We are caused to draw near and to approach (Jer. 30:21).

a. There is a natural distance between us and God as we are finite creatures and he is the infinite Creator. He is the Most High, exalted far above all blessing and praise. He is not a man as we are (*as the heaven is higher than the earth*, Isa. 55:9). This is and will be while God is God and man is man, and we should be affected with this distance in all our approaches to God. When we speak of an access to him and boldness in that access we must mean it so as not to impeach that awful reverent sense we are to have of this natural distance. God is in heaven (Eccles. 5:2). Abraham though the friend of God, and one that had near access to him, yet comes in a sense of this distance (Gen. 18:27; comp[are] v. 17, 23). Upon this account God is greatly to be feared even in the assemblies of his saints (Ps. 89:7; Lev. 10:3). We abuse the grace of God when we take occasion from this boldness of access to think meanly of him.

b. Nothwithstanding this natural distance our first parents in the estate of innocency had access to God, [and] were made in the image of God (Gen. 1:26). Man was his darling creature,

---

8. Greek, 'access' (Rom. 5:2).

his delights were in him (Prov. 8:31). Our first parents in paradise had access to God. The Sabbath day was instituted in paradise on purpose for this access. What intimate converse was there then between God and Adam immediately! The Garden of Eden without this would have been but a poor happiness. Admire the goodness of God to our first parents herein. The Psalmist cannot but wonder at it (Ps. 8:4, 5, 6). Some have thought that envy at it was the angel's sin.

c. Adam by sin lost this access. Eating forbidden fruit spoiled the intimacy and friendship that had been between God and Adam. Adam was afraid of God's approach (Gen. 3:8). God now appeared an angry judge. [He] drove him out of paradise, and to debar him access to God a cherubim was set (Gen. 3:23, 24). Sin bred a quarrel, a controversy between man and God. He had no longer boldness. Man having broken the marriage covenant God gave him a bill of divorce. The friendship ceased. He lost his boldness [and] could not now look God in the face.

d. We every one of us come into the world in a state of distance and estrangement from God. We were born in the far country (Luke 15:13), afar off (Eph. 2:12, 13), estranged from the womb (Ps. 58:3), alienated from the life of God (Eph. 4:18). There's a constant strangeness between God and an unregenerate soul – [there's] no access

i. by reason of guilt, which is as a partition wall between God and the sinner, cutting off all access, and intercourse. Sin separates (Isa. 59:2). God cannot endure to look upon iniquity. 'Tis this that makes the sacrifice of the wicked an abomination (Prov. 15:8). God knows them indeed but it is afar off (Ps. 138:6). He will not take the ungodly by the hand (Job 8:20; Isa. 1:11-15). God is a holy God, [who] cannot endure to look upon iniquity, and it would not consist with his infinite purity to grant an access to those that adhere to the pollutions of sin. What communion has Christ with Belial (2 Cor. 6:14, 15)? Guilty sinners may have access to ordinances but they have no access to the Father. They cannot with any confidence call God 'Father'. They are of their father the devil, and will do his works. [They are] rebels and traitors persisting, so cannot have the access of favourites.

ii. by reason of corruption. God is at a distance from them and they stand at a distance from him. They may not have access, no nor they *will* not. God saith to them, 'Depart', and they say to him, 'Depart' (Job 21:14). The carnal mind is enmity (Rom. 8:7). They turn their back to God and not the face (Jer. 2:27), not desirous to come near him. The desires are carried out so strongly towards an access to the creature that there [is] no desire of acquaintance with God. They have nothing to say to him. This is both the sin and misery of the unregenerate.

e. All true believers have access to God as a Father. The distance is cured and removed, not the natural but the moral distance. They are *brought* to God (1 Pet. 3:18) as the lost sheep is brought to the fold, the lost son to his father's house.

i. It is their character that they *seek* access to God, desire the knowledge of him, prefer his favour before life itself, sensible that they have left him, that they are undone without him. *O that I knew where I might find him* (Job 23:3)! The great gospel duty is expressed by seeking God (Isa. 55:6). Seek to him as to our King, our God, our husband. This is wrought in the soul by the blessed Spirit in conversion. Seek to him for guidance, government, happiness, turning the face to him. Can we witness to this? Have we sought access to God? *Lord, lift thou up [the light of thy countenance upon us]* (Ps. 4:6, 7).

ii. It is their privilege that they have access to God. They are *made nigh*. They dwell in God and God in them, and what freer access can there be (1 John 4:16). They are a habitation of God (Eph. 2:22). They are spiritual priests

(Rev. 1:6) to draw near unto God. That's the periphrasis[9] of the priesthood. They are a royal priesthood, a kingdom of priests (1 Pet. 2:5).

They have an *access* to God, an *introduction*, i.e.:

1. They have leave to come to him. The way is laid open to them. The golden sceptre is held out to them and they by faith have touched the top of it. *Come now* (Isa. 1:18). This guilt of sin which was the partition wall is taken out of the way. That which separated and suspended the introduction is removed. Those that have the wedding garment have an admission to the wedding feast, those that have not are intruders, and will be dealt with as such (Mat. 22:12). To them gave he ἐξουσίαν,[10] authority (John 1:12).

2. They have a heart to come to him. This is the *manuduction*. Where there is a principle of true grace there is a tendency or inclination towards God, like the needle touched with the lead stone. They have a spirit of supplication (Zech. 12:10), a spirit crying 'Abba' (Gal. 4:6). He shall say unto me, 'My father' (Ps. 89:26). All that are born again have this disposition of sons, bringing them to their Father. Those that are made nigh have that within them which inclines them to repeat their approaches, and to come nearer.

3. They have great encouragement to come to him. We have access. We have many and large inducements to apply ourselves to him. The relation he stands in to us, the promises, the advocate, the experience of all the saints, all that is encouraging so that they may come boldly, and cheerfully – not only access, but *access with confidence* (Eph. 3:12), having such ample assurances of acceptance, which faith fastens upon and produces this confidence.

---

9. *Periphrasis*, 'a roundabout way of saying something'.
10. Greek, 'authority', 'power'.

We have access to the Father – to God as a Father and [are] taught to call him so, to eye him as a Father in all our approaches to him, the Father of our Lord Jesus Christ and in him our Father (John 20:17).

I shall further open this privilege of access which believers have to the Father two ways:

1. By showing you the several ingredients which make up this privilege. This *access* to God includes:

  a. Acquaintance with God. There can be no comfortable access to one that we have not some knowledge of. We are alienated from the life of God by our ignorance (Eph. 1:18). Now the first step towards friendship is knowledge. One article of the covenant is, *they shall all know me* (Heb. 8:11), and that's in order to this access, for the more we know of God the more we are engaged to and encouraged in our approaches to him, especially when we know his glory in the face of Jesus Christ (2 Cor. 4:6), when his goodness passeth before us. 'Tis one great privilege of the saints that they are the people that know God (Dan. 11:32). He manifests himself and will manifest himself more and more (John 14:21; Hos. 6:3).
  b. Agreement with God. The angels have access to God, and need not this agreement there having been no quarrel, but fallen man can have no access to God without reconciliation, [no] communion till there be friendship (Amos 3:3). Acquaint thyself with him and be at peace (Job 22:21). [There can be] no acquaintance unless we be at peace. We have *access*, being reconciled, verse 16. This is the privilege of believers that the quarrel is taken up, God is at peace with them. There has been variance between God and the soul but now there's peace. God has engaged that he will be no more angry (Isa. 54:9). They have laid aside the enmity, consented to the reconciliation, accepted the terms, and here's peace. The

weapons of unrighteousness are laid down, and God's arm laid hold on. Aims and interests are happily twisted.

c. The likeness of God. We have *access to the Father*, i.e. we bear his image, are renewed after his image (Eph. 4:24). We are led into a conformity to him, made nigh, having his image and superscription. Sanctification is our access to God. Whilst we remain unholy we stand at the greatest distance from him. This difference [is] as great as between hell and heaven. Sanctification is an approach to him. We come to God in conversion. When we comply with his will, conform to his pattern, are holy as he is holy, this is an access to God. As obedient children (1 Pet. 1:14, 15) to draw nigh to God aright is to cleanse our hands and purify our heart (Jas. 4:8).

d. The love of God. We *have access* to him, i.e. he loves us, and we in some poor measure love him again (1 John 4:19). We have access to his heart, he loves us with an everlasting love, [he] rests in his love (Zeph. 3:17). The love of God is shed abroad in our hearts (Rom. 5:5; comp[are] v. 2). He loves us and comes to us, and invites us to him. The relation of a father implies love. We are introduced into his affections, are received in our approach as the prodigal with embraces and kisses (Luke 15:20).

e. Covenant with God. We have an access to the Father, i.e. we are introduced into the covenant, into covenant relations (2 Cor. 6:18; Hos. 2:19), are admitted into the covenant and to the promises and privileges of it. We pass into a covenant with the Lord (Deut. 29:12), joining ourselves to the Lord (Jer. 50:5). We have access to God as a God to us, and are to him a people, presenting ourselves to him (Rom. 12:1; 2 Cor. 8:5) and have access with the present.

f. Converse and communion with God. We have *access* to him, not only in respect of friendship, but in respect of fellowship (1 John 1:3, *truly our fellowship [is with the Father]*). We have an access to him as our Father

i. To receive from him. This is by faith. We are introduced to him to receive instruction and direction from him, to receive the law from his mouth (Job 22:21, 22), the word received as the Word of God (1 Thess. 2:13), access to his feet (Deut. 33:3), to his voice (John 10:27), to the secret of his covenant (Ps. 25:14; Prov. 3:32), the secret of his providence many times (Gen. 18:17). They have access to his attributes, [and] may derive from them as they have occasion strength and comfort and supply, access to his name (Prov. 18:10), access to his promises and all the good that is treasured up in Christ, access to God as to the fountain of all comfort, a fountain opened, in the whole course of our conversation, in every employment, condition, mercy, affliction.

ii. In address to him, in prayer and praise. Prayer is our approach to God and we have access in it. We may come boldly – παρρησίαν[11] (Eph. 3:12), come to speak all our mind. We may come with freedom, in solemn prayer, in ejaculatory prayer, alone, with others. We have access to his ear, 'tis always open to the voice of our supplications. We have access in all places, at all times. He is not hard of access. We have a manuduction, are many ways led to the duty, and led in it, taken by the hand as it were and brought to God in this duty.

(1) There's a throne of grace erected. We might have been summoned before a tribunal of terror, but we are invited to a throne of grace. A throne speaks majesty, but 'tis a throne in which grace sits (Heb. 4:16). Allud[de] to God's dwelling between the cherubims over the mercy-seat. Hence (Heb. 10:19) we are said to enter into the holiest in which the mercy seat was. A throne of grace speaks grace rich, and grace ruling – plentiful grace and powerful grace. This throne of grace is appointed, i.e. God has in the Word represented himself to his people as on a throne of grace.

(2) There's a spirit of grace poured out, to make intercession

11. Greek, 'boldness'.

in us, to plant and water and excite praying graces, and praising graces (Zech. 12:10); a spirit of adoption, to help our infirmities, our praying infirmities (Rom. 8:26), to instruct us what to pray for and how to pray, to draw up our petition for us, to indict it, and we have need of such help. 'Tis the spirit of adoption that is opposed to the spirit of bondage which straitens and hinders our access (Rom. 8:15).

(3) There's an answer of grace promised. God is a prayer-hearing God, [he] takes it among the titles of his honour, never said to Jacob seek in vain. The promise is full and express (Matt. 7:7; John 16:23). What can we wish more than to have what we will for the asking? The answer doth not always come speedily but it always come[s] surely. Prayer never rots in the skies. The answer if not in kind [is] yet in kindness.

(4) There's a mediator of grace appointed – an advocate with the Father (1 John 2:1), one that ever lives making intercession – perfumes our prayers with his own incense. His blood speaks for us. He is an authorized mediator, sanctified and sealed to be so, and he is a ready, righteous advocate.

Thus we have access to the Father. [We] may come boldly in the mediator's name.

2. By illustrating it with some similitudes.

Believers have access to God.

a. As a dutiful child hath access to his father. He may be free with his father. If any thing ails the child he may, he will have recourse to his father presently. We are taught by the precept and pattern of Christ to call God Father, and the Father himself loves us (John 16:26, 27). *Doubtless thou art our Father* (Isa. 63:16). There is that in the Father's bosom which makes the access easy, and our Saviour argues thence for our encouragement (Luke 11:11, 12, 13). When Absalom was denied access to his father and that justly, yet 'tis said the soul of David longed to go forth to him (2 Sam. 13:39). The bowels of earthly parents are cruelty compared with the tender mercies of our God (Luke 15:31).

b. As a diligent servant hath access to his master to receive orders from him, to attend him, to receive protection, provision, assistance, wages from him (Ps. 123:2). Thus Solomon's servants had access to him, and it was their happiness (1 Kings 10:8). 'Tis the privilege of believers that they are attendants upon God as their Master. Walk after him, as the servant walks after his master. *Where I am there shall my servant be* (John 12:26).

c. A loving wife hath access to her husband (Isa. 54:5). The covenant [is] a marriage covenant (Hos. 2:19). The desire of believers is towards God as their husband. Such is the law of marriage (Gen. 3:16). The husband is the covering of the eyes. True believers have free access to God, and frequent access, and endeared access. The devil and the powers of darkness cannot put asunder God and a believing soul, or hinder the access. Believers cleave to the Lord as the vine to the sides of the house.

d. As one friend has access to another – with the greatest freedom and affection, a friend as their own soul, an *alter idem*,[12] a *comes individuus*.[13] The saints are God's friends (John 15:14). Abraham [was] the friend of God (Jas. 2:23) and this honour have all the saints. There is a covenant of friendship established. How welcome do we bid our friends in their accesses! So doth God welcome his friends, his favourites.

e. As the inhabitant hath access to his house. He comes to it daily. There he's at home; there he's welcome. God is the dwelling place of his people (Ps. 90:1), their hiding place (Ps. 32:7). A man's house is his castle. Believers are at home with God, are where they would be (Ps. 116:7), and are as welcome

12. Latin, 'another of the same'.

13. Latin, 'an inseparable companion'.

as at home. Come to him for provision, rest and safety. Be free with him as a man is at his own house. True believers are heirs of God (Rom. 8:17) and by Christ we have access. Possession [is] given us of the premises.

f. As the rich man hath access to his treasure. He goes freely to it when he has an occasion. God is the *portion* of his people (Lam. 3:24). Their treasure is in heaven (Matt. 6:20) and they may have recourse to it for supply. Those who have not access go begging and borrowing from one creature to another and still remain empty, but the believer by faith can fetch strength and comfort from God, and finds him a God all-sufficient. A believer is one that is brought so to live upon God as to pass through the creature to God, to terminate all the joys in him, to enjoy God in all our enjoyments and when stripped of all to enjoy all in God.

27 Mar. 1692

WE BOTH HAVE AN ACCESS (i)

Doct[rine] That it is the unspeakable privilege of all true believers that they have through Christ an access by one Spirit unto the Father.

Show 2. How this access to the Father is through Christ by one Spirit. We have mention here of all the three persons in the blessed Trinity concurring in the work of our salvation. Understand it according to the economy of the work of redemption, in which each of the persons have a respective agency and operation – a mystery to be adored with love and thankfulness, but not pried into. As in the creation of man there was (to speak with reverence) a consult of the Trinity (Gen. 1:26), so in the new creation.

Our access is *to God* the Father, as Creator, i.e. as our rightful owner, sovereign ruler, chiefest good and highest end, *through Christ* as Redeemer, Saviour and mediator, *by the Spirit* as regenerator and sanctifier. Thus are those relations eminently ascribed distinctly to Father, Son and Holy Spirit.

1. Our access to the Father is *through Christ* – δί αὐτοῦ – *through him*, or for his sake.

   a. He is the door (John 10:9). We enter by him. The first step we take in this access is through Christ. The access in conversion is through Christ (Heb. 7:25). We are like the Sodomites struck with blindness and weary ourselves to find the door (Gen. 19:11), but in the gospel the door is opened, and it is a wide door. Whoever will, let him come. Through him we go *in and out*, i.e. do everything (Ps. 121:8). Many are in the outer court of a profession yet do not get within the door. This [is the] *gate of the Lord* viz. Christ (Ps. 118:20; comp[are] v. 22). This door will be shut shortly (Matt. 25:10). Faith is called the door (Acts 14:27) because by faith we receive Jesus Christ and so come to God through him. By faith we enter in at this door. Many climb up another way [and] think to have access to God by their own righteousness, the merit of their own performance, but such will be found bold intruders.

b. He is the way (John 14:6). Those that have any business to the Father, let them know that Christ is the way. By Adam's sin the way to the Father was blocked up, a cherubim was set. The great thing to be enquired after [is] how shall we get near to God again, and 'tis answered only by Christ. He is *the way and the truth*, i.e. the true way, in opposition to the types and figures (such as Jacob's ladder) that were of him under the law (Heb. 9:24), *the way and the life* – the living way (Heb. 10:20). The sacrifices under the law were, though, the appointed way but they died and rose no more. Christ rose again. This way is made plain. 'Tis a highway (Isa. 35:8), a good old way, the way in which all the saints have walked, and walked with comfort – and he is the only way (Acts 4:12).

c. He is the High Priest. The people had access to God by the High Priest who was ordained for men *in things pertaining to God* (Heb. 5:2), in all those things wherein men have to do with God. Once a year the High Priest entered within the veil. 'Twas a great solemnity (Lev. 16), and in him the people had an access, for he went in as the representative. See Exodus 28:12. There he sprinkled the blood and burned incense and so made atonement. The apostles grounded our access to God upon the priesthood of Christ (Heb. 4:14, 15, 16). He is entered for us (Heb. 6:20; comp[are] Heb. 9:24). See Jeremiah 30:21 applied to Christ. That Scripture is full to this purpose (Heb. 10:19, 20, 21, 22). Our access to God is by *the blood of Jesus*, the blood shed on earth to make atonement, the blood speaking in heaven to make intercession.

1. Christ died to make reconciliation, and so we have access. That which made the difference was sin. Christ by dying took away sin, [and] the rending of the veil of the temple at the death of

Christ (Mar. 15:38) signified that 'twas his death that gave us the access. Christ suffered for sin so to bring us to God (1 Pet. 3:18), to take that out of the way which hindered our access. The curse stood in our way, [but] Christ removed it (Gal. 3:13) – the wrath, Christ bore it. Thus was the enmity slain, justice satisfied, the demands of it answered. [He] took the piercings of the flaming sword into his own blessed side, so making peace. Thus we have an introduction. The High Priest had no access without blood (Heb. 9:7). That was his introduction, [for there was] no access for sinful man to a righteous God without something to plead as satisfaction. The blood of the sacrifices was typically so, Christ's blood is really so. 'Tis by that that we have access. We durst not approach to God without that to plead.

2. Christ lives to make intercession, and so we have access. We have *an advocate* with the Father (1 John 2:1). His blood is there speaking for us, i.e. the intercession is made in the virtue of his satisfaction. We have a friend in court, one that sits at the right hand of God (Heb. 8:1), which notes both the constancy and the authority of his intercession. The Apostle mentions this with an emphasis (Rom. 8:34). 'Tis the intercession of Christ that is the cloud of incense with which the mercy seat must be covered (Lev. 16:13, *that he die not*). Aaron may die indeed before the mercy seat if it be not so covered. Mere mercy would not save us – without Christ's intercession. Allu[de to] Job 42:8, *go to my servant Job*. More particularly, 'tis by Christ that we have access

   a. to the knowledge of God. [There is] no acquaintance with God but by Christ (John 14:8, 9). We have the knowledge of God in the face of Christ (2 Cor. 4:6). [The command is] *Know God and Jesus Christ* (John 17:3). 'Twas his errand into the world to declare the Father to us (John 1:18). What he was, what he said, what he did, what he suffered declares God to the children of men. He was himself God manifested in the flesh, his glory as of the first-begotten of the Father. We are amazed when we think abstractly of the divine essence, and are lost in the thought, but when we think of Immanuel, God with us, God in our nature, our understandings are in some measure relieved and our conceptions helped. He is *the image* (Col. 1; Heb. 1).

b. to the kindness of God. We have access to his favour and friendship and acceptance only through Jesus Christ. [There is] no acceptance for our persons or performances any other way (Matt. 3:17; 17:5), [by] our persons (Eph. 1:6), [by] our performances (1 Pet. 2:5). 'Tis Christ that is the mediator of that covenant of friendship which is between God and true believers. He is our peace (Eph. 2:14; 2 Cor. 5:20). 'Tis in Christ that we are beloved, laid in the bosom, owned, accepted. He's our Benjamin. [There is] no seeing the face of God without him (allu[de to] Gen. 43:3), no obtaining of blessing but in the garment of the elder brother. All the tokens for good that come from God to us are purchased by the blood of Christ, and we cannot receive those kindnesses but by pleading that purchase, and depending upon it. All spiritual blessings flow to us in Christ (Eph. 1:3).

c. to his throne of grace in the world – in ordinances, especially in prayer. 'Tis in Christ that we have leave to come, that we have any hope to speed in coming. Every petition must be put up in his name. 'Twas the practice of OT saints (Ps. 84:8, 9; Dan. 9:17, *for the Lord's sake*). Take Christ with you in every prayer. If you go without him you go without your errand. We may come boldly (Heb. 4:16).

d. to his throne of glory in the other world. 'Tis in Christ that we have access to heaven. He opened the kingdom of heaven to all believers. We have boldness to enter into the holiest (Heb. 10:19). We have a present entrance for our hopes, and 'tis grounded upon Christ's mediation (Heb. 6:19, 20). The veil is rent, so that nothing can come between a believer and heaven. 'Tis Christ that is the author of eternal salvation (Heb. 5:9).

3. 'Tis by *one Spirit*. The satisfaction and intercession of Christ makes God accessible, takes away that which hinders on God's part, opens the door, clears the way, but still we are blind and lame and impotent, and which is worst of all, averse, so that till the distempers be in some measure cured we shall never draw near to God, and that's done by the Spirit. We have access *through Christ* by way of impetration,[1] *through the Spirit* by way of application. Christ lays open the way, the Spirit puts us into it, and leads us in it. The Lord Jesus has dealt with God and satisfied him. The work of the Spirit is to deal with us, to make us willing. 'Tis by the Spirit that souls are *drawn* (John 6:44), a powerful work wrought upon the will. The Spirit doth it, and it is one Spirit that works upon all the saints.

a. 'Tis by *the Spirit*. We should never come to God of ourselves. Our natural bent is to backslide *from* him (Hos. 11:7). The unrenewed will is prejudiced against God, still starts aside from him. By the Spirit we have access, are brought nigh. *The Spirit* doth this

i. as an enlightening Spirit. The Spirit opens the eyes and turns from darkness to light, and so turns from the power of Satan unto God (Acts 26:18), convinceth us of our distance from God, the sinfulness and misery of that distance, the possibility and desirableness of being made nigh. The way of access [is] opened for us by the blood of Christ. The ordinary means of this illumination is the Word through which the Spirit works.

ii. as a uniting Spirit. The Spirit is the bond of our union. We are a habitation of God through the Spirit (Eph. 2:22) and the temples of the Holy Ghost (1 Cor. 6:19; comp[are] chap. 3:16). Those that are joined to the Lord are therefore said to be one Spirit with him (1 Cor. 6:17). The Spirit of Christ is said to be in us (Rom. 8:9). The Spirit dwells in us not by way of radiation, but by way of abiding influence

1. *Impetration*, 'the act of obtaining something by a request or petition'.

and operation. 'Tis given radically and immediately to Christ our head, and from him derived to us.

iii. as a sanctifying Spirit. Wherever there's grace there's a disposition to draw near to God. Grace moves towards God as the sparks fly upward. Wherever there is a spirit of grace he is a spirit of supplication (Zech. 12:10). Where the will is changed the bent of it is towards God. All that are sanctified have said and will say that it's a good thing to draw nigh to God, that it's best with them when they are nearest to God. As soon as ever Paul was converted, behold he prayeth (Acts 9:11).

iv. as a spirit of adoption (Rom. 8:15), working in us his nature and witnessing to the relation of sons. The Spirit by clearing up to us our sonship gives us a manuduction,[2] [and] enables us to come. Whither should a child go but to his Father, and to come with boldness, to cry, 'Abba, Father'? This allures the soul. These are bands of love. 'Tis the Spirit that sustains us while our souls follow hard after God (Ps. 63:8), puts strength into us while we are seeking for him (Job 23:3, 6). When we prevail in our address 'tis by his own strength (Hos. 12:3).

b. 'Tis by *one* Spirit, and that one Spirit is

i. the same in all the saints, viz. in this great point of access to God. In other things they differ but in this they are all agreed, to come to God as to a Father.

ii. sufficient for all the saints. There's light and life enough with this Spirit for all poor dark and dull souls that lay themselves under his influence. The Spirit that was given to Christ as mediator was enough for all the saints. He had not the Spirit by measure [John 3:34].

Some by ἐν ἑνὶ; πνεύματι[3] understand our own spirits. Our

---

2. *Manuduction*, 'introduction by the hand'.

3. Greek, 'by one spirit' (1 Cor. 12:13).

access to God is spiritual, not local (Ps. 139:6), and there must be a oneness of spirit else [there is] no acceptable access to God. Unite my heart (Ps. 86:11), *one heart* (Ezek. 11:19).

Show 3. That this is the unspeakable privilege of all true believers and them only – *we both* – we that are reconciled, whether Jew or Gentile.

1. It is the privilege of *all true believers*. This is one branch of that *common salvation* (Jude 3). All that are in covenant with God, and are born again have access to God as a Father. Those that are at a distance from each other in many things yet meet in this that they have access to God.

    a. At a distance in place, that never saw one another, nor are ever likely to see one another in this world. The elect of God are scattered abroad (John 11:52). Saints will be brought from all quarters of the world (Matt. 8:11), from the four winds (Matt. 24:31), out of all nations and kindreds and people (Rev. 7:9). The saints are the salt of the earth scattered. Notwithstanding this distance they have all access to God. This is that spiritual communion of saints which is very comfortable where there cannot be local communion. This is sweet, that we are not alone in our approaches. See Acts 10:34, 35.
    b. At a distance in outward condition – high and low, rich and poor, bond and free meet in this that they have a like access to God. There's no respect of persons with God in these things. The poor in the world [are] rich in faith (Jas. 2:5). The poor have not a freedom of access to the rich, neither their doors nor their ears are always open, but they have a freedom of access to God. Therefore the poor are not to be trampled upon.
    c. At a distance in their apprehensions about lesser things. The saints will never be all of a mind in every thing till they come to heaven, and their difference of opinion is too apt to breed a

strangeness and a difficulty of access one to another, but they both have access to God. There's the centre of the saints' unity – one in us (John 17:21), not one in the Pope or a general council, but one in God and Christ (Eph. 1:10).

d. At a distance in degrees and gifts, graces, and comforts. Some are weak, others strong, some babes, others grown men, but they both have an access to God. Though one can speak more fluently and accurately, and come with more assurance, yet they have all an introduction. 'Tis rendered as a reason why the strong should not despise the weak, nor the weak judge the strong, for *God hath received him* (Rom. 14:3, etc). None are so strong as to be above this access, none so weak as to be below it.

Thus 'tis the privilege of *all* true believers, for

i. they are all children of the same Father – *we both* have one Father, as creatures, as new creatures (Mal. 2:10; Eph. 4:6). They all receive the same adoption, all make but one family (Eph. 3:15), all taught to address themselves to God as *our Father* in heaven. They all bear the same image, are renewed after the image of God (Eph. 4:24), as far as sanctified are all conformed to his likeness. Therefore all have the same access.

ii. they are all united to the same Jesus, and all that are in Christ have access to God. Every true member of the body has a real union with the head though all are not of the same bigness, use and honour. We all receive from Christ's fulness (John 1:16). Christ is that same spiritual Rock which all Israel drink of (1 Cor. 10:4). All the world has light and influence from the same sun. All that have an interest in Christ have by him access to the Father.

iii. they are all animated by the same Spirit, as all the members of the body by the same soul, though the operations be diverse (1 Cor. 12:4). Grace is for substance the same in all the saints. Their faith is alike precious (2 Pet. 1:1) though not alike strong. 'Tis the common faith (Titus 1:4). They all have the same access for they all have the same disposition to it, [the same] desire of it. 'Tis one thing in which all the saints are agreed, that it's good to draw near to God (Ps. 73:28), as face answers to face (Prov. 27:19).

iv. they are all interested in the same promises. *Every one* that asketh receiveth (Luke 11:10). In this particularly there's no difference between *Jew and Greek that whosever shall call on the name of the Lord shall be saved* (Rom. 10:12, 13). 'Tis by the promise that we have access. 'Tis in the covenant that the throne of grace is erected, and there all the saints meet.

What an engagement should this be to us to love one another (Eph. 4:3, 4). We all meet in our access to God, who is nigh to us. Why then should there be any difference among ourselves? Let us not reject any whom God has received. Let us put an end to feuds and differences among Christians. In this we are *brethren* (Gen. 13:8). *We both have access*.

2. It is the privilege of true believers only – we that are reconciled in distinction from those that yet persist in their enmity. They are *afar off* (Eph. 2:13).

a. Those that are *without Christ* have no access. They that are out of Christ are out of the way. [There is] no coming to the Father but by him. [They are] without Christ and therefore *afar off* (Eph. 2:12, 13). They are without Christ that [have] no relation to him. None are in Christ but those that are *new creatures* (2 Cor. 5:17). Those are without Christ that never *received him*, never consented to the gospel offer.

b. Those that are *without the Spirit* have no access. Those that walk after the flesh, and fulfil the lusts of the flesh (Rom. 8:1), those that are sensual (Jude 19) [have no access]. They may come to ordinances but they have no access to God in ordinances. Their sacrifice is an abomination (Prov. 15:8).

The condition of such is very sad. Those that have no access to God have no access to the fountain and springhead of all good. [They have] no true fellowship with God, though they pretend to it. See 1 John 1:6.

c. It is a very precious privilege. 'Tis the greatest happiness that a poor creature is capable of, to have access to his Creator, to be introduced to the King of Kings. 'Tis spoken of as the happiness of Solomon's servants that they stood continually before him (1 Kings 10:8). 'Tis the privilege of saints that they are a people near unto him (Ps. 148:14; see Ps. 65:4).

i. It is an honourable access. 'Tis promised to the diligent (Prov. 22:29). *He shall stand before kings*, but what's that compared with the saints' access to the King of Kings? Hushai [was] the king's friend (2 Sam. 15:37; 1 Kings 4:5). Haman put his access to the king and queen as the crown of all his honours (Esther 5:12), but what's that to this? Seemeth it a small thing (Num. 16:9)? When God visits a man, or receives his visits he magnifies him (Job 7:17, 18; Ps. 91:15). *I will honour him*. How? Why*, he shall call and I will answer*, which notes near access. David admires at the honour that God hereby put upon him (1 Chron. 17:16, 17). This honour have all his saints (Ps. 149:9). We are ambitious of it (2 Cor. 5:9). Thus they are even now like the angels which always behold the face of our Father, and are round about the throne.

ii. It is a comfortable access. 'Tis this that makes wisdom's ways ways of pleasantness (Prov. 3:17), and a day in God's courts better than a thousand (Ps. 84:10). 'Tis walking in the light of the Lord, and truly light is sweet. 'Tis this that is the heaven upon earth, puts sweetness into every ordinance, into every providence that we can see God near to us in all. This made David's *a goodly heritage* that the Lord was continually at his right hand (Ps. 16:6, 8). Nearness to God makes every land a land flowing with milk and honey – a Canaan, sat down with *great delight* (Can. 2:3).

iii. It is a gainful access. There's much to be gotten by it (Job 22:21). Ask those that have been near to God, and they'll tell you how good it is (Ps. 73:28; comp[are] v. 27). People are enquiring for good (Ps. 4:6), but this is the chief good, the crown of all. O the income of grace and peace and glory you receive and outward good things as far as they are indeed good for us by our *access* to God in Christ!

Those that have freedom of access to God have

1. a companion ready in all their solitudes, so that they are never less alone than when alone. Do we need better society than fellowship with the Father? – in *the night watches* (Ps. 63:6), *when I awake* (Ps. 139:18), sitting alone and keeping silence, in the clefts of the rock, then we have a God to talk to. Those that are weary of being alone either have not this access to God, or know not how to use it.
2. a counsellor ready in all their doubts. We are often at a loss in this wilderness. [We] do not know to do, what course to steer. Those that have access to God have access to a guide (Ps. 73:24), who has promised to direct with his eye, to lead us in the way wherein we should go. We have one to ask advice from, as David often [did].
3. a comforter ready in all their sorrows. Other comforters often stand at a distance, [and] will not know our souls, but if we have access to God we shall find him ready. Though we are sometimes tempted to think him far off (Lam. 1:16), yet take Paul's experience (2 Cor. 1:3, 4). Those that have access to God have access to an exalted cordial which will support sinking spirits, and be the strength of a fainting heart.
4. a supply ready in all their wants. They that have access to God have access to a full fountain, an inexhaustible treasure, a rich mine. Wants for the body [are] supplied in kind or kindness, [also] wants for the soul (Ps. 23:1; Ps. 34:10, *[they] want no good thing*), nothing that infinite wisdom sees really good. Those that have access to God have access

to him as El-Shaddai,[4] a God all-sufficient, have access to a full breast of consolation.

5. a support ready under all their burdens. They have access to him as *Adonai*,[5] my stay and the strength of my heart (Ps. 73:26), have access to the everlasting arms, so that they cannot sink. He will bear them up when they are fainting. See Psalm 73:23.
6. a shelter ready in all their dangers, a city of refuge near at hand. The name of the Lord is a strong tower (Prov. 18:10). [They have] access to God as to a castle of defence (Ps. 18:2). Access to God is our security and relief when we are in the midst of trouble, even in the valley of the shadow of death (Ps. 23:4), access to God as the chickens to the hen (Ps. 57:1; Matt. 23:37).
7. strength ready for all their performances in doing work, fighting work. He is their *arm every morning* (Isa. 33:2). Strong in the Lord, faith is a strengthening grace as it fetcheth in strength from heaven, and goes forth in that strength.
8. salvation insured by a sweet and undeceiving earnest. What's heaven but an everlasting access to God, and present access is a pledge of it. If he thus guide us by his counsel he will receive us to glory. Those that have access to God have access within the veil, and have livery and seisin[6] given them of the inheritance.

---

4. Hebrew, 'God all-sufficient'.

5. Hebrew, 'my Lord'.

6. *Livery*, 'distinctive clothing often given by a person of rank to his servants'; *seisin*, is an old legal term borrowed from the French *saisine*. It means the taking possession of land by freehold or the land so possessed.

3 Apr. 1692

WE BOTH HAVE AN ACCESS(ii)

D[octrine] That it is the unspeakable privilege of all true believers that through Christ they have an access by one Spirit unto the Father.

Application The doctrine must be applied to sinners that have not this access to God, and to saints that have this access.

1. To unbelieving sinners that are afar off and have not this access to God. There are many such even in the visible church – many that are near to God in name and profession but are far from him in affection. [They have] access to ordinances, but no access to God. [They are] near in their mouth but far from their reins (Jer. 12:2; comp[are] Matt. 15:8).
   In dealing with such I must say something.

   a. To discover them. Who are they who though they come to ordinances yet have no access to God? [They] are *afar off* (Eph. 2:13), in a state of distance and estrangement notwithstanding their seeming approaches. 'Tis the case of hypocrites – not who by name.
      i. Those that are spiritually blind have no access to God. Where there's reigning ignorance, there is an alienation *from the life of God* (Eph. 4:18). Those that are in the dark do but feel after God (Acts 17:27), groping as blind men. This is the case of many who are destroyed for lack of knowledge, ignorant of God and Christ and another world, and willing to be so. [They] walk on in darkness. *Strait is the gate*, too strait to be hit by a blind soul. Do take heed that this be not your condition, that you be not ignorant in the midst of gospel light. Those that are dead have no access to God.
      ii. Those that are spiritually leprous have no access to God. Those I mean that continue in the love and liking of sin,

which is the leprosy of the soul – guilty and filthy, and overspread with it. Lepers were to be shut out of the way, to be put at a distance. God is a pure and holy and sin-hating God. Those that wallow in uncleanness and drunkenness and profaneness, to be sure those have no access to God. His soul loathes them. He beholds them afar off. He will *not take the ungodly by the hand* (Job 8:20 [KJV] margin), and we shall never come near to him if he do not take us by the hand and lead us. They shall *not stand in his sight* (Ps. 5:5). Hath he need of mad-men (allud[de to] 1 Sam. 21:14, 15)? See how he answers such (Ezek: 14:4).

iii. Those that make no business with God have no access to him. The wise governor of the world entertains no idle visitants. Our business with God is to confess our sins and to get them pardoned, to acknowledge our corruptions and to get them mortified, to deal with him about a covenant of peace and reconciliation. Now those that are unconcerned in these things mind them not, are indifferent about them, care not which end goes foremost in their spiritual state. Whether sin be pardoned or not, God reconciled or no, such make no business with God, and so have no access. They desire not the knowledge of God's ways (Job 21:14, 15). Those that come without an errand are likely to go away without an answer. So in particular duties. When we neglect the business of the duty, we have not access to God.

iv. Those that wrap themselves in the filthy rags of their own righteousness have no access to God, that trust to it as a righteousness. See what our righteousnesses are (Isa. 64:6). Paul in his access to God desires not to be found in his own righteousness. [He] disclaims it as a righteousness (Phil. 3:9). Those have no access to God, that do not come to him in Christ in a dependence upon him, relying only upon his merit.

This was it that ruined the Pharisee who sped not in his access because he was proud, and confident of his own righteousness (Luke 18:11, 12). See how the Gentiles gained this access and the Jews lost it (Rom. 9:30, 31, 32; 10:3).

v. Those that cleave to the world and the things of it have no access to God. God and the world, God and Mammon, are often mentioned as opposites, and we cannot adhere to and follow after both. Those have no access to God whose hearts go after their covetousness while they sit before God as his people sitteth (Ezek. 33:31). Those that follow after the lying vanities are so far from having any access to, that really they are forsaking and running away from their own mercies (Jon. 2:8). The world in the heart is a clog in our approaches to God. Worldly, earthly-minded people whose hearts are carried out strongly towards the creature, have not, cannot have any access to God (Jas. 4:4).

b. To convince them. And, O that I knew what to say that might convince them! The condition of such is very miserable as [they] have no access to God. You have heard what a blessed thing it is to have access to God. Now what is it to want that access? It doth certainly include all misery. If it be so good to draw near to God then it's an evil and bitter thing to be far from him. See the woes, Hosea 7:12; comp[are] Hosea 9:12. This distance or want of access to God implies:

i. Poverty. God is the spring-head of all good. In him are all our springs. Those that have no access to God are empty (Jer. 2:13) and know not whither to go for supplies – wretched and miserable and *poor*. Those that are far from God are far from all-sufficiency. The conduit pipes are hereby cut off (Isa. 59:1, 2). That which separates between us and God hides all good things from us, like the prodigal (Luke 15:13). Prayer is the messenger that fetcheth in supplies. Those that have no access to God want that messenger (comp[are] Jer. 5:5). Those that are without God are without hope (Eph. 2:12). [They] are in want and the wells of salvation are shut up to them. [There is] no peace to those that have no access to God.

ii. Peril. Those that have no access to God are in danger and have no protection, lie exposed every day and have no guard. Those that are separated from God are not only separated from all good, but separated to all evil (Deut. 29:21). Those that are at a distance from God are in the hand[s] of their enemies, pursued by the guilt of sin, the curse of the law, the malice of Satan, and have no shelter. [They are] in the midst of fiery darts, and [have] no shield. Those that are far from thee shall perish (Ps. 73:27). The whole creation is at war with those that are at war with God. 'Twas Saul's sad complaint (1 Sam. 28:15).

iii. Horror. There can be no inward comfort and satisfaction of soul where there is not an access to God. When Cain was driven out from the presence of the Lord, and denied access to him, he went into the land of Nod (Gen. 4:16), the land of shaking, or floating, tossed with terrors.[1] Those who are once departed from God can never find rest anywhere else. [They are] continually fluctuating like Noah's dove when she was at a distance from the ark. How horrible is it to the saints to want the comfort of this access! Much more to sinners who want the title to it!

iv. Hell. Want of access to God is a hell upon earth. What's hell but to lie for ever under the power of the soul-sinking word, *Depart from me* (Matt. 25:41), and the *gulf fixed* to cut off all access (Luke 16:26). [There is] no coming nigh to God then. Sin is the gulf between God and the sinner. Whilst you are here in the world that gulf is not fixed. While there's life there's hope. Sin may be taken

1. Matthew Henry is here referring to the derivation of the word Nod, which comes from a Hebrew verbal root that means 'to shake [the head]'.

away and a door opened to God, but if it be not done now while the golden sceptre is held out 'twill be a gulf *fixed* shortly. Those are deep and heavy words, *destruction from the presence of the Lord* (2 Thess. 1:9).

c. To direct them. You that want this access to God, will you suffer a word of exhortation? Though your condition be sad, blessed be God it's not desperate. You may have access to God for all this if you take the right course. O what welcome doctrine would this be to poor damned sinners in hell, who feel what it is to want access to God! But I am not to preach it to them but you, O men, I call.

i. Mourn over your estrangement from God. Mourn over this as both the sinfulness and misery of your natural estate that it is a state of distance from God, lest you mourn at the last (Prov. 5:11). Your want of access to God was long of yourselves. You may thank yourselves for it. You would not come. You have forgotten the Lord your God (Jer. 3:21). *None saith, Where is God* (Job 35:10)? Think from whom you have been estranged, one that is not far from you, one that has not been unmindful of you, but has done you good. [You are] unmindful of the rock that begat you (Deut. 32:15, 19). Think for what you have been estranged – for broken cisterns (Jer. 2:13), how long you have been estranged – from the womb (Ps. 58:3). Bewail your folly, your ingratitude, the rebellion of your estrangements. Mourners might not have access to the King (Ezek. 4:2), but here,

ii. Desire an access to him, and go to him by prayer and tell him so. *Draw nigh to God and he will draw nigh to you* (Jas. 4:8). Be convinced of the pleasure and profit of access to God, and let that conviction stir up your desire. O that I knew where I might find him! Do not rest contented with any good, as the most of men do, any good short of God's favour (Ps. 4:6, 7). You are called to seek the Lord, for yet he may be found (Isa. 55:6). Let your hearts consent to this call (Ps. 27:8). When trouble is near, enemies near, death near, judgment near, then you would desire an access to God. Therefore desire it now, for none of these things are very far off. You'd desire access to God hereafter. Desire it now. *Engage your hearts* (Jer. 30:21).

iii. Break off your league with every sin. There cannot be an access to God till there is a recess from sin. There is such an eternal irreconcilable quarrel between God and sin that it is utterly impossible to keep in with God and keep in with sin too (1 John 1:6, 7). To think to approach to God with sin in your embraces is to provoke him, not to please him. See 2 Corinthians 6:14, 15, 16, 17; Job 11:14; James 4:8. Those that would have fellowship with God must have no fellowship with the unfruitful works of darkness. Keep at a distance from sin, or else that will keep you at a distance from God. 'Tis sin that makes us unfit that we may not, guilty that we dare not, weak that we cannot, forward that we will not, draw near to God.[2] Nothing else hinders, poverty, contempt.

iv. Submit your souls to the conduct of the blessed Spirit. 'Tis by *one Spirit* that we have access. Give up yourselves to the Spirit. Receive his teachings, resign yourselves to his conduct. Take heed of grieving him (Eph. 4:30). Walk not after the flesh but after the Spirit. Beg of God to give you his Holy Spirit. He will not deny those that ask him. Get the spirit of adoption, the spirit of sons, and that will bring you to God.

v. Make mention of Christ's righteousness, even of his only in all your access to God. Be sure to take Christ along with you in the arms of faith and love, else *no access*. 'Tis *through Christ*. Let him be all in all to you. Our access is

2. In the margin at this point Matthew Henry has noted *Tuck*. This is most probably a notation that this sentence is drawn from the writings of the Puritan scholar Anthony Tuckney (1599–1670).

by faith (Rom. 5:2), because faith is the grace by which we accept of Christ, and close with him. [There is] no coming to the Father but by him (John 14:6, 7). No agreement, no acceptance, no answer but through Jesus Christ. Look to it then that you *be found in him*. Kiss the Son (Ps. 2:12). Make him your friend (allu[de to] Acts 12:20). Come in a dependence upon the merit of his death, the prevalency of his intercession. 'Tis a horrible thing to think of God out of Christ. 'Tis by the better hope that we draw nigh to God (Heb. 7:19). And now, *who is he that will engage [his heart]* (Jer. 30:21)?

2. To believing saints that are made nigh and have this access to God through Jesus Christ. I hope I speak to some such, that are of the people *near unto him*, that have been introduced in conversion, passed from death to life, introduced in communion daily, receive from him, return to him – in Jesus Christ.

a. Know the dignity of such – not to be proud of it, but to preserve it in yourselves and to value you it in others. Surely God's people are a precious people. They are his favourites. 'Tis this that is the praise of the saints (Ps. 148:14). If the world did but know the worth of good men they would hedge them about with pearls. The saints though poor and low, despised in the world, yet upon this account [are] truly honourable and precious. This honour should make all the saints with a holy height and generosity to abhor every thing that's base and unbecoming their dignity. Look with a gracious scorn and contempt upon all the vanities of this world. Disdain to stoop to the pleasures of sin. Value yourselves by this. Honour [it] more than any thing else. Be not fond or puffed up with other honours. Do not envy yourselves to others. You are *a royal priesthood* (1 Pet. 2:9; comp[are] vv. 11, 12). *It is not for kings* (allu[de to] Prov. 31:4). Use this as an agent against sin.

b. Know the duty of such and do it.

i. Thankfully admire the condescending goodness of God in admitting them to this access. Speak of it to his praise. Surely this is a privilege of the covenant which challengeth the greatest wonder. *Lord, how is it* (John 14:22)? 'Tis a sign we have not this access if we do not admire it and be not thankful for it. *Behold what manner of love* (1 John 3:1). In heaven, where the access will be immediate, the wonder and thankfulness will be completed. Begin your heaven now. God must have all the glory. See Revelation 5:9, 10. 'Twas he that made us nigh, or we had never been nigh.

To help you in this thankful admiration consider:

1. Who he is and what we are, his greatness and our meanness, his holiness and our sinfulness. See 2 Samuel 7:18, etc. How undeserving we are of such a favour. How ill-deserving! We may say as Mephibosheth to David (2 Sam. 9:7, 8), that was the kindness of God, verse 3. Whence is this to me that not the mother of my Lord, but my Lord himself should come to me and take me to him (Luke 1:43)? Think what a rebellious distance we had been at, how long we had stood it out. [It's] a wonder of mercy that we were not long since fixed on t'other side of the great gulf.
2. What it cost him to bring us to this access. 'Twas no such easy matter. The contrivance of it was wonderful, the application more so. Think of the price it cost, no less than the blood of his own Son (Rev. 1:5, 6). The veil of his flesh [was] rent to break the partition wall. God seemed at a distance from him (Ps. 22:1) that we might have access. O bless God for Jesus Christ!

Think of the power it cost, an almighty power that made us of unwilling, willing. Think how we were drawn to it (John 6:44). What a powerful grace it was that inclined our hearts! Think how long he stood at the door and knocked (Rev. 3:20), and at last put in his hand by the hole of the door (Cant. 5:4; Isa. 65:1).

3. How much we gain by it. 'Tis not he but we that have gotten by it. O what a comfortable change hath hereby been made in our souls! See with what a holy triumph the Apostle speaks of it (Eph. 2:13). *But now* – a happy now. O let all this stir up thankfulness (1 Tim. 1:17). This thankful wonder [is] repeated in every access. When you have had any sweet communion with God in an ordinance reflect upon it with wonder and thankfulness, that we should have had such an invitation, such encouragements to come, should be so entertained when we do come.

ii. Take heed of doing any thing to prejudice or obstruct your access to God. 'Tis a precious privilege. Be very chary of it. *Keep yourselves in the love of God* (Jude 21).

Two things especially obstruct our access.

1. Guilt. That provokes God to hide his face. [It] rebuilds the partition wall, helps to alienate the affections from God, flatters the desires, deadens the pursuits after God. 'Tis as a cloud that comes between us and the sun. Guilt sealed up David's lips, therefore he prayed, *Lord, open my lips* (Ps. 51:15). Watch against sin. It will come against you in your access to God. Guilt concerning Joseph dampened his brethren when they had access to him (Gen. 42:21; 50:15).
2. Fear. Hard thoughts of God, distrust of him, these hinder access. The evil heart of unbelief [hinders]. God will be served without fear (Luke 1:74), i.e. without a fear of amazement. This prevailing fear obstructed David's access (2 Sam. 6:9, 10). Look upon God in his

greatness but withal remember his goodness, and come boldly. That which spoils our holy boldness is an enemy to our access.

iii. Make use of your access to God. It's a privilege which is to be improved. Have you access to God? Then visit him. What use doth the favourite make of his access to the King, and his interest in him? The same use should you make of your access to God. Come to him. You that are come to him in conversion, come to him in communion. Come to him to hear from him, to speak with him, else you receive the grace of God in vain.

1. Come frequently. Every day in every thing you should have recourse to God. Visit him the first thing you do in the morning (Ps. 5:3), and so in the evening, and often in the day (Phil. 4:6, *in every thing*), when any sudden emergency happens (Prov. 3:6). No time [is] amiss, the throne of grace is always open and you need not fear being burdensome (as Prov. 25:17) if you come aright.

Whatever the occasion is, still have recourse to God (Prov. 3:6). When you are in doubt come to him for direction, in danger come to him for protection, in temptation come to him for strength, etc. David and Daniel [came] thrice a day. Thus improve the privilege – the oftener the better, the more welcome (Ps. 27:8).

2. Come boldly, [with] a humble boldness, not as if you were giving bread to an elephant, as Titus said to the trembling petitioner (Heb. 4:16). You have leave to speak all your minds (Eph. 3:12). This boldness must be wholly built upon the merit of Christ, and his intercession for us, which leaves no room for our distrust if we have but an interest in him.
3. Come reverently. Your access is to a great God and therefore it must be very reverent. Our boldness must

not degenerate into rashness and presumption. Come into the presence of God with a holy awe (Rev. 10:3), without distraction (1 Cor. 7:35). Take heed of doing any thing to disturb your visits (Cant. 2:7), [come] as the publican (Luke 18:12; Heb. 12:28).

4. Come for others as well as for yourselves. Improve your access to God for the benefit of your friends. Spread their condition before the Lord, as those that have their king's ear petition for their friends. Thus [did] Moses (Exod. 33:12, 13). We are taught to say, *Our Father*. Make supplication for all saints (Eph. 6:18).

iv. Let God have access to you in his Word and in his providences. Throw open the doors of your souls (Ps. 24:7; comp[are] 25:1). Let him come and take possession of you, let his Word have a place in you (John 8:37), dwell richly (Col. 3:16). When the beloved knocks, rise to open to him and do not lie still making excuses (Cant. 5:2, 3). Let the blessed Spirit have free access to your souls in conviction, direction, consolation. Come and meet him in his approaches to you. Rejoice to hear the bridegroom's voice (John 3:29). Though he come with the rod, yet bid him welcome, and do not shut the doors against him (1 Sam. 3:18, *It is the Lord*).

When he stands at the door and knocks, be ready to answer (Rev. 3:20; Ps. 27:8). Take all well that God doth, and say, 'Gold is the word of the Lord' (Isa. 39.8). Make it to appear by the entertainment that you give him in every ordinance and every providence that you do really bid him welcome.

v. Take the comfort of this access to God. 'Tis a privilege that has much in it for the consolation of all the Lord's people. Whatever ails them they have an access to God for direction, strength, supply – this is indeed the summary of the saints' comforts.

'Tis in a special manner comfortable.

1. When we want the opportunity of public ordinances, [we] sojourn in Mesech and Kedar,[3] confined and restrained by sickness or persecution, yet even then we have *access to God*, which we cannot expect in a willing absence from instituted ordinances but may in a forced absence. Enemies may keep us from ministers and one from another but they cannot keep us from God (Ps. 42:6, 8; 63:1, 6; 84:3, 9, 11). Hezekiah when he was sick and could not go to the house of the Lord, yet turned his face to the wall and prayed (Isa. 38:2).
2. When we want the comfort of other friends, they at a distance from us, in place or affection, that we cannot have that access to them which we would desire yet we have access to God. Others perhaps stand aloof from us, [as] 'twas Job's case (Job 19:12, etc.) and David's (Ps. 38:11; 55:12, 13) and it's very melancholy, but when we have no body else to go to it's some comfort (and instead of all comfort) that we have a God to go to, to whom we may freely unbosom ourselves. He's a friend that never fails nor forsakes. The way to heaven is always open, and the word of promise nigh you.

vi. Covet a nearer access to God. You that have access to God will say it's good to draw near to God (Ps. 73:28) and therefore the nearer the better. The more we have of the sense of God's love to us, and the more our hearts are carried out in love to him every day the nearer is our access. When we see and enjoy more of him, here's a nearer access, our friendship more confirmed, our fellowship more continued.

---

3. The allusion is to Ps. 120:5.

1. Press after a nearer access to God in grace here. Build up yourselves (Jude 20). Labour after more knowledge of him, follow on to know (Hos. 6:3), [seek] after more of his love and likeness. Grow in grace (2 Pet. 3:18). Do not rest in any measure attained. Paul that had been in the third heaven yet is pressing forwards (Phil. 3:13, 14). Delight in those things which bring you nearer to God – Sabbaths, sermons, sacraments (Ps. 27:4). Engage your hearts to approach unto God in all these. Aim at an access to God in them (Ps. 63:2).
2. Pant after the nearest access to God in glory hereafter. We are yet but in the outer court. Long to be within the veil. The access there will be immediate, uninterrupted and eternal, present clouds [shall be] dispelled, and the approach more sensible, no longer by faith but by sight. Let the comfort of present approaches whet your appetite after that. What's heaven but to be with God there (1 Thess. 4:17, at his right hand), bathing ourselves at the fountain head? O when shall it once be! Why are his chariots so long in coming (Cant. 8:14)?

8

Ordinances in the Covenant

10 Apr. 1692

8. ORDINANCES IN THE COVENANT

Moreover I will make a covenant of peace with them – and will set my sanctuary in the midst of them for evermore, my tabernacle also shall be with them (Ezek. 37:26, 27).

The uniting of the two sticks, the stick of Judah and the stick of Joseph, in the prophet's hand was a teaching sign, and is supposed to point not only at the coalescence of the poor remains of the ten tribes with the two tribes at the return out of Babylon, but under the type of that to represent the union of Jews and Gentiles in the gospel church. Comp[are] Ephesians 2:14, which if so astonishing in the accomplishment must needs be much more mysterious in the prediction.

Several precious promises follow upon this union for where brethren dwell together in unity the Lord commands the blessing (Ps. 133:1, 3). The bringing of God's people together is the first step towards their prosperity – the Philadelphian period, the happy period. These promises must need point at gospel times. The text contains part of these privileges of which Jew and Gentile should be joint partakers.

1. In general, *a covenant*. 'Twas by the covenant that they were first taken to be a people, and now retaken having been long *lo-ammi* (Hos. 1:9, 10),[1] but now 'tis called a covenant of *peace*, implying there had been a quarrel, which must be taken up. The covenant between God and fallen man is a covenant of peace and it is *an everlasting covenant* (see Isa. 54:10). God will not, we must not, forget it.

1. Hebrew *lo-ammi* means 'not my people'.

2. In particular, ordinances in that covenant – *I will set my sanctuary*. OT prophecies relating to gospel times and gospel ordinances are usually clothed with OT language, borrowed from the ceremonial institutions (as Isa. 19:19; 66:21; and often elsewhere). So [they are] here. Not that there should be any one holy place as there was under the law (1 Tim. 2:8; Mal. 1:11, *in every place*), but they shall have the privilege of gospel ordinances instead of the legal institutions – a spiritual sanctuary instead of the worldly sanctuary. So 'tis called [in] Hebrews 9:1. We read much of the sanctuary in the OT, the service of the sanctuary and the offering of the sanctuary, and the charge of the sanctuary, and the purification of the sanctuary, and the vessels of the sanctuary. 'Twas the instituted place of public worship which God chose to record his name there. Now something instead of that, and which should be tantamount, is here promised.

– *my tabernacle also*. The OT administration is called the tabernacle (Heb. 13:10) because it was to be of short continuance, but here God promises a tabernacle to continue, the true tabernacle (see Heb. 8:2).

Now this comes in as part of the everlasting covenant and is joined with God's being to us a God.

Doct[rine] That sanctuary tabernacle privileges are the precious privileges of all those that are in covenant with God. Or thus,

That gospel ordinances are precious privileges belonging to the covenant people of the God of heaven.

I need not tell you what gospel ordinances are. You have most of them together (Acts 2:41, 42). *Baptism*, the door of admission into the visible church – *in the apostles' doctrine*, or under the apostles' teaching – church *fellowship*, the communion of saints in Christian conference and charity, mutual aids – *breaking of bread*, the Lord's Supper; and prayers in public – singing of psalms we have (Col. 3:16), a standing ministry and the Christian Sabbath, or Lord's Day, are gospel ordinances instituted as means, appointed for the due and regular administration of other ordinances. These bear the stamp of a divine appointment, therefore we call them ordinances. In them we have more immediately to do with God. God's covenants with the children of men have still had some such ordinances annexed. [They are] appointed methods of intercourse, channels for the conveyance of covenant comforts and reciprocal returns of covenant duties, acknowledgements, and engagements.

Now there's two ways of being in covenant with God according to which the doctrine requires a distinct consideration.

1. In profession and name. So are all visible church-members, all that profess faith in Christ and obedience to him, and the infants of those that do so, and to all such, according as they are capable, gospel ordinances do belong.

   The *sanctuary* and the *tabernacle* are entailed upon the visible church. Therefore [it is] called God's Israel (Ps. 76:1, 2). To them pertain the *glory* (Rom. 9:4). Ministers are set in the visible church (1 Cor. 12:28), given to the church (Eph. 4:11, 12, 13; 1 Cor. 3:22). All external professors are entitled to external privileges.

   Gospel ordinances to visible professors and mixed communities, are

   a. an honour. They are dignifying and distinguishing even there where they are not sanctifying and saving. The church is therefore said to be a crown of glory (Isa. 62:3). Ordinances are the *glory* of a nation (Ps. 85:9). When the ark goes, the glory goes (1 Sam. 4:22; Ezek. 9:3). [They are] a singular honour (Ps. 147:20;149:9). 'Twas upon the account of ordinances that the national church of the Jews was called a kingdom of priests (Exod. 19:6). When God takes away his ordinances he is said to break the staff of beauty (Zech. 11:10). Ordinances of worship are the *beauty of holiness* (Ps. 29:2).
   b. an opportunity. Those that are in profession, God's covenant people, have the ordinary means of salvation, and that's a great privilege. They are within hearing of the joyful sound

(Ps. 89:15), in those streets where wisdom cries. The church, though [it is] not the fountain of truth, yet it is the channel of conveyance. Many mighty nations want this opportunity. See what a privilege it is for a people to have God's sanctuary among them (Rom. 10:14, 15, 17). They are a step nearer heaven than other people, [they] are in a fairer way for salvation.

Those that have gospel ordinances among them as we have in this nation,

i. they have clearer discoveries of gospel light. Where ordinances are, light is, truth is. The church is the pillar and ground of truth (1 Tim. 3:15), as the pillar which has an inscription upon it, or to which a proclamation is affixed, and so held forth to the view of all, even to the principalities and powers as known *by the church* (Eph. 3:10). Where ordinances are, light is (Matt. 4:16; Luke 1:79). Therefore the churches in which those ordinances are administered are called *candlesticks*, and the ministers of the ordinances *stars* (Rev. 1:20). While we have ordinances the light is with us. 'Tis day time. The Word and sacraments exhibit Christ crucified (Gal. 3:1).

ii. they have more inviting displays of gospel love. In the sanctuary God doth not only manifest himself but manifests himself upon the mercy seat. For our encouragement common goodness is made known in providences (Acts 14:17), but gospel grace is made known only in ordinances, and without the knowledge of that there's but small encouragement for a guilty sinner to come to him. 'Tis in ordinances that the proclamation of grace is given out, this act of indemnity exhibited, the golden sceptre held forth. The promises [are] sealed conditionally in the sacraments to all visible believers.

iii. they have fuller directions for a gospel conversation. Ordinances are not only a light to our eyes but a light to our feet. Those that have them have not only received what they ought to know but how they ought to walk (1 Thess. 4:1). 'Tis in the ordinances that we have the best helps for engagements to, and encouragements in, that which is good. We are instructed by ordinances what we must do and how we must do it. Sacraments are guides, and spurs, and bonds, and oil to the wheels of our obedience. [They are] goads and nails (Eccles. 12:11).

Use 1. Bless God for the national enjoyment of sanctuary privileges, that we live in a land where ordinances are administered, a Goshen[2] that we have Bibles, and ministers, and Sabbaths, and sacraments, and solemn assemblies, that God's *tabernacle* is with us. Our eyes see our teachers (Isa. 30:20, 21) notwithstanding the restless contrivances of popish enemies, yet hitherto God has been a defence upon our glory (Isa. 4:5, 6). The Scripture [is] fulfilled (Isa. 42:4, *the isles shall wait [for his law]*). Ordinances are the beauty, strength and wealth of the nation. Oppose this to the grievances which some complain of. Though we have reason to be humbled for our corruptions and the disagreeableness of our conversations to our privileges yet we have reason to be thankful for our privileges, that the voice of the turtle is heard in our land.[3] Ordinances [are] administered with freedom, under the countenance and protection of authority, a wonder of mercy that [they are] yet continued notwithstanding barrenness (Isa. 5:5).

2. Acknowledge with thankfulness our own particular interest in sanctuary privileges. Bless God for your visible church membership, that you were baptized and so gathered under the wings of the divine majesty, added to the visible church (1 Cor. 12:13), planted in the vineyard (Luke 13:6). Bless God for your share in public ordinances – the Word, and prayer, and

2. Goshen, the part of Egypt in which the Israelites lived.

3. See Song of Sol. 2:12.

communion of saints. Blessed are the eyes which see these things (Matt. 13:16, 17; Luke 10:24). 'Tis a great mercy that we have a nail in God's *holy place* (Ezra 9:8), settled, stated, constant means, dwelling in God's house (Ps. 84:4). Who are we that we should be where God's sanctuary is, where his name is known? That your lot should be cast in times and places of gospel light, where God has a glorious high throne, and now where Satan's seat is (Rev. 2:13), of the seat of the beast? O the days of the Son of Man that we enjoy! A wide door opened! We have seen the outgoings of our God and our King, for the sanctuary, in the sanctuary (Ps. 63:2; 68:29), that the sanctuary is not desolate, the vineyard [not] laid waste.

3. Be earnest with God in prayer for the continuance of gospel ordinances and sanctuary privileges to us, that we may never know the want of the means of grace which we do enjoy. Put that promise in suit (Isa. 33:20). Pray that the open door may not be shut (Rev. 3:8), that the candlestick may never be removed, nor the entail of the gospel [be] cut off. Pray against all corruptions in ordinances, obstructions of ordinances. Lord, let it alone (Luke 13:8). Do not cut down the tree, or remove the dressers, or pluck up the hedge, or withhold the dues. If the glory goes God goes, and all good goes. Dread the fate of Shiloh, and the seven churches of Asia. Pray that God's sanctuary may be with us for evermore. 'Twill be well if there be peace and truth in our days, but better if likewise left to those that shall come after. Pray against the cutting off of the line of profession so the nail we have in the holy place may be clenched.

4. Rest not in external privileges but give all diligence to make a right improvement of them. A man may go from the sanctuary to hell. Judgment begins there (Ezek. 9:6). Nadab and Abihu died at the door of the tabernacle, Uzzah by the ark. The ordinances are means of salvation but to multitudes ineffectual means, and will aggravate the condemnation. See Luke 13:25, 26. Ordinances are good things and it's very well if they do us good but if not to

remember that we have received these good things that will pour oil into the flames shortly (Luke 13:25). 'Tis sad for men to be lighted to utter darkness by the light of the gospel, to go laden with sermons and Sabbaths and sacraments to hell. You that enjoy vineyard privileges bring forth fruit accordingly, else they will but make you the more inexcusable. Rest not in the form, the name, but press after the power, the thing (see Jer. 7:4).

5. In power and reality. Such as have truly consented to the covenant of grace – Christians indeed – and gospel ordinances are precious privileges belonging to them in another manner than they do to others. These are the church of the first-born (Heb. 12:23). God's sanctuary is in a special manner with them. They are the temples of the Holy Ghost (1 Cor. 3:16). Those that have God to be to them a God have a peculiar interest in gospel ordinances.

Show 1. How gospel ordinances do in a special manner belong to true believers.

a. They have a right to ordinances secured to them, the most special ordinances. Wicked people come to ordinances, but they are trespassers and usurpers while they go on in their sins. *What hast thou to do [to declare my statutes]* (Ps. 50:16; see Isa. 1:11, 12, etc.; comp[are] vv. 16-18). True believers are welcome to the solemn assemblies. For their sakes ordinances were instituted (2 Cor. 4:15). These have a right to the wedding feast that have on the wedding garment. As for others, *Friend, how camest you in [not having a wedding garment*] (Matt. 22:12)? The servants are not chidden[4] for letting him in. The wedding garment is the secret thing. These may have a right to ordinances *in foro ecclesia*[5] yet have no right *in foro coeli*.[6] They that are friends are invited (Cant. 2:4; 5:1).

4. *Chidden*, the past participle of the verb 'chide'.
5. Latin, 'in the court of the church'.
6. Latin, 'in the court of heaven'.

b. They have the ends of the ordinances secured to them.

i. Acceptance with God. Others want this, come to ordinances but do not meet with God there (Jer. 6:20; Amos 5:21, *but him will I accept*; Job 42:8; 1 Pet: 2:5). Ordinances are appointed to be the way of testifying our homage and obedience to our Creator and Redeemer. 'Tis in them that we pay our rent. Wicked people bring this rent in brass money, and will God accept it? [He will not accept the] torn and the lame for sacrifice (Mal. 1:8, 13), but God smells a sweet savour from believer's services (Gen. 4:4; 8:21; 2 Cor. 5:13).

ii. Advantage to themselves. God teacheth them to profit, teacheth them with a strong hand. They have the blessing of ordinances which were instituted for the perfecting of the saints (Eph. 4:11, 12). If you be Christ's, Paul and Apollos are yours (1 Cor. 3:22; *helpers of your joy*, 2 Cor. 1:24), your servants (2 Cor. 4:5). [There is] a special charge to feed the lambs, the sheep (John 21:15, 16, 17). Show particularly – What are gospel ordinances to true believers?

(1) They are golden pipes, by which the oil of grace is conveyed from Christ the olive tree to their lamps (Zech. 4:12). Channels of conveyance are they to us that Christ makes them convey to us what he puts in them. By them we receive from his fulness (John 1:16). Our oil fails and our lamps go out when the golden pipes are stopped up. There were seven pipes, [Zech. 4] v. 2 – noting a sufficiency of supply. 'Tis by the Word and prayer and sacraments that quickening grace and strengthening grace are conveyed. We are receiving, depending creatures and God has appointed this method of communication.

(2) They are green pastures (Ps. 23:2) and they are only the sheep of Christ that find them so – pleasant, refreshing, fattening (Ezek. 34:14, 15) – proper, suitable food. The great shepherd leads his flock into the

pastures, makes them *lie down* there. These are likely to find good by ordinances that lie down by them, that fix to them not a bit and away. Those are not Christ's lambs that wander in a large place (Hos. 4:16), but that abide by the given pastures. We are directed to go forth by the footsteps of the flock (Cant. 1:7, 8). 'Tis in communion with God's people and under the conduct of his ministers, the under-shepherds that we may expect these green pastures, and you may know the flock by their footsteps. The way of ordinances is the good old way, the beaten path. None find pastures in ordinances but those who by faith enter through Christ (John 10:9).

(3) They are fountains of salvation (Isa. 12:3), wells of living water – not salvation itself, but wells of salvation, means of conveyance, out of which we may draw if we have a bucket ready. They are *rivers of water* (Ps. 1:3; comp[are] Ps. 36:8), like the waters of the sanctuary (Ezek. 47:1). Some [are] plain and easy, others more deep and mysterious but all to fructify the holy land, and to make glad the city of our God (Ps. 46:4). They are fresh, still flowing as a river, never drawn dry (Isa. 55:1).

(4) They are a feast of fatlings, meat for the soul (Hos. 11:4), plenty and variety, as at a feast (Isa. 25:6). The Word, sacraments and prayer are spiritual feasts to those that come to them with a spiritual appetite (Prov. 9:2, 5; Matt. 22:4). A feast was made for fulness, for friendship, for fellowship – for love, for laughter – replenished with the dainties of heaven. In ordinances the saints have meat to eat that the world knows not of.

(5) They are beautiful clothing. The *fine linen* is δικαιώματα,[7] the ordinances of the saints (Rev. 19:8). God has appointed our appearing before him in the

7. Greek, 'righteous deeds'.

ordinances, as the priests of old in their linen garments. 'Tis in these that the bride, the lamb's wife, is made ready. These are the clothing that is of wrought gold (Ps. 45:13, 14). Except there be *glory within* ordinances will not be as clothing.

(6) They are breasts of consolation – full breasts if we can but draw by faith. We may from thence *suck and be satisfied* (Isa. 66:11). There's nourishment in them, nourishment for babes, sincere milk (1 Pet. 2:1, 2), and we have need of it till we get to heaven. Then we shall come to the perfect man, and be past the breast.

(7) They are galleries of communion (Cant. 7:5) where the Lord Jesus meets his people, and converseth with them, hears from them, speaks to them, shows himself to them (Cant. 2:9), like Mount Horeb where God appointed Moses to meet him (Exod. 34:2). This communion with God in ordinances is a riddle to the carnal foolish world (1 John 1:3). 'Tis the working of the gracious affections in the soul agreeable to the ordinance we are engaged in, the soul's receivings from God and out-goings towards him.

(8) They are the gate of heaven (Gen. 28:17). In them we have the views of heaven, and are in the way to heaven. When John was in the Spirit on the Lord's Day he saw a door opened in heaven (Rev. 4:1), so true believers in ordinances. They are our Peniel, where we see the face of God and live,[8] our ladder by which we receive from heaven in mercy, and make returns to heaven in duty. 'Tis by these that we have access into the holiest.

Thus true believers have God's tabernacle with them.

Show 2. That this is a very precious privilege thus to have gospel ordinances. Blessed are such (Ps. 84:4; 89:15).

---

8. See Gen. 32:30.

a. There's safety in it – perhaps exposed to the world and the rage of persecuting enemies by it but safe in God (Ps. 27:4, 5). God's tabernacle will be a special shelter for defence in the evil day (see Isa. 4:6). The sanctuary was a place of refuge, so are ordinances to gracious souls (*help from the sanctuary*, Ps. 20:2). God in ordinances is a little sanctuary to his people (Isa. 8:14; Ezek. 11:16). When David was haunted by temptation he never found relief till he went into the sanctuary (Ps. 73:17). Ordinances are a branch of that name of the Lord which is a strong tower to the righteous (Prov. 18:10).

b. There is satisfaction in it – abundant satisfaction (Ps. 65:4). In ordinances we see God and the riches of his grace, and that's satisfying. That was it that David thirsted after (Ps. 63:1, 2, 5). We unbosom ourselves before him, make known our condition with freedom, and that's satisfying. [We] receive pardon, peace and grace and these are satisfying (Ps. 36:8). The bread of ordinances is satisfying to the poor of his people (Ps. 132:15).

c. There is sanctification in it. Ordinances are precious things to believers for they help to make them more like to God, to work them up into a greater conformity to him. Sanctuary privileges are precious for they help to mortify sin, and to make us meet for glory. 'Tis by these that we partake of a divine nature. They are means of *grace*.

d. There is salvation in it. Sanctuary privileges are both means and earnests of salvation. 'Tis by them that we are made wise to salvation (2 Tim. 3:15). In these the grace of God bringeth salvation (Titus 2:11). These are the field in which the true treasure is hid, the foretaste of glory.

Use 1. Try your state by this. You see what ordinances are to true believers. What are they to you?

a. What do you do in them? Anything or nothing? Many that come to ordinances do nothing in them or nothing to the purpose. What are you thinking of and minding when you are praying and hearing? Do you stir up yourselves *hoc agere*?[9] Do you stir up all that is within you (Ps. 103:1)?

b. What do you get by them? What *have* you to show for so long trading in ordinances? What knowledge, grace, comfort, strength? What water have you drawn? Wherein have you been the better for all the means of grace you have had? Has the profiting appeared? What fruit?

2. Suffer a word of exhortation, you that by faith are truly in covenant with God, to whom gospel ordinances do belong.

a. Understand gospel ordinances. Know the particular meaning of every service. Much of the learning of a Christian consists in his acquaintance with the particular intendment of every institution of Christ's. Understand not only how to improve an ordinance just while you have it, but how to improve it long *after* – Baptism, the Lord's Supper, the Word, Prayer. The efficacy is not tied to the administration.[10] They do not work as charms, or by physical agency, but as moral instruments.

b. Value gospel ordinances. Put a high estimate upon them. Rank them among your treasures, your glory. Prefer a day in God's courts before a thousand elsewhere (Ps. 84:10). Everything should be valued by the relation it has to God, the soul and eternity.

c. Desire gospel ordinances. Let your souls press after communion with God in them (Ps. 42:1, 2; Ps. 84:2). Come with an appetite to every ordinance, pant after opportunities of praying, hearing, sacraments. Be sensible of your continual want of them as of your daily food. Lord, evermore give us this bread.

d. Delight in gospel ordinances. Take pleasure in them. Sit down under Christ's shadow with delight. Call the Sabbath a delight (Isa. 58:13). Say, 'It's good to be here', as they [the whole

9. Latin, 'to do this'.
10. This appears to be an echo of the Westminster Confession of Faith, 27:3; 28:6.

assembly did in Hezekiah's time] (2 Chron. 30:23). Sing in the ways of the Lord (Ps. 138:5).

e. Labour to answer the ends of every ordinance. Be in a suitable frame [of mind]. Lift up your souls to God in every prayer. Bow down your souls before him in every sermon. What's the wedding garment, the suitable agreeable frame?

f. Long to be there where though there shall be no ordinances yet there shall be no need of them. The lamb shall be the temple (Rev. 21:22). Let sanctuary privileges make you long to be within the veil.

9

Providences in the Covenant

17 Apr. 1692

9. PROVIDENCES IN THE COVENANT

And we know that all things work together for the good of them that love God, to them who are the called according to his purpose (Rom. 8:28).

Two things are observable in these words.

1. The character of the saints – who are here described by such properties as are common to all those that are truly sanctified.

    a. They *love God.* Wherever there is a principle of grace the love of God is shed abroad in the heart (Rom. 5:5), love to God drawn out by his love to us. Love to God includes all those outgoings of the soul's affections towards God as the chiefest good – prizing him above all, choosing him, desiring him, delighting in him, returning to him as the rest of our souls (Ps. 116:7; Ps. 73:25). This is the main character of God's people, for 'tis the first and great commandment (Matt. 22:37). Admire the riches of gospel grace which proposeth and ensures heaven and happiness upon so just and reasonable a condition as loving God. The master doth not use to bargain for his servant's love, but this is it that God requires from us that we should love him. And he accepts nothing we do for him if we do not love him (1 Cor. 13:1, 2, 3, *and have not charity* – or *love*).

    b. They *are called according to his purpose* – effectually called according to the eternal purpose. Those are effectually called that come at the call, from self to God as the highest end, from sin to Christ as the chosen way, from earth to heaven as their portion – called to be saints. To those that are truly holy that call is effectual, that boasting may be for ever excluded and every crown laid at the feet of free grace. This call is effectual not according to any merit or desert of ours but according to God's own gracious purpose. Whom he did predestinate them he called, verse 30.

It concerns us all to examine ourselves by these characters. We are all called with the common call, which is more extensive than the saving choice, for *many are called that are not chosen* (Matt. 20:16), but the text speaks of a call that follows upon the choice – a call that is effectual.

2. The privilege of the saints – *that all things work together for good to them.* An answer of peace to our prayers was promised, verse 27, but it might be objected, How doth God hear the prayers of his afflicted when notwithstanding he continues the affliction upon the loins? 'Tis true many times he doth so but 'tis for their good. In this the Spirit's intercession is always effectual, that however it goes, with them it's all for good.

– and this *we know*. Οἴδαμεν[1] – we know it for a certainty, know it from the Word of God, from our own experience and the experience of all the saints. It's a full proof of the truth.

Doct[rine] That it is the unspeakable privilege of all those that are truly in covenant with God that all things shall work together for good to them.

Πάντα συνεργεῖ εἰς τὸ ἀγαθόν.[2]

Show 1. What are those things that shall work together for the good to them? I understand it in general, of all the *Providences* of God that are concerning them – all that God performs he performs for them (Ps. 57:2), which will answer a question sometimes disputed upon this text, whether the sins of God's people are intended here among those things that work for their good. God is not the author of sin. Those are not things of his performing,

1. Greek, 'we know'.
2. Greek, 'all things work together for good', or, 'he makes all things work together for good'.

but God's permitting of sin doth work for their good (see 2 Chron. 32:31), so that as far as God *performs* he doth it *for them*. Thus providences are theirs in the covenant.

a. Merciful Providences. I call these so which are generally accounted in favour of us – creature comforts, enjoyments, supplies, deliverances which tend to the gratifying of sense and the pleasing of our apprehensions.

These are all of God's ordering – all from above, every creature that to us and no more that God makes it to be. If the cisterns be full of sweet waters, 'tis he that fills them. Suppose comfort in relations, a comfortable place of abode, a growing estate, a good name, a healthful body, all that [your] heart could wish.

These providences are for hurt to wicked people (Prov. 1:32), who have many times a greater plenty of outward comforts than other people (Ps. 73:5). They are their *good things* (Luke 16:25), good in themselves but bad for the wicked, as delicate fare to a foul stomach. Many a one hath been ruined by such providences as these. But they are for good to the people of God – *good things* indeed to them. Sometimes they have a share of these things (*the promise of life that now is*, 1 Tim. 4:8), and 'tis this promise in the text that secures to them the happiness of the promises, yet what they have of the life that now is shall work for good to them.

b. Afflicting Providences. Such events as are commonly reckoned grievous and displeasing to flesh and blood – pain and sickness of body, losses and crosses in the estate, discontent and trouble in relations, reproach and ignominy in the home, every thing that is uneasy. These things are indifferently distributed to good and bad (Eccles. 9:1, 2). Both alike [are] born to trouble, and even saintship [is] no exemption from the common lot, so that 'tis impossible to make an unerring judgment of any man's spiritual estate upon the view of his temporal. This Job said and stood to (Job 9:22). In public calamities, sword and pestilence make no distinction (Ezek. 21:2), *righteous and wicked, green tree and dry tree* (Ezek. 20:47).

So as to perpetual afflictions – waters of a full cup are *wrung out to God's people* (Ps. 73:10, 14), *every morning*, as duly as the morning comes, and yet compassions [are] new every morning (Lam. 3:23). The events themselves are the same both for good and bad, but observe how different the design (Jer. 24:5, 9), some *for their hurt*, some *for their good*. These afflicting providences seem against them (Job. 13:26). Jacob thought all was *against him* (Gen. 42:36) but it proved on the contrary that all was for him. Afflicting providences [are] for good as well as [being] merciful.

Show 2. What is that *good* which these work for towards the people of God. Good is two-fold.

a. Temporal good – and the merciful providences have indeed a direct tendency to that, and to them they are truly *good* – for the Lord is for the body. But sometimes even the afflicting providences work for the temporal good, as in the case of Joseph, whose way to the second chariot of the kingdom lay through the pit and the prison. This God meant even for temporal good (Gen. 50:20). If Daniel had not been carried captive he had not been a Privy Counsellor to the King of Babylon. Very strangely and by unaccountable methods doth the divine providence sometimes bring about the advancement and enrichment of his people. Israel [was] enriched by the Egyptians. The wealth of the sinner [is] laid up for the just. But this is not [to] be always counted upon. If 'twere good for them they should have it (Ps. 34:10), and infinite wisdom will be the judge.

b. Spiritual and eternal good – and that's it that all things *work for*. That's good indeed that's good for the soul, the better the immortal part, not *any good* (Ps. 4:6). The soul is the man. Now providences *work together* for this good. Either directly or indirectly every providence has a tendency to the spiritual good of those that love God.

i. That's for their good that teacheth them every providence has a lesson, every rod the blossoming rod, and the chastening rod has a voice. Mercies teach as they give opportunity for learning, afflictions as they dispose the heart. Mercies teach us the goodness and sweetness of God, afflictions teach us the holiness and justice of God. The book of providence helps the learning of the saints (Ps. 107:43; Hos. 14:9). Chastenings are in a special manner teaching (Ps. 94:12). God teacheth with briars and thorns (allu[de to] Jude 8:16). Providences teach us the meaning of the Scriptures. When we see the Word of God fulfilled we understand it better. There's a great deal that the saints learn by *experience*, and that sticks (Rom. 5:3, 4). As Laban (Gen. 30:27), the saints have found God in his providences making good what he has spoken, and that has made many good scholars in the Scriptures. Thus have they learned many a good lesson. Thus God is teaching the saints from their youth up, even by his wondrous works (Ps. 71:17).

ii. That's for their good that tries them. Prosperity and adversity are both trials. [They] discover the people of God, not to God [for] he knows them but to themselves as 2 Chronicles 32:31, that they may take the comfort of what is good, and the shame of what is bad. Their graces are tried, their sincerity is tried, that they may come forth *as gold* (Job 23:10), approved, and improved. See 1 Peter 1:7. Troubles are trials, the touch stone of uprightness. See Daniel 11:35. Discover what metal we are made of. Variety of conditions is designed for the trial and exercise of variety of graces. We must be tried with each condition that we may be fit for any.

iii. That's for their good that breaks them from sin, humbles and reforms them, turns the heart from and against every sin. This every providence helps to do. Mercies help to shame us out of sins (Deut. 32:6; Ezek. 16:63), afflictions to startle us (Ezek. 6:9). Troubles have a great tendency to the embittering of sin, and mercies do it by sweetening the goodness of God. Providences have done more sometimes towards the separating between us and sin than ordinances. This is the fruit, even *the taking away of sin* (Isa. 27:9; Hos. 14:8). This effect the captivity had upon the Jews. Particular providences [are] designed to part between us and particular sins, perhaps the beloved sin.

iv. That's for their good that brings them nearer to God – nearer to his Lord, to his likeness. Providences do this. Mercies endear him to us, afflictions make us partakers of his *holiness* (Heb. 12:10). Holiness [is] the brightest glory of his nature, the richest gift of his covenant. Providences are the cords by which God draws his people to himself. They are means of sanctification. The will of God is done concerning us in every providence. Now as the will of God in the Word where it makes a due impression upon the soul is sanctifying, so the will of God in providence. We are made conformable to God's image when we are delivered into the mould of a providence. What's holiness but a compliance with God's will (Matt. 26:3)?

v. That's for their good that engageth them to duty. Our hearts are very treacherous and deceitful. Providences help to bind and fix them. Mercies oblige in gratitude to serve God. Afflictions oblige us in point of interest. Providences quicken us as to our work and in our work. *That they might observe his statutes* (Ps. 105:45). Providence is as a spur in the side to put us forward when we begin to draw back. Providences mind us of forgotten, neglected duties. Sometimes God doth by strange providences revive the sense of our obligations, especially [by] afflictions.

vi. That's for their good that encourageth them in duty. That's oil to the wheel of their obedience. Providences work together for the comfort and joy of those that love God, even afflicting providences (2 Cor. 1:5). Therefore it's said to be a matter of all joy (Jas. 1:2). Thus doth God give songs in the night, much more merciful providences (Deut.

28:47). These enlarge the heart in duty, [and] are intended to make us cheerful in the ways of God. The same meats that are clogging to some stomachs are cheering to others.

vii. That's for their good that frees them from this present world, that weans them from it and loosens their affections for it. Providences do this, merciful providences. Those that are savingly enlightened, the more they have and the more they see of the world the more they see of the vanity and insufficiency. Solomon, by enjoying the things of the world, discovered the emptiness of them. Much more [so with] afflictions. God puts wormwood upon the breast, to put us out of love with it.

viii. That's for their good that fits them for a better world, recommends it to them, quickens their longings after that world, disposeth them for it by a delight in the work and company and pleasures of that state. This providences do, merciful providences, as partial enjoyments make them long for the eminency and perfection of all these. Afflicting providences make them look beyond all these things and converse within the veil (2 Cor. 4:18). Thus are they made meet to partake of the inheritance. Watchfulness [is] quickened, [and] afflictions trim the lamps.

Show 3. Whence is it that providences thus *work together* for good – συνεργεῖ[3]?

a. They *work*, as physic[4] works, [in] various ways according to the intention of the skilful physician but all for the patient's good. There's a great deal to be done for the good of a soul. We are naturally so bad, nay, so averse to that which is good that it's no easy matter to bring us to embrace that which is really good for us. Understanding and will [are] both depraved and vitiated (Eccles. 6:12). As some bodies, so our souls are

---

3. Greek, 'work together'.
4. *Physic*, 'medicine'.

hard to work upon. There's humbling work, refining work, changing work, preparing work. It's a work of time and labour, like the working of stone for a building. That product doth not perhaps appear presently – it's in the doing.

b. They *work together*, as several ingredients in a medicine concur to answer the intention. *God has set the one over against the other* (Eccles. 7:14). The proportion, coherence and correspondence of providences conduce to the good of the people of God, as both rain and sunshine contribute to the fruitfulness of the earth.

Συνεργεῖ – a verb, singular, in conjunction with a noun plural,[5] noting the harmony of providence and its uniform designs. All the wheels [are] as one *wheel* (Ezek. 10:13). Like the lines that meet in the centre from every part of the circumference, though they may seem to thwart across one another yet they have all the same tendency. Like the wheels of a watch, all [is] one work. Now the work that providences do to those that love God is not from any specific quality in themselves for there are multitudes under the same providences that are never the better but the worse for them. But providences are theirs because God is theirs. *He works all things for good.* So some read it. 'Tis the work of God to bring so much good to his people out of providences. 'Tis he that has *made all these things.*

i. The will of God orders the providences themselves so as to be for good. *He performeth the thing that is appointed for us* (Job 33:14). Whatever befalls us and however things go with us, 'tis God that orders and disposes all. He sits at the upper end of all second causes. [He] makes every creature to be that to us and no more that it is. He gives and takes (Job 1:21; Lam. 3:27, 28), [he] wounds and heals, kills and makes alive, doth what he pleases with us and ours.

5. In Greek a neuter plural subject takes a verb in the singular.

Now in every will of God there is

(1) a counsel (Eph. 1:11, *after the counsel of his own [will]*). His will is his wisdom (Isa. 28:29). There's an admirable depth of design in the providences of God (Rom. 11:33). He doth not do things at a venture, haphazard, but all that he doth is the product of infinite wisdom. 'Twas an eternal counsel upon an infinite prescience.[6] He knows all his works from the beginning to the end at one view (Acts 15:18; 1 Sam. 2:3).

(2) a concern for his people. See 2 Chronicles 16:9. Wisdom is a faculty that directs to the use of means proper for the attainment of the desired end. Now God's end in all his counsels is the good of his people (Deut. 32:8, 9). All things are for their sake (2 Cor. 4:15). 'Tis a concern for the salvation of the chosen remnant. The appointment of every event concerning the elect is subservient to the main counsel of love concerning their eternal salvation. When he decreed salvation as the end, he decreed this or that condition as the way. Hence it is that all's for good, because it's all for heaven. Therefore the management of all is committed to Jesus Christ the Saviour.

ii. The Lord Jesus hath by dying taken the evil out of every providence. Hence it is that all works for good because the malignity of it is taken out by the dying of the Lord Jesus, which corrects the hurtful quality. Therefore it is that all works for good because Jesus Christ has taken the sting out of every affliction, and so it ceases to be hurtful. He has overcome the world (John 16:33), the good things of the world, the evil things of the world, so that they can do us no hurt. 'Tis through Christ that in these things, the providences that are concerning us, we are *conquerors*, nay, *more than conquerors* (Rom. 8:37), not only no

6. *Prescience*, 'foreknowledge'.

losers but great gainers. Providences not only not hurt us but do us good, not only not keep us out of heaven but help us forward in our way to heaven. This is owing to Christ's victory. By faith in that we overcome the world (1 John 5:4). Christ's victory [is] made ours. Not only [are we] delivered out of Egypt, but enriched with the spoil. The world [is] not only our inn, but our ship to help forward our motion. 'Moab to the spoil' (2 Kings 3:23).

iii. The blessed Spirit sanctifies providences to us. All the good we gain by providences is owing to the influences and operations of the Holy Spirit. Ordinances work for good no further than the Spirit works with them. So [with] providences. 'Tis true of providences that they are received *ad modum recipientis*.[7] The Spirit disposes the recipient. See Philippians 1:19. *This shall turn to my salvation through the supply of the Spirit* – ἐπιχορηγίας[8] – a contract pension or exhibition of the Spirit. Neither mercies nor afflictions would of themselves do us any good, but the corrupt nature would rather pervert them to our hurt, but 'tis the Spirit that subdues the corruption and disposes the soul to comply with the design and to answer the end of every providence. 'Tis not the afflictions but the sanctified afflictions that are the spiritual promotions. The efficacy of these as of other means depends only upon the blessing of God. 'Tis he that *chastens and teaches* (Ps. 94:12). 'Tis not the rod alone but the rod and reproof that give wisdom, and the Spirit is the great reprover (John 16:8). The discipline would do little good if the Spirit did not *open the ear to it* (Job 36:10).

Use 1. Make sure your interest in this promise. 'Tis an unspeakable privilege to have all providences work for our good. Till this is

7. Latin, 'in the manner of a recipient'.
8. Greek, 'supply', 'provision'.

done all works for hurt to you. What can a man desire more to make him happy? Make this promise yours.

a. See to it that you *love God*. He hath said he will *love* those that *love him* (Prov. 8:17), and 'tis that love of God that makes all work for good to us. 'Tis the father's love that makes him consult his child's good in every thing he doth for him, though earthly parents are oft mistaken, but our Heavenly Father is wise and knows what is best for us. Besides, our loving of God will dispose us and put us in a frame to get good by *all things*. Nothing makes us get hurt both by mercies and afflictions but want of love to God. The good or hurt of providences is as we are good or bad. They that love God will take all well that he doth and bless him both giving and taking (Job 1:21), receive both good and evil (Job 2:10), and providences certainly work for good to those that are in this frame. Examine your love. Is it a sincere, strong, superlative love? Those that love God love everything that is his for his sake – his Word, his day, his people.

b. See to it that you be effectually *called*. Make your calling sure and then thereby make your election sure (2 Pet. 1:10). Come at the call. Many say, 'I go Sir', yet stir never a step (Matt. 21:30). These are not effectually called. 'Tis a holy calling, a heavenly calling. What holiness, what heavenliness can you witness to? We are called to glory and virtue, not only to glory as the end but to virtue as the way. What answer do you give to the calls of the Word, calls from sin, to duty? Is it not a delaying, excusing, denying answer? Those that are called according to his purpose are happy according to his purpose.

Use 2. Make use of this promise accordingly. You that do love God, you cannot deny but you love him. *Thou knowest all things* (John 21:17). Improve this promise. *All things shall work together for good.*

a. Reckon that good for you that's good for your souls. Measure goodness by the right standard. God is the chiefest good. Account that best which makes us likest to him. Reckon the soul to be the man, and that it fares with you well or ill as it fares with your souls. Believe that there is such a thing as soul prosperity (3 John 2), and value it as the best prosperity, and put a rate upon every thing as it promotes or hinders that.

b. Labour to comply with the design of God in every providence. Get that good by mercies and afflictions that he intends you in them. Study the meaning of every event, whether it makes for you or against you. You are all enquiring, 'What's to be gotten?' Ask, 'What's to be gotten for my soul by this providence?' Study your duty of the day (Eccles. 7:14). That providence works for our good which we do the duty of. Especially take heed of getting hurt by providences, mercies, afflictions. Physic doth hurt those that will not submit to the rule in the taking of it.

c. Perplex not yourselves with inordinate care and solicitude about future events (1 Cor. 7:32; Phil. 4:6; 1 Pet. 5:7). Be satisfied in the general that all shall be for good, if you keep yourselves in the love of God. Let it be your care to please God, and to [be] found in the way of duty, and you cast all your other cares upon God. *Provoke me not, and I will do you no hurt* (Jer. 25:6). We have to do with a wise God that knows what's good for us better than we do for ourselves.

d. Submit cheerfully to the will of God in every affliction. This is a reason why we should not only bear tribulation but even rejoice in it. *Bless God* (Job 1:21, *receive it*). Bless God for that good he will bring to you out of the affliction though you do not know how. Bitter potions are for good. Never sway at them (John 18:11). Take affliction as physic, not as poison. *Let him do [to me as seemeth good unto him]* (2 Sam. 15:25, 26). Not only he may do so subscribing to his sovereignty, he can do, subscribing to his power, but let him do, subscribing to his goodness. You know not what all this tends to (John 13:7). 'Tis but it need be (1 Pet. 1:6). When you come to heaven you'll see that you could not have been without it. Judge nothing before the time. The house is yet but in the building.

e. This should engage us to the duty of prayer in all conditions. God will be sought unto even for promised mercies. 'Tis prayer that must fetch out this good. We have need to pray not only in adversity but in prosperity (Phil. 1:19, *through your prayer*). Pray against the snares of every condition (Prov. 30:8, 9). Pray continually, 'Lord, do me good by this mercy, by this affliction'. See Psalm 57:2.

f. Let God have the glory of all the good which we get by every providence. Glorify his wisdom, power and goodness. If all be of him all must be to him (Rom. 11:36). 'Tis distinguishing. Magnify the designs of providence, the counsels of the divine love, how God in all considered our frame, how proper and suitable the applications were. If he works all together for our good, we must labour to work all together for his glory. He performs all for us; let us perform all for him (1 Cor. 10:31).

10

Angels in the Covenant

24 Apr. 1692

10. ANGELS IN THE COVENANT

Are they not all ministering spirits, sent forth to minister for them that shall be heirs of salvation? (Heb. 1:14).

The scope of the Apostle in this chapter is as a faithful friend of the bridegroom to advance the honour of the Lord Jesus, and particularly to prove his preference above the angels, his exaltation far above all principalities and powers (Eph. 1:21). The angels are confessedly the most excellent and glorious creatures – the chief of the ways of God, the most splendid inhabitants of the upper world, the morning stars (Job 38:7), but Jesus Christ [is] far above them. Now one argument is taken from the office of the angels, they are *ministering spirits*. He *sits at God's right hand*, verse 13. Sitting [is] a posture of rest, but the angels are sent forth every day, always upon the wing. Sitting [is] a posture of rule, he reigns there, but the angels are servants, verse 7, and he that is sent is not *greater than he that sends him* (John 13:16). Thus in all things Jesus Christ is to have the preeminence (Col. 1:18). Let him have it accordingly in your souls (Cant. 5:10).

That which is said concerning Christ's honour tends very much to the saints' comfort, for his advancement is our concernment. He's head over all things to the church. His headship over the angels is to the church (Eph. 1:22), for the good of the church.

Observe in the text a summary of the saints' privileges.

1. The privileges of their home. They are *heirs of salvation*. 'Tis salvation, eternal salvation that is set before them and they are *heirs* to it, which is a sure, a sweet, but a self-denying title. [They are] heirs under age (Gal. 4:1, 2). *If children then heirs* (Rom. 8:17), not else.

τοὺς μέλλοντας κληρονομεῖν[1] they shall possess by

1. Greek, '[for] those who will inherit [salvation]'.

inheritance. They are not yet in possession but they shall be. How doth a young heir please himself with the thoughts of his inheritance? And should not we delight more in the contemplation of the joy that is set before us, and live more upon the hopes of it?

2. The privilege of their way – that the angels are ministering spirits *sent forth to minister for them*. They are not ministers or servants of the saints but ministers or servants of Christ for the saints and for their good. The shepherd is not a servant of the sheep, but for the sheep.

Doct[rine] That this is the great privilege of true believers that the blessed angels are ministering spirits sent forth to minister for their good. When we speak of angels we must speak with all humility. An arrogant pretending to an acquaintance with the world of angels more than is revealed in Scripture was the bane of many of the heretics in primitive times. Some such there were even in the apostolic days (Col. 2:18).

1. 'Tis certain there are angels, holy spirits, the inhabitants of the higher worlds, of a different nature both from the divine and human. The Sadducees denied it (Acts 23:8) but the Scripture is plain and express in it, though we see them not. They have no body as we have, though they have sometimes assumed a human shape. Some of the Platonic Fathers[2] will have some sort of material bodies proper to the angels, but the Scripture calls them *spirits* (Heb. 1:7), not infinite and omnipotent as God is, but finite intelligences, created in the beginning (Col. 1:16, 17), though their creation is not recounted by Moses for he designed the history of the church in this lower world, and the history of creation has therefore a special regard to that, though the angels are

---

2. The Platonic Fathers were philosophers who developed a later form of the philosophy of Plato from the third to the fifth century AD. In general they believed that the highest form of reality did not involve material existence.

certainly included under *the hosts of heaven* (Gen. 2:1) for they are frequently so called, as Psalm 103:20, 21; 148:2. [They were] probably created the first day, for when he laid the foundation of the earth the morning stars newly risen sang together (Job 38:6, 7). Their number [is] great (Dan. 7:10).

But for their several orders and dignities (which the Pseudo. Dionysius[3] in his celestial hierarchy makes so bold with and the schoolmen from him), their locality, intellect, will and power, whilst we are in a world of sinners, we are very unfit to talk of it (Deut. 29:29).

2. 'Tis as certain that the angels are *ministering spirits*. The name of *angel* speaks not [of] their nature but their office – as messengers (ministers are called angels) to teach us to acquaint ourselves more with their office than their nature. 'Tis the will of God we should converse most with that which we are most concerned in. Angels are called watchers (Dan. 4:13), soldiers[4] (Luke 2:13), messengers. They are *all* ministering spirits. Though several angels have their respective charge, we read of some sent on one message, some on another. Some think a proud disdaining to stoop to this ministration was the sin of the angels that fell. They thought themselves too good for it, and so deserted their station (Jude 6), but the rest kept their first estate.

Show 1. What the ministration of the angels is to the saints and for their good. In general they perfectly obey the will of God. Whatever they do 'tis at his command (Ps. 103:20), hence he's called Lord of Hosts. They are his ministers and his messengers (Ps. 104:4). [They] go when he bids them go, come when he bids them come, do what he bids them do. They are to us that and no more that God makes them to be. Not that God has any

3. Dionysius, the pseudo-Areopagite (c.AD 500), was a mystical theologian wrongly identified with the Athenian converted through Paul's ministry (Acts 17:34).

4. The Greek text of Luke 2:13 has στρατιᾶς οὐρανίου, 'heavenly army'.

need of angels or their services, as he made all by a word, so he can govern all, but he uses the ministration of angels to dignify them as workers with him, to comfort the saints and especially for his own praise and glory, in the ministration of such noble creatures. More particularly the ministration of angels relates

a. to Christ the head, as mediator. They are his servants in carrying on his undertaking, and those ministrations are for us, for the good of the heirs of salvation.

i. They did minister to Christ when he was in the world. They brought the tidings of his conception to Mary (Luke 1:26), to Joseph (Matt. 1:20), of his birth to the shepherds (Luke 2:10, 13), gave warning to Joseph of his peril (Matt. 2:13, 19), ministered to him after his temptation (Matt. 4:11), not as seconds when he was in that conflict for his own arm wrought salvation, but when 'twas over, in his agony (Luke 22:43), though appearing at a distance, as if the angels seemed to draw away from him. We find nothing that that angel said for we never find any angel speaking when Christ was present, lest he should seem to receive instructions from them. He could have had legions (Matt. 26:53). They attended at his resurrection to roll away the stone, to give notice of it (John 20:12), [and] at his ascension (Acts 1:10). Though for a while he appeared a little lower than the angels (Heb. 2:9), yet even then the angels were his humble servants. [The] mystery of godliness (1 Tim. 3:16) [is that he was] seen of angels (comp[are] 1 Pet. 1:12). This speaks him great.

ii. They do minister unto him now he is in heaven. They are *his* angels (Rev. 1:1; 22:16). They are ready to go where he send them, to do what he bids them. They are continually about the throne adoring him (Rev. 5:11, 12; 7:14) in ordering the affairs of the church foretold in the Revelation. We read much of Christ's using the ministry of angels. The trumpets sounded and the vials [were] poured out by angels.

iii. They will minister unto him at his second coming. He shall come attended with his mighty angels (2 Thess. 1:7; Matt. 25:31) to attend upon his person, to minister in the process. 'Twill be a busy day with the angels, [as] *the reapers are the angels* (Matt. 13:39, 41), the archangel (1 Thess. 4:16) perhaps [being] Christ himself.

b. to the church the body, in reference to those public concernments of it, or some parts of it. The ministration of angels was much used in the affairs of the OT church, especially

i. in giving the law (Gal. 3:19; Acts 7:53; Heb. 2:2; comp[are] Deut. 33:2; Ps. 68:8). 'Twas a representation of the day of judgment. The earthquake, lightnings, etc. were by the ministration of angels. It speaks much of the honour of the law, and should frighten us from the breach of it.

ii. in fighting their battles. God has used the ministry of angels for the ruin of his church's enemies (the Egyptians, Exod. 12:29; Sennacherib, Isa. 37:36). 'Twas an host of angels that went before David against the Philistines (2 Sam. 5:24). The angel of the Lord persecutes them (Ps. 35:6). Some observe that when God has any destroying work to do he uses the ministry of but one angel, or two at the most. One angel slew the first-born, routed the Assyrians, plagued Jerusalem, but many angels protect Elisha, guard Jacob. Three angels come to promise the birth of Isaac but two only went to destroy Sodom. The angels were created primarily for the preservation of men, not for their destruction. How far God doth still use the ministry of angels in the public concernments of the church we know not. We have seen victories strangely won. Whether God has not used an army of angels more than an army of soldiers who can tell. We find the angels active about the church (Zech. 1:8; 6:1, 5).

c. to particular believers the members, that are in covenant with God. When God in the covenant becomes our friend the angels become our friends likewise. The meanest of Christ's members have *their* angels (Matt. 18:10). The angels [are] theirs in the covenant.

'Tis queried whether every particular saint has a guardian angel, his *comes individuus*.[5] The Papists are so confident of it as to pray every day to their guardian angel, but there's no such thing in Scripture. We find many angels attending upon one saint. What need we plead for a guardian angel, when every saint has a guard of angels? He shall give his angels charge (Ps. 91:11, 12). They [the Catholics] urge Acts 12:15*, it is his angel,* but it doth not reach it. That was said by the people in the house who might speak it for a vulgar error. Rather, it is *his* messenger, one that makes use of his name to get admission.

The ministry of angels to the saints is various, even about the ordinary concernments of their lives.

i. The angels oppose the malice of evil spirits that seek to do them a mischief. The devil goes about as a roaring lion (1 Pet. 5:8), fighting against us. The good angels fight against him, engaged under Christ against the great dragon, in a constant war (Rev. 12:7, 9). More *disputes* of this kind they have with the devil than we are aware of (Jude 9). [We may wonder] whether this may not be the meaning of that difficult passage, Daniel 10:13, *the Prince of the kingdom of Persia*. The devil is called the *prince* of the power of the air, whether that might not be some evil genius that incensed the Persians against the people of God.

ii. The angels defend and preserve the bodies of the saints. See Revelation 20:1, 2. They have a particular charge concerning them by night and by day (Ps. 34:7), as the lifeguard encamps about the person of the king. Jacob when the angels of God met him said, 'This is God's camp' (Gen. 32:1, 2), Mahanaim,[6] two hosts, like an army divided

5. Latin, 'an inseparable companion'.

6. Hebrew, the dual form of the Hebrew word for a 'camp' or 'encampment (of soldiers)'.

into the rear and the van-guard. Jacob was between two angry people, Laban and Esau, but the angels were his guard both before and behind. Thus Elisha (2 Kings 6:17) and in general (Ps. 91:11, 12) [they] bear them *in their hands* as mothers or nurses carry little children with care and tenderness. The devil quoted that scripture (Matt. 4:6) but left out that which made against him, *in all thy ways*. When we are asleep the angels are watching over us, else we should soon be a prey to the powers of darkness.

iii. The angels teach and instruct the saints as the prophets (Dan. 10:21), and Zechariah often. How far truths may be brought to the understanding of the Lord's people by the ministry of angels we know not. Angels have great knowledge, [and are] full of eyes (Rev. 4:8). The devil we are sure is to many a lying spirit, and a spirit of error, and is there not as quick an access to our spirits for the good angels as for the evil? And have not they as much love for us as the evil angels have enmity against us? An angel was Philip's guide (Acts 8:26). Not that we are to expect visions and revelations as formerly the saints had, but ordinary instructions, furthering the means of our salvation, not to supersede the Scriptures of truth. Angels suggest that is the way.[7]

iv. The angels comfort and excite the souls of God's people, persuasively. They have certainly as much power to move us to duty as devils have to tempt us to sin. They are no further off us nor less able to hurt us, and it appears that they have a great good will to the children of men in that they rejoice in the conversion of sinners (Luke 15:10), and are present in the congregations of God's people (1 Cor. 11:10) where they are not idle spectators. Not that they take the work of Christ or the Spirit out of their hands but

7. There is a marginal note *Turretin* against this paragraph. This is probably an indication that this paragraph represents a position taken by this post-Reformation scholar.

are used by them as ministers which doth not at all derogate from the honour of God. There is no loss of the presence or efficacy of God for the service of angels.[8]

v. The angels convey the departing soul into the bosom of Abraham (Luke 16:22), though a poor beggar full of sores. *Angels* – not one but many, as if there were a strife among them who should carry it. Amasis of Egypt had his chariot drawn by four kings but what's that to Lazarus' triumph? If the soul be conveyed through the airy inferior region where the prince of darkness had his dominion how safely will it *charge* through the infernal hosts rather as in triumph than as in battle, under such a convoy? Thus they can never perish (John 10:28).

vi. The angels shall gather the saints together at that great day, not only as Christ's servants but as the saints' friends (Matt. 24:31; Mark 13:27), so exactly that none shall be missing from that πανήγυρις.[9] He has given his angels charge concerning them and then they shall deliver up their charge. An end will hereby be put to their ministrations. They will no longer need to wait upon them in a troublesome world when they shall have landed them all safely in everlasting rest.

Show 2. What kind of ministers the angels are to the saints.

a. They are strong, mighty angels (2 Thess. 1:7), great in power and might (2 Pet. 2:1). Strong indeed when one angel in one

---

8. Against this paragraph there is a marginal note: Baxter, Rutherford, Ambrose, Hall. This probably indicates that these Christian writers shared the view taken in this paragraph. Richard Baxter (1615–1691) was a Puritan writer who was a favourite with Matthew Henry. Samuel Rutherford (1600–1661) was an eminent Scottish minister, professor and writer. Isaac Ambrose (1604–64) was a Puritan minister who was ejected in 1662. Among his other writings was his work entitled *War with Devils – Ministration of Angels* (1661). Joseph Hall (1574–1656) was Bishop of Norwich. His book *Heaven upon Earth* (1606) was reprinted by John Wesley in his Christian Library.

9. Greek, 'a festival assembly'. Though a classical Greek word, it only occurs once in the New Testament in Heb. 12:22.

night slew 165 thousand of the Assyrians. [They] excel in strength (Ps. 103:20). We are weak for work, for conflicts, but the angels are strong, so that they that be with us are more than they that be with them, and more powerful (2 Kings 6:16). Principalities and powers are against us, but if the angels be for us principalities and powers are for us too. Angels are *the chariots of God* (Ps. 68:17), the militia of heaven. The militia of the times consisted much of chariots.

b. They are swift. They are ready to and quick in their ministrations. [They] always *behold the face of the Father* (Matt. 18:10), ready to receive the least hint or intimation of the divine will and pleasure. They are represented with wings (Isa. 6:2), fly swiftly (Dan. 9:21), like a flash of lightning (Ezek. 1:14). Our dangers are often sudden, our enemies near, but then the ministering spirits are not far off. They had not the clog of the bodies as we have. They are a flame of fire.

c. They are unanimous. When servants quarrel, one draws one way and another t'other, the work is not likely to go on, but it is not so among the heavenly hosts. The God of peace makes and keeps peace in his high places (Job 25:2). Though they are thousands of thousands yet they are all of a mind in doing the will of God (see Ezek. 1:9, 10, 12, like a disciplined army). The many angels that have the charge of the saints are called *the Angel* (Ps. 34:7).

d. They are unseen, viz. to bodily eyes. □They minister to us and we know it not. Our eyes see our teachers, but these teachers we see not, though they are not far from us. Their *hands* were *under their wings* (Ezek. 1:8). What they do is without noise or notice. They come not with observation. If you ask after their names as Manoah did, *it is secret* (Jude 13:18). The kindnesses they do us are not so discernible. The ministry of angels is in the sea and in the great waters. He makes his angels wind – so some [interpret it] – because you canst not tell whence it comes nor whither it goes.

e. They are condescending. 'Tis a great piece of condescension in the holy angels to minister for us mean creatures as we are, nay so sinful, in a world of so much sin and folly – to carry the soul of a Lazarus to heaven. 'Tis condescension for the inhabitants of the upper world to have any thing to do in this lower region – and yet they never repine[10] it. We should be so to our brethren.

f. They are constant – never discouraged from or tired with their work. They never leave the saints nor neglect their office. They keep us *in all our ways*. We are often tired with our work but the angels never faint nor worry. They have a spirit that is willing and no flesh to weaken them. They *always* behold the face of the Father, ministering continually – [there is] nothing to divert them or to disturb them. They are undaunted in their ministrations, never weary of doing the will of God. [They] rest not day nor night (Rev. 4:8).

Applic[ation] 1. Do not abuse this doctrine, as the Papists who from hence justify their practice of praying to the angels, and giving divine honour to them. The sun, moon and stars were worshipped by the heathen because of the great benefit that the world has by them, but still the sun is שֶׁמֶשׁ[11] a servant (Deut. 4:19). So the angels [are worshipped] by the Papists. Colossians 2:18 is express against it, and Revelation 19:10; 22:9 is most express. Angels are our fellow-servants, [and] therefore not to be worshipped. 'Tis robbing God of his due (Matt. 4:10). Many testimonies are produced against it from the primitive church. Nor should we covet any visible or sensible communion with angels. That's to expect an alteration of God's stated government. Should he go out of the way for us? The appearance of angels to us would rather affright and confound us, and leave us in doubt whether it might not be an illusion, for Satan can transform himself into an angel of light but this spiritual communion is much more agreeable to our present state.

2. Use this doctrine [in] three ways.

---

10. *Repine*, 'complain', 'fret'.

11. Hebrew, 'sun'.

a. For your instruction. Are the angels ministering spirits for the good of the Lord's people?

i. Then the saints are a very happy and a very honourable people – that have such attendants. *Lord, what is man* (Ps. 8:4)? Happy the people that is in such a case. Honour the saints accordingly. Let the people of God be precious to you. 'Tis the character of a citizen of Zion that he honours those that fear the Lord, and have we not reason to honour them? Let it be proclaimed before all the saints, 'Thus shall it be done to the man whom the King of Heaven delights to honour'. This should oblige us to be truly godly, and to get into the covenant with God. Though this honour do not look gay in the eyes of the world yet it will look great shortly.

ii. Then wicked people that go on in wicked ways are in a sad condition – for they have no benefit by the ministration of angels. The angels are their enemies, and have been enemies to sinful man ever since (Gen. 3:24) when the cherubim was set, and will be so till they are reconciled to God. Do you think the holy angels will minister for the good of those that are wallowing in their sins and lusts? They are pure beings, and cannot endure to look upon iniquity. Their delight is in loving and praising God and will they attend upon those that slight and forget him? Let this consideration persuade you out of love with your sins.

iii. Then blessed be God for Jesus Christ, for it is in him that the angels are our friends. He's the ladder upon which the angels *ascend* and *descend* (Gen. 28:12; comp[are] John 1:51), ascend to give an account of their ministration, and to receive new orders, and to carry up departing souls, descend to minister to the saints. All our intercourse with heaven is through Christ. 'Twas he that removed the cherubim and the flaming sword. 'Tis in Christ that things in heaven and things on earth are brought together (Eph. 1:10). He's the captain of the hosts.

b. For your comfort and encouragement if you be *true* believers. This makes much for the consolation that the angels are ministering spirits for your good. When angels appeared to saints the first word was, *Fear not*. 'Tis in a special manner comfortable

i. when we are in imminent perils and dangers by night or by day, going out or coming in, in journeys by sea or land. The great comfort is that the Lord keeps us (Gen. 24:7, 40), but it is withal comfortable that the angels are ministering spirits for our preservation. They have a charge concerning us, and they are and will be mindful of their charge. If God would but open our eyes (2 Kings 6:17)! They are always ready to us, provided we keep close to the way of duty, and do not tempt God.

ii. when we are buffeted by Satan's temptations, terrified with that roaring lion, the ministry of angels is very refreshing. Michael and his angels will prevail over the dragon. Triumph in this, that there's more with us than against us. God is able and faithful (1 Cor. 10:13), but he has given us the ministry of angels for the encouragement of our faith in him, to strengthen our confidence in his almighty power. God is able to keep what we have committed to him, and these secondary aids should be buttresses to our hope.

iii. when we suffer for righteousness' sake. The angels are in a special manner employed to minister to the saints then, as to the apostles (Acts 5:19, Peter; Acts 12:7). [There are] many instances in the histories of the martyrs. No prisons can keep out angels. John in Patmos had the sweetest converse with the angel, [as did] Elijah (1 Kings 19:4, 5).

iv. when we come to die. The attendance of the angels about our death-beds should make them sweet and easy. To think of the convey we shall have to glory! Though poor and sickly, and deformed, yet if we belong to Christ we shall be carried into everlasting habitations, like Elijah with the chariots of fire and horses of fire (2 Kings 2:11).

c. For your direction. This doctrine speaks a great deal of duty. Learn it and do it.

i. Acquaint yourselves with the relation we stand in to the angels, as belonging to the same family of which Christ is the head (Eph. 3:15). Our immortal souls being spiritual beings are akin to angels, lower though but little lower (Ps. 8:5). [We are] much more if sanctified and renewed after the image of God. Angels are the sons of God, so are the saints. We are fellow servants. Angels having the charge of the saints doubtless have a special love to them. They are the inhabitants of that city which we are heirs to. We are come to an innumerable company of angels (Heb. 12:22).

ii. Bless God for the ministration of angels and pray for the continuance of it. Look upon it as part of Christ's purchase for true believers and prize it accordingly. Let your prayers and praises terminate not in the angels but in the Lord of the angels. We receive and need the benefit of the ministration of angels more then we are aware of every day, [for] 'tis God's good pleasure that they fulfil. In signal deliverances though the sovereign power of God is to be principally eyed, we must not forget to be thankful for the ministry of angels in them (Dan. 6:22).

iii. Do nothing to forfeit the ministration of angels. Do not put yourselves out of their protection by withdrawing from the allegiance to the sovereign prince. Keep close to and constant in the way of your duty. Ask, Am I in Christ? Am I in my way and then it's well enough (Dod)?[12] Walk as becomes the heir of salvation. Do nothing unworthy of your hopes, for then you forfeit the ministry of angels. Keep yourselves in the love of God. Do not make him your enemy for then angels cannot be your friends.

---

12. The reference is to Henry Dodwell 'the elder' (1641–1711). He was noted as a scholar of the early church fathers, and he also edited the posthumous writings of John Pearson (1613–86) including his *Exposition of the Creed.*

iv. Converse much in your thoughts with the world of angels, [for this] 'twould help to make heaven familiar to us. 'Twould raise our adorations of the Lord Jesus to think of him thus attended. If it seem but a small matter that he is the head of the church on earth, think of him as head of the angels, worshipped by them (Heb. 1:4, 6). When we see the badness and baseness of this world, think how desirable the world of angels is among whom there's perfect holiness and harmony. When we come so short in our praises think how the angels do it (Ps. 103:20, 21).

v. Walk with a reverence of the presence of the angels especially in the worship of God. It should awe us into a seriousness. See 1 Corinthians 11:10. Be not guilty of errors before the angels (Eccles. 5:6). That's an awful charge (1 Tim. 5:21, *before the elect angels*). Especially, think how serious they are in the praises of God (Isa. 6:2, 3).

vi. Labour to do the will of God as the angels do. We are taught to pray so, and must endeavour it accordingly. As they minister to us we should minister to one another, [and] do what good we can to each other. A life of praise and a life of usefulness is a true angelical life. Do it from love to God as they do it. Be free to it, be fervent in it as they are. Thus our conversation should be in heaven. Desire and endeavour that earth may be like heaven.

vii. Long to be like the angels, and with the angels in the kingdom of heaven. Glorified saints are like the angels (Luke 20:36), and is not that desirable? Should not we press after the society and work of angels? Who that has any acquaintance with the angels and any hopes of being with them would be in love with such a world as this? Long to converse with them immediately, to stand with them in your lot at the end of your days.

11

Creatures in the Covenant

1 May 1692

11. CREATURES IN THE COVENANT

– for all things are yours, whether Paul, or Apollos, or Cephas, or the world, or life – or things present (1 Cor. 3:21, 22).

The Apostle is here dealing with those that disturbed the peace of the church by quarrelling about ministers, saying, *I am of Paul* – verse 4, and having *men's persons in admiration* (Jude 16). To shame them out of it he here tells them what little reason they had to dote upon one since they were all theirs, and not ministers only but other things, which with his usual fluency of expression he here reckons up, and sums up the particulars in a comprehensive general – *all are yours,* which is grounded upon this, *you are Christ's.* 'Tis therefore too mean a thing for you to glory thus in any creature. It's below a Christian thus enriched to adore any creature, since all is for the church's sake (2 Cor. 4:15).

The text is a true, and (allowing for the comprehensiveness of some of the particulars) a *perfect* inventory of the personal estate of the church, and of all those that belong to Christ. Though God hath chosen the poor (Jas. 2:5) and the base (1 Cor. 1:28), yet all [is] yours. 'Tis one of the Apostle's paradoxes (2 Cor. 6:10), *as having nothing and yet possessing all things*, and the text will help us to unriddle it.

1. Ministers are yours – *Paul and Apollos and Cephas* – three of the most prominent lights of the church put for all the rest because these were names that were abused by the Corinthians in their party making. [They were] variously gifted and endowed, Paul for enriched knowledge, Apollos for eloquence, Cephas for courage – but *all* [are] *yours*, servants of Christ for your good – as angels. If Paul and Apollos and Cephas, such great men, be yours, much more ordinary ministers whom you so much cry up.

He takes off the excessive respect to their ministers by the same argument that Christ urges against the Pharisees, superstitious regard to the Sabbath day (Mark 2:27). *The Sabbath was made for man and not man for the Sabbath.* Ministers were made for you and not you for them. *They have no dominion over your faith* (2 Cor. 1:24) yet to preserve your due esteem of your ministers notwithstanding he subjoins chapter 4:1, *let a man account of us as ministers of Christ.*

Note: That it is the privilege of those that are in covenant with God that Christ's ministers are theirs – theirs to do them good according to the utmost of their ability and opportunity. Theirs in the same sense that other *ordinances* are theirs – theirs as instruments that God ordinarily uses for the beginning and carrying on of the good work – theirs to intrust and teach them, to pray with them and for them, to direct and warn and comfort them – theirs as stewards to give them their portion of meat – theirs as shepherds to lead them into the green pastures – theirs as watchmen to give them warning – theirs as guides, overseers, to go before them.

a. Ministers are given by Christ to the church. They are the fruits of his ascension, love tokens that he left to his church, when he went to heaven (Eph. 4:8, 11, 12). God has set them there (1 Cor. 12:28). He gave them to be subservient to his glory in the administration of his mediatorial kingdom, as Prophet, Priest and King. The Father sent Christ and he sends his ministers (John 20:21, *as my Father*). [This is] not meant of an equality of power but a similitude of mission. The Father with his commission gave him qualifications. So Christ gifts those whom he sends. Therefore it follows there verse 22, *Receive ye the Holy Ghost.*

b. Ministers have given themselves to the church – devoted and dedicated their whole selves to the good of the church – and the edifying of the body. We preach ourselves *your servants*, without a complement (2 Cor. 4:5). All that are faithful have done so – willing to spend and be spent for you.

Int[roduction] 1. This speaks duty to ministers. Were I to preach to a congregation of such, how might I press them from hence to seek the good and welfare of souls – to study the edification of the body – those that do not do so defeat the design of the donor – and frustrate the intent of their commission. The Lord helps us all to write after Paul's copy – *not lording it over God's heritage* (1 Pet. 5:2, 3).

2. It speaks duty to the people. If ministers be yours,

a. Learn what value to put upon your minister. They are yours, your servants, for the good of souls and you are to make neither to deify them not to vilify them. Receive them as the fruits of Christ's ascension. Bless God for them. *Esteem them highly in love* (1 Thess. 5:12, 13), not for their person's sake but *for their work's sake*.
b. Learn what use to make of your ministers. Improve by their ministry. Do not receive the grace of God herein in vain. *Enquire at their mouth* (Mal. 2:7).

3. The *world* is yours, and *things present*. Of all things one would think there were least reason to put this into the inventory. Those that are Christ's have commonly so little of the world, and meet with so much hardship and opposition and persecution in it, and yet *the world is yours*. Not only [is] heaven yours shortly but the world now, though you are called out of the world. Abraham as the father of the faithful is called the heir of the world (Rom. 4:13) though he was never possest of more ground than a burying place. So his spiritual seed. That covenant of grace, *I will be a God to you* (Gen. 17:7) is enough to restore all God's covenant people to their original possessions, which Adam by sin had forfeited. *Things present*, i.e. the things of this world, things seen that are temporal and sensible; not only Paul and Apollos, the gifts of the prime luminaries of the church, but the common gifts of the world.

Doct[rine] That it is the unspeakable privilege of all those that are Christ's that the *world* is theirs, and things present.

[It's] theirs in possession, that's certain. Dominion and propriety are not founded in grace. We preach no such levelling doctrine. The worst of men we know as men have a kind of a title to that which we have in the world. Though Balaam was a wicked man, yet his ass confesses once and again that he was his (Num. 22:30), and therefore property is not to be invaded upon any *such* pretence. The Word of God sufficiently witnesses against such irregular practices (see Luke 12:13). We see *the earth given* (by providence*) into the hands of the wicked* (Job 9:24). How then is it said that the world belongs to those that are Christ's? 'Tis theirs not κτήσει[1] but χρήσει.[2] 'Tis theirs i.e. 'tis for their good – for their sake's, for their use.

Show 1. How and in what sense the world is theirs. It may be understood:

a. Of the church of God in general – considered as a complex body. 'Tis Christ's – his spouse, his fold, his family, his kingdom, continued in succession from generation to generation and the world is for the church. Christ is head over all them *to the church* (Eph. 1:22).

i. The continuance of the world is for the church. The world stands to this day for the church's sake. There are chosen vessels that are yet to be born in the world which belong to the election of grace, other sheep that must be brought in (John 10:16), much people [who are] yet uncalled (Acts 18:10). If all that belong to the election were effectually called in, the world would be set on fire presently. The world stands as the dressing room of the lamb's wife. While any remain uncalled she's unready (Rev. 19:7). When the mystical body is completed, the intermediate counsels of

1. Greek, 'by possession' (Acts 7:5).
2. Greek, 'by use' (Rom. 1:26).

God's love concerning the church accomplished, then cometh the end. The world is reprieved as condemned women with child, not for the sake of the guilty mother, but the innocent babe in her womb. The wicked world is therefore not destroyed because there is *a blessing in it* (Isa. 65:8). There's a promise of new heavens and new earth in the future state.

ii. The inferior creatures are for the church, all put under the feet of Christ as head of the church (Heb. 2:8), and many times these hosts of the Lord have been pressed into the service of the church – *the stars in their courses* (Jude 5:20) and many other instances. As far as sin and wickedness prevails the whole creation groans, as in slavery (Rom. 8:22), but when the church flourisheth *the field is joyful* (Ps. 96:12). 'Twas for the church's sake that the curse which sin brought upon the creation is far removed, as it is, and the ground blessed, otherwise it had never brought forth any thing perhaps but thorns and thistles (Gen. 3:17, 18 comp[are] Gen. 8:21; 9:9, 10). 'Tis for the church that God makes a covenant with the beasts of the field (Hos. 2:18).

iii. The government of kingdoms and nations is for the church. The Scripture takes little notion of the kingdoms of the world or the affairs of them further than the church was some way or other concerned in them, for God's common providence is for the special good of the church (2 Chron. 16:9). In ordering other affairs he consults the advantage of his church (Deut. 32:8) and the reason [is] rendered (v. 9). When heaven and earth are shaken, political heights and powers translated, 'tis with a design to introduce and establish the things that cannot be shaken (Hag. 2:6, 7; Heb. 12:26, 27; see Dan. 2:44, 45). Cyrus was raised for the church's good (Isa. 45:1-13). In all the amazing revolutions of states and kingdoms the Lord is founding Zion (Isa. 14:32). The providential kingdom is twisted in with the mediatorial kingdom. All judgment of this kind [is] committed to the Son. He has the heathen given him (Ps. 2:8; 22:28). All power is committed to him in heaven and in earth (Matt. 28:18), in the church and in the world – *[therefore I will give] men for you* (Isa. 43:4).

iv. The common gifts of wicked worldly men are for the church. The wit and learning and policy of such is given them for the church's good, as the workman strengthens and sharpens his instrument for the sake of the work he intends to do with it. God designs Egyptian wealth for tabernacle service. The earth is often made to help the woman (Rev. 12:16), not out of any love for the church but from some other principle, in pursuance of some design of their own – as Isaiah 15:4. Howbeit they mean no such thing (Isa. 10:7). The improvements that have been made by the children of this world in useful learning was for the church's good. The skill of the Tyrians was for building the temple.

v. The church will judge and condemn the world at the great day in subordination to Christ. The saints shall judge the world (1 Cor. 6:2). Thus the world is theirs, for the upright shall have dominion (Ps. 49:14). 'Tis theirs in reversion.[3] They shall judge the world not by convicting the criminals or giving the judgment. That's Christ's work, but by approving and applauding the sentence. They will help to stop the mouths of sinners and to render them inexcusable.

Thus the world is given to the church. These glorious things are spoken of the city of our God (Ps. 87:3, 4). It's good embarking with Sion's interests:

b. Of particular believers. *The world,* i.e. *things present*, the good things of the world, are theirs. Godliness has the promise of the life that now is (1 Tim. 4:8). The world is so theirs that if it were necessary to their happiness that they should have possession of all the world they should have it.

---

3. *reversion*, an archaic term for 'the residue', 'the remainder'.

'Tis not easy to understand how the world belongs to God's people. They have not their portion in it. 'Tis not their treasure. They are delivered from it, and yet still it's theirs. That is,

i. They have and shall have as much of it as infinite wisdom sees good for them. Some have more, others less. Some have five talents, others two, but each according *to his several ability* (Matt. 25:15). Those that have never so little of the things of the world yet have that which God sees best for them, he knows our frame, our temper, our distemper. What temptations would be too hard for us? If the wise God had seen what we have too little, he would have given us such and such things (2 Sam. 12:8). God sometimes gives abundance of the world to his covenant people especially in OT times – as Abraham, however Jehovah-jireh.[4] See Psalm 37:3, 25. They shall not want (Ps. 23:1). The Lord is for the body.

ii. What they have they hold by a good title, be it little or much, the tenant's good, and that's a desirable thing. 'Tis the gift of God, in Christ. 'Tis an honourable title, they hold *in capito,*[5] in Christ their head. 'Tis a sweet, a sure title. 'Tis an unquestionable indefeasible title. They hold all by the promise – and a promise without possession is better than profession without [the] promise. Their good things are dispensed to them not out of the basket of common providence, but out of the ark of the covenant. *God give thee dew of heaven* (Gen. 27:28).

iii. What they have comes from love. They have their daily bread from God as a *Father*. This love is it that makes a dinner of herbs better than a stalled ox (Prov. 15:17). 'Tis not like the food provided for a malefactor reprieved to keep him alive for execution but like the food provided for a child under age to keep him alive for the inheritance. 'Tis the love of God that sweetens all their enjoyments and

4. Hebrew, 'The LORD will see [to it]'.
5. Latin, 'in the head'.

makes creature comforts comforts indeed. [He] gives to *his beloved sleep* (Ps. 127:2).

iv. What they have they have with a blessing. The basket and the store [are] blessed (Deut. 28:4, 5). The Lord commands the blessing. 'Tis the blessing of the Lord that so makes rich as to add *no* sorrow with it (Prov. 10:22). The *habitation* of the just is blessed (Prov. 3:33). Though but a poor mean dwelling, yet it's sanctified with the blessing of God.

v. What they have is clean to them – *to you all things are pure* (Titus 1:15). All lawful things are lawful to them. The pollution which sin has brought upon the creatures is taken off to them by the blood of Christ (Rom. 14:20; all clean, Luke 11:41). Under the law there were several creatures that were by a ceremonial appointment unclean, and might not be eaten of, yet ceremonial uncleanness is removed for all. Nothing is now to be refused (Acts 10:15), but there is still a moral defilement of the creature for all whose mind and conscience is defiled. See 1 Timothy 4:4, 5, *sanctifed*, viz. to them who being in covenant with God will and should use it for God. Thus the *unbelieving wife is sanctified to the husband* (1 Cor. 7:14), sanctified by the Word and prayer to those that have faith to eye the word and make the prayer.

vi. What they have is comfortable to them. God gives them to rejoice in it (Eccles. 5:19). The *world* is theirs because they are content with what they have. Those have all that have enough. Godliness with contentment is all the wealth in the world (1 Tim. 6:6 and v. 8; having food and a *covering* τούτοις ἀρκεσθησόμεθα.[6] *In these we shall have enough* – so Dr Ham[mond].[7] We Christians shall in

6. Greek, 'with these we shall be content'.

7. The reference seems to be to Dr Henry Hammond (1605–1660). He was an Anglican minister and scholar, and though nominated to the Westminster Assembly, did not take his seat. In 1653 he published his *Paraphrases and Annotations of the NewTestament.*

this be sufficiently provided for. He's not to be reckoned rich that has much but he that has enough. 'Tis the privilege of those that are in covenant with God that they have enough to content them though they have but little in the world (Eccles. 9:7). Agur's wish is food convenient (Prov. 30:8), and that's enough and enough.

vii. What they have is an opportunity of glorifying God and doing good. The *world* is *theirs* for it helps them forward in their way, and is improvable for holy and heavenly purposes, to honour God with (Prov. 3:9, 10), to serve their generation, to make friends of (Luke 16:9). Grace is the true philosopher's stone that turns all into gold, enjoys God in all, glorifies God with all, in eating and drinking (1 Cor. 10:31). Creatures to the saints are instruments of holiness.

viii. What they have of the world will serve to bear their charges through it to a better. The world is theirs, not for their portion, but for their passage, and when they are got through it they will be above it, and have no need of it. The world is so theirs that they shall not want bread to eat, and raiment to put on till they come to their Father's house in peace (Gen. 28:20, 21). The world is theirs to go through as Israel through the wilderness to Canaan. It serves them as an inn upon the road till they come home. *Things present* are their spending money.

Show 2. How come the saints to have such an interest in the world that it should be theirs.

a. It's theirs by promise. Godliness has the promise even of the life that now is (1 Tim. 4:8). These promises [are] to be understood with the usual proviso as far as is for God's glory and our own good. The meek shall inherit the earth (Ps. 37:11). Nay, it's a NT promise (Matt. 5:5). Wisdom (that is, Christ) is brought in proffering her largesses, and see what they are (Prov. 3:16). Either outward prosperity is not good for us, or we shall have it. Many a one has lived upon the promises in the want of other good things (Ps. 37:3, *pasceris fide*[8]). Thou shall be fed by faith. There have been strange instances of God's providing for his people in want. Send providence to market.

b. It's theirs by conquest. Christ has conquered it for them (John 16:33), and they conquer it by faith in his victory (1 John 5:4). Nay, they are more than conquerors (Rom. 8:37). Faith so conquers the world as not only to prevent our getting hurt by it but to enable us to do good with it. This is dividing the spoils (Luke 11:22). The world is an enemy. [It] has slain its thousands, but it's given into the hands of believers conquered. Christian, to the spoil! Those that by faith have got the world under their feet have it in its place, as a servant in subjection. Men of the world are slaves to it. Better have one servant obeying than many ruling.

c. It's theirs by marriage. Jesus Christ is heir of all things. All [is] put under his feet. True believers being espoused to him, are interested in all that he hath. The wife has an interest in all the husband's possessions though she have them not all in her closet, or under her management. The world is yours, for you are *Christ's*. Thence arises the title.

Use 1. If this be so then *godliness is profitable unto all things* (1 Tim. 4:8). Let this recommend to your love and esteem that which so many despise and persecute, godliness. 'Tis the way to make us happy in both worlds. It appears by this that religion and piety is the best friend to outward prosperity and yet the way of serious godliness brings outward blessing along with it. *The Lord is for the body* (1 Cor. 6:13). Let this help to keep up the credit of godliness among you.

2. – then, *a little that a righteous man hath is better than riches of many wicked* (Ps. 37:16), a godly man's little better than a wicked man's much – better for him – sweeter and safer – every

8. Latin, 'you shall feed by faith'.

way better. Upon this account the righteous is *more excellent than his neighbour*. Those are rich that are rich towards God, for the *world* is theirs. Esau had *much*, that had Mount Seir for a possession, but Jacob (though all his estate lay in a drove or two of cattle) had *all* (Gen. 33:9, 11).

3. – then *let not thine heart envy sinners* (Prov. 23:17). Do not envy them the large share they have of outward prosperity, more than heart could wish, that which is all their happiness is the least part of the saints' happiness, and that is the world – and what they have they have no title to, no comfort in. They have it but they have it with a curse. Nothing is pure to them.

4. – *then seek first the kingdom of God and the righteousness thereof* (Matt. 6:33). Mind the soul in the first place. Soul-prosperity will either bring outward prosperity along with it or will sweeten the want of it. In all your choosings let the concernments of the soul determine the choice. Do not say, 'Make sure the world and for grace hope for the best', but make sure grace and hope for the best for the world, for godliness has the promise of the life that now is, but the life that now is hath not the promise of godliness. Let it be your first care to make that sure which will be made sure.

5. – then *use the world as not abusing it* (1 Cor. 7:31). You will not abuse that which your own. The world is yours. Don't abuse it. The world is abused when it's put to other uses than 'twas intended for – to a higher use, as when it's suffered to rule the soul, to a baser use as when it's made to serve the lusts, and becomes food or fuel to them. This makes the creation groan.

6. – then *let your conversation be without covetousness, and be content with such things as you have* (Heb. 13:5). Be satisfied with the world as far as it is yours in the promise, and be not eager in grasping after the possession. Whatever your condition is bring your minds to it. He's an insatiable man indeed that will not be satisfied with all.

To conclude. If you be Christ's, the world is yours, but:

1. You that have much of it, enjoy God in all. 'Tis infinitely more to you that God is yours than that the world is yours. Glorify God with your abundance. Let not your delight terminate in the creature. Acknowledge God's goodness, all this and heaven too, and do not we serve a good Master? The more you have of the world the more God expects from you (Prov. 6:9, 10).

2. You that have little of it, enjoy all in God. The less you have the less you have to account for at the great day. The less you have the more loose you should sit to it. Cast all your care upon God. He will provide for you and yours. Leave your fatherless children in the covenant, and then the world is theirs. They cannot want. You'll have never the less glory in t'other world for your having but little wealth in this world.

12

Afflictions in the Covenant

8 May 1692

12. AFFLICTIONS IN THE COVENANT

If his children forsake my law, and walk not in my judgments; if they break my statutes, and keep not my commandments; then will I visit their transgression with the rod and their iniquity with stripes. Nevertheless my loving kindness will I not utterly take from him, nor suffer my righteousness to fail (Ps. 89:30, 31, 32, 33).

'Twas a very dismal time with the church of God when this Psalm was penned. The hedges [were] broken down and the strongholds brought to ruin, etc. (v. 38, 40, etc.), but the design of it is to comfort and encourage the church's friends notwithstanding, and the comfort is drawn from the covenant. Whither else shall we go for comfort but to that covenant in which 'tis treasured up? 'Tis sometimes hard to reconcile providence with promises – and the cross with the covenant. This stumbled Gideon (Jude 6:13).

Now the text will help to reconcile them at such a time. Faith should be acted upon that part of the covenant which will direct us to put a right construction upon providences – our disquietments are commonly grounded upon our mistakes.

The covenant of grace is here set before us in the language of the covenant of royalty which was a figure of it, the everlasting covenant made with David as the type (2 Sam. 23:5) but with Christ as the antitype. He is called David (Hos. 3:5; Jer. 30:9) and that passage v. 26, 27 is applied to Christ (Heb. 1:5). The text hath reference to 2 Samuel 7:14, 15, but that which is there supposed concerning Solomon, *if he commit iniquity,* is here applied not to Christ but to the saints, *if his children forsake*, though Christ was made *sin* for us (2 Cor. 5:21).

Observe:

1. A supposition of sin committed (vv. 30, 31), set forth in a variety of expression, and yet no tautology – like that in Hebrews 8:12 – *unrighteousness, sins, iniquities*, omissions and commissions – *forsake my law, and walk not.*

2. Warning [is] given of correction for that sin – *then will I visit.* There are visits in mercy but this is spoken of a visit in wrath and displeasure. They shall be sure to smart for it, and that sharply – *the rod of men* (2 Sam. 7:14).

3. An assurance of the continuance of the covenant love and truth notwithstanding (v. 33, *nevertheless*). Neither the one nor the other shall break the covenant.

   a. The covenant with Christ shall not be broken by it – *my loving kindness will I not take from him*, i.e. the promise made to Christ of the advancement of his kingdom shall not be defeated by the apostasy of some that professed relation to him. Though some forsake him yet others shall cleave to him – *though Israel be not gathered* (Isa. 49:5). Observe a change of the plan, from *him.* Christ will have a name above every name for all this.
   b. The covenant with the saints shall not be broken by it. The covenant of works made no provision in case of sin. By that covenant, *If his children forsake my law*, I will cast them off and never have more to do with them. But the covenant of grace provides a remedy in such a case (1 John 2:1, 2). The loving kindness shall not be taken from *him*, i.e. from Christ the head, in whom 'tis treasured up, by whom and for whose sake it is conveyed.

Doct[rine] That the covenant of grace hath enough in it to secure the comfort of Christ's children under the greatest afflictions they may meet with in this world.

I put the doctrine thus general that under it I may take all that in the covenant (as it is here set down) relating to afflictions. Only two or three things must be promised as implied in the text.

1. That true believers are the *children* of the Lord Jesus Christ. He is the everlasting Father (Isa. 9:6; Heb. 2:13). They are called his children because he transacts for them as the father for the child. Adam was a common father to all mankind and in him we all die. Christ the Second Adam, [is] a common father to all believers and in him they are all made alive (1 Cor. 15:22). They are *the seed* that was promised him (Isa. 53:10). He owns them for his children, provides for them (John 21:5), disposeth of them, takes up when father and mother forsake. He will present them to his Father at the great day as his children in his right to be put in possession of the inheritance.

2. That even Christ's children do sometimes fall into sin. There are spots that are the *spots* of God's children (Deut. 32:5). Sins of infirmity – overtaken in a fault – not allowing themselves in it, but bewailing it, mourning over it. [There is] no such thing as sinless perfection in this life (1 John 1:8). We read of Noah's drunkenness, Lot's incest, David's adultery and murder, Peter's denying his Master, yet the saints as far as they are born of God cannot sin – but 'tis the other law in their members. This should not encourage us to sin (Rom. 6:1). Those that from hence infer that they may have peace though they go on [in sin] are none of Christ's children. That's covenanting with death. But this should make us jealous over ourselves (1 Cor. 10:12), and encourage us when we have sinned to repent.

3. That Christ's children meet with affliction in this world. 'Tis a truth that needs no proof. Our own experience sufficiently seals to it – *waters of a full cup are wrung out to them* (Ps. 73:10). Afflictions are various, in the body, name, estate, relations. You are all sensible of your afflictions and can soon point to the sore place. Those of you that have little to trouble, you at present should hear for the time to come. Lay up cordials in store. Now the covenant of grace is the great comfort of God's people. The promises of the covenant are your songs (Ps. 119:54, 62), even when the house is not so with God (2 Sam. 23:5). 'Tis a salve for

every sore. My business today is to open it, and 'twill lie upon you to apply it.

[There are] several things in the covenant to sweeten affliction, and make that ours.

1. Affliction to true believers is but a *rod – visit their transgressions with the rod* – a rod, not an axe, not a sword – for correction not for destruction. Sin turned the rod into a serpent but the covenant of grace turns it into a rod again. 'Tis said of wicked people that there's no *rod* of God upon them (Job 21:9). The reason is because God has a sword in store for them or if a rod 'tis a rod of iron (Ps. 2:9) to break in pieces. 'Tis a rod, yet note:

   a. Gentleness in the affliction. He corrects in measure (Jer. 30:11; Isa. 27:8) like the refiner's fire, not the destroyers fire. Like physic[1] for a child, in exact proportion, not as poison for noxious creatures, without measure. 'Tis *the rod of men* – so the parallel, see 2 Samuel 7:14, i.e. such a rod as men may wield. The rod of אֲנָשִׁים,[2] a weak man that cannot strike hard. When God comes to destroy, he threatens, I will not meet you as a man (Isa. 47:3). When he comes to correct he meets as a man, doth not put forth all his power.

   Or, *the rod of men*, i.e. such a rod as men may bear. [There is] no temptation but such as is common to men (1 Cor. 10:13). He considers our frame (Ps. 78:38, 39; 103:13, 14). 'Tis not the rod of devils, but the rod of men, weak men that cannot bear much. God is Lord of his anger.

   Stripes, or touches – that break no bones – some sensible [which] smart for the present, but do no great hurt. Not wounds, only stripes.

   b. Good [is] intended us by the affliction. A rod is to give wisdom, and to drive out the folly. The execution of a malefactor is not

1. *Physic* is an old word for 'medicine' or 'drugs'.
2. Hebrew, 'men'.

for his good, but to ease the country, and terrify others, but the correction of a child is for his good and amendment, not to cut him off from the inheritance but to fit him for it. The rod has a voice (Mic. 6:9). 'שֵׁבֶט טוֹב,[3] a sceptre of rule for good. 'Tis a shepherd's rod (Mic. 7:14; Ps. 23:4).

The rod of affliction is like Aaron's rod that budded and brought forth fruit. Though unlikely, afterwards it yieldeth the peaceable fruit (Heb. 12:11).

– Well, learn by what names to call your afflictions. Call them a *rod*. We are apt to make the worst of our afflictions. When sin sits light, crosses sit heavy, and we miscall them. Hear the rod. Kiss the rod. Be thankful it's not worse.

2. 'Tis a rod in the hand of God – *I will visit*, I that am in covenant with them. As this sweetens creature comforts yet they are God's sending so it sweetens crosses likewise and makes them easy, yet they come from his hand. The rod of the wicked shall not rest (Ps. 125:3). No, 'tis the rod of a good God. David desires to fall into the hands of the Lord (2 Sam. 24:1), and yet (Heb. 10:31) 'tis a fearful thing to fall into the hands of God as an avenging judge, but desirable to fall into the hands of God as a Father.

He that lays the rod upon us is God himself.

a. He's wise and knows what he doth – chooseth out the afflictions which he sees best for us – proportions the burden to the strength – affliction and spiritual physic, and the physician is skilful (see Isa. 28:27, 28, 29). We do not know what's good for ourselves but God knows what is good for us. Many parents are guilty of great folly in the correcting of their children but God is wise (Heb. 12: 9, 10).

b. He's just and will do us no wrong. Whatever comfort he takes from us 'tis but what he gave, and he may do what he will with his own. Whatever burden he lays upon us 'tis less than

3. Hebrew, 'rod' or 'sceptre'.

our iniquities deserve (Job 11:6). There's no unrighteousness with God in any dispensation. I *will visit* – the word signifieth a judicial process, according to the eternal rule of equity.

c. He's faithful and doth all according to promise – *afflicted in faithfulness* (Ps. 119:75). Every affliction is sent in pursuance of the great promise of the salvation of the remnant, by the cross to the crown. First to suffer and then to reign was part of the bargain. He that afflicts us is one that we may be sure doth not break one of his promises in so doing, for they are sure, infallibly sure, to all the seed.

d. He's gracious and pities them under all their afflictions. He doth not *afflict willingly* (Lam. 3:33). 'Tis his strange work. He doth not willingly grieve the *children of men*, much less the children of God, if not the prisoners of earth (v. 34) much less the free born citizens of heaven (comp[are] v. 32 *according to the multitude*). His causing of grief is not according to the greatness of his power or the multitude of the demands of wronged justice. To those his punishments bear no proportion, but his compassions [are] according to the multitude of his mercies (see Isa. 63:9).

e. He's theirs in covenant and designs their good in all. He's their *Father* – the Father of their spirits. In afflicting the flesh he acts as the Father of spirits (Heb. 12:9), takes care of the soul that that may be saved in the day of the Lord Jesus though the flesh be destroyed. The punishments of the wicked come from God, but not from God as *their* God. Thus the covenant makes afflictions ours by making God ours.

See the hand of God in every affliction (Job 23:14). Let this quiet your spirits (Job 1:21). If God do it we must not gainsay. 'Tis both our duty and interest to submit.

3. That God never lays the rod of affliction upon his people but when by reason of sin there's great need of it. *If his children forsake my law – then will I visit* – not else. Now for a season, *if need be* (1 Pet. 1:6), and 'tis sin that gives the occasion. He

doth not afflict *ex mero motu*,[4] unprovoked. *Provoke me not and I will do you no hurt* (Jer. 25:6).

Not that there's need of it to satisfy a vindictive justice, or to answer the challenges and demands of that. Christ has made full satisfaction. In him God has received double. The greatest afflictions of God's people are not the effects of the rigorous justice of the law of works as unremoved. And yet God hath an eye to sin in those afflicted. They are punishments (Ezra 9:13*), rebukes and corrections*, the most gentle names for them imply a fault. This is consistent with pardoning mercy (Ps. 99:8; 2 Sam. 12:13, 14). But God *visits transgressions with the rod,*

a. to vindicate his own honour, and to make it appear to all the world that though he doth indulge the soul he neither doth nor will indulge the sin, but hates iniquity wherever he finds it, and the more when he finds it in those that are his children. 'Tis a reflection upon the parents' prudence if a shrewd untoward child go unrebuked. Therefore judgment begins at the house of God (1 Pet. 4:17) for God is jealous of his own glory, and will be sanctified of all that are about him (Num. 14:20, 21). This is comfortable to a child of God that when he's under a smarting rod yet God is thereby glorified. This quieted Aaron (Lev. 10:3). Aaron had lost his sons but if God hath gotten honour by it 'tis well. If God be sanctified, Aaron's satisfied.

b. to reduce and recover his people from their sins. When he takes the rod in hand 'tis with a design to part between us and our sin. Afflictions in the covenant are medicinal, a refining fire, ours to do us good. The waters of affliction are to cleanse us.

God visits with a rod,

i. to discover sin and to bring it to our remembrance. He sends the rod to set the sin in order before our eyes (see 1 Kings 17:18). The rod is sent to rub up our memories, and to bring to mind forgotten sins of omission, of commission.

---

4. Latin, 'out of pure feeling'.

We are verily guilty (Gen. 42:21). Affliction has a great influence upon conscience to stir up that to do its office, to awaken it out of its slumbers. Sometimes the affliction directly answers the sin as in Adonibezek's case, and then it's easily discovered. Sometimes there's need of a strict scrutiny, an enquiry like David's (2 Sam. 21:1). Pray with Job (ch. 10:3). Consider Ecclesiastes 7:14.

ii. to embitter sin and to break the heart for it. The bitterness of sin may be tasted in the bitterness of affliction. This softens the heart. Affliction is sent to open the spring of sorrow and then 'tis more easily put into the right channel. The rod of affliction like Moses's rod fetcheth streams out of the rock (see Jer. 31:18). See sin robbing those of this and t'other comfort. Sin [is] the source of pain and sickness and try what it will do to humble you for it. How gracious wilt thou be when pangs come upon you?

iii. to purge out sin and to part us from it (Ps. 119:67, *but now*). Thus is all the fruit (Isa. 27:6). Afflictions in the covenant are the furnace to separate the dross and so purify the silver (Isa. 48:10), as the hedge of thorns (Hos. 2:6; and see what follows, v. 7). Thorns are pricking, but useful in the hedge. A thorn in the flesh kept Paul humble. Afflictions are the lancet to let out the corrupt blood – healed by his stripes.

iv. that notwithstanding all this, covenant love is sure to all true believers. *Nevertheless my loving kindness will I not utterly take from him nor cause [my loving kindness to fail]*. It implies that this loving kindness may be in part taken away. God was displeased with David (2 Sam. 11:27) – a child of God though never again a child of wrath, yet a child under wrath. At least the sense of this loving kindness [is] suspended (as Ps. 77:7, 8, 9) – no light appearing, the favour of God eclipsed, and yet there's life in the root. For all this, my God, my God, even when he seems to forsake (Ps. 22:1; Isa. 50:10). God is said to continue his loving kindness to his people (Ps. 36:10, Heb. *draw it out*[5]).

1. Notwithstanding these provocations, *yet I will not.* Every transgression in the covenant doth not put us out of covenant. Though we sin if we do not allow ourselves in sin, though we fall if we get up again, God will not utterly take away his loving kindness. The covenant of works left no room for repentance but we are under grace (Rom. 6:14). There's a pardon ready, an advocate ready, if the habitual frame of the heart and tenor of the life be according to covenant rules and principles. A false step shall not ruin us (Isa. 63:8, *my people*). Though a provoking people yet [they are] mine, *because children that will not lie* – not disdain the relation, not deal *deceitfully* in the covenant (Ps. 44:17), though foolishly yet not *falsely*.

2. Notwithstanding these afflictions – *nevertheless* – though David's seed be chastened yet it doth not follow that they are disinherited – though cast down yet not cast off – *perplexed but not in despair* (2 Cor. 4:8, 9). Pain and sickness and poverty do not separate us from the love of God (Rom. 8:35, etc.). Though God take away our relations from us, this and t'other creature, yet it doth not therefore follow that he had taken away his loving kindness.

God may turn his people out of their comforts and yet not turn them out of covenant. Israel was a sinful nation and often under the rod, and yet God challengeth them to show a bill of divorce (Isa. 50:1). Every frown doth not dissolve the relation.

Qu[estion] How comes it to pass that notwithstanding these provocations and afflictions yet the loving kindness is not wholly withdrawn?

A[nswer] Not for your sakes be it known to you (Ezek. 36:32), but there are two reasons implied in the text.

---

5. The Hebrew verb that commences this verse basically means to extend or make long. It is used in passages such as Jer. 31:3 in the same sense as here in Ps. 36:10.

1. 'Tis for Christ's sake, *My loving kindness will I not utterly take from him*. There's a change in the person – to teach us that 'tis to him we owe our continuance in the covenant. If it were not for him the loving kindness would soon be taken from us. We may thank ourselves for the rod, our ways and doings procure that, but we must thank Christ for the love *in* the rod, and *notwithstanding* the rod, 'tis his satisfaction and righteousness that procures that – *from him*, i.e. from them in him. 'Tis by virtue of our union with Christ that we keep in with God. He's the surety of the covenant (Heb. 7:22). He's the advocate of the Father.

2. 'Tis for the covenant's sake, implied in the words, *nor cause my faithfulness to fail*. The loving kindness would soon fail if it were not kept up by the *faithfulness*. Therefore the Lord has set his love, so firmly, so immovably, because he would *keep the oath* (Deut. 7:7, 8). This is insisted upon with an observable emphasis after the text (vv. 34, 35). 'Tis gone out of his lips, tis confirmed by an oath, *sworn by his holiness*, the glorious attribute of his (Heb. 6:13, 17, 18). This promise is made to Christ the head – *not lie unto David*. He's the proffer in trust. And what is this covenant? Why (see Isa. 54:10), 'tis an everlasting covenant which shall never be forgotten.

Use 1. Count upon affliction in this world. We are born and born again to trouble. While there is so much corruption within no marvel there is so much affliction without. Do not expect to find it all carpet way to heaven. You that are now in circumstances of peace do not say, tomorrow shall be as this day. For it's more than you know. God had one son without sin but never any without sorrow. Let affliction when it comes be no surprise to you. Sit loose to creature comforts. The way to the crown is by the cross, and shall the earth be forsaken for us? God has told us the worst of it (Rev. 3:20; Heb. 12:7, 8).

2. Come into the bond of the covenant that you may be ready for affliction. Since by a fatal necessity man is born to trouble it's

wisdom to take that course which will make the trouble least troublesome. Affliction is not that to a child of God that it is to another. Faith in Christ turns not only water into wine but poisons into antidotes – cures the wound by dressing the weapon. Give up yourselves to the conduct of this excellent physician. Submit to his methods. The best preparation for a deluge is to come into the ark (Heb. 11:7) – the ark of the covenant, yet the door stands open (see Ezek. 20:37).

3. Comply with the design of God in every affliction. When he visits with the rod learn obedience by it. Believe it [is] sent to separate between you and your sins and let it have that effect upon you. Hear the rod (Mic. 6:9). Labour to answer the intention of the cross. The more we taste the bitterness of sin the more good we get by every affliction. Let your ears be open to discipline. 'Tis a great condescension in God that he will take the trouble of correcting us (see Job 7:17, 18). Listen to the teaching with the chastenings.

4. Carry it aright under every affliction, in the mean between the extremes of despising the chastening of the Lord and fainting under it (Heb. 12:5, 6). Do not despise correction for when God judgeth he will overcome. If we be senseless under a less affliction he'll send a greater. Do not faint. 'Tis but a rod (Prov. 24:10; Jer. 12:5). You that belong to Christ make it appear that afflictions are that to you which you are not to others by carrying it better under affliction than others do – justifying God, judging yourselves. Let silence all murmuring thoughts. The afflictions spring from the covenant.

5. Comfort your hearts under the heaviest cross. To be content under a cross is too low an inference from this doctrine. Rejoice in it. See it not only consistent with but flowing from covenant love. Solace yourselves with the never-failing loving kindness of God, even when you are most afflicted (Ps. 73:26). Chide yourselves out of your disquietments (Ps. 42:11). Learn to live

by faith in the covenant when you have nothing else to live by. Live upon the promise (Heb. 13:5, 6).

6. Cleave close to God and the covenant of grace notwithstanding your afflictions. You see God keeps covenant with you notwithstanding he afflicts. Do you then keep covenant with him. God loves you never the less. Do you love him never the less? Make it appear that afflictions break no squares between you and Christ. Christ eats the honeycomb with the honey, and so should we. Make it appear that you look upon Christ as your friend by taking all in good part that Christ doth. Take Christ with his cross, and learn to love Christ and trust him as friend even when he seems to come forth against you as an enemy (Job 13:15).

13

Death in the Covenant

15 May 1692

13. DEATH IN THE COVENANT

All things are yours, whether – life or death – ...
(1 Cor. 3:21, 22).

Life and death are yours, that is,

1. The life and death of your ministers – *Paul* and *Apollos* and *Cephas*. So some understand it.

    a. Their *life* is yours. 'Tis prolonged for your good, for the service of your faith and comfort. God continues them in the world for your sake's, that they may perfect what is lacking (see Phil. 1:24, 25). And this is it that makes it καρπὸς ἔργου,[1] *operae pretium*,[2] worthwhile for a minister to live in the world. Faithful ministers make all the other affairs and concernments of their life to truckle[3] to the work of their ministry for your good (see 2 Cor. 5:13). Their life is yours for it is the great comfort of their life to see you flourish in grace. *Now we live* (1 Thess. 3:8), as on the other hand 'tis the great grief and burden of their lives if you walk unworthy of your profession.

    b. Their *death* is yours. 'Tis intended to do you good (2 Tim. 2:10, *I endure all things for the elect's sake*). If called out to suffer martyrdom, that's yours, intended for the confirmation of your faith, *offered upon the sacrifice and service of your faith* (Phil. 2:17). Their natural death is thus far yours that they never die till they have *finished their testimony* (Rev. 11:7) – never fall asleep till they have done the work of their generation. Their death is yours to do you good, to startle

---

1. Greek, 'fruit of labour'.
2. Latin, 'reward of work'.
3. *Truckle*, 'submit', 'accept an inferior position'.

and awaken you to consider that they are taken from the evil to come that you may know that there has been a prophet among you.

Labour therefore to get good by the life and death of your ministers. Concern yourselves in it. Glorify God in them and in any good they are the instruments of to you. Let their life be yours to do you good, lest they be taken away in wrath to you to harden you (Ezek. 3:26).

2. Your own life and death. 'Tis yours for your good and comfort, yours for you will glorify God with it, and our life and death are never more ours than when they are God's, when we live to the Lord and die to the Lord. See Romans 14:7, 8.

a. *Their life is yours* – not only eternal life, but the present life. It's yours for your good. The comfort of it is yours, the continuance of it yours. The saints only live, truly. As for others they are dead while they live (1 Tim. 5:6). Life is theirs for they know how to value it upon a right principle, how to use it for the right one. They know how to husband life, and to make the best of every inch of it.

Life is theirs for they have enough of it. 'Tis the privilege of the saints that they die *full of days* (Gen. 25:8), satisfied with living. Life is theirs, for the life be forfeited by sin yet in Christ Jesus to them the forfeiture is taken off, and their right restored with double comfort and assurance. Christ is to them the life. They breathe in the air of free grace. God is to them their life and the length of their days (Deut. 30:20).

b. Their *death* is yours. [This is] a surprising paradox. It must be meant of the death of the body. We see good people die, but the property is so altered that the death is theirs.

Doct[rine] It is the unspeakable privilege of all that are Christ's that by virtue of the covenant of grace death is theirs. *Death is theirs* if they be Christ's.

It needs no proof that those that are Christ's are subject to the stroke of death. We have instances of it daily. Piety is no security from the grave. Death is passed upon all men. The death of Christ delivers us from eternal death, but for the temporal death we are only delivered from the malignity of it.

This is a subject you are all concerned in. For what is the work of life but to get ready for death, for when we die there is not an end of us.

Show 1. How and in what sense death is yours if you be Christ's.

a. It's not your enemy to do you any hurt. It's yours, i.e. 'tis conquered and subdued for you, so that it is not against you. Death is a hard work, and sounds very dreadful. 'Tis *the king of terrors* (Job 18:14, τῶν φοβερῶν φοβερότατον[4]). Death is the separation of soul and body, these two old intimate friends, turns the body to the grave. [It] lodgeth that in the chambers of darkness, turns the soul out of its old habitation and instates it in an unchangeable condition of weal or woe. This is *death* – a serious thing. But for all this it's no enemy to a child of God. The malignity of it is taken out. 'Tis unstung (1 Cor. 15:55). It may hiss but it cannot hurt. 'Tis disarmed.

Death cannot hurt us, for,

i. It cannot separate us from the love of Christ (Rom. 8:38, 39). Christ retains his kindness for his people even when they are dying. Death separates from the love of other friends and relations. Their love and hatred perish together (Eccles. 9:6). Sarah had been the delight of Abraham's eyes but death separated her from his love (Gen. 23:4, *bury my dead out of my sight*). But 'tis not so between Christ and believers. The death of Christ draws them to Christ (John 12:32), and the death of the saints doth not

4. Greek, 'the most fearful of fears'. The Hebrew text of Job 18:14 has 'king of terrors'.

drive Christ from them. His love as it took rise before we were born, so it will continue *beyond* death. So some read Psalm 48:14.

The soul is taken into nearer and closer embraces, and the body though separated from all the living yet sleeps in Jesus (1 Thess. 4:14). [It] remains united to Christ, and there's a covenant with the dust remaining in full force and virtue. God is *the God of Abraham*, though he be dead.

ii. It cannot hurt the soul, and that's the man. The body is but the shell; the soul is the kernel. *Animus cujiusque is est quisque.*[5] He only loses himself that loses his soul (comp[are] Luke 9:25 with Matt. 16:26). 'Tis but the outward man that doth decay (2 Cor. 4.16). 'Tis only the earthly house of this tabernacle that is dissolved (2 Cor. 5:1). Death can *but* kill the body (Luke 12:5).

Death is an enemy to a wicked man's soul. It dislodgeth that, makes that to wander. They shall require *thy soul* (Luke 12:20). Now that's really an enemy to us that's an enemy to our souls. The *souls* of the saints are delivered from this lion, even their darling (Ps. 22:8).

Death is indeed called *an enemy* (1 Cor. 15:26) because it's commonly looked upon as such, and the bodies of the saints will continue under the power of death till Christ's second coming. But all things considered there's no great harm done.

b. It is your friend to do you good. Death is yours, your humble servant to do that for you that no one else could do for you. 'Tis yours for it's *gain* (Phil. 1:21), great gain for you.

If you are Christ's, death is yours for,

i. It is the period[6] of your grievances. Job's desire of it was too passionate but there is a gracious desire of it which is

5. Latin, 'the soul of each one, that is the person'.

6. *Period*, in the sense of 'end'.

good. Of the Master it was said that he was a man of sorrows and acquainted with grief, and 'tis true of all the servants (John 16:33). Now that which puts an end to all this is death, nothing but death. ''Tis that that brings them to their desired harbour (allu[de to] Ps. 107:30). We are here like a ship at sea, tossed with tempests, but there's rest (Job 3:17; Isa. 57:1, 2). Death wipes all tears from our eyes, ends that trouble which we are born to, and born again to, a salve for every sore. Death strikes but one stroke and that stroke doth relieve us.

Death is yours to put a period

(1) to the burden of corruption. The sin that dwells in us, the law in the members, is cancelled by nothing but death (the body of this death, Rom. 7:24). 'Tis the Red Sea in which all the Egyptians are drowned that have been as thorns in our eyes.

Sin dwells in us, and nothing but death that destroyeth the soul will dislodge the sin. The corruption resulted from that union of soul and body, and nothing but the parting of them will free us from that corruption. He that is dead is free from sin (Rom. 6:7). 'Tis like the ivy in the wall, the leprosy in the house. Death dischargeth us from that conflict. Sin brought death into the world, and nothing but death will carry sin out of the world. We have thought ordinances a great kindness that help to keep corruption under, and to weaken now and then a limb of the old man, but death will quite destroy it, lays the axe to the root of bitterness, and kills all at one blow, frees us from the very being of sin, all the relics of corruption.

(2) to the assaults of temptation. The devil is still pursuing the saints while they are here in the world with his fiery darts, thorns in the flesh, disturbing their peace, defiling their purity, and it's very grievous. Death puts an end to all these. That unclean one goes to and fro through the

earth, but no further. [He will] not enter the new Jerusalem (Rev. 21:27). Death dischargeth us from that war. We meet with temptations from wicked men. [We] are in the midst of a tempting world. Sheep and goats herd together now, but then [they will be] parted for ever. [There will be] no more dwelling in Mesech (Ps. 120:5).

(3) to the difficulty and fatigue of the duty. Though the spirit through grace is willing yet the flesh is weak and draws heavily. Many a weary step we have in our pilgrimage. Our hands tire, and our knees grow feeble. This body of flesh is a heavy clog to us. Death frees us from that clog. Duty is now hard, because the flesh is weak, but when we shall put off the body, we shall never again be weary of Sabbaths, weary of praising God. *They rest not day nor night* (Rev. 4:8).

(4) to the trouble of all our fears and sorrows. They shall all vanish and be no more when death comes. This follows upon the former. If there be no more sin, there will be no more trouble.

(a) No more desertions. Sometimes God seems to withdraw and hide himself but death draws back the curtain, and brings us to see him face to face. There shall be no more sense of his frowns, no more lamenting after the Lord, no more of the terrors of the Almighty. When we quit the body we put off that which is the veil of partition. While we are here we often lose the sight, but death puts a period to the disquietments.

(b) No more persecutions. Death puts an end to the rage of men, *actio moritur cum persona*[7] (Eccles. 9:6). It may sometimes ridiculously vent itself upon the dead body, as Revelation 11:8. So Bucer's bones and Wycliff's were burned, but there's no great

7. Latin, 'action dies with the person'.

matter in that. Death opens up the prison-door, and lets the oppressed go free. That which stops the breath stops the sorrowful sighing of the prisoners.

(c) No more afflictions. Death is a period to pain and sickness, aches and distempers. It cures all disease. [There's] no hunger or thirst in the grave, no complaint of Lazarus' sores. Losses in the estate, unkindness of death of friends and relations, these are sorrows which those that are dead are freed from. Death is a period to our fears. [We are] taken away from the evil to come (Isa. 57:1), as Josiah, though killed in battle (2 Kings 22:20). Death puts us in to the shore when a storm is coming, houses us in the ark upon the approach of the deluge, as Zoar to Lot. [It] delivereth us from all our fears. [It is] an outlet to all our miseries.

2. It is a passage to your happiness. Were it only an outlet from grief, what advantage then has the Christian (1 Cor. 15:19)? But it is withal an inlet to glory, a positive happiness. [We] depart and be with Christ (Phil. 1:23; 2 Cor. 5:8). Death is yours as the wagons that Joseph sent to fetch Jacob (Gen. 45:27). 'Tis a messenger that's sent to fetch us home, a transport ship to convey us to our inheritance.

a. It's a passage from darkness to light. We are here in the body cooped up in a dungeon. We know but in part, and see through a glass. Death that closeth the eyes of the body opens the eyes of the soul, and dispels the cloud and brings us to see face to face (1 Cor. 13:9, 10, 11, 12). Death will bring us to the knowledge of many things which we were before ignorant of. What we know not now we shall then know, when the mystery of God shall be finished. 'Twill be a lovely sight to see the amiableness of providences, their harmony and dependence. It doth not yet appear (1 John 3:1, 2).

b. It's a passage from distance to nearness. We are here afar off, absent from the Lord but death brings us near, when the soul shall take flight into the purer regions, and presently be with Christ *in paradise* (Luke 23:43), to be with Christ where he is (John 17:24). The angels are then ready to convey the soul, to carry it to its rest. God is not far from every one of us, but we shall be after another manner near to him in heaven.

c. It's a passage from sin to holiness. We shall not only put off the body of sin but be clothed with the garments of righteousness. The spirits of just men shall then be made perfect (Heb. 12:23), a perfect conformity to the will of God and the likeness of Christ, like Adam in innocency, no contrariety, or contradiction, but a complete harmony, the whole soul in tune. It's a passage to holy work, and holy company, only, wholly, for ever so – to converse among the holy myriads. 'Tis the passage to an everlasting Sabbath.

d. It's a passage from sorrow to joy. Death is an *entrance into the joy of our Lord* (Matt. 25:21), the return of the ransomed of the Lord to Zion (Isa. 35:10). Delight in God who is the gladness of our joy will there be summed up in an immediate uninterrupted fruition. True joy is the rest of the soul in the adequate object of its desires. When the soul goes to God it goes into the enjoyment of all good, to drink of the rivers of pleasure, pleasures evermore (Ps. 16:11). Death to the wicked is a passage from joy to sorrow.

e. It's a passage from war to peace. We live in a world that's little better than a great cock-pit. [There are] fightings within, and fightings without too. Our life [is] a warfare, we dwell with those that *hate peace*. The church is militant. We are to be always upon our guard, being in the midst of enemies. At death we put off the harness, and enter into peace. [We] soar above the stormy region into that that's quiet and serene. [There will be] no pricking briar and scratching thorn. [There] the end is peace (Ps. 37:37).

f. It's a passage from a wilderness to Canaan, like the way through Jordan. Our life is a wilderness state, a life of wants and wanderings, hurried to and fro, still at a loss. Death is our passage to a land flowing with milk and honey, when we shall have no more occasion for manna, [and be] the glory of all lands.

This passage is immediate. As soon as ever we are absent from the body we are present with the Lord (2 Cor. 5:8). The soul doth not sleep or go to purgatory, but immediately passeth to glory.

Show 2. What makes death so much ours if we be *Christ's*? What has altered the property so strangely?

a. The covenant of grace. In the covenant of works death stood as the revenger, to execute the divine wrath for the breach of it (Gen. 2:17, *surely die*), but in the covenant of grace death has another office. The *executioner* is turned into a *messenger*, and no more but a messenger.

This covenant makes death ours as it secures to us:

i. The presence of God with us in death (Ps. 23:4). [I will] fear no evil even in the darksome valley, for *thou art with me*. That takes off the terror. That presence is guarding and guiding, *a rod and a staff*, a sustaining left hand, and an embracing right hand (Cant. 2:6), [providing] living comforts in a dying hour. When death assaults us and God is departed 'tis sad indeed (1 Sam. 28:15), but if God be present there's no danger (Ps. 4:8).

ii. A portion, in the heavenly inheritance beyond death. This is it that makes death *ours*, that heaven is ours. 'Tis the everlasting habitations, into which we shall be received when we fail, that takes off the terror of the failure (Luke 16:9). To be dissolved is not desirable, but to depart is (Phil. 1:23). Not that we *would be unclothed* (2 Cor. 5:4). That's not it that makes death so much ours, but *clothed upon*. This is the gain of death. More than ever the most busy Christian gains in this world. 'Tis sudden, quick gain, but one stile more and we shall be home.

b. The cross of Christ. 'Tis by virtue of this that death comes to be so much ours. Christ by dying has *abolished death* (2 Tim. 1:10). 'Tis owing:

i. To the victories of the cross. The cross conquered death, and subdued it under our feet (Heb. 2:14). Thus did Christ spoil principalities and powers (Col. 2:15). Christ by dying conquered death, made atonement for sin and therefore [took] the sting of death. He removed that and then there's no harm in it. See 1 Corinthians 15:55, 56, 57. The sting of death stuck in the side of the Lord Jesus. This victory is made ours by faith. When Christ conquered him that had the power of death what could death do? Christ our Joshua divides Jordan.

ii. To the purchase of the cross. The blood of Christ bought heaven for us, which is therefore called the purchased possession. That made death ours which made heaven ours. 'Tis in Christ that all are made alive (1 Cor. 15:22). Thus Christ was the death of death (Hos. 13:14).

Use 1. If death be ours, then admire the wisdom, power and goodness of Christ the Redeemer that made it so, and speak of it to his praise. 'Twas a sovereign skill that brought meat out of the eater, and sweetness out of the strong. O the virtue of Christ's blood, that he should overcome death by submitting to it! O the depth! Mention it to the honour of the captain of our salvation as a noble stratagem. Herein we are more than conquerors through Christ (Rom. 8:37). Thus is Christ a complete Saviour in bringing sons to life and glory by death, his own death as the purchase, theirs as the passage.

2. If death make so much for those that are Christ's, then it makes against those that [are] none of his, a terrible inference from this comfortable doctrine. To those that are not in Christ, death is the period of all their joys, the ruin of their hopes (Job. 27:8). It strips them of all their comforts, the expectation perishes (Prov. 11:7). They must leave all that behind them which they placed their happiness in. The joy is gone like the crackling of thorns

under a pot, and nothing will remain but the torturing remembrance of them which will pour oil into the flame (Luke 16:25).

Death is a passage to all their miseries, an arrest to appear before the flaming tribunal, or like the sheriff that comes to fetch out the malefactor to execution. They shall *require thy soul* (Luke 12:20). 'Tis the greatest loss, for it's the loss of the soul (Matt. 16:26), eternally, irrevocably lost, *like sheep* for the slaughter (Ps. 49:14; comp[are] v. 15). At death [there] will be the great difference between the godly and the ungodly (Luke 16:22, 23). Sinners in appearance may die very quietly, [with] *no bands in their death* (Ps. 73:4), but there's chains on t'other side of it. [But there's] something *after* death. Death will be a great change, either for the better or for the worse.

3. It concerns us all to make it sure to ourselves that we are Christ's that so death may be ours. You know very well you must not be here always. As sure as we are now alive we must shortly die, our souls in our hands, and are we not concerned to make sure an interest in Christ for that and nothing else will stand us in stead in a dying hour? Secular birthrights will not do. *Riches profit not* (Prov. 11:4). Let this quicken us all with a double diligence to do it now which we shall most wish we had done when we come to die.

   We have a journey to go, a battle to fight, a cause to be tried, an account to give up, and doth it not concern us to be ready? Would you not make death your friend, then? Make Christ your friend by a lively faith. You that are young have your breath in your nostrils and when you come to die you'll wish you had done this. You see how the case stands. I leave it between God and your own souls. You think now we are too earnest with you to leave your sins and accept of Christ, but when you come to die, you'll see the meaning of this earnestness. We see death at your backs.

4. If this be so, then we should not sorrow as those that have no hope for them that sleep in Jesus. 'Tis their gain and should we envy them (1 Thess. 4:13, 14)? They are not lost but only gone

before, and when the way is foul and the weather stormy, happy they that get home first. We have reason to praise the dead (Eccles. 4:2). The condition of dead saints is upon many accounts better and more desirable than the condition of living saints. We are yet in our pilgrimage; they are at home. We have here no continuing city but they have a city that has foundations. We are yet at sea; they have arrived to the port. We have yet the sharpest encounter before us but they through grace are got triumphant through it.

5. Then those that are Christ's have no reason to fear death but to desire it rather. Do not fear it for it's not an enemy. It's disarmed and unstung. Christ died to deliver us from the fear of death (Heb. 2:15). Consider the worst it can do. It can *but* kill the body. It can but dissolve the earthly house of this tabernacle.

Nay, desire it rather as a friend, as the hireling desires the shadow (Job 7:2). Yet this will not justify our breaking prison before we have a legal discharge. Our times are in God's hand and not our own. But we should meekly and submissively long for our change. Desire to depart and to be with Christ (Phil. 1:23). In this we should groan (2 Cor. 5:1, 2). Thy kingdom come. When shall an end be put to the days of sin and misery? Make haste my beloved. Why are his chariot wheels so long a coming? Be ready to welcome death when it comes, as a good friend.

14

Heaven in the Covenant

22 May 1692

14. HEAVEN IN THE COVENANT

In the hope of eternal life which God that cannot lie promised before the world began (Titus 1:2).

You have heard much of the perfect enjoyment of the saints by virtue of the New Covenant, the riches they have in hand, and the provision made for them while they are under age, but after all 'tis very true if their hope in Christ were confined to this life their happiness would fall infinitely short of those great things which are intended by that fundamental article of the New Covenant that God is to them a God (Heb. 11:16; see 1 Cor. 15:19, *[we are of all men] the most miserable*) – both upon the account of damage for the present and disappointment for the future.

And therefore we must certainly look upon the promised future happiness of the saints as the most considerable conveyance of the New Covenant. What's laid out is much, but what's *laid up* is more (Ps. 31:19). The happiness in possession is nothing compared with the happiness in reversion.[1] This is the crown of covenant love. There's heaven in it. That's it that answers the dimensions of that great word, *I will be to them a God* (see Rev. 21:3, *and God himself shall be [with them]*).

The text doth fully express the grant of this happiness. 'Tis part of the description that Paul gives of the religion he professed and preached. Christianity is a *truth according to godliness* (v. 1), not a mere speculation, but a truth in order to practise, a truth not only to be known, but to be acknowledged and live up to. That's Christianity, and the gains of it are rich. 'Tis a religion whose advantages lie much in expectation, and the text describes that expectation. 'Tis *in hope*. Our holy religion is something expressed by *the hope of it* (1 Pet. 3:15). Those that will deal with God must

1. *Reversion*, an archaic word for 'the residue', 'the remainder'.

deal upon trust. The happiness is wrought for them that *trust* in him (Ps. 31:19). 'Tis mentioned as the end of our ministry to bring people to heaven.

Observe in the text.

1. The happiness granted – *eternal life*. Life is sometimes put for all good. There's the life of the body and the life of the soul, but this is *eternal* life, the life of the body and soul united and glorified. The happiness of the soul at death is this happiness inchoate[2] (Rom. 6:23).

2. The grant. 'Tis *promised* – ἐπηγγέιλατο.[3] Some understand it of the purpose and decree which is the promise in the embryo, rather than the promise properly so called, the declaration of the purpose. A promise supposeth the things future and not in present possession.

3. The grantor, *God that cannot lie* – ὁ ἀψευδὴς θεός,[4] an unlying God. The gods of the heathen were *a lie* (Isa. 44:20), teachers of lies (Hab. 2:18), but the Lord he is the true God, a God of truth and in whom there is no iniquity. *Every man [is] a liar* (Rom. 3:4). No confidence is to be put in man, but God cannot lie. 'Tis impossible (Heb. 6:18). [There is] no diminution of the omnipotence of God that he cannot lie (*posse malum non est posse*).[5] To be able to lie is a defect and impotency, no act of power. God cannot deny himself (2 Tim. 2:13). The veracity of God is the great foundation upon which our faith and hope is built. He is faithful *that has promised* (Heb. 11:11).

4. The date of the grant – *before the world began* (πρὸ ϡ χρόνων αἰωνίων[6]). Those who by the *promise* understand the decree

---

2. *Inchoate*, 'just begun'.
3. The Greek word ἐπηγγέιλατο is the simple past tense middle of the verb 'to promise', 'he promised'.
4. Greek, 'the God not guilty of falsehood'.
5. The Latin phrase means 'power to do evil is not power'.
6. Greek, lit. 'before eternal times', 'before the world began' (NIV).

and counsel of God, understand this of *the eternity* of the decree, before the foundation of the world (Eph. 1:4). Those who understand it properly of the revealed promise, understand this of the *antiquity* of the promise – promised *before long ages* (comp[are] Rom. 1:2). Some think he refers to these promises, Genesis 3:15; 15:1; 17:1. From the beginning of the world there had been some revelation of this purpose of God's good will. This eternal life was shadowed out to Adam by paradise, to Abraham and his seed by the land of Canaan. In those eternal life was promised. 'Tis an ancient grant, which adds to the credit of it. 'Tis that which all the saints have been saved by.

5. Our dependence upon this grant. We live *in hope* of it. There's this duty which this calls for from us – to hope for this glory. For this end 'tis proposed and promised. Other scriptures direct this hope. It must be the way of faith and obedience.

Doct[rine] That God that cannot lie hath in the covenant of grace promised eternal life to all true believers. 'Tis the unspeakable privilege of true believers who are in covenant with God that heaven is theirs.

Show 1. What this *eternal life* is. Let us apply our minds a little to think of it. You all either have, or may have a title to it. 'Tis offered to all. The gospel dispensation is *the kingdom of heaven*. 'Tis settled upon all true believers.

By eternal life I mean the future state of bliss and happiness which is reserved for and entailed upon the people of God after this life, which the soul is put in possession of at death, and soul and body at the resurrection.

a. 'Tis difficult to know. 'Tis spiritual, and therefore lies quite out of the road of sense (*eye hath not seen*, 1 Cor. 2:4). 'Tis hard to understand that which is spoken of heavenly things (John 3:12). It doth not yet appear [what we shall be] (1 John 3:2). The words that were heard in the third heavens were unspeakable words (2 Cor. 12:4). Those are too daring that go further than they have Scripture to guide them. We are apt to judge of t'other world by this and so are deceived.

b. 'Tis desirable to know – not merely as a curious speculation gratifying to the intellectual faculties, but for the warming of our affections, the quickening of our motions, and the directing of us in our whole conversation. 'Tis the mark we aim at, the prize we run for (Phil. 3:14) and therefore it's good to know what it is. Have we any hopes of being there for ever, and is it not desirable to know what kind of state it is?

c. 'Tis duty to know – for this end it is revealed to us that we might study it and get acquainted with it. Christ came into the world on purpose to make it known to us, and as far as it is manifested 'tis our duty to labour after the knowledge of it.

'Tis *eternal life*. So the text calls it. Christ is called eternal life (1 John 1:2; 5:20) because he is the spring and author of eternal life. Grace being heaven and glory begun is called eternal life (John 17:7; John 6:54; 1 John 5:13). But 'tis here taken for the happiness of the blessed in the future state.

1. It's *life*. The covenant of works threatened death for disobedience (Gen. 2:17), and so death passed upon all men (Rom. 5:12), but Christ is come that we might have *life* (John 10:10). He is the life (John 14:6). In him we have it more *abundantly*, more abundantly than Adam had it in innocency, than we have it in this world. Life is sometimes put for all good. In God's favour is life, i.e. all happiness (Ps. 30:5). Heaven is *life* for it is the perfection of all good. 'Tis the only true life, *the words of this life*. 'Tis the land of the living (Ps. 27:13). The world is the land of the dying. Sometimes 'tis called only *life* (Matt. 7:14; 19:17) for it is the only true life. Life is the perfection of God. *As I live*, saith the Lord.

Now that which constitutes this life is *God*. He's the only *beatitudo objectiva*.[7] 'Tis he that is *all in all* in that happiness (1

7. Latin for 'objective blessedness'.

Cor. 15:28). The *beatitudo formalis*[8] is the most noble outgoings of the soul towards God as the chiefest good. Some call it the operation of the soul, concerning God, not a transient but an immanent operation, not sensitive but intellective.[9]

This heavenly life consists of three things.

a. The vision of God. We shall see him as he is (1 John 3:2), behold his face (Ps. 17:15). The face of God is his glory represented. This was it that Moses was so desirous to see (Exod. 33:18). No man in this present life has seen him or can see him (1 Tim. 6:16), but in heaven we shall see him, [we shall] see his glory (John 17:24) and 'twill be a great thing, much beyond our present conception. This vision will not quite transcend the sphere of created nature but no doubt shall fully come up to it, so as to satisfy the most elevated, enlarged, contemplative power of an immortal spirit. The glory we shall see is the most *excellent glory* (2 Pet. 1:17). The glorified body of Christ may more easily be considered as the object of this vision than the divine essence. A ray of Christ's glory was almost the death of John (Rev. 1:17) because he was in a state that could not bear it, but the full manifestation of this glory will be the life of the saints. We shall see face to face (1 Cor. 13:12), see God in my flesh (Job 19:26), God clothed with a body – a very great word.

b. The fruition of God – to see God so as to enjoy him – to be united to him. The life of the body consists in its union with the soul, so the life of the soul consists in its union with God. Spiritual life is that union begun, eternal life is that union perfected. The glory is not only set before us but given to us (John 17:22, 23).

To see God and not to see him as ours would be a torture rather than a happiness, but that which makes up the life is the enjoyment – the receiving of all that love and favour from him

8. Latin for 'formal blessedness'.

9. *Intellective*, adjective, 'with reasoning powers'.

and the return of all that adoration and affection to him which results from the highest assurance of our interest in him and our relation to him.

Fruition is the crown of desire. All those desires of sanctified souls after God which are here moving towards him shall then be satisfied (Ps. 42:1, 2; 73:25). The language of every look will be, this glory is mine.

c. A likeness to God. We shall be *like him* (1 John 3:2) and this likeness [will be] satisfying (Ps. 17:15). Man was made in God's image (Gen. 1:26, 27). That image was defaced by sin, begun to be restored in grace, perfectly renewed in glory – not like the Most High (Isa. 14:14). That's the sinfulness of sin that it steps into God's throne, but like the Most Holy that's the excellency of grace that it clothes us with the image of God.

This is the heavenly life.

2. It's eternal life. Our present life is but for a moment, few days and full of troubles (Job 14:1). Old age is evil days (Eccles. 12:1). But the heavenly is eternal for:

a. There's no death to put a period[10] to the life itself. Death is abolished. After millions of ages 'twill be as far from an end as the first moment. In eternity there's no succession of ages, but an endless τὸ νύν.[11] Methuselah died at last, but [there is] no death in heaven.

b. There's no old age to put a period to the comforts of it. As there's no death so no burdens, no weariness, pain, sickness. Many have been weary of this life, perfectly surfeited with it, but the last of glory is the true glory (Prov. 25:27) because of the eternal weight of glory.

I shall further open to you the nature of this eternal life by showing

10. *Period*, in the sense of 'end'.

11. Greek , 'now', 'the present'.

you the several ingredients that constitute this happiness, especially as it is the happiness of the soul.

1. Perfect Knowledge. Such a perfection of knowledge as the created intellect is capable of. So strong are the deficits of knowledge that our first parents hazarded all their happiness to attain it, and yet woefully missed of it.

   The knowledge we attain here is at best partial, uncertain, unsatisfying (Eccles. 1:18), but in heaven we shall know as we also are known (1 Cor. 13:9, 10, 12), not by the operose[12] deductions of reason, that pleasing toil of the rational faculties, but by a clear and open view. In that paradise the tree of knowledge will be no forbidden fruit but so engraffed into the tree of life as at once to enlighten the understanding and to transform the mind. The veil rent, the lattice taken down, the glasses broken and we shall all behold with open face (2 Cor. 3:18). We have now a door opened into heaven but then heaven itself shall be opened (Rev. 4:1; 19:11). Difficulties will then be solved, and nothing will remain to puzzle us with its depth or its doubtfulness, but everything clear and certain. The mystery of God will then be finished, the platforms of divine counsels laid open. What we know not now we shall then know (John 13:7, *[but thou shalt know] hereafter*). We shall then know the meaning of the providences that which are now so perplexing. All riddles shall be unfolded and every thing made plain. We shall then see the beauty and harmony of providence and understand what infinite wisdom has been driving at. This will set us a wondering and set us a praying, and should make us long for the glory that *shall be revealed.*

2. Perfect Rest. There remaineth a rest for the people of God, and this is the rest (Heb. 4:4). Canaan was a type of it. Christ's errand will be to bring to them that are troubled *rest* (2 Thess. 1:7). This

---

12. *Operose*, from the Latin *operosus*, an Old English adjective, 'toilsome', 'heavy'.

is a world in which we must not look for rest (Mic. 2:10), but in heaven there's undisturbed, uninterrupted rest.

a. Rest from our labours (Rev. 14:13). The working time is while we are here in this world. In heaven we shall have rest. We have here a salvation to work out, a generation to serve, but that's the world of retribution. Heaven will be most welcome to the most laborious saints that lay out themselves most for God. The sleep of the labouring man is sweet (Eccles. 5:12). We shall then be past the burden and heat of the day. Necessary duties which are agreeable enough to the new nature yet become uneasy by the contradiction they give to flesh and blood, that makes them toilsome, but that flesh and blood cannot enter into the kingdom of God. The body shall be a spiritual body, and so the praise [will] be the everlasting work of heaven. There will be no labour in it, no difficulty. Sweat and toil came in with sin, and will go out with it (*[many . . . shall] sit down*, Matt. 8:11).

b. Rest from all our troubles. Satan's temptations, indwelling corruptions, outward afflictions, enemies' persecutions, we shall rest from all of these as a ship in a safe harbour after a tempestuous voyage, no more hurried and tossed with tempests, but all quiet and serene. The sun *that scorched shall no more light on them* (Rev. 7:16). These are the times of *refreshing* (Acts 3:19). Heaven will be a great *refreshment* to the weary soul. Storms blown over, no pricking briar nor grieving thorn. Heaven is a city of refuge.

3. Perfect Holiness. Heaven is a holy place. No unclean thing shall enter into that new Jerusalem – that holy of holies. The divine image shall be perfectly stamped upon the soul, and the whole man reduced to its primitive purity and rectitude. The state [is] a holy state, and the heart holy for that state. The work [is] holy, the company [is] holy.

'Tis an everlasting Sabbath, a holy day. Holiness will become that house for ever (Ps. 93:5). 'Tis the beauty of heaven, signified by those precious stones (Rev. 21:19). Holiness is a becoming thing.

a. There shall be perfect freedom from sin. No unclean thing shall enter therein, none of the remainders of corruption, no spots in the feast of love, no evil nor any appearance of it, no distractions, or vain thoughts. The prince of this world hath nothing there. Therefore it is that heaven would not be heaven even to an unsanctified soul that persists in the love of sin, no more than a well-furnished room would be agreeable to a swine that would rather be tumbling in the mire. Those that delight in wicked company can take little pleasure in heaven for there's no such company there.

b. There shall be a perfect compliance with the will of God. Holiness to the Lord [is] written upon everything there (Zech. 14:20). Glorified saints are said to be priests of God (Rev. 20:6), i.e. entirely devoted to God and to his immediate services as the priests were under the law. God's holiness is in a special manner adored in heaven (Rev. 4:8).

And how little will this agree with an unsanctified soul? Those that are weary of a short Sabbath, an hour of praise, will sure be weary of the long Sabbath of eternity, an eternity of praise.

4. Perfect Love. Heaven is [a] world of love. God is love, and what's heaven but God there. We live in a world of hatred, Esek and Sitnah,[13] contention and enmity, but the land of light is a land of love.

a. Perfect love to God. We are here much straitened in our love to God, and that straitens us in our obedience. We are cold and flat in our affections to him overpowered by the prevailing

13. These two names refer to the two wells over which Isaac's herdsmen and the herdsmen of Gerar quarrelled. Isaac named the first one *esek* (dispute) and the second one *sitnah* (opposition). See Gen. 26:19-22.

love of other things, but in heaven love will be made perfect. Our love to God is drawn out by his love to us (1 John 4:19). The polished steel reflects the rays but as it receives them in heaven where the communications of God's love will be the most full and immediate the outgoings of the soul to God will be the most strong and fixed. What's heaven but the eternal reciprocation of God's love between God and the saints? Having not seen him, we love him (1 Pet. 1:8), much more when we see him as he is.

b. Perfect love to the saints. They will then be perfectly joined in one body, and knit together by the strongest ties of union. Remaining darkness, and remaining corruption cause the cooling of love among Christians, but in heaven where there's perfect light and holiness, there will be no dividing principles and then they will all be one. The new Jerusalem is a city compact together. 'Tis this *charity* or love that will abide when faith shall be swallowed up in vision and hope in fruition (1 Cor. 10:13).

This makes the happiness of heaven a good and a pleasant thing that brethren shall there dwell together in unity (Ps. 133:1) – no clashing or dividing, Judah [shall] no longer vex Ephraim [Isa. 11:13].

5. Perfect Joy. We shall there enter into the joy of our Lord (Matt. 25:21). Though now we see him not yet we rejoice much more when we shall see him immediately (1 Pet. 1:8). Heaven is therefore called paradise (Luke 23:43) because it's the perfection of all delights.

a. There will never be any matter for sorrow. Sin and affliction, these two fountains of tears, will then be dried up for ever, all tears wiped away (Rev. 21:4). If there be a remembrance of sin, yet the pleasures of seeing it pardoned and conquered will drown any trouble which that remembrance may create. Not a heavy heart, not a weeping eye, not a melancholy look among all those holy myriads. We are now by our own folly making work for repentance, every day sowing tears but the harvest will be with joy.

b. There will ever be matter for joy. The enjoyment of God the chiefest good must needs put a transcendent gladness into the heart (Ps. 4:7), and that constant and uninterrupted, ever fresh, never failing, therefore called a *river* of pleasures (Ps. 36:8 *labitur et labetur*[14]), pleasures evermore (Ps. 16:11), everlasting joy (Isa. 35:10), spiritual, pure, unmixed joy. Present joys are fading and transitory, like the crackling of thorns under a pot, but the joys of heaven [will be] still flourishing. The light of joy is an everlasting light (Isa. 60:19, 20) which is held too high to be blown out by any of the blasts of the lower region. We have now the pleasures of ordinances, drops of joy, but we shall then bathe ourselves in the ocean of delights.

6. Perfect Satisfaction. The result of all this is, *I shall be satisfied* (Ps. 17:15). 'Tis the repose of the soul in God and a solacing of itself in the midst of infinite and inconceivable delights – resting in our love, having found an adequate object.

The happiness is satisfying because

a. it is suitable. We can desire nothing else for this will do. 'Tis agreeable to the soul's capacities. The Lord is my portion and therefore the lines are fallen in a pleasant place (Ps. 16:5, 6). 'Tis now the common sentiment of every sanctified soul that it's good to draw near to God. This [is] the general breathing of all the saints, Whom have I in heaven but thee? O the satisfaction of the soul in God (Ps. 116:7, *return to thy rest*)!

b. it is full. As we need desire nothing else, so no more of that. There is a present satisfaction in the suitableness of our spiritual enjoyments but yet there's not fulness. Grace is pressing forward (Phil. 3:13). In heaven there is not only joy but a

14. Latin, 'it flows and it will flow'.

> fulness of joy. Here we are hungering and thirsting, though not for more than Christ, yet for more of Christ, but if we can but get to heaven, our longings will be completely satisfied. We *shall hunger no more no thirst any more (*Rev. 7:16).

To conclude, you see what heaven is, now,

1. Do you truly like it? Do you love this salvation? If you do, then love the work of heaven now.

2. Do you truly long for it? Desire a title to it. O that this happiness might be mine! Desire the possession of it. Come Lord Jesus, come quickly!

29 May 1692

IN HOPE OF ETERNAL LIFE

D[octrine] That God that cannot lie hath in the covenant of grace promised eternal life to all true believers.

We have already given some faint and scanty account of heaven's happiness, and the nature of it, but the thousandth part hath not been told you. The admiration of the saints when they come to heaven will be like the Queen of Sheba's (1 Kings 10:6, 7). However, it is good to be here (Matt. 17:4). 'Tis very sweet dwelling in our thoughts upon this subject, pitching with Moses upon M[ount] Pisgah from thence to take a view of the land of promise.

We shall therefore make some further enquiry into the nature of this happiness, that we may be powerfully invited to accept the offer of it and in some measure affected with and engaged by the believing view of it. 'Tis good to be frequently meditating of heaven especially on Sabbath days.

Besides, what hath been already considered which are the principal ingredients of this happiness, let's apply our minds to think

1. of the happiness of our bodies in heaven. 'Tis in a special manner the salvation of the soul (1 Pet. 1:9), but the body being part of Christ's purchase will be a sharer in the happiness at the resurrection.

   'Twill be the happiness of our bodies

   a. that they will be perpetually glorifying God. 'Tis now our duty to glorify God with our bodies. They should be instruments of his honour, but they prove too often rather impediments to our glorifying God than instruments of it. The flesh is weak (Matt. 26:41). But there that weakness will be done away, and the body for ever fitted to secure the soul in glorifying of God.

      'Twill be a *spiritual body* (1 Cor. 15:44), light and agile.

Now though the spirit be willing and not weary of the duty, yet the flesh is weak and often wearied with the duty. But there the flesh itself will be so spiritualised as not to be capable of weariness (*equal to the angels*, Luke 20:36). We shall never according as we pray do the will of God as the angels do it that are in heaven till we come to be equal to the angels. The bodies of those that shall be found alive must undergo a change (1 Cor. 15:57). [There shall be] no need of meat or drink or sleep.

b. that they will be perfectly glorified with God according as the body is capable of glory. Though a *vile body*[1] yet [it will] be made like to the glorious body of Christ (Phil. 3:21), raised in glory (1 Cor. 15:42, 43). A specimen of the glory of Christ's body we have in his transfiguration (Matt. 17:2), and something like that shall the bodies of the saints partake of in heaven. They are now clods of the earth, but shall then shine as the sun (Matt. 13:43), no more subject to the deformities and infirmities of the perfect state, no more wasting or decay, but *all glorious* not within only, but without also (Rom. 8:13). How should this oblige us to glorify God in our bodies, seeing there is so much glory reserved for our bodies! Shall we make them instruments of sin or defile these bodies which we expect to be thus glorified (Rom. 12:1; 1 Cor. 6:20)?

2. of the happy work that there we shall be employed in. The heavenly paradise is not intended for a place of idleness no more than the earthly. The work of heaven is praise (Rev. 4:8). They that dwell in God's house will be still praising him (Ps. 84:4). Herein the temple was a type of heaven (Ps. 134:1). Now praise is *good* (Ps. 92:1), 'tis *pleasant* (Ps. 135:3).

We find praise sweet and pleasant work while we are here, the most delightful employment, the Sabbath, the day of praise,

---

1. The word 'vile' at the time of the AV and when Matthew Henry was preaching meant 'weak', 'humble'. The AV expression 'vile body' was the translation of the Greek phrase τὸ σῶμα τῆς ταπεινώσεως, 'the body of humiliation'.

the sweetest day in the week. But what then will that eternity of praise be?

a. There will be full and abundant matter for praise. Here the cup is mixed – April days[2] – our sins make work for repentance, our troubles make work for prayer, and these do very much take us up, but in heaven there will be neither sin nor trouble but all grace and love, and so nothing but praise. The mystery of redemption will there be cleared. The mercy of redemption will there be completed, the impressions of redeeming love will be stronger, communications of the divine favour more immediate. Now our praises are faint because our faith is so. Doubts prevail to stop the mouth of praises, our praises are lost in our complaints.

b. There will be a free and fixed heart for praise. Here we never want *matter* for praise, we have reason in everything to give thanks (1 Thess. 5:18), but we want a *heart* for praise. We are often out of tune and unfit for the duty, but there will be a perfect harmony, the heart awakened and fixed (Ps. 108:1, 2). The vision and fruition of God drawing out an enlarged love to him will open the lips to show forth God's praise. Then and not till then all that is *within us* will praise God (Ps. 103:1). Here we have much within us that is averse to the duty. Sin dwells in us, but there all that is within us will be employed in praise. No disturbance, deadness, distraction. Allellujah [will be] the burden of the song (Rev. 5:9, 10). This is work that the angels are now doing (Ps. 103:20). This should make us love the duty of praise and delight in it, and abound in it. Begin our heaven here and now. We are now in our apprenticeship.

3. of the happy company we shall there be joined to. Company adds much to the delight of any place. In heaven there will be good company, the πανήγυρις[3] (Heb. 12:22), all gathered

2. *April days*, days of changeable weather.

3. Greek, 'a festival assembly'.

together (Matt. 8:11) and it will be a great meeting (Rev. 7:11), a public meeting in the air (1 Thess. 4:17).

We shall have good company in heaven for we shall be

a. with all the saints. Here the salt of the earth is scattered but there 'twill be all gathered, all that ever were, that are, or that ever shall be, all the Old Testament saints that got acquainted with a Christ to come by the dark shadows of the law, all the New Testament saints to whom life and immortality is brought to light by the gospel, all the great and famous saints, men of renown, Abraham and Isaac (Matt. 8:11), Peter and Paul and all the patriarchs, prophets, apostles, martyrs, whose memories are yet precious, all the mean and obscure saints that never made any noise in the world. 'Twill be a general rendezvous, those that we never saw nor heard of, not one saint shall be missing, not one Thomas absent from the meeting of the disciples, a great meeting just when all God's spiritual Israel from Dan to Beer-sheba shall be gathered together. Those that we ourselves have known and been acquainted with, those that have been fasting and praying and hearing together on earth shall be feasting and singing and triumphing together in heaven.

   And 'tis generally agreed among divines that glorified saints will know one another, not after the flesh, as now (2 Cor. 5:16), not by stature or complexion, titles of dignity or affinity, but by the image of Christ and our spiritual relation through him to one another. The three apostles knew Moses and Elijah in Christ's transfiguration. Adam in paradise said of Eve, this is bone of my bone. If it will in any way conduce to the happiness of the saints doubtless they shall have it (1 Cor. 13:12, 13, love implies knowledge).

b. with none but saints – an unmixed society – here there are tares among the corn, chaff among the wheat, good and bad fish in the nets, Ham in the ark, Judas among the apostles, but there the bad shall be forever separated (Matt. 25:32, 33; 13:44). [There shall be] no spots in the feast of love. Then you shall discern both righteous and wicked (Mal. 3:17), no duty in that temple, no false brother to spy out our liberty. That will be a pure lump. No more vexation to the righteous souls, as now there is. No sinners to entice or to grieve. None crowding in to the feast without the wedding garment.

c. with saints made perfect. Here the best have their imperfections, their ignorances and follies, roughness and unevenness. We must all have grains of allowance. This often embitters society, but there every thing will be holy to make the society amiable. When the sons of God come together there Satan will not among them as now he doth to sow discord. Wars and fightings here come from our lusts, but there the lusts will be subdued, and Luther and Calvin will be of a mind. This should make us long for heaven, that we shall have such good company there, and we should choose such for our companions now (Ps. 119:63). Death gathers us to our people, changes our place but not our company.

4. The continuance and duration of all this happiness which adds much to the desirableness of it. 'Tis *eternal* life. 'Tis a happiness without period, never waxing old or decaying. 'Tis a meeting to part no more. If it were not for this the fear of losing it would very much embitter the sweetness of it, but when it is abiding it must needs be satisfying. 'Tis a perfection which we shall never see an end of, as we do of all subliminary perfection (Ps. 119:96).

a. Is heaven rest? It is a *remaining* rest (Heb. 4:9). Here our rests are very short. *Rest a while* is the most we can say, but there will be a long rest. The soul will then be in its centre, perfectly fixed.

b. Is heaven pleasure? 'Tis *pleasure* for evermore (Ps. 16:11). Our pleasures here are transitory and succeeded by pain. Sinners outlive all their pleasures (Luke 16:25). 'Tis but for a season (Heb. 11:25). The true pleasure will last as long as we shall last.

c. Is heaven joy? It is *everlasting* joy (Isa. 35:10). The joy of the hypocrite is but for a moment (Job 20:5), soon raised and soon lost, like Jonah's gourd. The joy of the upright is lasting

– God the object of this joy [is] eternal, the soul the subject [is] immortal.

d. Is heaven glory? It is *eternal* glory (2 Cor. 4:17). Nothing under the sun is more uncertain than glory. We see present glory stained and withered but the glory that shall be revealed is everlasting.

Dwell in your thoughts on these things.

Let us further discover to you something of the happiness of heaven by opening the several comparisons and similarities by which it is set forth to us in the Scriptures. Heavenly things are clothed with earthly expressions (John 3:12). The treasure [is] in earthen vessels that we may the better understand what it is. God lisps to us in our own language.[4] You'll all say that this is a sweet subject, and very comfortable – *juvat usq. morari*[5] – but take heed that it be not to you like sweetmeats to foul stomachs which turn into choler[6] and do hurt. See to it that the title to this happiness be first made sure by faith, and then you may take the comfort of it, otherwise you have no part nor lot in the matter.

What is heaven?

1. Heaven is a prize (Phil. 3:14, βραβεῖον[7]). It signifies the reward proposed to those that strove for mastery in any exercise, as in the olympic games, in which the prize striven for was commonly rich and valuable, glorious and honourable. But in other races the prize is given to one only, here to all who run well, and in the right way. See 1 Corinthians 9:24. Heaven is a prize, i.e. it is the recompense of all the pains we take in the service of God. 'Tis a *reward*, not for our works, but according to them (Matt. 5:12; Heb. 10:34), like the labourer's penny (Matt. 20:10).

a. It's a splendid prize – of glory that fades not away (1 Pet. 5:4,

---

4. This is a quotation from John Calvin, *The Institutes*, Book 1.xiii.1.

5. This Latin sentence is by the Roman poet Virgil (70–19 BC). It can be found in Aeneid 6.487, and means: 'They delight to linger still'.

6. *Choler*, 'yellow bile'.

7. Greek, 'prize'.

ἀμαράντιον[8]), not like the withering garlands, the common prize that runners strove for. But a true, lasting, solid, substantial glory. 'Tis to be honoured by the Father himself, the sole fountain of honour (John 12:26).

b. It's a suitable prize adapted to the nature and desires of an immortal soul, answering the labours of their present state – joy for their sorrow, rest for their labour, honour for their contempt, riches for their poverty. Infinite wisdom has so adapted it.

c. It's a sure prize. We do not run at uncertainties (1 Cor. 9:26). The prize is as sure to him that overcomes as infinite wisdom, love and faithfulness can make it. 'Tis laid up in heaven, a sure place (1 Pet. 1:4) given by a righteous judge (2 Tim. 4:8). 'Tis a sure reward (Prov. 11:18).

2. Heaven is a paradise (Luke 23:43; 2 Cor. 12:4; Rev. 2:7). The Garden of Eden was a type of heaven. Christ our Second Adam purchases for us and restores us to all that happiness which the first Adam lost for us, and as much above it as heaven is above the earth.

a. Paradise was a place of innocency. When Adam left his innocency he soon lost his paradise. The saints are free from sin in heaven, the image of God perfectly renewed with this advantage that no serpent comes in there by his subtlety to deceive us. Those that have a right to the tree of life shall eat and live for ever.

b. Paradise was a place of delight. So is heaven, not carnal pleasures, such a paradise as the Turks dream of, but true spiritual pleasure, arising from the vision and fruition of God – unmixed, uninterrupted pleasures. Even spiritual comforts are here mixed, and therefore we must rejoice with trembling, but there's no allay to the delights in heaven.

How should this quicken us to abound in the work of the

---

8. Greek, 'unfading'.

Lord, [with] yonder's pleasures to make amends for all the pain and sorrow and difficulty?

3. Heaven is a crown (2 Tim. 4:8), a crown of righteousness. 'Tis a happiness represented by the royalty of kings and princes, who are looked among as chief of the children of men. 'Tis a throne (Rev. 3:21), 'tis a kingdom (Luke 12:32), a kingdom that cannot be shaken (Heb. 12:28). A crown denotes

   a. dominion. The saints shall reign with Christ, [they shall] sit upon thrones. They shall participate in the honour which Jesus Christ will then have won by conquering and subduing all his enemies (Ps. 49:14). They shall have a complete rule over their own spirits. Sin and Satan and all the powers of darkness will then be perfectly trodden under their feet (Rom. 16:20), no more to rebel or to disturb them. Those that suffered with Christ shall reign with him and this reign [shall be] everlasting (Rev. 21:5, *reign for ever and ever*). Other reigns have their periods and revolutions. The crown doth not endure to every generation (Prov. 27:24). We see crowns falling from the head, but the kingdom that shall be given to the saints of the Most High is an everlasting kingdom (Dan. 7:27).
   b. dignity. Heaven is glory (Ps. 84:11), kingdom and glory (1 Thess. 2:12), eternal glory (1 Pet. 5:10), the body raised in glory. Those that have now honoured God shall then be honoured by him, and it is a weight of glory (2 Cor. 4:17). Every word is emphatical. The place of work, the company honourable, the attendants honourable. The angels are not only round about the throne of God but *about the beasts and the elders* (Rev. 5:11) which speaks not only [of] the safety but the honour of the glorified saints. The meanest saints though low in the world [are] advanced to the bosom of Abraham. This honour have all the saints.

4. Heaven is a city (Heb. 11:10; 12:22), a continuing city (Heb.

13:14). We have a large description of this city (Rev. 21:1ff.). Jerusalem was a figure of it – [a] united city, compact together (Ps. 122:3), beautiful for situation (Ps. 48:2). The name of the city [is] Jehova Shammah (Ezek. 48:35).[9] Holiness to the Lord [is] written upon everything in this city (Zech. 14:20, 21). *Jerusalem* is a holy city, *the vision of peace*, all [is] quiet there.[10] 'Tis a city of refuge, *no more sea* (Rev. 21:1), no waves and billows. 'Tis a city of righteousness, a faithful city, a city that has foundations.

a. Guarded as a city. The wisdom and power of God are a wall of defence round about this city, to keep out all that hurt and destroy. Where there are palaces there's need of bulwarks (Ps. 48:13). *The door was shut* (Matt. 25:10) as the door of the ark, not only to seclude those that were without but to secure those that were within. He that keeps the city neither slumbers nor sleeps. God himself is a wall of fire. The mountains [are] round about Jerusalem (Ps. 125:1).
b. Governed as a city – not as the fishes of the sea [but] a perfect exact order, for God is the God of order. 'Tis not only *urbs* but *civitas* (Heb. 12:22),[11] incorporated, and the denizens[12] of this city are the innumerable company of angels and the spirits of just men made perfect. Heaven must needs be a land of order where God is the Sovereign Ruler and his will the Sovereign Rule. He maketh peace in those high places. 'Tis a city where there's no want of any good thing.

5. Heaven is a house. 'Tis the saints' home. [It is] our *house* which

---

9. The Hebrew expression means 'The LORD is there'.
10. The allusion here is to the fact that the name 'Jerusalem' contains a variant of the Hebrew word for peace, *shalom*. The word 'Jerusalem' means 'let peace be established'.
11. The Latin word *urbs* means 'city', while *civitas* means 'a union of citizens', 'a state', 'commonwealth'.
12. *Denizens*, from the Old French, 'inhabitants', 'frequenters of a particular place'.

is from heaven (2 Cor. 5:1). Houses are necessary for our comfortable subsistence in this world but [it's] no house like that.

a. It's a capacious house, high and large, august and spacious [with] many mansions (John 14:2). [There is] room enough for all the saints. We need not fear being straitened. We may say of heaven as Isaac of his well (Gen. 26:22, *Rehoboth*[13]). There's room enough, and it had need be large that must entertain all the saints, the great multitude which no man can number (Rev. 7:9).
b. It's a convenient house. We here have our conveniences and our inconveniences but there all's agreeable and nothing amiss. 'Tis a well-furnished house, in which nothing is wanting – a paradise – which we should think of when we find any inconveniences in our present habitations. We must never expect to have everything to our mind till we come to heaven.
c. It's a lightsome house. There needs no sun [for] the Son of Righteousness is the light of it (Isa. 60:20). There's no night there. Darkness is for ever banished out of those pure regions. The house must needs be lightsome where there's perfect knowledge and perfect joy, and where he is all in all who is Light and in whom is no darkness at all.
d. It's a lasting house, an everlasting habitation (Luke 16:9), a house that can never totter for the foundations are strong and durable. 'Tis built upon the mount of Christ, the promise of God, the holy mountains (Ps. 87:1). It can never be invaded, never undermined. No thief can break through to steal (Matt. 6:20). All's safe there. It must needs be so when angels stand sentinel at every gate (Rev. 21:12).

6. Heaven is a *heritage* – in allusion to the land of Canaan, a heritage for Israel his people. 'Tis called *the inheritance of the saints* (Col. 1:12). Canaan was a good land, the glory of all lands, the fitter to represent heaven. 'Twas divided by lot, and the disposal

13. The Hebrew word means 'broad places.'

of that is of the Lord (Ps. 16:11). Heaven is given according to the appointment of the Father but to none but Israelites indeed. If children then heirs, not else (Rom. 8:17). We attain to it not by our own righteousness (Deut. 9:5). See what kind of inheritance it is (1 Pet. 1:4; Eph. 1:4).

a. 'Tis free as an inheritance. [It] costs us nothing. We are heirs of the *grace* of life. 'Tis the *gift* of God. We do not hold as purchasers, but as heirs purely by the act of God. [We] do nothing to any merit. Christ was the sole purchaser.
b. 'Tis firm as an inheritance. The saints through Christ have an unquestionable, indefensible title to it (Father I will, John 17:24). Everything that can be desired is done to confirm it, if we can but evidence our relation to Christ by faith (John 1:12). 'Tis firm for 'tis settled upon Christ in truth for all true believers and he as the captain of our salvation has engaged to bring many sons to glory.

To conclude.

1. Think much of heaven. These thoughts should be pleasant to us, more than thoughts of earthly things.

2. Talk much of it. Comfort one another (1 Thess. 4:18).

5 Jun. 1692

ETERNAL LIFE WHICH GOD THAT CANNOT LIE PROMISED BEFORE THE WORLD BEGAN

D[octrine] That God who cannot lie hath in the covenant of grace promised eternal life to all true believers.

We have endeavoured to open the nature of this eternal life what it is, I now proceed to:

Show 2. The promise of this eternal life. The promises of the New Covenant are reduced by the Apostle to two heads (1 Tim. 4:8).

a. The promises of *the life that now is* – which may include not only the temporal blessings but such spiritual blessings as are enjoyed in this life – the privileges of our way – what we have in hand – *now are we the sons of God* (1 John 3:2). The words of the gospel are the words of *this* life (Acts 5:20). In keeping, as well as after keeping, there is great reward (Ps. 19:11).

b. The promises of *the life which is to come* – goodness laid up (Ps. 31:19), spiritual blessings *in heavenly places* (Eph. 1:3), and this is purely in promise. The land of Canaan was in this a type of heaven yet it was *the land of promise* (Heb. 11:9). The heirs of heaven are called *the heirs of promise* (Heb. 6:17).

There are three great blessings that make so great a figure in the promises of Scripture that they are each of them called κατ' ἐξοχήν,[1] *the promise*. Christ was *the* promise to the O[ld] T[estament] saints (Heb. 11:38, 39). They received not *the promise*, i.e. the promised Messiah personally exhibited (Acts 13:32, 33). *The Spirit* was *the*

1. The Greek expression κατ' ἐξοχήν means *'par excellence'* (1 Cor. 2:1).

promise to the saints when Christ was here upon earth (Luke 24:49; Acts 1:4; 2:33). That was it they were then in expectation of. *Heaven* is *the* promise for the saints now – the great promise that we are waiting for the accomplishment of. 'Tis called *the* promise (Heb. 10:36; comp[are] Heb. 9:15; see 1 John 2:25).

The opening up of the several steps of this promise will be of use to us to direct our thoughts concerning this happiness, that we may know upon what ground we go in our expectations of it.

1. The promise of eternal life was founded in the counsels of everlasting love. God's promises are his revealed purposes (see Eph. 1:9). As all truth and being is consonant to the idea of the eternal mind, so all grace and mercy is consonant to the intentions of eternal love (see Eph. 3:11; so some understand the text *before the world began ...*). This speaks very much [of] the riches of divine love. God is love, and therefore his love [is] commensurate with his being, both [are] from eternity.

    a. God did from eternity design this happiness. The kingdom is said to be prepared from the foundation of the world (Matt. 25:34). Then that platform was laid by the measuring line of the divine prescience.[2] The life is a hidden life (Gal. 3:3), hid in God (Eph. 3:9), i.e. in the projects of his eternal counsel (1 Cor. 2:9). The saints will then participate of Christ's glory, and that glory is the same which he had before the world was (John 17:5; comp[are] 5:24). That must needs be a glorious happiness which was so long in the designing, so long in the preparing. Something great is always expected where there's great preparation, as for the building of the temple (1 Chron. 22:14). Heaven is a dinner prepared (Matt. 22:4). Now my creatures shall see what infinite wisdom, power and goodness can do to make them happy. This is the masterpiece of the divine goodness, the crowning favour, and therefore reserved to the last. This is that in which the Lord Jesus will be for ever

2. *Prescience*, 'foreknowledge'.

glorified and admired (2 Thess. 1:10). Canaan was a land picked out for Israel.

b. God did from eternity design a remnant to this happiness – and the promise is in pursuance of that design – the elect are chosen *to salvation*, as the end, *through sanctification* as the means (2 Thess. 2:13). Election is the first link in that golden chain which glorification is the last link of (Rom. 8:30). When the dinner is prepared the guests are intended. God would not provide such a happiness without determining who should be the monument of his grace in the enjoyment of it.

The names of those that are designed for heaven are written in heaven (Luke 10:20), as the names of the citizens are enrolled in the records of the city. As Israel was designed for Canaan long before they were put in possession of it (Deut. 32:8), so the spiritual Israel [is] designed for glory. And all that God doth for them is in pursuance of this design. They are *called* to this kingdom (1 Thess. 2:12), *begotten again* to this inheritance (1 Pet. 1:3, 4).

This mystery of election is not to be curiously pried into, much less presumed upon, but adored with wonder, love and thankfulness, as it will be to eternity when the mystery of God shall be filled up.

2. The promise of eternal life was purchased by the blood of Jesus Christ. The eternal promise was purposed in Christ (Eph. 3:11), the remnant chosen in Christ (Eph. 1:4). That's the consideration in this charter or grant. 'Tis for and in consideration of the death of Christ and the merit of that death. 'Tis indeed bottomed upon his whole undertaking. Heaven is therefore called *the purchased possession* (Eph. 1:14). This Canaan is promised not for your sakes be it known to you but for Christ's sake (Deut. 9:5, *not for thy righteousness*), and therefore he is said to give this eternal life (John 10:28).

a. 'Twas Christ that removed the forfeiture – our inheritance was mortgaged into the hands of divine justice by sin. The forfeiture was signified by the cherubim and the flaming sword (Gen. 3:24). We are altogether unable of ourselves to redeem this inheritance. We have by sin come short of the glory of God (Rom. 3:23). Now Jesus Christ as our Göel,[3] our next of kin redeems the inheritance, pays the debt and takes up the mortgage, opens the kingdom of heaven to all believers, making atonement for those sins that had incurred the forfeiture, satisfying God's justice, answered the demands of the law, the broken covenant of works, and paid not the *idem* yet the *tantandem*[4] – took away that which hindered (judgments, executions, encumbrances), nailing it to his cross (Col. 2:14), removed the flaming sword – redeemed us from the curse of the law (see for a full scripture for it Heb. 9:15; John 3:16).

b. 'Twas Christ that obtained the title. He did not restore us to our first state but to a new title. [He] purchased of the Father a promise of this happiness to all that believe and obey him. 'Tis the gift of God through Jesus Christ our Lord (Rom. 6:23). There could be no merit in our obedience by virtue of which to challenge such a reward, but Jesus Christ purchased a promise of it to those that do believe and obey, and so it becomes *a recompense of reward* (Heb. 11:26) – not as if God were a debtor to us, our goodness extendeth not to him – but a debtor to his own truth. We are said to be *saved* by his life (Rom. 5:10). 'Tis by the blood of Jesus that we have boldness to enter the holiest (Heb. 10:19, 20). 'Tis he that has gone before to take possession (Heb. 6:19), to prepare a place for us (John 14:2).

3. The promise of eternal life was revealed in some measure to the O[ld] T[estament] saints. 'Twas promised πρὸ χρόνων αἰωνίων[5] – *many ages ago* (Act. 26:6), *and in sundry times*

---

3. *Göel*, Hebrew for 'deliverer', 'redeemer', of a relative's lost blood, property or freedom.
4. *Idem* and *tantandem* are Latin for 'the same', 'the actual thing', and 'just the amount', 'the exact equivalent'.
5. Greek, 'before long ages ago', 'before time began' (NIV, NKJV).

and in divers manners (Heb. 1:1), though then it was but darkly made known over as it is to us now. Yet like the morning rays of the sun there were some prefaces to that revelation. They saw this promise though far off and did embrace it (Heb. 11:13). The O[ld] T[estament] saints lived and died in the belief of a future happiness (see Heb. 11:10, 14, 16, 26).

Yet 'tis strange we have so little notice taken of it in the law of Moses but temporal rewards and punishments were agreeable to the constitution of that dispensation and the ignorant world would be more allured by temporal blessings. Abn. Ezra[6] thinks there is a tacit intimation of eternal life (Deut. 32:39), death and *life* after it. David speaks clearly of it, and Daniel (ch. 12:2). When Christ was at the door the light increased (see 1 Pet. 1:10, 11).

The translation of Enoch was a revelation of heaven to the patriarchs before the flood. The land of Canaan was plainly intended to be a type of heaven. Thus was the gospel preached to them (Heb. 9:2, 3, 9). The translation of Enoch likewise but they could not steadfastly see to the end of these things (2 Cor. 3:13). There was a veil between the holy place and the most holy, which signifieth both darkness and distance.

And yet by faith in a Christ to come, by their receiving of and submitting to the revelation they had, they got to heaven then. Abraham and Isaac and Jacob are in the kingdom of God (Matt. 8:11). Heaven is represented as the *bosom of Abraham*, he being the father of the faithful. Bless God for the more full and clear discoveries that we have (Heb. 11:40).

4. The promise of eternal life is brought to a closer light by the gospel. The shadows are done away, the clouds scattered, the veil rent at the death of Christ (Matt. 27:51). Life and immortality [are] brought to light (2 Tim. 1:10), in due times manifested (Titus 1:3).

---

6. The reference here is to the medieval Jewish commentator known as Aben (or Ibn) Ezra (c. 1090–1164) who late in life wrote a commentary on the Pentateuch, the five books of Moses.

Truth is come by Christ in opposition to the types and figures of the O[ld] T[estament] (see Heb. 9:24). The gospel dispensation is therefore called the kingdom of heaven (Matt. 3:2) because in it the kingdom of heaven is more clearly discovered. *Great is the reward in heaven*. That's a N[ew] T[estament] promise (Matt. 5:10) not as the O[ld] T[estament], *that thy days may be long in the land.*

a. Christ himself discovered it to the world. He had lain in the bosom of the Father (John 1:18). He came to take people off from the pomp and grandeur of this world, to teach his followers not to expect happiness here, though could hardly be brought off from it. Thou shalt have treasure in heaven (Matt. 19:21).
b. He sent his ministers upon the same errand – Paul an apostle in hope of eternal life. The religion we preach is *a heavenly calling*, not only that it has its rise from heaven but its tendency to heaven.
c. For this end the Scriptures are written. The Scriptures of the N[ew] T[estament] help to make the O[ld] T[estament] plain and easy, and in them you may find eternal life (John 5:39). There we have an account of the other world and the glories of it. This is the gospel record (1 John 5:11). This is the treasure hid in the field, so that if we remain ignorant of or unconcerned about this eternal life we are without excuse living in a day of so much light. Enquire after this knowledge (John 17:3). The Scripture gives us a map of the country we are to trade with.

5. The promise of eternal life is offered to all upon reasonable terms. 'Tis proposed to all that if they will repent and believe in Christ and be new creatures, all this happiness shall be theirs (*whoever believes in Christ*, John 3:15). The Lord knows them that are his but he hath appointed us in Christ's name to proffer it to all upon gospel terms, that those who perish might be left without excuse. We are sent to offer the penny to all that are willing to work in the vineyard. As many as we find we must bid to the

marriage (Matt. 22:9). You may all be happy if it be not your own fault. The generality of the offer is *love to the whole world* (John 3:16). None are excluded that do not exclude themselves. I appeal to yourselves if the terms be not highly reasonable and sweet. 'Tis sometimes proposed as a *pearl* to be purchased (Matt. 13:46), sometimes as a *penny* to be earned (Matt. 20:2), sometimes as a *prize* to be run for (Phil. 3:14). Not that there is any meritorious proportion between any thing that we can do and this happiness, but 'tis proposed upon such and such conditions.

a. Is it not reasonable that those who would be saved by Christ should be ruled by him in the matter of salvation? Upon these terms 'tis offered (Heb. 5:9). *Hear ye him* (Matt. 17:5). [There is] no getting to heaven but by submitting to the conduct and government of Jesus Christ and can any thing be objected against that? This is believing in Christ, submitting to him as our Prophet, Priest and King. Those that would be brought by Christ to glory must *follow* him, yield to his direction (John 12:26).
b. Is it not reasonable that those who would be happy, i.e. holy, hereafter should be holy, i.e. happy, now? Heaven is a place of perfect holiness and is it not reasonable we should be sanctified and made meet for such a state? Is it not reasonable that those that would have a place in the new Jerusalem should repent and make themselves new hearts, that those who have by sin forfeited their happiness should repent of and forsake their sins before they be restored to the title? Is it not reasonable that the end and means should go together, salvation and sanctification?
c. Is it not reasonable that those who would soon see and enjoy God for ever should serve and enjoy him now? That those who would be to eternity there where God is all in all should make him their all in all now? Whom have I in heaven but thee (Ps. 73:25)? That's the frame of spirit required to give up ourselves to God as our owner, ruler, benefactor, chief good and ultimate end, and set him before us.

d. Is it not reasonable that those who would have their bodies and souls in heaven hereafter should have their affections and conversations in heaven now, that where the treasure is there the heart should be (Matt. 6:21; comp[are] Phil. 3:20; Col. 3:1, 2)? We must quit this world and for good reason (Matt. 19:21). Is it not reasonable that those who would be always living a heavenly life should live a heavenly life now?

e. Is it not reasonable that those who would reign with Christ should be willing [to] suffer with him (2 Tim. 2:12), especially considering that the sufferings of this present time are not worthy to be compared with that glory (Rom. 8:18)? Nay, they work for us that glory (2 Cor. 4:17). Well, upon those terms the promise of eternal life is offered to you as a good tenement for and under such and such rents and services. None are excluded that will come up to these terms, rich and poor, bond and free, servants (Col. 3:24), poor (Jas. 2:5), Gentiles, fellow-heirs (Eph. 3:6).

6. The promise of eternal life is made over to all true believers upon believing. Others may have a title, but they *have* (Rev. 22:14). Their title results from their union with Christ and relation to him. They have received the adoption of sons (John 1:12) and if children, then heirs (Rom. 8:17). Heaven is theirs. 'Tis *prepared* for them (Matt. 25:34), whereas (v. 41) hell is prepared for the devil. The happiness is *laid up* for them (2 Tim. 4:8), reserved for them (1 Pet. 1:4). They *have* eternal life (John 3:16; 6:54). Not the possession of it, [for] that's to come. Those that will deal with God must deal upon truth, but:

a. They have the promise of it. 'Tis the *land of promise*, and this the promise of one *that cannot lie*. The promise is their *magna charta*,[7] 'tis that which they have to show for it, [and] on which they ground their hopes.

---

7. The reference to *magna charta* is to the document given by King John of England in 1215, traditionally seen as guaranteeing human rights against the abuse of kingly power.

'Tis by promise

i. to secure it to them, for the promise is sure to all the seed. In this case a promise without possession is better than possession without promise. The angels had possession but soon lost it because they had not the promise of preservation which the saints have. The promise is the foundation upon which that city is built (Heb. 11:10).
ii. to keep them in expectation. God would reserve the best till last that his people might be encouraged to wait on him, and that their faith and patience may be tried. He doth it to train them up in hope.

This promise is as sure as can possibly be made. 'Tis written, 'tis sealed, 'tis backed with an oath (Heb. 6:17, 18), all the assurances imaginable. If we be but faithful we may be confident that God will never be false. God will have us to depend upon him. [He] gives us sufficient footing for faith and then requires us to stand upon it.

b. They have the earnest of it – the blessed spirit (2 Cor. 1:22; Eph. 1:14). The earnest binds the bargain and is part of the payment. They have livery[8] and seisin.[9] The sanctifying operations of the Holy Spirit are an assurance of the consummation of holiness in glory. Thus the inheritance passeth, and in vain do we pretend to the grant if we cannot prove the livery and the seisin executed upon it. By the Spirit we are *sealed* (Eph. 4:30), marked for glory, as goods are marked. The Spirit is called the anointing (1 John 2:27). The anointing of David did abundantly assure him of the kingdom, notwithstanding the many oppositions in the way.
c. They have the first-fruits of it. Spiritual life is eternal life begun.

---

8. *Livery*, 'distinctive clothing often given by a person of rank to his servants'.
9. *Seisin* is an old legal term borrowed from the French *saisine*. It means the taking of possession of land by freehold or the land so possessed.

Heaven is theirs, for what are their present comforts, communions and conformity to God but a heaven upon earth (Rom. 8:23; Heb. 10:34 *[knowing] in yourselves*). [The] present light and love [are] the beginnings of eternal light and love. Their citizenship is now in heaven, their conversation above. Though as yet grace be like the smoking flax yet there's a spark that will be blown up into a flame shortly.

d. They have the power of God engaged for their preservation to it. *They* are *kept* by an almighty power to salvation (1 Pet. 1:5). They shall never perish (John 10:28) and there's need of such a power, they are in the midst of many oppositions and difficulties. There are many advantages, but he that hath opened the wide door will make it effectual and none shall shut it (Phil. 1:6). Thus the promise is for the present made over to true believers, with all these advantages (*now are we* ..., 1 John 3:2).

7. The promise of eternal life shall certainly be accomplished at last to all true believers. They shall all at last be put in a full possession of this happiness. Not one true believer shall miss of it. Christ will bring the many sons to glory, and present them all together to the Father (Heb. 2:10, 13).

a. God is true to his Word. He is faithful that hath called us (1 Thess. 5:24). All the promises of God are Yea and Amen, and this particularly, *he cannot lie*. 'Tis impossible he should. 'Twould be an eternal reproach to the faithfulness of God if any believing, sanctified soul should miss of heaven. We may venture our souls upon the word which God hath spoken. He hath spoken in his holiness and we may rejoice in hope. The word of man is yea and nay, every man a liar, but God is not a man that he should lie.

b. Christ is true to his undertaking. He hath undertaken to conduct all that were given him safe to glory (John 6:28, 39, 40). When he went away he promised to come again (John 14:3). The authority he hath is put into his hands for this end that he might give eternal life to the chosen remnant (John 17:2) and accordingly he claims it for them with authority (v. 24, *Father, I will* ...). All this assures us that the promise will not fail, but where God gives grace he will give glory. Glorified saints will be eternal monuments of the divine faithfulness. Christ will then be admired in them that believe when they shall be brought all together in glory.

8. The promise of eternal life is the crown of all the promises of the New Covenant. This is the topstone of the building, 'tis the principal article.

   a. 'Tis this that completes the happiness of believers. We have hope in Christ in this life, but if our hopes did not extend further we were of all men most miserable (1 Cor. 15:19), because of that hazard we run of all our outward comforts by our profession. We have hard work to do, troubles to undergo and if we were to have our labour for our pains 'twere sad indeed. But now we seek a *better* country (Heb. 11:16).
   b. 'Tis this that answers the extent of that great promise of the covenant that God will be to us a God (Heb. 11:16). *He is not ashamed to be called their God, for he hath prepared* [*a city for them*]. If he had not so provided for them he would have been ashamed to be called their God. What God did for them in this world, if that had been all, would have been a product no ways answerable to the pregnancy of the promise, *I will be a God to you.* Therefore thence Christ fetcheth an argument to prove the reference and a future state, because else God had not made good what he had said to Abraham (Matt. 22:31, 32). For God to be a God to any person must needs imply something great. The present happiness of the saints doth not answer to it. Therefore there must be something in reversion[10] to fill it up.

---

10. *Reversion*, an archaic term for 'the residue', 'the remainder'.

To conclude.

1. Study the promise of eternal life. Dwell much in your thoughts upon it – by whom, through whom and to whom 'tis promised.

2. Strengthen your faith and hope in that promise. Live upon it. Draw comfort from it. Do all in hope of eternal life.

12 Jun. 1692

IN HOPE OF ETERNAL LIFE WHICH GOD WHO CANNOT LIE PROMISED

Doct[rine] That God who cannot lie hath in the covenant of grace promised eternal life to all true believers.

Use 1. By way of instruction and information.

a. Mix faith with what hath been said concerning the glory that shall be revealed. Believe that there is such a happiness set before us, and promised to us in the gospel. 'Tis not a fool's paradise, but a real thing. Though out of sight faith doth evidence and substantiate it (Heb. 11:1). This word will not profit if it be not mixed with faith (Heb. 4:2). 'Tis faith that realiseth unseen things. 'Tis by faith that we look at the things that are not seen (2 Cor. 4:18).

b. Meditate upon it. Dwell in your thoughts upon this glory that shall be revealed. The reason why that which in the general we believe and acknowledge has not that influence upon us that it should have is because we do not think seriously and particularly of it as we should. Be more frequent and intense in your thoughts of this eternal life and deduce from it these inferences.

i. If this be so then the people of God are a very happy people. We may from hence conclude, *Happy art thou, O Israel* (Deut. 33:29; comp[are] v. 28). The fountain or *the eye*[1] of Jacob is upon *a land of corn and wine*. The saints are therefore happy not because of anything they have in this world. If their happiness were confined to the present time they were miserable people (1 Cor. 15:19), but their eye

1. The Hebrew word can mean either 'fountain' or 'eye'.

being upon such a good land we conclude them truly happy. They are heirs under age (Gal. 4:1). [There is] much is prospect, in reversion.[2] *Blessed is the people that is in such a case* (Ps. 144:15).

Let this increase

(1) our honour of them. 'Tis the character of a citizen of Zion, that he honours them that fear the Lord (Ps. 15:4). Though poor and low and despised in the world yet upon this account they are truly honourable (see Jas. 1:5; comp[are] 1, 2, 3). Not that I would overthrow civil respects as they are due, but establish sacred respects. Think what this poor despised Christian that fears God and works righteousness will be shortly, though now trampled upon. A jewel is a jewel though it lie in the dirt. Think how the tables will shortly be turned, and esteem things as they will [be] then. Vile[3] bodies will then be changed (Phil. 3:21). *We fools counted his life madness. Wisd.*[4] The corruptions and infirmities of the saints now lessen our esteem of them but think how they will be, *black* now but *comely* shortly (Cant. 1:5, 6).

(2) our concern for them. Our kindness should extend to such as these (Ps. 16:2, 3). We should therefore do good to the household of faith (Gal. 6:10). You see what God intends to do for them and therefore as there is occasion we should take a pleasure in doing for them, for their bodies, for their souls, especially for their furtherance in the way to this eternal life. Make them

2. *Reversion*, an archaic word for 'residue', 'the remainder'.
3. The word *vile* which occurs in the AV of Philippians 3:21 meant at that time 'weak', 'humble'. The AV expression 'vile body' was the translation of the Greek phrase to; σῶμα τῆς ταπεινώσεως, 'the body of humiliation'.
4. The quotation (Wisdom 5.4) is from the apocryphal book *Wisdom*, written in Greek in the last century BC, but purporting to be by Solomon.

your friends (Luke 16:9). Christ therefore takes what is done to them as done to himself because they are heirs of this kingdom.

(3) our delight in them and in their company. Do then covet to keep great company. Keep company with those then that fear God for they are truly great. You have heard that God is with them, and they shall be for ever with him, and therefore say, *We will go with you* (Zech. 8:23).

c. If this be so then it is not in vain to serve God. There's nothing lost by our doing or suffering for God. It seems there have been those that have said so, and 'tis reckoned among the *stout words* spoken against God (Mal. 3:13, 14, *It is vain to serve God*). Probably it refers to the error of the Sadducees which arose in Malachi's time denying a future state of retribution, implying if there be not such a state of retribution it will be in vain if you take the service all together, with the sufferings. Christ had respect to the joy that was set before him (Heb. 12:2).

There's nothing lost by losing for God. We may be losers for him but we cannot be losers *by* him in the end (Matt. 19:29; Prov. 19:16; Prov. 11:14, 15). There are three sorts of persons that do in effect say *it is vain to serve God.*

i. Those that serve him not at all, that like the devil's wages so well that they are for serving him and for serving their base lusts, and are not for the service of God (see Job 21:14, 15; 22:17). They do in effect say that they do not believe it worth while to serve God, that they do not believe him able or willing to make them amends, or do not rely upon the faithfulness of his word, question[ing] whether he has been serious in the promise. Tell them of the duty of prayer and repentance. They know nothing that's to be got by them and they will not trouble themselves about them.

ii. Those that serve him slightly and carelessly, that do what they do in religion coldly and indifferently with half a heart, as if they did it not. Those do in effect say, *it is vain to serve God.* Those that said so were the same that brought the torn and the lame for the sacrifice (Mal. 1:13), as if any thing would serve, the worst they had.

iii. Those that serve him dejectedly and under prevailing disquietments, that drive on heavily in religion, that reflect upon the ways of God as if there were nothing to be got by them. The Psalmist was under a temptation of this kind (Ps. 73:13, 14). If it be so, why am I thus? If such a happiness as this be promised certainly I have not cleansed my hands in vain (Isa. 45:19). But *seek and find.* Believe this truth that it is not in vain to serve God. 'Tis vain to serve sin (Hab. 2:13; Rom. 6:23). But none that serve God said in the end (whatever thought they might have had in the hour of temptation) that 'twas in vain to serve God.

d. If this be so then blessed be God for Jesus Christ. Nothing can endear Christ to us more than a foresight of his glory. 'Twas he that prepared it, that purchased it, that is gone before to take possession of it, and will come again to fetch us to the possession of it. And have not we then abundant reason to be thankful? 'Tis the gift of God through Jesus Christ (Rom. 6:23).

i. We owe our title to Christ. We claim by, from and under him. Heaven is ours by virtue of our union with Christ. We are joint heirs with Christ (Rom. 8:17), and therefore blessed be God for the mediator. All this flows to us in the stream of Christ's blood. He's our Göel[5] that redeems the mortgaged inheritance, and 'twas infinite wisdom that found out this way of salvation. 'Tis in Christ that this promise is Yea and Amen, sure and steadfast. We have for the present cause to be thankful.

ii. Our possession will be owing to Christ if ever we get to it. 'Tis he that prepares us for it and preserves us to it by his

5. *Göel*, Hebrew for 'deliverer', 'redeemer', of a relative's lost blood, property or freedom.

Spirit, that will shortly bring the many sons to glory. And therefore how thankful should we be for redeeming love. How this should fill us!

Think how undeserving, how ill-deserving we were. Think what it cost Christ to purchase this eternal life for us. 'Twas by means of death (Heb. 9:15). Nothing less would open the kingdom of heaven. The veil must be rent, viz. his flesh (Heb. 10:20). Look upon heaven and you'll see how much we are beholden to Christ.

e. If this be so then 'tis the greatest folly imaginable to choose a portion in this life. Multitudes do so (Ps. 17:14), and it is for their ruin. That's a man's portion which he depends upon as his happiness.

'Tis folly to choose a portion in this life for,

i. 'Tis the choosing of that for a portion which will not satisfy us. 'Tis not in it to make us happy. 'Tis husks, 'tis wind, 'tis not suitable to the nature of a soul. 'Tis part of the vanity of the creature that it will soon surfeit but never satisfy (Eccles. 4:8). A man's life consists not in the abundance of those things (Luke 12:18).

ii. 'Tis the refusing of that which would. O the madness of the most of men that neglect so great salvation (Heb. 2:3), [that] refuse such an offer! [They] will not come to Christ, no, not that they may have such a life (John 5:40). [They] will not hear, no, not the *rest and refreshing* (Isa. 28:12). What folly is it to choose our good things in this life (Luke 16:25), to make such poor things as these our *reward* (Matt. 6:2), our *consolation* (Luke 6:24) when there are such better things set before us for our reward and consolation.

Do not choose like fools, nor prefer trash before treasure.

f. If this be so then we serve a good Master. Let what hath been said of heaven raise and keep in us good thoughts of God. Is he not a kind Master

i. that hath provided such a recompense of reward for our poor services, so far, so infinitely transcending all pretensions of ours? *Is this the manner of men* (2 Sam. 7:19)? An eternal joy for a moment's pains? A glory such as eye hath not seen? 'Tis owing to the free grace of God. Those that were prepared to glory are called *vessels of mercy* (Rom. 9:23).

ii. that hath given us such discoveries and such assurances of it? [There are] so many promises of it, so much to clear our sight of it and to confirm our faith concerning it. [There are] so many previous pledges and earnests [there is] no room left for doubting. We do not run at uncertainties. Great men intend large bounties to their servants many times when they give them no assurance.

iii. that daily loads us with so many benefits in our way towards it, gives us such larger provisions to bear our charges – blessings of the nether springs, promises even of the life that now is, good things for the body, not only for necessity but for delight and ornament. All this and heaven too. Do not we serve a good Master then?

Use 2. By way of trial and examination. Is there such a happiness as this promised to some and not to others? Then it concerns us all to enquire whether we have any title to it, any interest in it. What well-grounded hope have we of this eternal life?

What Christ hath done for us is the ground and foundation of our title, but there must be something done in us to be the evidence of our title, and that's the place and interest of *good works* in the business of salvation – Christ *in you* the hope of glory (Col. 1:27).

I shall endeavour

a. to give you some motives to persuade you to try yourselves. 'Tis a spiritual duty and against the grain to your corrupt nature. Most people are willing to take it for granted without putting themselves to the trouble of an enquiry. [They] fancy themselves in a good condition however. Suspect yourselves (Isa. 44:20). I beseech you, do not rest in such a fancy, but *prove your own selves* (2 Cor. 13:5).

Consider,

i. The matter to be tried is a thing of consequence. 'Tis not for a pebble but a pearl. All you are worth lies at stake, your whole happiness. If you had an estate of great value which you were to have a trial for, how solicitous would you be about it? And will you have no care or concern when the matter to be tried is no less your eternal welfare? 'Tis not a small thing for 'tis *thy life*, the life of thy precious soul, and souls are precious things (Matt. 16:26).

   How jealous should you be over yourselves with a godly jealousy. Believe it to be no trifle but a matter of great weight, whether heaven be yours or no.

ii. 'Tis a very easy matter to be mistaken. A man's easily imposed upon with counters for gold. Counterfeit grace is so like true grace that a man may presently be deceived with one for t'other. The heart is very deceitful in all things (Jer. 17:9), and in nothing more than in this. The life is a hidden life, hidden many times from ourselves.

iii. 'Tis a thing which multitudes have been mistaken before us, that have thought themselves in the way to heaven, but proved in the road to hell. 'Twas Laodicea's mistake (Rev. 3:17). Many that have thought themselves in a good condition till death and hell have undeceived them, *a whole generation of such* (Prov. 30:12). The foolish builder hath had a great many followers in his folly.

iv. We have that in us which disposeth us for and leads us into such a mistake. Pride and self-love disposes us to entertain every thing that seems to make for us. Men are generally averse to believe any thing ill concerning themselves. We have reason to suspect ourselves for our hearts have a great many turnings and fetches. We are apt to go upon wrong hypotheses.

v. A mistake in this matter is of very dangerous consequence. If we have not title to this eternal life we are certainly liable to eternal death. [There is] no mean between the two. Creature comforts may be lost and recovered again, as Job, but this eternal life if lost is irrecoverably lost without retrieve. Do you know what it is to miss of eternal life? To come short of this glory?

Let us therefore fear (Heb. 4:1), and look diligently (Heb. 12:15).

b. Some marks by which to try yourselves – and now conscience do thine office. Be willing to undergo the test. Come to the touchstone. Let's see who the Scripture saith shall go to heaven and who not. Not who by name, but who by character. 'Tis certain not all, not the most [shall go] (Matt. 7:13, 14; Luke 13:23, 24). Therefore examine each for himself. Let's enquire:

i. Who they are that have no title to this eternal life, [that] have no part nor lot (Acts 8:21).

(1) Ignorant people have not title to this happiness. 'Tis a land of light and these have no right to it that allow themselves in gross ignorance of God and Christ and their souls and this other world. O what abundance doth this cut off from all claims, that are willingly ignorant in the midst of all the means of knowledge, destroyed for lack of knowledge (Hos. 4:6), *that know not God* (2 Thess. 1:8). Those that are to this day in the condition in which they are born are excluded (John 3:5).

(2) Those that live in any gross sin have no title to this happiness. The wicked shall be turned into hell (Ps. 9:17). See several black catalogues, exclusion bills (1 Cor. 6:9, 10; Gal. 5:19-21; Eph. 5:5; Rev. 22:15), particularly those that live in hatred (1 John 3:14, 15). Though these sins may be kept close from the eye of this world yet they will appear shortly to shut the sinner out of heaven. That's no place for such cattle. 'Twould not consist with the holiness of the sin-hating God to lay such as these in his bosom.

(3) Those that rest in the form of godliness without the power of it have no title to this happiness. Hypocrites are certainly excluded. The church triumphant admits of no false brethren. Those that deceived men with false pretences will find a God too wise to be deceived. You know the case of the foolish virgins.

(4) Those that continue in unbelief and impenitency have no title to this happiness. No sin would of itself exclude people from heaven if this were not added to it (see Heb. 3:8). Unbelief is the sin against the remedy. 'Tis against our appeal – *he that believes not the son of God* (John 3:36). [There is] no way of escaping perdition but the way of repentance (Luke 13:3, 5). That's the plank thrown out after shipwreck.

ii. Who they are who have a title to this happiness (see Ps. 15:1; 24:3). Not who in person, [for] that's known to God only (Matt. 20:23), but who in character.

(1) All those and those only that truly repent of and from every known sin have a title to this eternal life. Those that sorrow for sin and forsake it shall come to heaven, that state of sinless purity. The future state shall be a time of refreshing to those only that repent and are converted (Acts 3:19). Those only that mourn shall be comforted (Matt. 5:4). Those that sow in tears shall reap in joy (Ps. 126:5, 6). Repentance is a separation from sin, and that must be else the soul is unmeet for heaven. Can you witness to this repentance? What trouble did your sins ever cost you? What anxious thoughts, what carefulness, what indignation? What fruits have you been meet for repentance? Those that keep their garments pure are worthy, i.e. meet to walk in white (Rev. 3:4).

(2) All those and those only that by a lively faith give up themselves entirely to Jesus Christ as their Prophet, Priest and King have a title to this eternal life. Christ is

the door, and the way. By faith we enter in at this door and walk in this way. The covenant of works required sinless obedience. The covenant of grace substitutes faith in the room of it. See John 3:36; 20:31. Faith is the interesting grace. We believe to the saving of the soul (Heb. 10:39). What federal transactions[6] have there been? Faith is a receiving grace, and resigning grace, a depending grace, a grace that leads us out of ourselves and makes Christ all in all.

(3) All those and those only that are sanctified and renewed after the image of God have a title to this happiness. [There is] no seeing God without holiness (Heb. 12:14) and purity (Matt. 5:8), as he is pure (1 John 3:3). None are fit for the new Jerusalem but those that have a new heart and a new spirit. This is being made *meet for the inheritance* (Col. 1:12), as one intended for a place or office has education accordingly to fit him for it, as the stones of Solomon's temple were before squared and fitted for it. The beatific vision is attained in the way of *righteousness* (Ps. 17:15), put there for the whole of sanctification. This sanctification consists much in a disclaiming the world, depending upon heaven for a portion.

(4) All those and those only that seriously endeavour to keep the commandments of God have a title to this happiness (Rev. 22:14). 'Tis not talking of them but doing of them that will entitle us to *blessedness* (Ps. 119:1, 2). Christ is the author of this salvation to those only that obey him (Heb. 5:9), those that would reap in glory but sow in duty. 'Tis not perfect obedience that is required as necessary to salvation, but sincere endeavour. That's a gospel word – pressing towards perfection. Love to instituted ordinances is a good sign

6. The English word 'federal' comes from the Latin *foedus*, 'a covenant', 'a bond'. Here the reference is to God's covenantal dealings.

of meetness for heaven. A disposition to the work of heaven evidences some measure of preparedness for heaven.

(5) All those and those only that *love God* have a title to this happiness (1 Cor. 2:9, *prepared for them*; Jas. 2:5, *promised* to them that love him). To love God is to have the affections drawn out towards him, fixed upon him, as the chiefest good. This love must be a superlative love, more than anything else. Many say they love him whose hearts are not with him. Those love God indeed that love him in all conditions. See James 1:12. The crown of life is promised to them *that love him*. When they are in affliction love to God is then tried – whether we can love him when he slays us. Those that love God will *love his appearing* (2 Tim. 4:8).

(6) All those and those only that hold on and hold out to the end shall inherit eternal life. Perseverance in grace is a commanded duty as well as a promised mercy, and 'tis that only that obtains the crown (Matt. 10:22). Drawing back is to perdition. We lose what we have gained unless we persevere (2 John 8). Under the law if a Nazarite were polluted after his vow he lost all his former days (Num. 6:12). The former righteousness shall not be mentioned if we apostatise (Ezek. 18:24). The crown of life is sure to those only that are faithful unto death (Rev. 2:10).

To conclude. Bring your hearts to the trial, and do not leave it until you have brought it to an issue. Let the verdict be impartial and proceed accordingly. Of those that do get to heaven

1. some are saved yet *so as by fire* (1 Cor. 3:15), i.e. with great difficulty – scarcely saved. Take heed of such a hazard. Say not, a man may get to heaven in such a way, but it's an unusual part to run a venture in a matter of such moment.
2. others have an *abundant entrance administered to them* (2

Pet. 1:11), as a ship that comes into a harbour with full sail. And they are such as take pains in self examination to get assurance (v. 10).

19 Jun. 1692

ETERNAL LIFE WHICH GOD THAT CANNOT LIE PROMISED ... (Titus 1:2)

D[octrine] That God has in the covenant of grace promised eternal life to all true believers.

Use 3. By way of exhortation. When the Apostle had been speaking of heaven's happiness he concluded (1 Thess. 4:18), *wherefore comfort one another*, παρακαλεῖτε,[1] *exhort one another* (so it signifies) *with these words*. There's matter for exhortation to be drawn from that which is revealed in the Word concerning heaven, and will you *suffer* this word of exhortation?

Exh[ortation]

1. Be all of you exhorted to give all diligence to secure to yourselves a title to and an interest in this eternal life. Here is such happiness set before you. Make it your own. I am this day to *set life* before you, therefore *choose life* (Deut. 30:15, 19). In other things 'tis easy to persuade people to choose the good and refuse the evil, but in the affairs of their souls how unpersuadable are they? In other things the serious offer of a good bargain is enough. There needs no rhetoric to persuade one that's seeking to take hold of a cord, and yet how is this salvation neglected?

   My exhortation to you is in the words of the Apostle (1 Tim. 6:12), *lay hold on eternal life*, as he that wins the race lays hold on the prize. It notes great earnestness and diligence. Lay hold on it with a holy violence.

   a. It is a thing that may be done. 'Tis very possible that all this happiness may be their own. We do not put you upon

1. Greek, 2nd person plural present imperative of the verb to 'comfort' or 'exhort'.

impossibilities. 'Tis true the gate is strait and the way narrow (Matt. 7:14), but 'tis as true that the gate is *open* and way is *plain.* 'Tis true that multitudes miss it and are lost for ever, but it's as true that it's long of themselves if they do. I am sure you may be happy if you will. The offer is free and general. Wisdom is introduced with *length of days* in her hand, proffering eternal life to as many as will embrace her (Prov. 2:16). 'Tis in the close of the fullest description of this glory that we have this invitation, Revelation 22:17, *whosoever will let him come.*

b. It is thing that must be done. We are not left at our liberty about it whether we will accept of it or no, but are commanded to *seek the kingdom of God* (Matt. 6:33). God has so far consulted our happiness as not to leave us wholly at our liberty, but to interpose his own authority, and command us to believe. 'Twas one great end for which we were sent into this world to glorify God and enjoy him. He hath twisted interests with us, our own happiness with his glory.

c. If it be not done we are undone for ever. There's no mean between infinite happiness and infinite misery to eternity. If heaven be not ours, hell is. ἕκαστοι εἰς τὸν ἴδιον τόπον χωρεῖν μέλλει (Ignation).[2] Judas that fell by transgression went to *his own place* (Acts 1:25), the place that was fittest for him, the place that he had merited by his own sin. There are but two places that will receive all the children of men to all eternity – either Abraham's bosom, or hell torment (Luke 16:22, 23). And it will be a mighty aggravation of the ruin that when time 'twas possible not only to have prevented it but to have obtained eternal happiness. To see Lazarus in Abraham's bosom will not pour so much oil into the flames as to remember that *then in thy lifetime receivest thy good things* and particularly a fair offer of life and happiness, which thou wouldst not accept (Luke 16:25; Prov. 1:24). This will sting for ever.

---

2. This Greek quotation comes from chapter 5 of the early church father Ignatius' *Letter to the Magnesians* and reads: 'Each shall go to his own place'.

Let me in short tell you as plainly as I can

i. what you must do. I'll suppose you coming to me with the gaoler's question (Acts 16:30), or the question of the young gentleman that came to Christ (Luke 18:18). He came like a man in earnest (Mark 10:17) with a serious question, *What shall I do to inherit [eternal life]?* Not a curious question like that [of] Luke 13:23, or a captious question like that [of] Matthew 22:17, but a very good question about eternal things – and 'twas proposed with a very good design – not to tempt him, as Luke 10:25, but to be instructed by him.

If I were now to put you in a way how to live long in this world, or how to inherit a great estate here, how attentive would you be but because we preach about an unseen world, how careless are most of the people. *Hear*, i.e. hear and obey, and *your souls shall live* (Isa. 55:3). The directions will be nothing new. Perhaps you may expect as Namaan (2 Kings 5:11, 12), but I have no new gospel to preach. I have no commission to show you any new way to heaven but what I have told you often I now tell you weeping (Phil. 3:18), weeping for the obstinacy of those that neglect so great a salvation. If this is the first time you had had this offer made you, how would you catch at it, or if you were sure it would be the last. The first indeed it is not, but you know not but it may be the last.

Let me ground the directions upon the particulars in the text.

(I) It is *eternal life* that is set before you, and therefore if you would have it

(a) you must sit loose to temporal life. Be more concerned about the things that are not seen yet are eternal than the things that are seen yet are temporal (2 Cor. 4:18). This is the first step towards heaven, to sit loose to the things of sense and time as vanity and vexation of spirit, and to be dead to them – to be more solicitous about our everlasting condition than about our present state. Those that were heirs of that better country confessed themselves *strangers and pilgrims* in this world (Heb. 11:13). Those that would seek the kingdom of God so as to find must take no anxious solicitous thought about present things (Matt. 6:32, 32, 34). Our Lord Jesus lays a great stress upon this (Matt. 19:21; Luke 14:26). The stream of the affections must be turned out of this earthly channel (Col. 3:1, 2). Life itself must not be dear compared with this eternal life (Acts 20:24).

(b) you must make sure [of] *spiritual* life, for that's the beginning and first-fruits of eternal life. Grace is the life of the soul. If you would see the everlasting light you must awake and rise from the dead (Eph. 5:14) – life unto life (2 Cor. 2:16), life spiritual to life eternal. See to it that there be a true living principle of grace planted in your souls. Holiness is the life of the soul, and conformity to God. You must live the life of heaven. There must be heavenly breathings, heavenly motion. You must have your conversations by the *grace of God* (2 Cor. 1:12). You must be *holy*, that's the life of heaven.

(II) It is *eternal life promised,* and therefore

(a) we must fulfil the conditions. 'Tis not promised absolutely to all, then none would perish, but conditionally, and the conditions are very reasonable. 'Tis true in all this that God doth work what he requires, gives them a heart to fulfil the conditions, but he requires the duty of all, as the condition of the promise. You have the conditions (Acts 20:24).

(i) *Repentance towards God.* All that would have eternal life must repent of their sins, i.e. must be sorry for what's past and have no more to do with sin for the future. Christ died to save us not in our sins but from our sins (Matt. 1:21). You must renounce every sin else you cannot call heaven yours. The love and allowance of sin will not consist with a title to this eternal life, for

(b) by sin we forfeit this eternal life. Sin is treason against the government of heaven, and we justly lose our share in heaven's privileges when we withdraw our obedience to heaven's laws. Though every sin be not an irremediable forfeiture so well-ordered in this covenant of grace and so sure, yet every sin unrepented of is – every beloved sin is. 'Tis the meritorious cause of our exclusion from heaven. No unclean thing shall enter (Rev. 21:27).

(c) by sin we disfit ourselves for this eternal life. Therefore sin must be renounced as that which renders us utterly uncapable of enjoying God. Sin doth alienate the heart from God and builds up the partition wall, sets us at a distance, separates between us and God (Isa. 59:1). The dismal sentence, *Depart from me*, is the sinner's choice.

(i) *Faith towards our Lord Jesus Christ.* Those that would have life must come to Christ for it (John 5:40; Matt. 11:28). The salvation is put into his hand to be disposed of by him, and all that will have it must have it from Christ (Acts 16:31). Believe in Christ, i.e.:

(d) Rely upon Christ's righteousness. Be found in Christ. Put in your claim through Jesus Christ our Lord. Come in a dependence upon the ability and willingness of Christ to save you, having no confidence in the flesh. Walk in Christ as the only way to heaven (John 14:6). [There is] no coming to heaven but by him. Build all your hopes upon his merit.

(e) Resign yourself to his rule. Submit to the government of Jesus Christ. He is the author of this salvation to those that obey him (Heb. 5:9). The moral law is put into the hand of the mediator, and we are required to observe it in faith. True faith works in obedience. Christ saith, 'Love one another'. Christ enjoins sobriety, righteousness. The grace of God teaches this (Titus 2:11, 12).

(III) We must be willing to wait for the performance. 'Tis a happiness in promise, and we must be content to deal upon trust. 'Tis promised to those that love and look for Christ's appearing (2 Tim. 4:8). The heirs of heaven must be heirs of promise. [They must] embrace a promise (Heb. 11:13). 'Tis the character of Christians indeed that they *wait* for his Son (1 Thess. 1:10).

You see what's to be done that this eternal life may be yours. Let me tell you

ii. how you must do it:

(I) Do it speedily – today before tomorrow. Do not give sleep to the eyes nor slumber to your eyelids until it be done. Do not rest till you have finished the thing. (allu[de to] Ruth 3:18). Delays in this case are highly dangerous. Many a one has left a good bargain by delays. Therefore strike it immediately. Just now renounce your sins and give up yourselves to Christ. You that are young do not put it off until you are old. *Seek first* (Matt. 6:23). Postpone a care about your portion in this life.

(II) Do it sincerely. This eternal life is promised by God, *that cannot lie*, and those are his people that will not lie (Isa. 63:8), that will not deal deceitfully in the covenant. Never expect a real happiness for a feigned holiness. Be upright in the choice and consent, upright in your purposes and promises.

(III) Do it steadfastly and with a holy humble resolution. 'Tis a thing that should engage all that is within us. Resolve to take up with nothing short of this happiness. *Strive to enter* (Luke 13:24) ἀγωνίζεσθε.[3] Strive as in agony, as for a matter of life and death, as one in earnest. Not only ask and seek but knock. With the greatest importunity, beg for heaven as one that's starving begs for bread.

Exh[ortation]

2. To those who through grace have title to this eternal life, an interest in the promise of it. I hope I speak to such as are called by Christ to his kingdom and glory, to whom pertains the inheritance. You are all of you ready to pretend to it. Be persuaded to make sure work for your souls in this matter, and you, do your duty and take the comfort. These two go abreast. Neither [is] to be neglected. Many are willing enough to separate them. They love with Ephraim *to tread out the corn*, but not with Judah *to plow*, and with Jacob to *break the clod* (Hos. 10:11, 12). [They] love to hear of comforts, those are smooth things, but not to hear of duty. But what God has joined let not us think to separate.

a. Do the duty that this calls for from you. Dignity calls for duty. Are you in the hope of eternal life, Christians? Live up to the hope. Let eternal life be always ready to you. Abide continually under the influence of it.

i. Let your thoughts be filled with it. Thoughts are the first-born of the soul, and resemble the parent, the beginning of its strength. As he thinketh in his heart so is he. Those whose hopes refer no higher than the world, their thoughts are wholly conversant about the world (Ps. 49:1), but if the hope enter into that within the veil it cannot but take the thoughts along with it (Matt. 6:21). If you were in hope of some great estate to fall to you shortly, how frequently

3. Greek, 'strive', 'agonise (as in an athletic contest)'.

and with what delight would you be thinking of it – and should not you think of heaven. Get a scriptural map of this Jerusalem and study it well. Make heaven familiar to you (Ps. 48:12, 13). (Some think that rapture of Paul's [2 Cor. 12:2, 3, 4] was only by a profound abstraction of his soul from his corporeal senses, God entertaining with an internal sense of that glory.) But he said *whether in the body*.

ii. Let your temptations be baffled with it. Are you in the hope of eternal life, and will you defile yourselves with the sordid pleasures of sin (see 2 Cor. 7:1)? Use your hopes of heaven as a bridle of restraint to keep you in from all manner of sin. Let it break you forever of Satan's assaults when he would draw you to pride, or passion, or worldly mindedness. Think, doth this become one that's in the hope of heaven? *It is not for kings, O Lemuel* (allu[de to] Prov. 31:4). Hold fast your crown (Rev. 3:11), it's worth holding. This hope should purify us (1 John 3:3). What can Satan offer to invite you to sin which can pretend to out-weigh eternal life? Moses foiled the temptations of this world with this (Heb. 11:24, 25, 26). When you are going forth against your spiritual enemies bathe your swords in heaven (see 2 Pet. 3:13, 14).

iii. Let your desires be raised by it, raised above the poor little trifling things of sense and time. Will you that are in the hope of treasures in heaven pant after the dust of the earth? The believing views of this glory should enable us with a holy disdain to trample upon the things of this world as unworthy of our love. The woman in heaven that was clothed with the sun had the moon under her feet (Rev. 12:1). Manage the things of this world with an indifferency (1 Cor. 7:29, 30). They have no glory by reason of the glory that excelleth. But let your desire be enlarged toward heaven. Set your affections on it (Col. 3:1). We should groan earnestly (2 Cor. 5:2). Desire *that better country* (Heb. 11:16). Is it not thy home, thy father's house, and do not you long to be there? What do you see in this world to court your stay? Come Lord Jesus (Rev. 22:20)!

iv. Let your designs be fixed by it. Aim at heaven in every thing. Make unseen things our scope (2 Cor. 4:18, σκοπούντων[4]), our mark. Take aim at this eternal life in everything you do. *Seek for this glory and honour* (Rom. 2:7). No body comes to heaven by chance, nor stumble upon the crown of glory as Saul did upon the crown of Israel while he was seeking his father's asses. No, the face must be set Zion-ward (Jer. 50:5). That which distinguisheth a true Christian from an hypocrite is that he's one that designs for heaven. That's the port he's bound for, and he steers accordingly. The most of men look at other things, as the Pharisees (Matt. 6:5). A true Christian is one that prays and hears and talks and lives, and all for eternal life. Do not look a wry look to any other satisfaction.

v. Let your diligence be quickened by it. Hopes of heaven should be as a spur in our side. This eternal life should excite our spiritual liveliness. We are very apt to grow dull and slothful and indifferent. When such a distemper grows upon you, think, Do I work now as one that's working for heaven? Is this running, striving, wrestling? Will not eternal life make me rich amends for all my labour (1 Cor. 15:58; 2 Cor. 5:8, 9; Gal. 6:9)? When Jacob had had a vision of glory, then Jacob lift up his feet (Gen. 29:1, margin).[5] Paul had his eye upon this when he pressed forward at that rate (Phil. 3:13, 14). Think how all this will pass in your account. Let it make you delight in dealing with others to bring them to heaven. [Be] diligent in building up yourselves. Do more than others.

---

4. The Greek verb σκοπέω means 'look upon', 'gaze upon', while the noun σκοπός means 'a mark' (to be aimed at). The English word *scope* comes from the Greek noun.

5. The reference is to the marginal reading in the AV at Gen. 29:1, where it gives the literal rendering of the Hebrew, 'he lifted up his feet'.

vi. Let your discourse be seasoned in it. Are you in hope of eternal life? Be often talking of it when you come together. 'Tis a pity Christians when they meet should part without talking of heaven. If two of the same country meet in a strange country with what pleasure do they talk of home. Our language should be the language of Canaan, not mixed as in Nehemiah 13:2. The very air of a man's discourse discovers what country he's of (see John 3:31). Corrupt communication, the language of hell, ill becomes the heirs of salvation (Col. 4:6)

vii. Let your courage be steeled by it. Fear not neither be faint-hearted. In reference to the difficulties of doing work, suffering work, let this strengthen the weak hands and confirm the feeble knees. The way's straight and afflicted (ὅδος τεθλιμμένη)[6] but there's life at the end of it (Matt. 7:14). Let none of these things move you (Acts 20:24). Having cast anchor within the veil be steady in your motions. This is that which has supported the martyrs and has brought them triumphantly through flame – a sharp breakfast but a supper with the Lamb.

viii. Let your conversation be throughout guided and governed by it. In every step you take in the way fetch directions from your end. In doubtful cases ask what's to be done by one that's bound for heaven. We should live as those who are going to eternal life. Our conversation should be in heaven (Phil. 3:20). A heavenly conversation would be a humble, holy, even conversation. 'Twould make us reverent in serving God (Heb. 12:28). Love and joy and praise should sweeten our conversation.

b. Take the comfort that this offers to you. Have the hopes of eternal life. Live upon these hopes. Lay the mouth of faith to these full breasts and from thence suck and be satisfied. Do

---

6. The Greek quotation is from the words used in Matt. 7:14, 'the confined way.'

not put comfort away from you. 'Tis the will of God that you should be comforted (Isa. 40:1), and after all [there is] nothing like a foresight of heaven to comfort a *child* of God. Only make sure work in the foundation. Be right in the closing act, and then be comforted.

There is that in this which will mightily befriend.

i. A cheerful life in general. 'Tis the will of God that true Christians should rejoice in the Lord always (Phil. 4:4), and what [is] more likely to maintain and keep up that joy than hope of the glory of God (Rom. 5:2)? What refreshment must it needs be to the soul by faith to converse within the veil, to taste of the rivers of pleasure! Carnal sensual pleasure doth but sadden a gracious soul, and leave a damp upon the spirit, but how pleasant must the heavenly conversation needs be. None have so much cause to rejoice as the heirs of heaven have. This would fill the soul with joy unspeakable (1 Pet. 1:8), consolations that are not small. Spiritual solid substantial joy – this would put gladness into the heart (Ps. 4:7). This holy cheerfulness would please God, adorn profession, win upon others. The foretastes of heaven should put the sweetness into all our comforts, and furnish us with a continual feast.

ii. Our support under particular burdens. Our way lies through a vale of tears. Burdens of many kinds we must count upon. Hope of heaven should cheer up our spirit, and keep trouble from the heart. 'Tis a prescribed cordial (John 14:1, 2) and the saints in all ages have annexed their *probatum est*[7] – David (Ps. 27:13), Moses (Heb. 11:26), Paul (2 Cor. 4:16, 17). When we are cast down and disquieted one believing look within the veil would raise us up (Rom. 8:18). If it be so, why am I thus? If [I am] the King's son, why [am I] lean from day to day? A prospect of that joy that is before us, when all tears shall be wiped away, should help to wipe away tears now. The heirs of heaven should

7. Latin for 'it is approved', 'it is good'.

rejoice in tribulation. Their joy should survive their creature comforts, for it is not lodged in this lower region.

Take comfort from hence

1. in reference to the remainders of indwelling corruptions. This body of sin shall not torment us in heaven. No vain thoughts, no ungoverned passions, [no] unruly appetites there. None of the sons of Zeruiah[8] that are too hard for us [will be there], but all pure and regular and in frame, like Adam in innocency, with this advantage that the rectitude will not be loseable. [There will be] no law in the members to war against the law in the mind, no pricking briar or vexing thorn.

2. in reference to the strength of Satan's temptations. None of those fiery darts will touch us there to molest and inflame us. That unclean spirit was so cast out of these pure and quiet regions as never to return to them again. Satan will there be perfectly subdued (Rom. 16:20), the victory completed, the enemy so routed as never to rally again. Here if he departs 'tis but for a season (Luke 4:13), but there [for ever].

3. in reference to the eclipses of the divine favour. We are here often under a cloud. God hides himself, our beloved withdraws himself and is gone (Cant. 5:6), but there's no cloud in the upper region. We have here our comfort by glances, but there the views will be immediate and uninterrupted – communion not as here in ordinances.

4. in reference to our outward troubles and afflictions, whether the rebuke of providence or persecutions for righteousness sake. There's something in this eternal life which suits our trouble whatever it is. 'Tis a salve for every sore. Is it poverty, imprisonment, banishment, reproach? In heaven there's riches, freedom, glory (see Heb. 10:3).

---

8. See the AV of 2 Sam. 3:39, 'the sons of Zeruiah be too hard for me'.

5. in reference to the stroke of death – the death of our friends and relations. We hope to meet them again shortly in a better place. They are but gone before (1 Thess. 4:13). In reference to our own death, never fear it. Death to the saints is a passage to eternal life, like Joseph's wagons. Entertain it then with joy and bid it welcome. Comfort yourselves and one another with these words.

[Undated]

ETERNAL LIFE(i)

Having observed out of this text what it is to be religious, 'tis by a patient continuance in well-doing to seek for immortal glory, I come now to consider:

1. What is the recompense of reward proposed for those that by patient continuance in well-doing seek for it, viz. *eternal life.*

Doct[rine] That those who are truly religious in this world shall without fail be truly happy in the world to come. The righteous judge of heaven and earth will render the recompense of eternal life to all that patiently continue in well-doing.

Show 1. Upon what account God will confer this future happiness upon obedient and persevering believers – on what score will it come to them. Here 'tis represented as rendered to them by the righteous judge according to their works.

a. For certain *not of debt.* None can claim this happiness as having done anything to deserve it, or to take off the forfeiture of it which we have all incurred. We cannot atone for the wrong we have done to God by sin, much less can we be profitable to him (see Job 22:2, 3). We pay our servants their wages because we have need of their work, and they have earned their wages, but God doth not thus give this happiness to the saints for there is no proportion at all between their services and this recompense (see Job 35:5, 7). He will render this happiness to the saints *according to* their works, not *for* their works, otherwise there would be room for boasting, which must be excluded, and is so by the law of faith (Rom. 3:27). Our good works cannot in justice merit this happiness because we are already bound to them (Luke 17:10), because we can do nothing but by the grace of God working in us both to will and to do, and because the best of our services are attended with many infirmities and imperfections, and give us cause to expect rather a breach than a blessing, such a blessing. All that are fitted for heaven are made sensible of their unworthiness, and are made willing to take it not as *due* wages, but as a *free* gift. Every crown [will be] there cast at the footstool of the throne (Rev. 4:10, 11) and all the saved remnant acknowledging how much they are beholden to the Lord Jesus Christ.

b. But of grace (Rom. 6:23), *the gift of God*, opposed to that wrath which is *the wages of sin*. Free grace is the spring, and first wheel. All the rest flows from this. *By grace we are saved* (Eph. 2:5, 8, 9). 'Grace, grace', must be cried to every stone in that building (Zech. 4:7). This is a truth we must hold fast, that the eternal happiness of the saints is owing purely to the grace of God in Jesus Christ, who is the author of this eternal salvation (Heb. 5:9).

But to illustrate the harmony of the divine attributes and the economy of God's government and his relations to man the acts of his *grace* are annexed to the acts of his *dominion*. And he confers his gifts as benefactor by such rules and measures as tend to advance his honour and interest in the children of men as their *Lord* and *Ruler*. And therefore in setting up his kingdom among men he hath proposed and promised this future happiness upon condition of sincere obedience to his command, and to those that are so and so qualified for it. And this eternal life comes to be rendered to those that do well and continue in it. More particularly,

i. This happiness was designed for them in the counsels of everlasting love. Election is the first link in that golden chain which glorification is the last link of (Rom. 8:30). As God was from eternity designing this happiness (Matt. 25:34), so he was designing a remnant to this happiness (2 Thess. 2:13). God's favours to eternity will be disposed according to his purposes from eternity (Eph. 3:11; see John 17:2;

6:39). The names of those that are intended for heaven are written in heaven (Luke 10:20), for it would not consist with the divine wisdom to provide such a happiness without determining who should be the monuments of his grace in the enjoyment of it. O the depth of this wisdom and grace!

ii. 'Twas purchased for them for the blood of the Redeemer, and upon this score 'tis given them. Hence it is called the purchased possession (Eph. 1:14). The inheritance was mortgaged. Christ as our next of kin (that was able to do it) redeems it. [He] took that out of the way which hindered, all judgments, executions and other encumbrances (Col. 2:19). He opened the kingdom of heaven to all believers (Heb. 10:19, 20). He purchased this glory to himself and his spiritual seed, and so obedient believers come to it (see Heb. 9:15). For your sakes he sanctifies himself (John 17:6, 19, 24). Thus 'tis the gift of God *through Christ* (Rom. 6:23) 'Tis in consideration of Christ's undertaking for us and the price he paid that God renders eternal life to those that *obey Christ* (Heb. 5:9). He being empowered to give the law, he is empowered to make the promise and make it good (John 17:2).

iii. 'Tis promised to them in the everlasting covenant. Though God is debtor to no man yet he is pleased to make himself a debtor by his own promise, and he will render to men according to their works, because he has said he will (Titus 1:2; see John 3:15, 16). The promise is offered to all, but true believers upon their believing come to have an interest in it, by virtue of their union with Christ and relation to him. They are the children of the promise and to them the promise is sure (Heb. 6:17, 18, 19). Heaven is the true Canaan, the land of promise. The promise of eternal life is the crown of all the promises of the everlasting covenant. 'Tis that which will complete the happiness of the saints (1 Cor. 15:19), and which will answer the extent of that great fundamental promise of the covenant that God will be to them a God (see Heb. 11:16), so that he is *faithful* in giving eternal life to obedient believers (1 Thess. 5:24). This was part of the legacy bequeathed by the New Testament in the blood of Christ so that though 'twas free grace that bequeathed it, according to the nature of a legacy, yet being bequeathed 'tis an act of justice to pay it.

iv. They are prepared and made meet for it by the blessed Spirit as a sanctifier. God will give eternal life to those that by patient continuance in well-doing seek for it because that good work which is now wrought in them is a preparation for that happiness (2 Cor. 5:5). Nay, it is the earnest of it (2 Cor. 1:22; Eph. 1:14). God will *give glory* as the perfection of the *grace* he has given in this world, the crown of his own work towards which the beginnings are working (Col. 1:12). They that are truly religious have the first-fruits and therefore must have the harvest. They have the *anointing* (1 John 2:27) and therefore must have the kingdom. Patient continuance in well-doing is a foundation on which a fabric shall be reared as high as heaven, and he that has begun to build is able to finish.

v. There is great tendency in the present state, character and disposition of the saints towards that happiness. Consider what the saints are and you'll see under that notion to look upon their eternal happiness, for it is variously represented in Scripture.

(1) The saints are the *children* of God and heaven is their inheritance, and the righteous Father will give to the sons the inheritance of sons. If *children, then heirs* (Rom. 8:17). They that do well are God's children for they are *like God* (Eph. 5:1). They bear his image, they partake of his nature, and will he not then give them children's portions? And less than heaven's glory will not portion an immortal soul (see John 3:1, 2)? If sons then they abide in the house for ever. They are now under tutors and governors but 'tis to prepare them for the inheritance.

(2) The saints are *travellers* in the good way, and heaven is their home, their journey's end. They walk in the way of good men, the narrow way, which leads directly to life (Matt. 7:14). A religious course and conversation is the highway that will bring us to happiness according to the appointment and designation of God (Prov. 12:28). Those who continue in well-doing go on in the way, and though it be tedious yet it will end in life. The Word of God hath said, *This is the way*, walk in it, and you shall find *rest* (Jer. 6:16). Walk in this way and it will bring you to heaven.

(3) The saints are *labourers* in God's vineyard and heaven is the reward of their labour, their *penny* as it is in the parable (Matt. 20:9). They that work God's work, and make it the business of their lives shall certainly be rewarded for it. God will not forget the labour of love (Heb. 6:10). Though the best saints in the world could recover nothing *quantum meruit*, yet upon an *assumpsit*[1] they may recover no less than heaven, pleading not our desert but God's promise (see Rev. 14:13, *their works follow them*). Good and faithful servants that are found doing shall enter in the joy of their Lord.

(4) The saints are *vessels* of mercy, and eternal life is that and that only which will fill those vessels. Therefore God will give them this happiness because they are his workmanship now created for it (see Rom. 9:23, *prepared unto glory*). Therefore he will give them this glory because he hath wrought in them an aptitude and disposition to it. He will not open the desires of his people towards this glory and raise their expectations of it and then frustrate them. That would be unkind.

(5) The saints are *running* the race set before them, and

1. In Latin *quantum meruit* means 'as much as he deserved', while *assumpsit* means 'he has undertaken', 'he took'.

heaven is the prize they run for. Those that continue in well-doing are striving, not for a corruptible crown but an incorruptible crown, and the righteous judge will give it to those that faithfully finish their course (2 Tim. 4:7, 8; see Phil. 3:13, 14; 1 Cor. 9:24, etc.). 'Tis not so much the labour as the success that is rewarded, and glorious things are spoken of those that do overcome (Rev. 2 and 3). He that strives lawfully shall be crowned (2 Tim. 2:5).

(6) The saints are wise *merchants*, and heaven is the *pearl* of price which they were willing to take at the rate on which it is offered, and why should they not have it? We are called to buy, to buy freely, and yet to part with all we have. If we come up to the terms we shall certainly have our bargain, that which we agreed with God for (see Matt. 13:45, 46).

(7) The saints are often losing for God, and heaven is the recompense of their losses. Our continuance in well-doing *has need of patience*, and the terms of our profession are forsaking houses, lands, etc. and will God suffer us to lose by him? Nay, hath he not engaged to make up all these losses with an eternal life (Matt. 19:29) and so to recompense us in the resurrection of the just (Heb. 10:34)?

(8) The saints are the citizens of the new Jerusalem and shall have the rights and privileges of their citizenship. Their conversation is in heaven, and therefore their eternal abode shall be there (Phil. 3:20; Heb. 11:16). There's room in the heavenly city for all that belong to it, and we are to come to it (Heb. 12:22).

Show 2. What this future happiness is which all that are truly religious shall have in the world to come. In general:

a. It is a complete happiness, the highest degree of happiness the children of men are capable of. 'Tis a happiness that will not admit of any *allay*, nor desire *any addition*. There will be nothing to *embitter it*. There will be nothing to *increase* it. It must be complete for it is *entire*, the happiness of the whole man in all its faculties and interests, and it's all within itself. Here what happiness we have is compounded and patched up of many pieces, and *ex quolibit defectu oritur malum*,[2] wine mixed with water, *sollicitum aliquid latis introvenit*,[3] some *but* or other. But the happiness of heaven is perfect. [There is] nothing wanting, no jar in the harmony, no inconvenience in the conveniences, whatever [the] heart can wish. Solomon observed all his grievances were *under the sun* (Eccles. 1:3), none above it.

b. It is a continuing happiness. The permanency of it adds much to the perfection of it. We have seen an end of all subliminary perfection (Ps. 119:96) but no end of that perfection, no delay or tendency towards a period, no doubt or fear of period.[4] Were there any such fear that would embitter the comfort, but 'tis a continuing city (Heb. 13:14). The soul that is made happy being an immortal soul, and the God that undertakes to make it happy from himself immediately being an immortal God, the happiness itself must needs be of an endless duration.

c. It is such a happiness as in our present state we cannot conceive of (1 Cor. 2:9). 'Tis a glory that is *to be revealed* (Rom. 8:18). It doth not yet appear what we shall be (1 John 3:2). 'Tis a happiness transcending not only all the comforts but all the conceptions of our present state. We speak of it as children do of preferments and employments they never saw (1 Cor. 13:11, 12), or as blind men do of colours. Only this we are sure of, that it will be a happiness perfective of our nature. God will show what he can do to make a beloved creature happy. Thus shall it be done to every man whom the King delights to honour.

---

2. Latin, 'out of any defect trouble comes'.
3. Latin, 'some care or other enters [even] those who are happy'.
4. *Period*, here in the sense of 'end'.

d. It is a happiness in which God will be all in all (1 Cor. 15:28), the most noble outgoings of the soul towards God as the chief good. 'Tis an immediate and uninterrupted communion with God – God himself with them and their God (Rev. 21:3).

i. It is to see God as he is (1 John 3:2). This was the sight Moses was so ambitious of (Exod. 33:18) but we are not capable of it in this present state (John 1:18). [We] see God in Christ, [see] God in my flesh (Job 19:26). A faint ray of the glory of Christ was almost the death of John (Rev. 1:17) because he was in a state which could not bear it, though in the Spirit, but the full manifestation of this glory will be the life of the saints face to face (1 Cor. 13:13), to see him whom the angels adore, whom our souls love.

ii. It is to enjoy God, to see him as ours. He that hath the bride is the bridegroom. The life of the body consists in its union and communion with the soul, so the life of the soul in its union and communion with God. 'Tis to see God as our reconciled Father, our covenant friend, to drink in the rays of his glory as that which we are sharers in. You know what it is to enjoy a beloved friend. God and glorified saints converse together. They dwell with him, walk with him. [There is] nothing in them to alienate them from him, nothing to interrupt between them and him.

iii. It is to be like God. Without a conformity to him, there could be no happiness in communion with him. We shall be *like him* (1 John 3:2), changed into the same image (2 Cor. 3:18). That image of God which is stamped upon the soul in sanctification, and is here like the rude draft of a picture. [It] will there be finished and the last hand put to it.

iv. It is to be perfectly satisfied in all this (Ps. 17:15), the soul reposing itself in God, and resting in him. 'Tis where it would be. All the desires of sanctified souls after God which are here moving towards him shall then be satisfied (Ps. 42:1, 2; 73:25; John 9:14). With more than God? No, nor nothing more of God, [but] resting in his love.

[There are] two things in this happiness.

(1) A perfect freedom from all evil. Whatever we can imagine grievous or uneasy to us, there's nothing of it in heaven. 'Tis rest from all our labours (Rev. 14:13) and the toil and fatigue of them (Heb. 4:4), rest from all our troubles, Satan's temptations, indwelling corruptions, outward afflictions, persecution of enemies. As a ship in a safe and quiet harbour after a stormy voyage, no rocks, nor waves, nor tempests, nor pirates – no grievance (Rev. 7:16), all tears wiped away (Rev. 21:4), no pain, nor sickness of body, no deformity, infirmity, decay – nothing to disturb the peace. No cares, no fears, no enemies and best of all no sin. No pricking brier nor grieving thorn, a kingdom without war and tumult, a church without scandal and schism, a family without any uneasiness, a society without any mixture, no spots in the feast of charity, no false brethren,

(2) A perfect fruition of all good. 'Tis not a negative happiness, 'tis a positive. All the soul's desires [are] satisfied and swallowed up in delights. Take nine words and think of them.

(a) *Life* So 'tis called in the Psalms and often elsewhere. Death includes all evil, and it passed on all men for sin (Rom. 5:12), but Christ is the life (John 14: 6), our life (John 10:10), *more abundantly* than Adam had it in innocency, and yet we have it in this world. Heaven is the land of the living (Ps. 27:13), 'tis life (Matt. 19:17), the only true life. 'Tis a dying life we live here, but 'tis a life indeed that the saints live in heaven, sunning saints in the refreshing beams of divine favour (Ps. 30:5). If a man will give all that he has for so poor a life as this we live here (Job 2:4), what should we not be willing to part with for such a life as that?

(b) *Light* 'Tis a rational life, the life was the light (John 1:4). Here we live in a dark world and cannot order our speech by reason of darkness, but there all clouds will be scattered and we shall see as we are seen (1 Cor. 13:9, 10, 12). We have now some glimpses of light but they are in comparison with the heavenly light as that of a candle to the noonday sun. All difficulties will then be solved, all depths fathomed, doubts cleared, the mystery of God finished, the platform of divine counsels laid open – the mystery of redemption, the mysteries of providence – all revealed. The tree of knowledge will not be a forbidden tree in that paradise.

(c) *Love* Now we live in a world of hatred, esek and sitnah,[5] contention and hatred but the world of light will be a world of love, perfect love to God. Here we are much straitened in it, and thence ariseth the straitness of our obedience, but in heaven we shall love the Lord our God with all our heart. He will there let out his love, and so draw out ours (1 John 4:19). What's heaven but the eternal reciprocation of loves between God and the saints? There will be perfect love to the saints (1 Cor. 13:8, 13). How pleasant it is (Ps. 133:1)!

(d) *Purity* Heaven is a holy place. No unclean thing shall enter into that new Jerusalem, that holy of holies (Rev. 21:27), [with] the divine image perfectly renewed upon the soul, never more to be defaced or lost. Holiness becomes God's house (Ps. 93:5). The state [is] a holy state and the heart holy for that state, the company holy. Holiness to the Lord [is] written on everything there (Zech. 14:20). God's holiness is in a special manner adored there (Rev.

5. These two names refer to the two wells over which Isaac's herdsmen and the herdsmen of Gerar quarrelled. Isaac named the first one *esek* (dispute) and the second one *sitnah* (opposition). See Gen. 26:19-22.

4:8) and the saints made partaker[s] of his holiness. Hence it is that sanctification is so necessary a preparation for that happiness. Heaven would not be heaven to one unsanctified. Those that are weary of a short Sabbath will sure be weary of an everlasting Sabbath.

(e) *Pleasure* The river of pleasures (Ps. 36:8), pleasures for evermore (Ps. 16:6). 'Tis paradise, the Garden of Eden (Rev. 2:7), i.e. of pleasure, no sinful pleasures, the Turk's paradise, but spiritual pleasures, the fatness and sweetness of God's house. We have now the pleasure of the ordinances (Ps. 84:10) but we shall then bathe ourselves in the ocean of delights. The happiness of heaven is represented by a pleasant city, a pleasant dwelling, the company pleasant, everything agreeable, and therefore pleasant, pure, unmixed, uninterrupted pleasures, *sincera voluptus*.[6] If the ways be pleasantness, what will the end be?

(f) *Praise* The work of heaven is praise (Rev. 4:8). They that dwell in God's house will be still praising him (Ps. 84:4). Praise is good (Ps. 92:1), 'tis pleasant (Ps. 135:3). This work glorified saints shall for ever be employed in. They will have full matter for praise, and a freed and fixed heart for praise. Here our praises are often lost in complaints, and our harps hung upon the willow-trees, but in heaven there will be neither sin nor trouble but all grace and love and sweetness – a blessed Sabbath indeed.

(g) *Glory* The happiness of heaven is often called so. 'Tis the glory that is to be revealed, a *weight* of glory (2 Cor. 4:17), massy and substantial, not as the glory of all flesh, *like the flower of the grass*. O'Tis a participation of Christ's glory. Those who

6. Latin for 'genuine pleasure'.

sought for immortal honour and glory shall find what they sought – a glory that excelleth in comparison with which the creature has no glory. The glory of the kings of the earth and the nations is all in effect brought into this new Jerusalem (Rev. 21:24, 26). Is it not an unspeakable glory to attend upon the throne of God? To be *as the angels*, to have the body like Christ's (Phil. 3:21). Home 'tis represented as a crown, a throne, etc.

(h) *Gladness* Glorified saints enter into the joy of their Lord (Matt. 25:21). That's the harvest of joy for all who sow in tears (Ps. 126:1). Sin and affliction, these two fountains of tears, will then be dried up for ever. Not a heavy heart, not a weeping eye, not a melancholy look among all the thousands of the saints. Our way to heaven lies through a vale of tears, but when we come there everlasting joy shall not only fill our hearts but crown our heads (Isa. 35:6; 60:19, 20)? 'Tis represented by a *feast* which is made for laughter, *wine* in the kingdom of God which makes glad the heart, *a marriage* which useth[7] is to be attended with joy.

(i) *God himself* All will be swallowed up in God – ever with the Lord (1 Thess. 4:17). There could not be any eternal happiness but by the immediate communion with and communication from the eternal God, who is not only the author and giver but matter of that happiness. But what do I mean, to put the sea into an eggshell? The thousandth part has not been told you.

---

7. *Useth*, in the obsolete sense of 'to be accustomed'. Modern English only employs this meaning with the past tense, e.g. 'He *used* to come home every weekend'.

[undated]

ETERNAL LIFE(ii)

Show 3. What influence the prospects of this *eternal life* should have upon us to make us all truly religious. Wherefore are those things set before us but that we may be guided and governed by them in our present course.

Why are these things made known to us by the light of the gospel (2 Tim. 1:10) but that we may thereby be brought into obedience to the laws of the gospel. This happiness is set before us not as a matter of curious notion and speculation, but as a matter of consequence. We do not discourse of heaven as the philosophers of the material heavens, only to exercise their wits, but as merchants talk of the pearls of price they are trading for. We are speaking of that which is of the highest importance to every one of us. The assurances of eternal life, to those that continue in well-doing, may be of use to us.

a. As a general argument why we should be religious. I take it for granted you all believe that there is such a happiness set before us and attainable by us, that there is an *eternal* life after this temporal life. Work this then when you say that you believe upon your hearts and try what influence and effect it will have upon you.

1. That which is set before us is *eternal*, and therefore to be minded with the greatest concern and to be preferred before that which is temporal (2 Cor. 9:18). Religion teacheth us to deal in things that are eternal, and reason tells us that this do best deserve the serious intentions and regards of our souls. God is the *eternal, the King eternal* (1 Tim. 1:17) and all the things that are eternal depend immediately upon him, eternal life upon his *grace* and eternal death upon his *wrath*. The eternal judgment (Heb. 6:2) is his judgment. Now to be religious is to have a due regard to this God, on whom eternity depends, and is not that our greatest

concern? If we be bound for an eternal state to make sure an interest in the eternal God, to observe and obey him now with whom we certainly have to do eternally. Eternity is a thing that challengeth the most serious and awful regards.

2. 'Tis an *eternal life,* i.e. an eternal happiness that is set before us, and therefore to be pursued with the greatest diligence and desire. What can be a more powerful inducement to us to walk in the way of religion than to be assured of such a happiness as this in the end of our way?

For if it be so,

a. Then it cannot possibly *turn to our loss* to be religious. In making a bargain, in desiring a trade, this is our first care, not to lose by it. When we call upon people to be religious, and to set about the practice of serious godliness the devil and their own corrupt hearts tell them it will be to their loss, and damage, and they had better let it alone. Doth this thought arise in your minds at any time? We are content to join issue upon, and try this case. Christ would have us to sit down and count (Luke 14:28), and if such a happiness as this in the other world be the reward of religion, then though we may be losers for it, we cannot be losers by it.

i. If religion abridge us of our *pleasures* yet we shall not lose by it if we be recompensed with *eternal pleasures*. To be religious is to deny ourselves in that carnal liberty which others take, but alas that liberty is *bondage* (2 Pet. 2:19), and if we be restrained from that liberty, yet we have the liberty to draw near to God, which is the best pleasure. The pleasures religion forbids are brutal and sensual, mixed with pain, and followed with death. [It is] no great loss to lose them but since it seems something of a loss it shall be made up in the pleasure at God's right hand (Ps. 16:11; 36:8). Heaven is an everlasting *feast*, where there's all, plenty and all joy, laughter in the midst of which the heart is not sad, and mirth the end of which is not heaviness. Doth a wise man envy children the pleasure of children's play? Who would not deny the pleasure of sinful embraces, for the pleasure of the everlasting embraces of divine love? It is no loss to *enter into* life so *maimed* (Mark 9:43).

ii. If religion balk our *preferment* or blast our credit with men, yet we shall not lose by it if we be recompensed with *eternal glory*. Usually to be strictly and seriously godly is to be out of the way of preferment in this world, for that's a thing which they will have that seek it, and they will not seek it that know it and themselves. And is not this a loss? Never to rise nor make a figure but be always an underling and obscure, [is] no loss if we can but obtain heaven's glory. Is it not better preferment to be made unto our God *kings* and *priests* (Rev. 1:6), to sit down with Christ on his throne (Rev. 3:21; Luke 23:30)? If set at man's footstool (Jas. 2:3) will it not make amends for that to be set at Christ's right hand (Matt. 25:34; Matt. 5:11, 12), to wear the crown of glory?

iii. If our *estates* be hazarded and impaired by our religion yet we shall not lose by it if we be recompensed with *the eternal inheritance*. Religion may check us in those practices which others thrive by (Neh. 5:14). Their consciences will not let them take such courses as others take to get wealth, but if you get the favour of God, and the true riches, is not that better? If we forsake houses and lands for Christ will not heaven make up the loss (Matt. 19:29)? See Hebrews 10:14. If God give thee heaven, will he not give thee *much more than this* (2 Chron. 25:9)? If the saints are scattered strangers yet they are chosen as an inheritance (1 Pet. 1:4).

iv. If our *lives* be exposed and lost for our religion yet we shall not sit down losers if we be recompensed with *eternal life*. 'Tis certain when we come to Christ we must put such a value upon him, and upon our own expectations from him as to prefer them over against life itself which must therefore be *hated* (Luke 14:26), not loved (Rev.

12:11), not counted dear (Acts 20:24). We may be called to resist unto blood, but the hazards of a mortal life are nothing to the gains of an immortal life. See Matthew 16:25. The *better resurrection* will make amends (Heb. 11:35), i.e. a resurrection to a better life that this is. The loving-kindness of God, especially as is shall be given out to glorified saints, is *better than life* (Ps. 63:3). Here in the midst of life we are in death, but there shall be no more death (2 Tim. 1:10). This is a life which many a man is weary of (Job 10:1), but that's a life which though everlasting is not tedious. This is a life with the inferior creatures, that with God and glorious spirits. So that 'tis certain we shall never lose by our religion. Heaven is a good counter-security.

b. Then it will without doubt *turn to our gain* to be religious. 'Tis but a small encouragement to be assured that we shall not lose but yet the world cannot give that to its devotees. Our encouragements are much greater. We shall be gainers by it. Interest rules the world, and all people are for what they can get. Now, I tell you therefore, those that deal in wisdom's merchandise get unspeakably. See Proverbs 3:1-15. There are those who say that it is vain to serve God (Mal. 3:13, 14; Job 21:14, 15; 22:17). But if this be true that they that are holy here shall be thus happy hereafter, that suggestion is very false, for it is not *in vain*. Good men have been tempted to say, 'I have cleansed my hands in vain' (Ps. 73:13, 14). But go by faith into the sanctuary, the heavenly sanctuary, and you'll have other thoughts (v. 17). Will you but be wise for yourself (Prov. 9:12)? Men will praise you and so will God if you thus do well yourselves (Ps. 49:18). The Lord Jesus himself was encouraged by the joy set before him (Heb. 12:2). For this end the recompense of reward is set before us so that we may be assisted by it into the narrow way (Matt. 7:19). You that are wavering in your choice let this bring you to a point. In the choice of relations, callings etc. you are governed by your profit. Be governed by it in this matter.

If God will render eternal life to those that continue in well-doing, then the gain of religion is:

i. *Sure* gain and that's a great matter. The gain of the world lies at great uncertainty, buying and selling is winning and losing, but he that sows righteousness shall have a sure reward (Prov. 11:18). 'Tis one of the *sure* mercies of David (Acts 13:34). The promise is sure (Rom. 4:16). 'Tis future but 'tis reserved (1 Pet. 1:4), and therefore it concerns us to know that it is sure, else here we can not count upon it, or take any encouragement from it, or be induced by it. Why, in other things we reckon that our gain which we have not in possession if it be well secured to us – and why not in this?

(1) The husbandman reckons the corn upon his ground his gain though he must stay till harvest for it (Jas. 5:7, 8). He builds upon the promise (Gen. 8:22), but we are much surer of the crown of glory than he can be of the crop of corn, for though he be never so diligent he may be disappointed, but (Gal. 6:8, 9) *we shall reap* – the harvest will come (Ps. 126:5, 6; Eccles. 11:1).

(2) The tradesman reckons his debts upon good security his gain, though he must stay for them till the pay day come. The gain of eternal life is as sure as the bond of your God's truth can make it. He has promised (Titus 1:2) and the bond stands sure, and 'tis a good bond laid up in store (1 Tim. 6:19). The time set in the bond is not yet come, but it's sure, etc. We have good interest in the mean time.

(3) The servant reckons his wages his gain though he must stay for it till his year be up. He knows it's in good hands, his master will not wrong him of it, but we can be much more sure of the reward for our work than any servant can be of his wages, for we have God's promise confirmed by an oath (Heb. 6:17, 18), only we must wait (Job 7:2). 'Tis not till after a long time

that the Lord of the servants cometh and reckoneth with them (Luke 19:11; Matt. 25:19).

(4) The heir reckons his estate his gain if it be well secured to him though he do not enter upon it till he comes to age. If children, then heirs (Rom. 5:12), though now [he is] under tutors and governors (Gal. 4:1). The inheritance is sure though in reversion[1] after our life, and that our own, so that in other things the futurity of possession hinders not the sureness of interest.

ii. 'Tis great gain, a *great recompense* (Heb. 10:35). 'Tis very rich and great if compared

(1) with our services which will then be recompensed. The work is but small, and the sufferings small compared with the gain (2 Cor. 4:15; Rom. 8:18). We are but unprofitable servants, [who] do not deserve *thanks* (Luke 17:9). We much less seek a reward.

(2) with all the gains and profits of this world. The gain of religion far surpasseth the gain of any calling or employment in this world. See Philippians 3:7, 8. Those are dear bought, but the gain of heaven comes cheap. Those are vain and unsatisfying and scanty but that solid and substantial and sufficient.

(3) 'tis everlasting gain. What we get in the world we may lose again, 'tis ebbing and flowing, but in heaven it's always full sea. The riches of the world make themselves wings and flee away (Prov. 23:5), but that's a crown of glory that fades not away. 'Tis gain which will make rich to eternity, durable riches, an inheritance incorruptible (1 Pet. 1:4). The excellency of the gain of religion is that it is gain at death (Phil. 1:21, *to die is gain*). To the children of this world death is the greatest loss. It puts out all their light, strips them of all their comforts, puts them out of their stewardship and sends

1. *Reversion*, an archaic word for 'residue', 'the remainder'.

them a begging, but those that are truly religious have a happiness, a comfort which will stand them in good stead in a dying hour, when they fail (Luke 16:9). Let this recommend religion to you.

c. As an inducement to some particular instances, and branches of religion. Will the righteous God render eternal life to those that patiently continue in well-doing? The consideration of this should help to work in every one of us these good things.

i. *Thankfulness* to God. Will God thus richly recompense all our work and labour of love, and has he set before us such a happiness? And are we not bound to bless and praise him? Has he done so well for us, and shall not we then speak well of him? We are bound to be thankful not only for what we have in hand but for what we have in hope. David blessed God for the promise of the kingdom (Ps. 60:6). A life of religion should be a life of praise. To this we are called (1 Pet. 2:9). Consider this the work of heaven, the work we hope to be doing for ever, and therefore we should abound in it now. And is there any thing that calls more for our praises than this, that God has provided us such a happiness, discovered it to us, begotten us to it? See 1 Peter 1:3, 4, etc.; Ephesians 1:3, 11; Colossians 1:3, 5, 12. Especially blessed be God for Jesus Christ for 'tis God's gift through him (Rom. 6:23). Be much in praise, all other duties of religion must be in order to this.

ii. *Jealousy* over ourselves. Will God give eternal life to them that patiently continue in well-doing? *Let us therefore fear* (Heb. 9:1). Is there such a prize set before us, which we are striving for, should not we then be filled with a holy concern lest we should fail of it (1 Cor. 9:24, etc.)? Ask, Do I *do well*? Am I in a good state? Am I in a good way? Are not multitudes mistaken (Prov. 14:12)? And should I not then look diligently (Heb. 12:15)? Or if I do well, have not I reason to fear lest I should not continue in it? Have not I a subtle enemy to deal with, and a treacherous heart in my own bosom, and may not I be betrayed? We should be in agony in this matter (Luke 13:24). The more weighty the concern is, the more deep should our concern be about it. When the matter is of consequence it is not safe to take things upon trust. Suspect yourselves. *Is there not a lie* (Isa. 44:20)? Then trade high.

iii. *Watchfulness* against sin. Is there such a happiness set before us, let us then be careful that we do nothing to forfeit it, to disfit oneself for it or to weaken our hopes of it. See 2 Peter 3:13, 14. Have nothing to do with sin for that will stain your garments, displease your Lord, alienate your affections from this happiness, make you very unready for the Master's coming. Do we look for *eternal life*? Keep [your] conscience pure then from *dead* works. 'Tis a holy place we are going to into which no unclean thing shall enter (Rev. 21:27). Therefore harbour no uncleanness. When tempted to sin remember this (2 Cor. 7:1). Let this hope purify us (1 John 1:3), and mortify our members upon earth (Col. 4:5). Abstain from the appearances of sin.

iv. *Diligence* in holy duties, not only because our religious services will be thus rewarded but because in them we are working out this salvation, and getting ready for it, therefore *give diligence* (2 Pet. 1:5). We know whose errand we go upon, and who we are working for. Let us not be slothful in business (Rom. 12:11). Lay hold on all opportunities, rejoice in them, and learn to take pains in the improvement of them, to labour in religion as those that labour for eternal life. See 1 Corinthians 15:58; Galatians 6:9. Up and be doing for 'tis a crown, a kingdom we are labouring for. Wherefore lift up your hands that hang down. See Luke 2:35; 1 Peter 1:13; 2 Corinthians 5:5, 9. When Jacob had had a vision of glory he lift[ed] up his feet (Gen. 29:1, marg.[2]). Be not afraid of doing *too much* in religion. All

2. The reference is to the marginal reading in the AV at Gen. 29:1, where it gives the literal rendering of the Hebrew, 'he lifted up his feet'.

the danger is of trifling and doing too little. Work as those that are going to heaven. See Philippians 3:13, 14.

v. *Love* to our brethren. Our religion lies very much in this, and the fruits of it. 'Tis by this that faith works (Gal. 5:6). How should the thoughts of that world of love kindle to inflame in our souls a warm affection to all good people, discovered in a readiness as we have opportunity to do good to them? *Love* will there be perfected (1 Cor. 13:8, 13). 'Tis a heaven upon earth to dwell in love. They that do so dwell in God. Those that differ from us in lesser things, yet we should love them because we hope to be forever with them. The works and labours of love will there be abundantly recompensed (Heb. 6:10), even a cup of cold water (Matt. 10:42). Christ will there reward what was done to his people as if it had been done to himself (Matt. 25:35). Let this therefore make peace, and quicken us to abound in good works.

vi. *Joy* in the Lord. This is an essential part of religion (Phil. 3:3; 4:4). We should live a life of delight in God (Ps. 37:4), serving him with joyfulness and gladness, singing in his ways, and what greater matter of joy can be ministered to us here than the prospects of eternal glory? We may, we must rejoice *in hope* of that (Rom. 5:2; 1 Pet. 1:8, 9). Think what a good Master we serve, what a rich recompense we expect, and then say, 'Why art thou cast down?' Shall I enter shortly into the joy of my Lord, and shall not the joy of my Lord enter into me now? All tears shall then be wiped away. How is it that thou that art the King's Son art lean from day to day? Comfort yourselves and one another (1 Thess. 4:18). There's matter of comfort in this argument, all the burdens and sorrows of this present time, the temptations of Satan, the corruption of our own hearts, the eclipses of the divine favour, [will be gone]. Set this in the scale against all this. Eternal life will cure all.

vii. *Contempt* of the world. Do we expect eternal life in the other world? How poor and little should the things of this world appear to us, and how loose should we sit to them? And how indifferent should we be in our cares about them, and our pursuits of them? Moses had respect to the recompense of the reward, and see what a light matter he made of the things of this world (Heb. 11:24, 25, 26). Eternal life is *substance*, is *reality*, is *glory*, in comparison of which this world and all its pomps and pleasures are but a shadow. Therefore labour not to be rich (Prov. 23:3, 4). Lay not up treasure in these things (Matt. 6:19, 20; Col. 3:1, 2; 1 John 2:15). Let us not reckon ourselves to be *at home* here in this world (Mic. 2:10). We are very apt to have more sweet and pleasing thoughts of the delights of sense and our comforts here than of heaven. We settle here and build tabernacles, and say, 'It will be well with us' (Luke 18:19), whereas we should sit loose to these things. Do not call the couch thy bed, or the inn thine home.

viii. *Patience* under the cross. We have need of patience. One of the first lessons we must learn is to take up the cross (Matt. 16:24). Now the foresight of our happiness will help to make the cross easy (2 Cor. 4:16, 17). Let this keep trouble from the heart (John 14:1, 2), and prevent our *fainting* (Ps. 27:13). We have reason to bear our afflictions with patience because they are preparing us for this glory (Rom. 5:3), and we shall be abundantly recompensed for them in this glorious state (2 Tim. 2:12; 1 Pet. 4:13). We shall there rest from all our labours, and be eased of all our burdens. Let this therefore keep us from fretting at our troubles, or sinking under them or quarrelling with the will of God in them. Heaven will make amends for all.

ix. *Willingness* to die. Religion consists much in this, not only to sit loose to the comforts of life, but even to life itself, as those that have not in this world all they would have. It also provides an acquiescence in the will of God in whose hands our times are. And what can make us more willing to die than a prospect of this happiness t'other side of death? See 2 Corinthians 5:2, 6, 8. Thoughts of heaven will not only make death not dreadful, but it will make it desirable (Phil. 1:23). What do we see in this world to court our stay in it or to make us fond of it? Or what is there in death that should make us afraid of it? Is it not our passage to eternal life? Though rough and stormy yet 'tis but the short cut. It argues great unbelief of God, great coldness of love to him, and an inordinate affection to the things that are seen that we so loathe to die, nay, so loathe to entertain thoughts of it. We have need of our afflictions to cure this distemper.

x. *A cheerful expectation* of our future station. Herein lies much of religion, having our *conversation in heaven* (Phil. 3:20). The way of life is above (Prov. 15:24). Thoughts of this eternal life should draw us to mind the things that are to come, to set our affections on those things, to make them our scope and aim (2 Cor. 4:18), trading with heaven, receiving thence, returning thither, speaking the language of heaven, conversing with the heavenly society, and doing the work of heaven as far as is consistent with our present state. This is having our conversation in heaven as those that belong to and are bound for the new Jerusalem. Now the more we think of the joys and glories of our future state the more will our hearts be carried out towards it. Eternal life set before us will influence our spiritual life.

And now (brethren) shall I put some serious questions to you upon the whole matter.

1. Do you believe that there is such a happiness as this prepared for those that continue in well-doing? Do you think it to be a real thing? Faith is the *evidence* of it (Heb. 11:1). It is not a bare name. 'Tis not a fancy, a fool's paradise. You say you believe *the life everlasting*, but do you indeed believe it? Do you believe

that those that are holy now shall be happy shortly? That God has prepared a kingdom for those that love him?

2. Have you a mind of this happiness? You may have a share in it if it be not your own fault. No doubt you would rather have heaven than hell for your portion but would you rather have heaven than earth? Have you ever seriously put that question (Luke 18:18)?

3. What are you willing to do that you may obtain this happiness? Are you willing to forsake all your sins, and to give up yourselves to God in Christ as your God? You know you must keep the commandments (Matt. 19:17). Are you willing to bow your necks to that easy yoke? Are you willing to take Christ upon his own terms, Christ upon any terms, Christ and his cross?

4. What evidences have you to show for this happiness? Can you answer the character of the citizen of Zion (Ps. 15:1; 24:3)? What spiritual life have you, the beginning and earnest of eternal life? What evidences of sanctification and meetness for glory?

5. What do you use to think of this happiness? What room has it in your thoughts? We should be often meditating upon it, dwelling upon it in our thoughts. Set time apart for this meditation. What's the inward thought? What walks do you take in the holy city?

6. What influence have the thoughts of heaven upon you? What power have they over you? What use do you make of them? To what purpose?

15

Repetition

26 Jun. 1692

REPETITION

– and I will make an everlasting covenant with you, even the sure mercies of David (Isa. 55:3 latter part).

The covenant of grace with all its inestimable blessings is here tendered to us for our encouragement to hearken to Christ and to come to him. Ministers are called ministers of the *new testament* (2 Cor. 3:6). 'Tis [καινῆς διαθήκης[1]] – of the New Covenant. We are appointed to preach that – to set before them from the Word what God hath treasured up in the New Covenant for all those that repent and believe the gospel.

I have endeavoured in much weakness at large to open it to you, in many sermons. I am this day to conclude with a short reflection upon the particular heads that have been insisted on – to revive something of those truths that you have heard (see Phil 3:1; Heb. 8:1; 2 Pet. 1:15). All [this is] little enough. We are so apt to let them slip.

Observe in this text

1. that the God of heaven hath been graciously pleased to make a covenant of grace with all true believers. The covenant of grace is the gospel revelation of the will of God concerning man's duty upon his performance or non-performance of that duty. This covenant was founded in free grace, purchased by Christ's blood [Luke 22:2, *the New Testament in my blood*], revealed to the Old Testament saints, brought to clearer light by the gospel. [It] is externally administered in the visible church, as of old among the Jews [Rom. 9:4, 5]. It is savingly closed with by true believers. This covenant God proposeth to us all.

---

1. Greek, 'of the new covenant'.

2. that this covenant is an *everlasting* covenant. The continuance of it was from everlasting. The continuance of it [is] to everlasting. As it was in the beginning it is now and ever shall be. The terms of salvation are the same now that ever they were since Adam's sin and will continue so. The market is not risen, and it will not fall. In the application of it to true believers it is everlasting – a covenant that shall never be forgotten. 'Tis everlasting in regard to the consequences of it – the eternal condition of the children of men will be determined according to it.

3. the benefits of this covenant are *mercies*. They flow from God's mercy and are ordered hugely in kindness to us (*well-ordered*, 2 Sam. 23:5) for the glory of God, the honour of Christ, the encouragement of sinners to accept of it and the comfort of Christian saints that have accepted of it (well-ordered *in all things*). Sincerity is our gospel perfection (Gen. 17:1). Whatever is required in the covenant is promised in the covenant [Phil. 2:13]. Every transgression of the covenant doth not put us out of the covenant (Ps. 89:30, etc.) and our salvation is not in our own keeping but in the keeping of the mediator, the surety (Heb. 7:22).

4. they are the *mercies of David*, i.e. such mercies as God promised to David. Some think it refers to Psalm 89:24, 28, etc. (Greek, τὰ ὅσια,[2] *holy things* others to 2 Chron. 6:42). Herein the weak shall be as David (Zech. 12:5). This rather points at Christ of whom David was a type. They are *the mercies of David* being purchased by him, promised in him. He is the great trustee of the covenant. All [is] treasured up in his hand. Christ is all in all in the covenant of grace.

5. they are *sure* mercies. The covenant of grace is sure. In the general proposal 'tis sure, i.e. God is real and sincere in the offer, serious and in earnest, he is not a man – he's *Jehovah* (Exod. 6:3, 4, 6). 'Tis sure because [of] the mercies of David, i.e. Christ. 'Tis sure

---

2. Greek, 'the holy [things]'.

for it's written, it's published, sealed, sworn (Heb. 6:17, 18). In the particular application 'tis sure – sure to all the seed (Rom. 4:16), without repentance (Rom. 11:29). God will keep close to them (Heb. 13:5) and he will keep them close to him (John .10:28, 29; Jer. 32:40). God is faithful (1 Thess. 5:24).

These sure mercies we have been attempting to open to you, but the one half has not been told you. Eye has not seen (1 Cor. 2:9). However better a faint representation than none at all. There are unsearchable riches (Eph. 3:8) which must be understood as proferred to those that are without. You may all have an interest if you will, but [they are] promised to those that are within. Believers have an actual interest upon their believing (walk about this Zion, Ps. 48:12, 13).

It is the unspeakable privilege of all those who by faith are in covenant with God that God is theirs (Heb. 8:10). This is the main matter and includes all of the rest (a God to Israel, 1 Chron. 17:24). This is the very quintessence of heaven's happiness (Rev. 21:3). All the promises are summed up in this.

a. What God is in himself he will be to them, that which the creature neither is nor can be. He hath made himself known by his names and titles, and the comfort of each of them belongs to believers. They have an interest in the attributes of God. His incommunicable attributes do all make for them. His oneness, his spirituality, make for them he's infinite, independent, eternal, unchangeable, and it's well for them he is so, for then their happiness is so – a happiness that will satisfy their nature and supply their needs, satisfy their desires and run parallel with the duration of the soul.

   His communicable attributes are made over them, engaged for them, employed for them so that they depend upon them and portion themselves out of them, provided that there be an awful sense of distance. God is a living God and his life is theirs, the fountain of their life, a knowing God and his knowledge theirs to discover for them, to provide for them, to witness for them; a sovereign God and his sovereignty is theirs, to rule in them and to rule for them (Ps. 146:6); a wise God and his wisdom is theirs to counsel them, to contrive for them a powerful God and his power theirs (Gen. 17:1); his creating, controlling power theirs, his strengthening, sustaining power theirs, his delivering, destroying power theirs; a holy God and his holiness theirs to secure the covenant and to sanctify them; a just God and his justice theirs to pardon their sins, to plead their cause; a good God and his goodness theirs, 'tis their storehouse, 'tis their cordial, their plea, the rock that follows them, a faithful God and his faithfulness is theirs to secure all the rest to them (Ps. 144:15).

b. What God has said he will be to them, that he will be.

i. A Father (2 Cor. 6:18). All the comfort which children have or expect to have in a good father, that and infinitely more the saints have in God. He owns them for his children, gives them the nature and disposition of children. This is a NT revelation. OT saints rarely called God Father. They have their Father's eye and ear, heart and house, bread and blessing, tendence and teaching, care and comfort, rule and rod, besides what's reserved for them in the other world – the inheritance of sons – he pities and spare[s] them and delights in them. He's a rich and royal Father, a wise and watchful Father, pitiful and powerful, ever-loving and ever-living.

ii. A Husband (Isa. 54:5). He betrothes them to himself (Hos. 2:19, 20), dignifies them, dwells with them, directs them, delights in them, cherisheth them, communicates himself to them, provides for them, partakes with them in their joys and sorrows, makes them fruitful and makes over to them a rich jointure.[3] He's a suitable, splendid husband, a rich remaining husband.

---

3. *Jointure*, an arrangement by which a husband settles property on his wife for her use after his death.

iii. A Shepherd (Ps. 23:1). He is so to the church in general (Ps. 40:1) and to particular believers. He takes them into his fold. He loves them and leads them, protects them and provides for them quiet pastures and still waters, carries them when they are weary, cures them when they are sick, redeemeth them when they are wandering, and reserveth an eternal happiness for them. Use this for direction and comfort.

iv. A King (Ps. 44:4), King of saints (Rev. 15:2), King by conquest (Ps. 110:1), King by contract. As his people's King he prescribes their laws (writes his laws for them and in them), preserves their peace, forgives their offences, fights their battles, receives their addresses (their appeals and their request), rewards their services.

v. A sun and shield (Ps. 84:11), a sun to enlighten, search, warm and comfort them, and to make them fruitful, a shield to protect and defend them to protect their persons, their purity, their comforts, their crown. He's a shield ready for them, a shield round about them (Ps. 5:12; Gen. 15:1).

vi. A portion (Lam. 3:24), their portion, i.e their all. Every man has something that is his all, all his desire, his delight and dependence. Carnal people make profit of their all, their reward, their consolation. True believers have chosen otherwise. The Lord is the portion of their inheritance hereafter, their cup here (Ps. 16:5), a suitable, satisfying, ready remaining portion.

vii. A constant guide (Ps. 48:8), our guide to direct our actions, by his Word and Spirit to direct our affairs, to his own glory and our good – and this to death, through death and beyond death.

Use 1. Let us be to him a people then (Heb. 8:10). Accept of the revelation, avouch the Lord, yield ourselves to him, give yourselves. Say 'I am the Lord's', join yourselves to the Lord. Approve yourselves to God in the relation by affection to him, adoration of him, affections on him, adoration of him, affiance[4] on him, adherence to him, appeal and access to him, a knowledge of him, action for him.

2. That Christ is theirs, given for a *covenant* to them (Isa. 49:8). He purchased the covenant, ordered it, published it, confirmed it. He's the mediator of it – the blessed daysman.[5] His death gave life to the covenant. The promises of the covenant are Yea and Amen in him. Jesus Christ is all in all in this covenant. All the duty of the covenant is summed up in our being his, and all the happiness of the covenant is summed up in his being ours (1 Cor. 1:30). We receive Christ (John 1:12) as *a gift*. In particular, Christ is ours.

a. Our righteousness (Jer. 23:60), a righteousness we must have wherein to appear before God, for we are guilty, and God is just. We are of ourselves far from righteousness (Isa. 46:12). Christ has by dying brought in an everlasting righteousness (Dan. 9:24), answered the demands of wronged justice, the Father declared himself satisfied (Matt. 3:17). He is made of God to all believers righteousness (1 Cor. 1:30). By the grant and donation of free grace according to the tenor of the covenant they become interested in the satisfaction and the righteousness resulting from it (Isa. 45:24, 25). Nay, we are made the righteousness of God in him (2 Cor. 5:21), acquitted, accepted. He is Jehovah our righteousness, sufficient. Make mention of him (Ps. 31:16) to God as the plea, to yourselves as the quickening and comfort.

b. Our life (Col. 3:4), the life of the body (John 11:25), the life of the soul, which consists in its union with God. 'Tis through Christ that we are united to God, and so live the life of grace in this world. 'Tis hid with him (Col. 3:3). It depends upon him as the head and root, the life of glory in t'other world. He is the author and matter of that happiness. Heaven is to be with Christ there (Phil. 1:27; Luke 27:4). Live upon Christ and then walk with him (Col. 2:6; Phil. 1:28).

---

4. *Affiance*, 'trust'.

5. *Daysman*, archaic English for 'umpire', 'arbiter'.

c. Our peace (Eph. 2:14; Mic. 5:5), *peace with* God. The reconciliation and the loving kindness is owing to Christ. He's the mediator of that peace (1 Tim. 2:5), the maker (Col. 1:20), the messenger (Eph. 2:17), the matter (Eph. 1:6, 7), the maintainer of this peace (Rom. 8:34), therefore (2 Cor. 5:19, 20) peace with ourselves. 'Tis Christ that bought it for us, bequeathed it to us, creates it in us (Isa. 57:19), is the ground and foundation of it (Heb. 9:14). Peace with others, with enemies (Prov. 16:7; Mic. 5:5), with brethren. He commands peace, prayed for it. He is the common centre of unity (Eph. 1:10), has abolished the law of commandments.

d. Our hope (1 Tim. 1:1). He is the author of our hope (Heb. 7:14; 1 Pet. 1:3), the object of our hope and the summary of all the promises (Phil. 3:8); the ground of our hope, the foundation; the evidence of our hope (Col. 1:27). To have Christ in us is to be acted by his Spirit, drawn by his love, governed by his law and swayed by his interests. Christ is our hope in this life, beyond this life (1 Cor. 15:14). So now, improve this hope.

e. Our Redeemer (Job 19:25) – redeems our inheritance that was mortgaged, our Göel,[6] near of kin to us. He laid open for us the new and living way. All that are interested in that redemption are married to the Redeemer. He redeems our persons from slavery. We are all by nature sold for sin and sold under sin. Christ has satisfied the judge, subdued the jailor, sounded the jubilee trumpet and sent his Spirit to knock off the chains (Ezra 1:5).

f. Our High Priest (Heb. 3:1; comp[are] Heb. 5:1, etc.). He reconciles us to God, instructs us, intercedes for us, presents our persons and performances, blesseth us. He's a great and gracious High Priest, a righteous and remaining High Priest. Consider him thus. Make use of him for atonement, for acceptance, for advice. Come boldly (Heb. 4:15; 10:2).

g. Our captain (Heb. 2:10). Contrives for us, commands,

6. *Göel*, Hebrew for 'deliverer', 'redeemer', of a relative's lost blood, property or freedom.

conducts us, conquers for us, crowns us – given to us to be so (Isa. 55.4). A glorious captain, a generous captain, valiant and victorious (Rev. 6:2), very tender of all his soldiers, and very terrible to all his enemies. Be his soldiers, and good soldiers (2 Tim. 2:3).

h. Our forerunner (Heb. 6:20). His ascension to heaven [was] not only an act of glory, but an act of grace. [He has] run before not as a servant but as a sovereign. *For us* – as our Priest, as our Prince, as our attorney, as our advocate, as our head, as our harbinger (John 14:2, 3).

i. Our friend (Cant. 5:16) – a special friend indeed. He has been so, witness his dying for them. He is so. He loves them, visits them, writes to them, counsels them, reproves them, supplieth them, sympathiseth [with] them, communicates his secrets to them, pays their debts, comforts them, will be their friend at need, a knowing and kind friend, rich and ready, faithful and forgiving, pitiful and persevering?

j. Our all (Col. 3:12). *All in all* in point of wisdom, righteousness, strength, grace, comfort, salvation. All fulness dwells in him.

And should not we be his then (Cant. 2:16)? Receive his doctrine, bear his image, obey his laws, espouse his interest, acquiesce in his disposals, depend upon his mediatorship.

3. The Spirit is theirs (Eph. 1:13).

a. The Spirit is a spirit of promise – promised to Christ the head, to the church the body. 'Tis proferred to all (Prov. 1:23), assured to all the elect to begin and carry on the good work, to supply the want of Christ's bodily presence (John 16:7), to act and animate the mystical body, to prepare the saints for heaven (2 Cor. 5:5).

b. True believers are in Christ after their believing [is] sealed with his Spirit – i.e. they receive his sanctifying impressions (as the wax receives the impressions of the seal), exact, abiding (2 Cor. 3:18) and his comforting testimony. Sealing denotes something precious (Isa. 43:4), peculiar (Prov. 4:9), private (Col. 3:3), preferred (Rev. 7:3), promised.

The Spirit is to true believers:

i. A Teacher (John 14:26). The Spirit teacheth doctrines to be known and believed and so preserves them from ignorance and error, duties to be known and practised, and preserves them from mistakes and neglects. He opens the understanding (Luke 24:45), refreshes the memory, bows the will, influences the affections, works faith. None teaches like the Spirit with a strong hand, sealing the instruction. Those teachings are evermore humbling and changing.

ii. A Comforter (John 14:16). παράκλητος[7] – an advocate, or, comforter. The saints have their fears and sorrows and troubles and need comfort. The Spirit stills the storm, succours the heart, shows the cure, and refresheth the soul with joy and peace in believing. The Spirit sanctifies and so comforts, emboldens them in prayer, whispers good words and comfortable words. Expect the comforts thereof from the Spirit's hand, in the Spirit's way (the Comforter convinceth) and in the Spirit's time.

iii. A spirit of adoption (Rom. 8:15), witnessing to the relation of children (which witness is also agreeable to the Scripture and grounded on sanctification) working the nature and disposition of children, viz. a love of God and likeness to him and a dependence upon him, particularly *crying, Abba Father*. The Spirit stirs us up to prayer, holds praying infirmities (Rom.8: 26, 27), works praying graces, enboldens the soul.

iv. An earnest (2 Cor. 1:22) which binds the present bargain, is part of payment and assures us of the full sum – present light is an earnest of complete light, so present love and present likeness, present conquests, present communions and present comforts.

Grieve not the Holy Spirit (Eph. 4:30). Do not resist him, in his

7. Greek, 'helper', 'advocate', 'comforter'.

convictions, teachings, sanctifyings or comforts. Do not quench the Spirit (1 Thess. 5:19) by neglect, smothering it, withdrawing fuel, pouring on water.

4. Pardon is theirs (Heb. 8:12). 'Tis a most precious privilege of the New Covenant. Pardon of sin is an act of God's free grace whereby to a penitent believing sinner for the sake of Christ and his righteousness, the obligation to punishment which ariseth from the sinfulness of his heart and life is dissolved and ceaseth. Sin is not imputed (Ps. 32:2), God doth not enter into judgment (Ps. 143:3), the sinner shall not die (2 Sam. 12:13), anger taken away (Isa. 12:2), iniquity not the ruin, no condemnation. 'Tis the remitting of a debt, the removing of a burden, the cleansing of a spot, the curing of a wound, the covering of nakedness, taking away a cloud, taking up a quarrel. The first covenant left no room for pardon, but the second doth. Pardon is firstly offered to all upon their faith and repentance, chief of sinners not excepted. The offer is written, sealed, proclaimed. Pardon is effectually assured to all true believers. 'Tis free, 'tis full and 'tis the foundation of all other covenant blessings, *for I will*. Those are pardoned and yet must pray for pardon every day, pardoned and yet afflicted, pardoned but have not also the sense of their pardon. They are blessed that have their sins pardoned (Ps. 32:1, 2). Whatever you do make sure of your pardon. 'Tis offered, accept the offer. Come in and submit. Those who are pardoned love much. Go and sin no more.

5. Peace is theirs – 'tis bequeathed to them (John 14:27). Peace of conscience – a full and rational quietness and tranquillity of soul arising from a believing sense of our justification before God – quietness and assurance (Isa. 32:17), 'tis the copy of our pardons (Rom. 5:11), receiving the atonement. 'Tis the composure of our spirits (Isa. 26:3), the calm of our fears (Ps. 3:5, 6), the rest of our souls (Ps. 116:7). 'Tis our reconciliation with ourselves and the rejoining of broken bones (Ps. 51:8). This peace is how[ever] bequeathed by will, that the promises might be sure. The will is

written, 'tis published, 'tis sealed, there's an executor named (the Spirit, John 16:15). The Testator is dead, the will is proved, that which we have to do is to sue out our legacy – it belongs to all true believers, they have a title to it (Ps. 97:11). Their end is peace (Ps. 37:37). It belongs to them only. Wicked people may have the devil's peace, but none of Jesus' peace. 'Tis a precious legacy, which we should all labour to get and keep – the path of peace and path of deep humiliation for sin, dependence on Christ, delight in God diligent in duty.

6. Grace is theirs (John 1:16). Grace, i.e. the good will of God manifested to us, that loving kindness which is better than life, that good work of God wrought in us. Grace is granted to believers in the New Covenant – the planting of grace (Deut. 30:6; Ezek. 11:19; 36:26; John 6:37), the performing of grace (1 Pet. 1:5; Jer. 32:40), the increase of grace (Job 17:9; Prov. 4:18), the comfort of grace (Isa. 32:17), the consummation of grace (Phil. 1:6). This is received (1 Cor. 4:7, *all* received – that many, mean, miserable). 'Tis from Christ's fulness (Prov. 8:21). He received that he might give. *Grace for grace* notes this freeness of grace and the fulness of grace, the serviceableness of grace and the substitution of NT grace in the room of OT grace, the augmentation and continuance of grace, its agreeableness and conformity to the grace in Christ. Get grace then, be governed by it. Grow in it. Let your conversation be the grace of God. Promote grace in others. The great promise of grace is Hebrews 8:10, *I will put their laws into their minds* – the understanding opened to know the will of God, the will bound to comply with it. The law written in the heart is near to us and ruling in us.

7. Access to God is theirs (Eph. 2:18), an introduction, leave to come to God, a heart to come to him, and great encouragement to come, access to God to receive from him as from a Father, to address him as to a Father. There's a throne of grace created, a spirit of grace poured out, an answer of grace promised, a mediator of grace appointed – and what could we more? This

access is *through Christ*. He is the door and the way (John 14:6). He is the High Priest. He died to make reconciliation, lives to make intercession and both that we might have access. 'Tis *by the Spirit* as an enlightening Spirit and as a spirit of adoption. *We both* – both Jew and Gentile – those that in other things are at a distance meet in this, all united to the same Jesus. This is an advantageous access – to have access to God is to have access to good, them that are yet at a distance from God be persuaded to come to him – repent of their estrangements, desire an access, submit to the conduct of the Spirit. Them that have access improve it, get nearer.

8. Ordinances are theirs (Ezek. 37:26). Those that are in covenant with God but in profession have an external right to ordinances, which are to them an honour and an opportunity, but ordinances belong in another manner to true believers. The covenant secures to them a right to ordinances and ends of ordinances. Ordinances to them are golden pipes, and green pastures, fountains of salvation and feasts of fat things, beautiful clothing and breasts of consolation, galleries of communion and the gate of heaven. There's safety, satisfaction, sanctification and salvation to the saints in the ordinances. Labour to answer the ends of the ordinances.

9. Providences are theirs (8:28). All God's providences work together for good to God's people – merciful providences, afflicting providences – for spiritual good – to touch and try them – to break them off from sin and to bring them nearer to God, to engage them to duty, to encourage them in duty, to free them from this world, to fit them for heaven. He works all for good by his infinite wisdom and sovereignty (Phil. 1:19). Comply with the design of providences. Get the good that God intends you (Eccles. 7:14).

10. Angels are theirs (Heb. 1:14), their angels (Matt. 18:10). They ministered to Christ the head, to the church in general, to particular believers. Theirs to oppose the malice of evil spirits, to preserve

the bodies of the saints (Ps. 34:7; 91:11) as Jacob and Elisha, to instruct them and comfort them, to convey the departing soul (Luke 16:42), to gather the saints together at the great day. They are strong and swift, unanimous and unseen, condescending and constant in their ministrations. This is very comfortable to the saints in their dangers and sufferings. We should converse now in our thoughts with the world of the angels. Do nothing to forfeit their ministration. Do the will of God as they do.

11. The world is theirs (1 Cor. 3:21, 22). 'Tis for the church in general (Eph. 1:22) – the inferior creatures, national governments, common gifts for the church. 'Tis for particular believers (1 Tim. 4:8). They have as much of it as is good for them by a good title. They have it from love and with a blessing. 'Tis clear to them and comfortable to them. 'Tis an opportunity of glorifying God and doing good and what they will have serve to bear their charges to heaven. 'Tis theirs by conquest, by promise, by marriage, therefore (1 Tim. 4:1; Ps. 37:16; Prov. 23:17; Matt. 6:23; 1 Cor. 2:31; Heb. 13:5).

12. Afflictions are theirs (Ps. 89:30, 31, 32, 33). Christ's children do sometimes fall into sin, and fall under affliction, but it is their comfort that their affliction is but a rod whch speaks gentleness in the affliction and good intended by it. 'Tis a rod in the hand of God who is wise and holy and faithful and gracious and our God in covenant. God never heaps this rod of affliction upon his children but where by reason of sin there's great need of it, to vindicate his own honour, and to recover them from their sins. And notwithstanding all this, covenant love is sure for all true believers – *nevertheless my loving kindness* – notwithstanding their provocations and notwithstanding their affliction (Rom. 8:35). 'Tis for Christ's sake – not *take from him* – for the covenant's sake – *nor cause my faithfulness to fail.*

13. Death is theirs (1 Cor. 3:21, 22) – or *death.* 'Tis not their enemy to do them any hurt, cannot separate them from the love of Christ

nor hurt the soul. Nay, it is their friend to do them good. 'Tis the period[8] of all their grievances, corruption, temptations, difficulties, sorrows, fears. 'Tis a passage to their happiness – from darkness to light, from distance to nearness, from sin to holiness, from sorrow to joy, from war to peace, from a wilderness to Canaan. Thanks to the covenant of grace and the cross of Christ, the victories and purchases of the cross – meat out of the eater.[9] Then do not fear death...

14. Heaven is theirs (Titus 1:2) *eternal life*, consisting in the vision and fruition of God and likeness to him (Ps. 17:6). Perfect knowledge, rest, holiness, love, joy and peace – satisfaction in all these. Even the body will be glorified (Phil. 3:21). The work and company and continuance will increase the happiness. Heaven is a prize and a paradise, a crown and a city, a house and a heritage. This is promised in the New Covenant, the promises founded in God's counsels, purchased by Christ, revealed darkly to the Old Testament saints, more clearly to us. 'Tis offered to all upon reasonable terms. 'Tis made over to true believers, who have the assurances of it. It shall certainly be accomplished at last. 'Tis this that is the crown of all the promises of the New Covenant – and is it not our great concern to make this ours, and then to live accordingly, a heavenly conversation.

And thus we have given you some short hints of those things which have been largely opened and applied in 134 sermons. If any good has been done let God have the glory. I desire to take the shame of my weakness, deadness and folly, and that my mangyness[10] has been very disagreeable to the weight and worth of the subject. O how weak and faint and transient are the impressions of these great and precious truths. Bless God that our opportunities have been thus long continued notwithstanding our barrenness. And now,

8. *Period*, in the sense of 'end'.
9 .'Meat out of the eater', see Judg. 14:14.
10. *Mangyness*, 'shabbiness'.

in the close, will you labour to answer the end of all this – that it may not be altogether in vain that which I have designed in this subject (I hope) has been

1. to help your understanding of this covenant that you might not be in the dark about it. Beg of God to teach you to plead that promise (Ps. 25:14), know the extent, the fulness, the riches of it. Let not the things of the gospel be strangers to you. Acquaint yourselves with the charter. There is still more to be known.

2. to engage your meditations upon it. You that do understand it should be still spending your thoughts upon it. Let this be your inward thought. Let thoughts of the covenant of grace fill you. This is the way of extracting sweetness out of it.

3. to quicken your consent to it. All this is left and you do not accept the invitation, yet the golden sceptre is held out. Do not defer or make excuses. God willing (Ps. 110:3), you that are young learn to accept a good bargain. Come for all things are now ready (Jer. 50:5).

4. to direct your conversation by it. Live as a people in covenant with God. All the privileges speak duty that must be done. The privileges are peculiar and you must be so in your walking. Show forth the praises of him that called you.

5. to encourage your comforts in it. We are appointed to comfort them (Isa. 40:1), and the covenant of grace is your treasury of comforts. Derive from it as there is occasion. Live by faith in this covenant (1 Thess. 4:5). And now, brethren, I commend you to God and the word of his grace.

Other Books of Interest from Christian Heritage

CHRISTIAN HERITAGE
THE
PLEASANTNESS
OF A
RELIGIOUS LIFE
A Puritan's view of
the Good Life
Matthew Henry
Introduced by J.I. Packer

The Pleasantness of a Religious Life

A Puritan's view of the Good Life

Matthew Henry

Introduced by J.I. Packer

'Here is a bait that has no hook under it... a pleasure which God himself invites you to, and which will make you happy, truly and eternally happy... it is certain that there is true pleasure in true religion.'

Matthew Henry, the Great Puritan commentator, looks at what gives people real joy. He looks at 12 different types of Christian pleasure, reviews what God has done to bring sunners joy, demonstrates that Christian experience proves this and challenges the reader to join in!

This classic of Christian Living was Matthew Henry's last book and is brought to you by J.I. Packer who adds an extensive introduction to the book showing its significance and gestation from Henry's minstry.

'We too get told that being a Christian is a bleak and burdensome business, and not being a Christian would be more fun; we too like Henry's first hearers and readers, need to be reminded that it is absolutely not so.'

J.I.Packer

ISBN 1 85792 391X

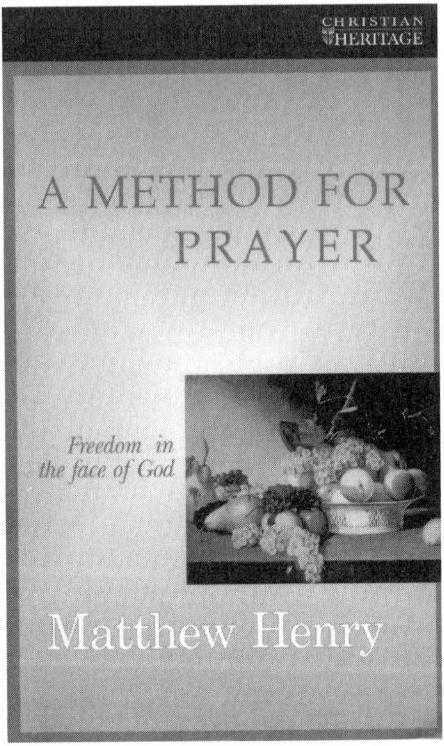
CHRISTIAN HERITAGE
A METHOD FOR PRAYER
Freedom in the face of God
Matthew Henry

A Method For Prayer

Freedom in the Face of God

Matthew Henry

Edited by J. Ligon Duncan III

True prayer comes from the heart, so why do we need method?

The great devotional commentator and pastor, Matthew Henry, shows that Christians benefit from discipline just as much as talking freely with God. You will discover the methods Jesus taught, look at styles of prayer, see helpful examples and be warmly introduced to communing freely with God on a new level of understanding.

Ligon Duncan had edited the original text to make it more accessible to the modern reader. He has also added Henry's sermons on prayer, his advice on spending each day in prayer, outlines for scriptural prayer and advice on leading in public prayer.

ISBN 1 85792 068 6

CHRISTIAN HERITAGE
JERUSALEM'S GLORY
A Puritan's view of what the church should be
THOMAS WATSON

Jerusalem's Glory

A Puritan's View
of what the Church should be

Thomas Watson

Edited by Roger N. McDermott

Thomas Watson was a renowned puritan preacher and writer in England during the 17th century. Born in 1619, he entered the Christian ministry and rapidly gained a reputation as a practical and godly minister, expounding the Scriptures faithfully and building up the church. Many of his writings have been republished today.

Written in 1661, this book, a rare gem which has remained unpublished for 340 years, contains all the hallmarks of what made the puritans great. It represents a clarion call to the church to recognize her failings and repent, turning to God and casting herself on his mercy. Here we have a puritan preacher of the gospel, speaking plainly to the ills of society and in particular to the church.

The text is simplified for the modern reader, with a biographical introduction added to the original work. It will, through time, come to be regarded as Watson at his most readable and best.

'There is a happy union of sound doctrine, heart-searching experience and practical wisdom throughout all his works...'

C.H. Spurgeon

ISBN 1 85792 569 6

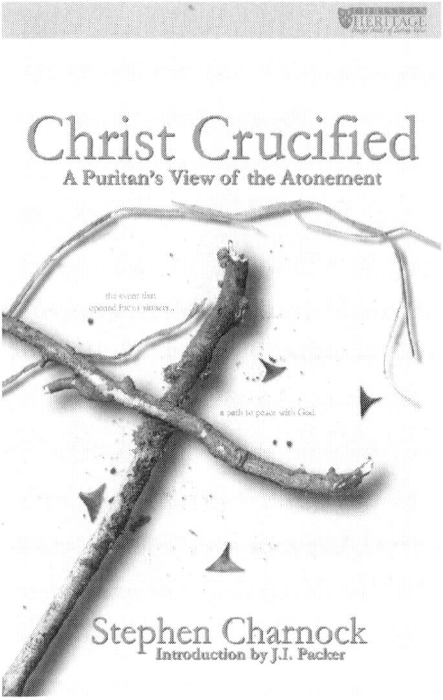

Christ Crucified

A Puritan's View of the Atonement

the event that
opened for us anew...

a path to peace with God

Stephen Charnock

Introduction by J.I. Packer

Christ Crucified

A Puritan's view of the Atonement

Stephen Charnock

Introduction by J.I Packer

In this stimulating work Stephen Charnock links the Old and New Testaments with this classic explanation of how the sacrifice of Jesus Christ fulfils the Old Testament sacrificial system. He particularly illustrates the importance of the Passover, and opens up our understanding of the differences which characterise the New Testament Church era. He shows that Jesus willingly submitted to the pain he knew he would go through, in order to bring us the blessings of a new covenant with God.

Stephen Charnock (1628-1680) was educated at Cambridge University after which he lectured at Oxford University. He was appointed chaplain to the Governor of Ireland, Oliver Cromwell's son Henry in 1655, where he soon gained a reputation for preaching. In 1675, years after the fall of Oliver Cromwell's Commonwealth, Charnock became a Presbyterian Minister in London. His works, mostly published posthumously, have the characteristic Puritan concern for central gospel themes and consistent application of Biblical texts to practical problems.

'Sentence after sentence in Charnock's ordered march lights up and glows in your heart'

J.I. Packer

ISBN 1 85792 076 7

Christian Focus Publications

publishes books for all ages

Our mission statement -
STAYING FAITHFUL
In dependence upon God we seek to help make his infallible word, the Bible, relevant. Our aim is to ensure that the Lord Jesus Christ is presented as the only hope to obtain forgiveness of sin, live a useful life and look forward to heaven with him.

REACHING OUT
Christ's last command requires us to reach out to our world with his gospel. We seek to help fulfill that by publishing books that point people towards Jesus and help them to develop a Christ-like maturity. We aim to equip all levels of readers for life, work ministry and mission.

Books in our adult range are published in three imprints.

Christian Focus contains popular works including biographies, commentaries, basic doctrine, and Christian living. Our children's books are also published in this imprint.
Mentor focuses on books written at a level suitable for Bible College and seminary students, pastors, and other serious readers; the imprint includes commentaries, doctrinal studies, examination of current issues, and church history.
Christian Heritage contains classic writings from the past.

For a free catalogue of all our titles, please write to:

Christian Focus Publications, Ltd
Geanies House, Fearn,
Ross-shire, IV20 1TW, Scotland, United Kingdom
info@christianfocus.com

For details of our titles visit us on our website
www.christianfocus.com